DISCARD

THE FAMILY
REVOLUTION
IN MODERN
CHINA

THE FAMILY
REVOLUTION
IN MODERN
CHINA

Marion J. Levy, Jr.

ATHENEUM   1968   NEW YORK

Published by Atheneum
Reprinted by arrangement with the author
Originally published by Harvard University Press in
cooperation with the Institute of Pacific Relations
Copyright © 1949 by Marion J. Levy, Jr.
Library of Congress catalog card number 63-20892
Manufactured in the United States of America by
The Murray Printing Company
Forge Village, Massachusetts
Published in Canada by McClelland & Stewart Ltd.
First Atheneum Edition

To My Parents

CONTENTS

Foreword by Talcott Parsons   ix

Author's Preface   xi

PART ONE
INTRODUCTION

 I *General Concepts*   3
 II *Concrete Distinctions*   41

PART TWO
"TRADITIONAL" FAMILY STRUCTURE

 III *The Kinship Substructure of Role Differentiation*   63
 IV *The Kinship Substructure of Solidarity*   164
 V *The Kinship Substructure of Economic Allocation*   208
 VI *The Kinship Substructure of Political Allocation*   232
 VII *The Kinship Substructure of Integration and Expression* 247

PART THREE
THE KINSHIP STRUCTURE OF "TRANSITIONAL" CHINA AND
THE PROBLEM OF MODERNIZATION

 VIII *The Situation and the New Forces*   273
 IX *"Transitional" Kinship Structure*   289
 X *The Problem of Modernization*   350
Bibliography   367
Glossary   381
Index   385

FOREWORD

It is a great pleasure to write a brief foreword to Dr. Marion Levy's study of the family revolution in China. The book is noteworthy because it is the first major work of a new type of scholar in the comparative study of social institutions. After his graduate study of sociology was already well under way, Dr. Levy made the courageous decision to equip himself *both* as a well-trained sociologist and as a full-fledged Far-Eastern specialist with all that the latter implied, particularly the knowledge of different languages. While pursuing his sociological studies, he therefore undertook the study of Chinese and then Japanese. The exigencies of the war fortunately enabled him to spend a year in China, where he could perfect his knowledge of the language and learn much about the life of the people.

This means that, unlike so many students of China who have been Sinologists only, Dr. Levy brings to his study of Chinese institutions the training of the general sociologist. This gives him a grasp of the significance of general problems, a set of analytical tools and a technically refined comparative perspective which the traditional Sinologist has lacked. At the same time, by his command of the language, knowledge of Sinological sources, and use of Chinese materials, Dr. Levy is able to do an empirical piece of work of which the ordinary general sociologist would not be capable. If our knowledge of the variability of human social arrangements is to be both broad and sound, we must have many such studies.

Dr. Levy has chosen as the field for this study the Chinese family system, which is most basic to Chinese society. Much of its empirical subject matter will be familiar to students of the Western literature. The contribution of this study must not be sought primarily in the new facts it brings to light, but in two other directions—the perspective through which the material and its problems are seen, and the consistency and rigor with which the author's analysis is carried out.

Dr. Olga Lang in her *Chinese Family and Society* has already given us a picture of the process of transition which has been going on in Chinese family relationships. This picture is considerably further systematized and placed in perspective by Dr. Levy's analysis, and is further illuminated by consideration of the relation between changes in the family structure and the industrialization of the economy, a relation which is very important for the family in the United States. Raising the question of the changes which would be necessary for a thorough industrialization of China gives Dr. Levy a strategic vantage point for analysis. The same contrast encourages systematic analysis of the "traditional" family as a sociological ideal type.

This analysis in turn enables Dr. Levy to illuminate certain of the important points of strain in the old system as in the father–son and the mother-in-law–daughter-in-law relationships. Knowledge that such strains existed helps greatly in understanding the tendency of the old system to break up relatively suddenly and completely.

This book is, in itself, a notable contribution to the literature of its field. It is to be hoped also that it establishes a perspective of problems within which the author can contribute many more detailed studies and thereby add to our understanding of the enormously important processes of social change which are taking place in China.

Talcott Parsons

AUTHOR'S PREFACE

This study attempts a systematic analysis of the family structure of "traditional" and "transitional" China with special reference to the role played by industrialization in the changes which are taking place. The results of this study do not masquerade as definitive, for it has not been possible either to see or to verify from facts gathered by others all the phenomena analyzed here. The data at present permit nothing in the nature of definitive statements on either the "traditional" or the "transitional" period in China because adequate statistical data are not at hand, and alternative materials on a large enough scale to replace statistics have not yet appeared. This study should therefore be viewed as an attempt to set forth the best available set of hypotheses based on the facts and their interrelations. I believe that the study does offer a systematic analysis which may be verified or disproved, in whole or in part, as material of a more definitive nature becomes available. It should at least eliminate some floundering about in future work on the subject and point out strategic areas for investigation and means of integrating further findings. In a field so little explored as this it must be the hope of every worker as a scientist, whatever his hopes to the contrary as a man, that within a reasonably short period he will find his work radically amended, if not superseded entirely. This study is not presented as an end product but as a bare beginning.

The data for this study have been obtained from three sources. First, there are materials from various written works, both European and Chinese, which are cited in the orthodox fashion whenever they are used. Most of these writings, insofar as they are scientific analyses, lack definitive character.

The second source has been informants, from which the bulk of the material has come. The number and range of informants is by no means as great as one might wish, but the usefulness of the material obtained from this source is still considerable. This material, along with the closely connected personal observation of the author during a year's stay in China from 1943 to 1944, is not cited specifically in each case, since to do so would add nothing toward a definitive character for the study and would burden the reader with numerous repetitious footnotes.

The informants consulted have in general been of four sorts: (1) Chinese social scientists and scholars, (2) Chinese students in the United States, (3) Chinese from various walks of life in China, and (4) Westerners with considerable experience in China.

In the first group three persons have been of greatest importance. Two of them, Shih Kuo-Heng and Ting Sheng-Shu, were in the United States when the study was written up and were available for many consultations. The third, Wu Wen-Tsao, was kind enough to offer much information and guidance to me when I was in China, though at that time the study lay far in the future. Above all he convinced me that work by Westerners in this field was not hopeless. At the same period in China a fourth man, Li Yu-I, was also of great help in our occasional talks, which were all too few. In general both in China and in the United States, Chinese scholars and social scientists were consulted whenever possible. Fortunately for the study, many were well grounded in the Classical literature of China and in Chinese history. Ting Sheng-Shu was especially helpful in this respect, and without his aid and that of others the reconstruction of the "traditional" picture would have been far more difficult. The scholars and scientists were equally helpful in the specific information they gave about present conditions and contrasts with the past. Their training in the field of social science made access to information far simpler than might otherwise have been the case.

A special word must be said of Shih Kuo-Heng. Professor Shih gave most generously of his time and talents. He was not only a mine of information; he gave valuable critical aid as well. Like all the persons helpful to this study, he cannot be held responsible for its shortcomings, but any success it may have will reflect its debt to him.

From time to time interviews with other Chinese scholars in the field have been conducted wherever possible. These interviews have always been of the focused rather than the unfocused variety, although care has been exercised to phrase questions in such a way as to prejudice the answers as little as possible. Since time was limited in dealing with men of the level of sophistication of those in this group, the focused interview produced better results than the unfocused interview.

In the second group many persons participated. Chinese students by no means furnish a cross section of Chinese society in any general sense, but constitute a highly selected sample. Some care was taken to sift their information for bias from this source. Many of these students were interviewed in China as well as in the United States. Fortunately, during the author's stay in China he was located in an area which contained several institutions of higher learning, including refugee medical schools. The students interviewed were from many parts of China. The interviews were both focused and unfocused. The focused interviews proved more satisfactory because the unfocused ones were diffuse and often idealized rather than accurate. The latter quality, however, afforded some insight into the aims and stresses pertinent to the Chinese student's role.

The year's contact with Chinese from various walks of life in China varied from a tobacco shaver in a small village to an extremely sophisticated author of poems, essays, and short stories. It included such diverse people as a bookseller who had studied and lived in Japan and an elderly woman reared in a highly "traditional" gentry family who had ended by affiliating herself in a supervisory capacity with the new educational system. These people were not professional students in any case, but some of them were unusually acute. With the more acute persons, focused interviews were used, but with the others interviews were unfocused. Since the author's spoken Chinese was bad, he resorted to writing or some passing Chinese interpreter who knew English or Japanese if the informant did not know English. Effort was taken not to give the impression that a study or cross-examination was in process, but rather that the inquirer was an interested curiosity-ridden spectator.

Contacts with Chinese in China were facilitated by the fact that the Chinese people were as curious about the foreigner as he was about them. After a few hikes through the area he became a familiar figure, and the people were always ready to talk awhile over a cup of tea.

Several Westerners of considerable periods of residence in China were interviewed. By and large, the people interviewed were not of the "Old China Hand" variety, but were persons who had come in close contact with the Chinese people. Among these were businessmen, doctors, teachers, missionaries, government employees, and the like. Several were persons born and brought up in China. Effort was taken to concentrate on persons who had learned something of the Chinese language on the rough hypothesis that those long residents of China who had learned nothing of the language were less likely to be valuable as informants than others. This is not always the case, but it is a generally reliable guide. These interviews were largely focused, but in only a few cases were the interviews so arranged as to be clearly interviews from the point of view of the informants. This was felt to be desirable in that it did not pose in the informant any specifically motivated wish to appear a profound student of the mysterious Orient.

Unfortunately, notes on the Chinese interviews were not kept. The author was in China under Navy auspices, and the Navy discouraged the keeping of any sort of notes or diaries, regardless of content. Furthermore, the imminent possibility of being moved militated further against any systematic note system. The interviewing carried out in the United States was recorded in rough notes which were almost immediately incorporated into the study. The interviewing technique used leaves much to be desired, but it did furnish insight and data for the hypotheses of which this study is composed, and its fruitfulness will be determined when definitive tests of these hypotheses are available.

Finally, there is material derived by analysis. When a gap exists in information from informants and other sources, theory is sometimes applied to associated material in order to derive an hypothesis about the facts. When this is done, the chain of reasoning involved is incorporated in the text. The danger of such a procedure is obvious; in highly developed sciences such as physics the use of theory to "outrun data" is a commonplace today, but in relatively undeveloped sciences like those in the social field the practice is subject to proportionately greater dangers. In support of this practice here it can only be said that both the "facts" so derived and the theory so employed have been subjected to thorough outside criticism.

On the "traditional" period definitive statistical proof will probably never be available since such figures as are given in the wealth of historical materials are unsatisfactory. It is likely that students of the "traditional" phenomena will forever be thrown back on the use of theory for proof: in this case, by the proof that alternatives are functionally impossible or highly improbable. It is to be expected that students of the "transitional" and future periods will not stand forever on such grounds. The future of China will require the development of statistical studies as well as other collections of material. The present study has been undertaken in the hope that a systematically developed and integrated set of hypotheses about family structure and the problem of industrialization in China might at least be of some service, not only in leading to its own verification or disproof, but in directing the type of research that will be fruitful for many practical ends in the future.

I owe a great debt to the university communities which trained me, that at the University of Texas and that at Harvard University, where men in the departments of Economics, Sociology, and Far Eastern Languages gave particularly of their time and effort. I owe a special debt to Talcott Parsons, who supervised this study in its form as a doctoral thesis and who instilled standards concerning systematic generalized scientific work in the social field. It would be gross ingratitude not to mention Clarence E. Ayres, who offers invaluable training in the critical approach to all his students. My primary indebtedness to the men and women in these fields is clear.

In the specific criticism of the ideas and materials of this study I am indebted to David F. Aberle, Joseph Levenson, Edwin O. Reischauer, Shih Kuo-Heng, Pitirim A. Sorokin, Francis X. Sutton, and others in great numbers. In general among the colleagues in my own age group, four, David F. Aberle, Morris Blumberg, Joseph Levenson, and Francis X. Sutton, have helped me in ways which defy identification. Ruth Whitman has earned my gratitude by her editing of the manuscript and by the preparation of the index for the volume.

I owe the leisure and resources which made this study possible to funds provided by the Social Science Research Council and the Chinese Cultural Scholarship. The men and women who administer these grants have made an art of providing necessary aid with a minimum of red tape. Gratitude is also due to the University Research Fund of Princeton University, which provided the funds necessary to prepare the manuscript for publication. An expression of indebtedness is also due the General Secretariat of the Institute of Pacific Relations with whose coöperation this volume is published. Needless to say, none of these organizations is responsible for the contents of the volume, though their aid was vital in its production.

Finally, mention must be made again of the Chinese who have aided this work. They are not, of course, responsible for its shortcomings, but without them it could not have been written. In the arduous course of Chinese studies the help extended by Chinese scholars is not only of great intrinsic value but makes possible a goal which might otherwise seem unattainable. The Western student has no greater asset in this field than the willingness and eagerness of his Chinese colleagues to help him.

MARION J. LEVY, JR.

PART ONE

INTRODUCTION

CHAPTER ONE

GENERAL CONCEPTS

IT is now generally agreed by anthropologists and sociologists that kinship structure—defined as that portion of the total institutional structure of the society which, in addition to other equally and often more important orientations, determines the membership of its units and the nature of the solidarity among its members by orientation to the facts of biological relatedness—is, as a matter of empirical observation, a feature of every known society. It may also be pointed out that the existence of some structure oriented in part at least to the facts of biological relatedness is also a functional requirement[1] of any society if only for the reasons (1) that in its absence the problem of allocation of responsibility for and of assignment of status to the members of new generations would become infinitely more troublesome and complex, and (2) that the random assignment of sexual relationships and the absence of any system of value orientations and institutionalized patterns are not only inconsistent with the fact that effective patterns are always present in sexual roles, but, under such conditions, would also result in a sort of sexual *bellum omnium contra omnes.*[2]

[1] A functional requirement of any system is a factor necessary to the continued operation of that system. The level of generality used in the definition of the system will determine the level of generality of its functional requirements.

[2] These two factors, the ubiquity of the phenomenon of kinship structure as a matter of empirical observation, and the parallel explanation of it as a functional necessity for specific reasons, serve as a significant example of the pairing of verification and explanation. This type of analysis and verification, while quite acceptable on general methodological grounds, is peculiarly liable to teleological misuse—a sort of "functional teleology" (I am indebted to Professor Sorokin for this term)—unless care is observed. Thus it is valid method to state that x is a functional prerequisite for y for reasons $a, b, c, \ldots$ and to deduce from that, that in the presence of y, x is always to be found. It is not, however, permissible to observe that the existence of a given phenomenon is the result of its being a functional prerequisite of the phenomenon of which it is a part. Its status as a functional prerequisite stands or falls on its necessity for the continued operation of the system of which it is a part.

The existence of kinship structure, whether viewed as an empirically ubiquitous phenomenon or as a functional prerequisite for specific reasons, is but the beginning of the problem. Given its existence for all empirical cases of the more generalized phenomenon of society, the interesting and difficult problem is the diversity of its multifarious exemplifications and its ability to vary, at least slightly and more often drastically, from society to society. Of the various possible methods of analysis of kinship phenomena two would seem to offer the greatest advantage. The first of these focuses on the relational aspects of kinship, that is, it analyzes kinship phenomena by taking an individual, generally designated as *ego,* and studying the permutations and combinations of types of connections, interactions, avoidances, taboos, and the like between *ego* and the other individuals related to him on a kinship basis. The second of these focuses primarily upon the organizational aspects of kinship, that is, it analyzes kinship phenomena by studying the structural features of the membership units in terms of which kinship activities are carried out.

Its existence cannot be assumed as necessary beyond the limits of the system of which it is a part, nor can its existence be considered as preordained. In the case of social phenomena, history is strewn with the relics of societies and civilizations whose rise, fall, reëstablishment and subsequent degeneration—or any portion of this process—testify to the incorrectness of a "functional teleology," to the invalidity of maintaining the necessary continued existence of any functional prerequisite in and of itself.

Thus it is not permissible to say that a given process of allocation of duties in a business firm exists because it is a functional prerequisite of that firm. That is teleology, pure and simple—not at all different from the statement, "legs were created to wear pants and noses to bear spectacles." It is permissible to say that if there is to be such a firm there must be a definite process of allocation of duties, that in its absence, the firm will cease to function.

On the most generalized level of consideration of social systems, it is no great problem to keep this consideration in mind, but as more concrete phenomena are studied, the tendency to assume the necessity of some particular factor independent of the phenomenon of which it is a functional prerequisite is more difficult to avoid. Such teleological arguments form the basis for many pseudorational discussions of social change. For example, discussions of the Chinese family by Chinese authors as well as others often fall into such difficulties. The continued existence of the "traditional" Chinese family pattern or some reasonable compromise thereof is often explained as necessary to the Chinese way of life, when, in fact, the way of life referred to has ceased to exist. This sometimes leads an author to ignore the fact that the family referred to may be a survival of an institution past its time as a functional prerequisite of the system in which it occurs rather than a prerequisite of the general system currently extant.

By far the largest part of kinship analysis in social science literature has been relational analysis; systematic development or use of the organizational approach has not appeared. The relational type of analysis focuses attention on individuals by virtue of the fact that it singles out an individual, *ego,* as a point of reference. The organizational approach focuses attention on membership units. Thus the kinship picture from the relational point of view is not identical for any two members of a society because no two members have exactly the same kin. Organizationally speaking, however, the picture is the same for all individuals of a given concrete membership unit. By and large the kinship structure of most societies functions largely in terms of membership units rather than in terms of individual relations.[8]

Social science is indebted to the relational approach for a vast amount of information and insight into social systems. The organizational approach, while it has lacked systematic formulation of the type given the relational approach, has appeared in all the first rate literature in the field of family organization. Complete analysis of kinship obviously requires the use of both approaches. This study takes the organizational approach as its starting point and uses elements of the relational approach wherever necessary, chiefly because our interest is in a functioning structure which in fact functions in terms of organizational units rather than in terms of a taxonomy of relatives from *ego's* point of view.

The *family,* which is the chief structural unit of this study, is used to denote the smallest kinship unit on a membership basis which is treated as a unit for generalized purposes by other parts of the society and by other parts of the kinship structure. As a membership unit, the family includes certain individuals and excludes others. A roll call can be made of the individuals constituting a given concrete family, and the membership and structure of the unit remain the same regardless of which member is taken as *ego.* It is essential that the term family be restricted to the denotations given it here, for in China, as in most other societies, the family is but one of several membership units oriented to kinship factors. The clan or *tsu* and its various subdivisions are all units of this sort. Although these

---

[8] The preoccupation of past social science literature with the relational type of analysis is interesting from the point of view of *wissensoziologie.* It is possible at least that analysis tended in this direction partly because preoccupation with such analysis developed in a society which not only placed a general emphasis on individualism but also had a kinship structure which was unusually individualistic.

units are important for many purposes, their organization is quite different and distinct from that of the family.

In each kinship structure there are certain generalized structural requirements which must be satisfied if the structure is to continue its existence.[4] For rough analytical purposes these requirements can be divided into five general categories of which the fifth is in considerable part a residual category. These are: (1) role differentiation, (2) the allocation of solidarity, (3) economic allocation, (4) political allocation, and (5) the allocation of integration and expression.

FIVE STRUCTURAL PREREQUISITES
FOR KINSHIP STRUCTURE

The empirical existence of structures oriented to the categories listed above is not generally called into question, but it is of some interest to seek an explanation of the status of the categories as prerequisites of kinship structure. Here a few remarks about the general nature of such a line of argument are in order. In relation to any system, a given function may be considered a prerequisite of the system if in the absence of its performance, the system can no longer continue to operate at all, or if in its absence the system disintegrates into smaller systems, or combines with other systems. In the field of biology, for example, one of the ultimate tests of this sort is whether or not the system "dies" if the function is not performed. In studying social systems, which are less amenable to experimentation and more refractory than the materials for biological study, the student is often forced back on the procedure of "proof" by assuming the contrary of what is to be "proved" and showing the incompatibility of the contrary position with the empirical data or other hypotheses on the one hand, and that it is the sole alternative to its opposite on the other. It is true as has been mentioned above in passing [5] that history has furnished many examples of social systems for which the requisites for existence reached so tenuous and unstable a point that the

---

[4] Note this does not rule out the factors of development and change. A given system can go through dynamic processes of greater or lesser magnitude involving considerable variation in the manner in which these requirements are handled and in fact always does. The absence of any one of them, however, would mean the dissolution of the system.

[5] See Chapter One, footnote 2.

societies disintegrated and in many cases, vanished leaving, as far as can be determined, only some of their less perishable artifacts to testify to their existence and nature. At the same time, the number of such cases in which sufficient empirical evidence or historical data remains to enable scientists to resurrect analytically their disintegration in terms of functional failures is small indeed. Despite work on specialized aspects of this problem,[6] such an analysis as this has not been worked out completely and in detail in the case of any of these societies.[7] At any rate, in the case of any given functioning social system, one can hardly fall back upon the expedient of depriving the system of certain elements and standing back to see what follows. In the main, the student is left with the following methodological tool. A given requirement can be termed a functional prerequisite of any social system if in its hypothesized absence the system would degenerate into the war of all against all, or if its members would simply cease to live, or if structural alteration on the level concerned would take place. In systems on a less generalized level, it is sufficient to show that the hypothesized absence of the requirement would have one of the above two results with regard to its own members or that the substructures would cease to have an existence distinct from other substructures in the total social system.

There is some need to point out one type of abstraction involved in separating the kinship structure and its substructures from the general social system for analysis. It should never be forgotten that these kinship substructures are inevitably in some cases and in some degree part of the more generalized substructures for the whole society. Take for example, the status of women relative to men. As will be brought out below, it is essential that some distinctions on a sexual basis be brought out in every kinship structure, but the same is also true for the society as a whole. The role differentiation of women relative to men in the kinship structure can never vary independently of that for women in the society at large. It is, however, methodologically permissible to abstract the kinship sector of the general status of women and hold it up for investigation. As a corollary of this, it follows that the analysis of the kinship sector of a general social substructure never completely describes the total substructure unless

---

[6] See P. A. Sorokin, *Social and Cultural Dynamics* (New York, 1937); also A. J. Toynbee, *A Study of History* (London, 1934).

[7] Perhaps the case of the fall of Rome has come nearest to exposition in these terms.

all the activities of that substructure are in terms of kinship, that is, conterminous with that section of the society which is the kinship structure.
The same is true on all scores, of course. It is quite obvious that such is
the case with regard to age, sex, generation, and similar roles, but it is
also true of the kinship substructures of economic allocation, integration
and expression, power allocation and, to a lesser extent, perhaps,[8] but al
ways to some extent, of the allocation of solidarity.

Another limitation of abstraction which should be kept in mind is
that the course of argument will deal with these factors one by one, with
an analytical limning of their spheres and contents as its goal, but that
is not to argue that these factors are found concretely embodied in this
form. Characteristically, they are not. There are, perhaps, certain aspects
of an individual's role in these substructures which may be defined solely
by one of these factors, but most often this is not the case. Age roles are
often coupled with sex distinctions, economic substructures are mutually
interdependent with the distribution of power and responsibility, and
so on through levels of complexity of interrelationship which vary widely
from one social system to another. In the concrete analysis which is to
follow, attempts will be made to draw attention to this aspect of the
particular cases in hand.

ROLE DIFFERENTIATION IN KINSHIP STRUCTURE

Role differentiation in kinship structure may be defined as the
distribution of persons among the various positions and activities distinguished in the kinship structure and hence the differential arrangement of the members of the structure. This immediately raises the question of the terms on which differential arrangement is made. It is, of
course, the variation in these terms which distinguishes among the various
possible types of role differentiation. The terms in which role differentia-

[8] It may well be possible to make out a case for the theory that in those societies
in which kinship solidarity is not the major social solidarity, the kinship solidarity is
somewhat less influenced by the general social definition of solidarity than is true
of the other factors mentioned here. Verification of this theory would require considerable comparative empirical research. Insofar as it is true, it might well be a
factor in the explanation of the stress on an individual who is passing from a stage
of primary relations with persons of his own kin unit to one of primary relations
with persons outside it, or the case of a society changing from a stage of primary
social emphasis on kin solidarity to another formulation, or some combination of
these two cases.

tion occurs, while crucial in its definition, do not alter the autonomy of role differentiation as a structural phenomenon. The members of society must always recognize some structure of role differentiation and orient their action to it. Therefore, although the primary basis of a given structuralization of role differentiation might be, for example, political, the phenomena involved cannot be understood solely in terms of the political variable. Whatever the basis of the differential arrangement of members in a society or group, the action of members of the group and of outsiders in their relations with this group must in part be specifically oriented to this inescapable arrangement. Thus differentiation may be to a marked degree interdependent with one or more of the other four structures to be discussed here, but it is never a dependent variable of one or of any combination of them. Before going further into this aspect of role differentiation, however, a word or so more needs be said on the functional background of the phenomenon.

Role differentiation may be said to furnish a method of coping with the following general problems. First, there is the distribution of individuals among the total number of positions of whatever sort in the structure under consideration. This must be done regardless of how numerous or varied either the positions or the individuals may be. The number and variety of both categories will, of course, have substantial effect upon the concrete result, but the status of the requirement as a requirement is not affected by these considerations. It is reasonably clear, of course, that random distribution of this sort is inconceivable and that failure to have a well-institutionalized method of handling this requirement, a structure of role differentiation, would result in the cessation of functioning of the larger structure of which it is a part, either because vital positions would not be filled, or because fighting would break out over who was to fill which position—or more likely, a combination of both. In any case the system could not persist.

Second, there must also be some differentiation among individuals due to the fact that they are by no means homogeneous. Even if one could hypothesize a social universe of completely homogeneous positions, the phenomenon of role differentiation would still result, in a functioning society, from the lack of homogeneity among the members. Babies are everywhere unable to subsist without the aid, not alone of other individuals, but also of other individuals differentiated from them in respect to physical and mental maturity, to mention only two criteria. Men are everywhere unable to bear children, and women everywhere must to some degree differentiate their activities with regard to childbearing. Actually in social systems the lack of homogeneity which must be integrated by institutionalized role differentiation goes far beyond such physical factors, but they will suffice for illustration. It should be pointed out that the totality of possible variation and differential arrangement, either in terms of positions or members in a social structure or substructure is never institutionally prescribed. The institutionalized portion of any given structure of social role differentiation must, however, cover such part of the role differentiation as is required for the functioning of the society. If it does not, change or disintegration or both will follow. Which will occur is, of course, subject to variation.

The terms on which the differential arrangement of members of kinship structures can be based might conceivably be extremely wide and varied, but in five respects, at least, there must be role differentiation to some degree. These five are age, sex, generation, economic position, and political position. It is perhaps not going too far to say that most types of role differentiation within kinship structures, particularly insofar as the role differentiation is institutionalized,[9] would fall into one or more of these five terms. There may be, and perhaps characteristically there are, other terms in the institutionalized kinship role differentiation, but there are always these five at least, however differently they may be emphasized.

The basic reason for age role differentiation lies ultimately in the fact that certain functions cannot be fulfilled by individuals of certain stages of physical and mental development. This factor, however, sets only the

[9] As pointed out above, the institutionalization in these respects never exhausts the totality of possible variations. Thus it is not merely conceivable that there exist some role differentiation within a specific kin unit that is not part of the institutionalized methods of role differentiation of the kinship structure of a given society, but the contrary is well nigh inconceivable. Thus in a given family in the southwestern part of the United States one might find a differential arrangement of the members in terms of their ability to ride horses or herd cattle, or in a given academic family there might be a differential arrangement of the members on the basis of intellectual promise and attainment, and these special differentiations of role might be of crucial significance in the families concerned, but, nevertheless, they could hardly be considered part of the institutionalized kinship structure of that geographical or occupational sphere.

minimum level of age distinction in kinship units, and the distinction is never quite so rudimentary in any specific case. Thus in all kinship structures there must be some differentiation of role as between adults and children, but the ways in which these lines can be drawn are exceedingly various. There might be several steps largely defined on the basis of age though with some admixture of criteria of prowess or achievement within these two major groups. In addition to these more or less absolute age groupings, there is differentiation based on relative age. The Chinese family structure places great emphasis on both absolute age groups and consideration of relative age.

Role differentiation based on sex is another of those minimally required orientations to the limiting factors of human heredity and non-human environment which are always present in such structures and which can always be said to go considerably beyond the minimal requirements of orientation to the physical factors involved. It is a generally accepted empirical fact that all known societies go further in distinction between sex roles in regard to occupations, ceremonial roles, authority, or a number of other considerations than is physiologically required. The same is true of kinship structures. Perhaps the most familiar kinship differentiation along these lines is combined with the question of the allocation of power. One of the primary modes of role differentiation in terms of power distribution is that of sex, and it is here that the familiar terms of matriarchy and patriarchy arise.

Virtually conterminous in familiarity with its role in the distribution of power is the focus on sex differentiation in the rearing of children. Even in societies which tend to equalize sex roles in the family the primary duties in the raising of children are heavily concentrated on the female side, especially in the early stages of the child's development. Economic roles also tend to crystalize in considerable degree along sex lines. This is particularly true of occupational roles. For example, housekeeping, however low its esteem, is nevertheless an economic role from the social point of view, and it is a commonplace of a great many societies that this is "woman's work." The differentiation goes far beyond this, however, and mingles with the general occupational distinctions on a sex basis which appear in such societies.

Finally, there is a familiar differentiation of roles along sex lines for the purpose of ritual activities. This may be absent from the kinship structure,[10] but it often plays an important role. The lines drawn between the sexes in these respects is sharp in China and is one of the main factors in the consideration of the population problems of China. There are, of course, other possibilities of variation along these lines which could be elaborated at some length, but those already indicated should be sufficient to indicate the type and tenor of such proliferation.

One other interesting aspect of role differentiation on a basis of sex distinction is that it is so frequently a focus for stress in changing social systems. This is apt to be peculiarly true when the changes being made are in the direction of industrialization. The institutional basis of industrialized societies must lay peculiar stress on the differentiation of individuals on a universalistic basis. This usually puts considerable pressure on those patterns which institutionalize a sex differential regardless of objective criteria. The influence of this is ordinarily quickly felt in the kinship structure, and the growth of industrialization and the spread of its influence have been everywhere accompanied by moves for the emancipation of women both within the family and within the society generally.[11]

Kinship role differentiation on the basis of generation is always drawn to some degree, though the importance attributed to the factor may vary widely. Again, there is a minimal recognition of this difference due to the birth of children, their rearing in kinship systems, and their general state of dependency in their early stages. The obverse side of this is, of course, the necessity of distinguishing parents and the problem of old age. Here again kinship role differentiation along the lines concerned goes considerably beyond the minimum. One of the important aspects of this category is its closeness to that of age. In some societies the two tend to merge, and the distinction is not crucial. But perhaps this is less often

[10] In the family system of modern Western society, this distinction along sex lines is not ordinarily drawn, but it is drawn quite distinctly in the major religious systems of that society.

[11] That these movements have been in an overwhelming number of cases accompanied by feminist movements follows from the fact that in the societies affected, it is the female role which has held the lesser power, privilege, and prestige. Presumably, had the reverse been the case, the agitation would have come from the men. In this connection it is interesting to recall that where groups other than sex groups have been differentiated on particularistic grounds as regards power and privilege especially (*e.g.*, social classes), industrialization has been inevitably accompanied by agitation for removal of particularistic discrimination.

true than the reverse. As will be demonstrated below, the distinction is of vital significance in China, early and late.

Generational role differentiation in kinship systems is most important in connection with the distribution of power and the administrative aspects of the economic sphere of the family's life, however crude and simple these may be. In kinship units which give considerable attention to generational differentiation, economic and political functions are certain to be defined in generational terms to some degree. Other functions may also be divided along generational lines. Ceremonial functions often are, for example. In social systems undergoing change from highly particularistic patterns to more universalistic ones, the delineation of economic and political functions along generational lines is one of the factors most apt to become a source of friction among the individual members of a given kinship unit.

Another important aspect of generational role differentiation is the role it plays in the determination of the basic unit of solidarity of the kinship structure. The general question of solidarity in kinship units is taken up below, but it may be pointed out here that the differing content of the basic kinship units as between two societies is often in part determined on the basis of generation inclusion. Thus ideally the multilineal conjugal family unit contains only two generations. A patriarchal family unit such as that which formed the classical ideal in China, contains at least three generations and preferably more.

Consideration of the factors involved in role differentiation along economic lines tends to blend with the more general discussion of the structural aspects of economic allocation which will be carried on later in this chapter. The basic explanation for kinship role differentiation on an economic basis lies in the necessity of distributing roles of production and consumption among the various members of the kinship units. Roles of production must be distributed if the family is to survive. Without income and management of this phase of activity, the family would, in the last analysis, starve. Without a definite system of distribution the way would be open for a competition limited only by the respective distribution of command over physical force. In addition, depending on the delineation of roles in other respects, certain individual members must participate differentially in both the production and the consumption of the kinship unit. Kinship role differentiation on an economic basis is not of necessity strongly emphasized, but it is commonly the focus of considerable attention.

It is not conceivable that the distribution of the consumption of income be identical with the distribution of the earning of it, if only for the reason that very young children are incapable of economically productive effort sufficient to meet their minimum needs. This is true despite the fact that the points at which some societies set the limits in these respects are very much lower than those of others. The obverse of this is equally true. There must be some consumption by the earner if only that he may continue to live and earn. Within these two limits, however, concrete solutions are to be found. Role differentiation on the grounds of consumption are apt to be more highly correlated with other aspects of role differentiation than with production. The converse is equally true.[12] The two important criteria of role differentiation in these respects are: (a) the distinction between consumers and producers, and (b) the distinction between types or degree of production or consumption.

The kinship role differentiation based on political position within the family is always of crucial significance, involving, as it does, the allocation of power and responsibility. The implications of this are more fully dealt with in the section on the substructure of political allocation. Role differentiation along these lines is required by two basic facts. In the first place, if a given unit of the kinship structure is to have relations with other units or parts of the society, some member or members must take responsibility for the acts of members of this unit and the fulfillment of their obligations to other units. The same must be done with regard to its internal relations. In addition, there must be some definite allocation of power to back up the assignment of roles, tasks, and so forth, in order to punish deviation, if necessary, and in the last analysis, in order to limit the use of force by others according to whim or in the implementation of institutionally illegitimate ends.

[12] *E.g.*, in the state of Texas, a subsection of the general American community, there is no question but what the male is regarded as the proper major income earner of the family, but regard for the equality of women in certain respects is such that the wife has legal right to fifty per cent of all the husband's income subsequent to the marriage, regardless of her own activities.

SOLIDARITY IN KINSHIP STRUCTURE

The allocation of solidarity in kinship structure has been defined above as the distribution of relationships among the members of the kinship structure according to the content, strength, and intensity of the relationship. Considerations of this sort have played a large role in the literature which has been built up in anthropology, sociology, and psychology on the general subject of kinship. Solidarity, as used here, will cover a phenomenon of infinite gradation between two poles. The negative pole will be taken to mean complete antagonism—war at sight, as it were. The positive pole will be taken to mean complete agreement and complete and mutual affective accord. The only element of discontinuity of the variation between these two poles is at the point of perfect neutrality. This point is ruled out with reference to the relations of members of the basic kinship unit of solidarity in particular and of kinship units in general, because some affective orientation of members of kinship units toward one another is always institutionally enjoined.

In the definition of the term solidarity in use here, the subsidiary terms content, strength, and intensity have appeared. By the term content is meant the definition of the type of relation which is to exist and the members between whom it is to exist. Thus all kinship structures have a solidarity relationship of some sort between mother and child, covering at least the early stages of the child's development. The content of the solidarity would include the mother and child as the persons involved. The type of relationship might vary considerably, but it would commonly include obedience of the child up to a point, care of the child by the mother, strong emotional attachment of the mother to the child and vice versa, and so forth. This will serve as a much simplified example.

By the term strength we mean the relative precedence taken by this relationship over other relationships of its general sort, and over other obligations and commitments in the larger social sphere, or vice versa. As an example, the relationship between father and son in the "traditional" Chinese family may be contrasted with that between male siblings. The former definitely takes precedence should any conflict arise, and hence is to be considered "stronger" from this point of view.[18] It is possible

---

[18] In the concrete case, events might actually work out quite otherwise, depending on personalities involved, but here the discussion is in terms of the institutionalized patterns.

that in these relations the strength of A's relation with B will not coincide exactly with the strength of B's relation with A. Here again the Confucian ideal furnishes a good example. No relation in that ideal pattern is stronger than that of son to father from the son's point of view; but from the father's point of view, the relation with his father would take precedence over that with his son.

By the term intensity we mean the state of mutual affect involved in the relationship. The intensity of solidarity is subject to two major planes of variation. There is first the question of the type or types of affect involved: respect, love, fear, and so on. Though there are many different affects which may be listed according to whatever psychological taxonomy may be preferred, the important thing to note here is a dichotomy of avoidance and intimacy. The intensity of the affective relationship between a Navaho man and his mother-in-law is great, but he must avoid all contact with her. The intensity of the affective relationship between husband and wife in the family system of the United States is expected to be great and the relation intimate—involving a great deal of direct personal contact with overt display of affect. The essence of avoidance used here is the tendency to minimize direct contact and have such as does exist on a relatively formal basis. The essence of the term intimacy is the tendency to emphasize direct contact, informality, and overt display of affect. Certain affects are generally more easily combined with avoidance than with intimacy—for example, respect and fear—but this is a highly relative matter.

Second, there is the degree of the affective involvement of the relationship. It must be noted, relative to these two planes of variation, that there is the possibility that in a given relation, A's affects relative to B may differ from B's to A in type or intensity. If the relation between husband and wife in the American family is taken as an example of this aspect of kinship solidarity, it may be noted that the types of affect involved are institutionally expected to consist chiefly of romantic love and enthusiastic admiration of the individual's total character. There may be, and commonly are, others, but these two would seem to predominate. Even here, although the two are of undeniable importance, the former predominates. If the gap between the two is too great, problems may be created. The position of either husband or wife then tends to degenerate. The wife may tend toward the "Hausfrau" role, or the husband may tend toward the role of the "weak man" or the "bad husband." [14] Neither tendency has social approval. The degree of affective involvement of the American husband and wife is supposed to be high indeed. Here again the emphasis is on the factor of romantic love. It is to be noted that in general in the example given both husband and wife are expected to have roughly the same affects and the same degree of affective involvement. There are concrete cases, of course, in which there is considerable variance in these respects between the parties.

One of the most important points about these three aspects of kinship solidarity is that the latter two factors, strength and intensity, may each differ not only as among the parties to the relation but also from one another. The relationship may be quite strong and yet have relatively low intensity, or it may be quite intense and relatively weak. Since there is always some degree of affect involved in kinship relations, the relation can never be completely neutral so far as intensity is concerned. [15]

To consider the necessity of kinship solidarity for the kinship structure, it is necessary to differentiate between two aspects of kinship solidarity. First, there is the solidarity which a particular kinship unit presents relative to the members of the society outside the particular kinship unit. Second, there are the various solidarities among the various members of a particular kinship unit itself. The status of the former as a prerequisite is a corollary of the status of the kinship structure itself as a prerequisite. If a kinship structure must exist if there is a society, then its members must, in their relationships toward other members of society, have certain content, strength, and intensity, institutionally prescribed on the basis of their being members of a particular kinship unit. The degree to which this is so, and particularly the strength of kinship solidarity relative to other solidarities in the social system, is subject to a wide range of possibilities, but, if it did not exist to some degree, the separateness and distinctness of the kinship units would be dissolved. One aspect of comparison between

[14] There are other directions these tendencies may take, but these would seem, by and large, to be the major ones.

[15] In the institutionally prescribed case, the solidarity patterns of kinship structures cannot well be negative save in specific types of relations (*e.g.*, incest, see below), since the kinship system is presumably a unit of high solidarity in the general social system. In the concrete case, however, this may in fact result. The type of difficulty that such a result brings is well exemplified in the case of the Chinese family. This type of result may be brought about through the latent effects of an otherwise fairly well integrated pattern. The so-called Oedipus complex is a case in point.

the American family and the "traditional" Chinese family pattern in these respects will illuminate what is meant here. In the American case many obligations take precedence over family considerations. Notable among these are certain relations with the government. For example, in time of war, loyalty to the nation takes precedence over loyalty to the family. This is not the case with the Confucian ideal.[16] Emperors have specifically forgiven traitors whose action was motivated by family considerations. No doubt many other examples will come readily to the reader's mind.

The variations in regard to the distinction of solidarities within a given kinship unit itself are well known to students of these matters. As has been observed above, this phenomenon together with that of role differentiation has received the primary focus of attention of anthropologists, sociologists, and psychiatrists. The status of this level of solidarity of kinship units as a prerequisite of those units depends on much the same line of reasoning followed in the case of role differentiation. In the accomplishment of the various duties required for the existence of the kinship unit, and in the allocation of its fruits, whether they be economic goods or affection, there must be a reasonably stable structure of relationships. The stable structure is role differentiation: the force which gives the structure its relative stability is the institutional prescription of the content, strength, and intensity of the relationship—its structure of solidarity.[17]

Kinship structures may differ in many ways. One of the most significant of these modes of difference for purposes of comparative social analysis is the difference in what constitutes the primary unit of solidarity of the kinship structure.[18] The number of relational terms distinguished

[16] Even in the American case the family takes precedence in some fairly extreme situations. A woman cannot be forced to testify against her husband, regardless of the seriousness of the crime of which he is accused.

[17] The interrelationship between role differentiation and solidarity emerges clearly here.

[18] Professor Talcott Parsons, in lectures and private conversation, has laid considerable emphasis on this mode of differentiation and that of differentiation of kinship units by differentiation among role structures within more or less identical primary units of solidarity. Thus the Japanese family and the German family have different primary units of solidarity. The American and German families have roughly equivalent primary units of solidarity, but a radically different definition and distribution of roles within the units.

relative to *ego* vary from approximately twenty-four to well over three hundred. People in all these relations in the societies concerned are members of one relational system, but these systems are always further broken down. The smallest portion of any individual's total relational system which operates as a membership unit for generalized purposes relative to the remainder of that system and other aspects of the society is the primary unit of kinship solidarity. This primary unit of solidarity is identical with what this study has defined as the family. As institutionally prescribed it always includes parents and nonadult children as a minimum and commonly includes several other members.

In the operation of the incest taboo the question of solidarity is clearly put, both as regards the basic unit in relation to other units, and as regards the relations between members of the basic unit. In any society, heterosexual intercourse [19] is prohibited between certain members of the society. The incest taboo is comprised of those prohibitions on heterosexual intercourse which are specifically oriented to the kinship structure,[20] namely, where the sexual nexus might in the absence of the taboo take place between two relatives without any special notice being taken of it for this reason. That is to say that the incest taboo outlaws a particular sort of kinship solidarity, solidarity on a basis of heterosexual intercourse between certain members of the kinship units. The actual definition of incest for a particular society is subject to variation. Empirically, however, the incest taboo always covers certain biologic and affinal relationships. These are the relations between direct ancestors (parents, grandparents, greatgrandparents, and so on) and children, between siblings of the opposite sex, and between direct ancestors and their children's spouses.[21] It

[19] The incest taboo does not seem to cover homosexual relationships. Relationships of this nature, if prohibited, are generally handled on the basis of the type of relationship concerned rather than the particularistic definition of the members of the relationship. This is quite different from the incest taboo in which the emphasis definitely focuses on the particularistic definition of the members of the relationship.

[20] This study does not see fit to confine the term "incest" to sexual relations between consanguineous relatives, since in many societies this taboo is extended to certain affinal relations as well. Usage here differs in this respect from that of Professor R. Fortune in his article for the *Encyclopedia of the Social Sciences* (New York, 1932), 7, 620–622.

[21] There have been segments of societies to which these taboos did not apply (*e.g.*, the royal house of Egypt), but there is no authenticated case of a total social system in which these taboos do not apply to the population at large.

would appear, therefore, from the evidence of various empirical observations that, although the incest taboo ordinarily outlaws many heterosexual relationships beyond the limits of the primary unit of kinship solidarity, it always outlaws them between blood relatives within the limits of the primary unit of kinship solidarity.[22] Within that unit, some relations of this sort between affinal relatives are frequently excepted from the incest taboo, for example, the relations between siblings and the spouses of their fellow siblings, and obviously this is true in the case of relatives classified relative to one another as husbands and wives (or functional equivalents and variations thereof, for example, concubines).

What is the basis of this peculiar taboo? In a short article on the subject Professor R. Fortune shows that the simple biologistic theories of inherent revulsion and the like fail to account for the phenomenon itself, and one might add that these theories also fail to account for the differing patterns of the incest taboo in different societies.[23]

It has been suggested above that a kinship structure is required for the stable existence of any society, and that this in turn requires solidarity on the part of the kinship units, both with regard to internal and external affairs. The primary unit of kinship solidarity operates in considerable degree as a unit in economic, political, and other matters relative to other persons and groups within the larger kinship units of which it is a part and/or to persons and groups in the society outside those units. Thus any forces working to break down the strength of the solidarity of this unit [24] must be held in check as completely as possible.

Modern social scientists generally agree that the emotional involvements of sexual relations are peculiarly intense and deep seated. Perhaps

[22] Empirical proof of this point would require careful comparative documentation and is beyond the scope of this study. Consultation with anthropologists, however, has failed to produce any case to the contrary which holds over a society as a whole. As mentioned above, there have been segments of certain societies which have been exempted from these taboos.

[23] *Op. cit.,* pp. 620–622.

[24] The permission of heterosexual relations between members of the primary unit of kinship solidarity other than those in the position relative to one another of husband and wife (or functional equivalent thereof) might increase the intensity of, say, the father and his daughter for some extended period, but this would in all likelihood be offset by a degeneration of the intensity of solidarity between husband and wife, daughter and mother, and so on. There is every reason to believe the strength of the solidarity of the unit would not be increased even temporarily.

modern workers in this field have gone too far in these respects and overemphasize the role played by such phenomena, but certainly they have proved the importance of such considerations past all doubting. It may well be that the basic factor in explaining the existence of the incest taboo is the necessity of reducing rivalry between members of the family unit to a minimum. The incest taboo inhibits solidarity of a sort which would almost certainly be disruptive of other necessary solidarities. In all family structures the relations between parents and children and between siblings are always of primary importance, and it is precisely these relationships which are always included in the incest taboo.

This is by no means a sufficient explanation of the phenomenon, however, since this factor is certainly unable to account for all the variations in definition of the incest taboo in different societies. Other considerations enter. One of the commonest is the factor of insuring security of the family unit by means of allying it with other groups in the society. If the society places a premium on security gained in this fashion, all members of the extended kinship groups concerned may be included in the incest taboo, thus necessitating an alliance with some new kinship group with each marriage. This factor is often taken as the primary factor in the explanation of the incest taboo because of the frequency with which it crops up empirically.[25] As the sole explanation it is not tenable since it fails to account for the presence of such a taboo in societies which institutionalize kinship endogamy, and since it fails to account for the fact that a specific core of relatives is always included in the incest taboo, whatever its variations. There are, no doubt, other factors which enter into the explanation of the exact definition of any particular incest taboo, but it would seem that there is no case in which the maintenance of internal family solidarity can be ignored, whereas the other considerations which enter can be ignored in certain cases. Insofar as this position is a valid one, the particular definition of the incest taboo in a given society will serve as a highly strategic tool for social analysis, since the specific definition of the incest taboo will always throw some considerable light on the primary foci of solidarity within the units concerned. Furthermore, with changing definitions of the incest taboo changing family conditions will certainly be found. Whether they be disruptive changes or changes in the direction of greater stability and integration will depend on the concrete case. The

[25] See R. Fortune, *op. cit.*, pp. 620–622.

changes will, however, go far beyond the matter of sexual relations; the question of solidarity in general is sure to be involved. Finally, in any concrete case in which heterosexual relationships are not found to be taboo between direct ancestors and children, siblings, and direct ancestors and the spouses of children, the family or families concerned will be: (a) a family or families occupying a very particular and peculiar status in the social system as a whole—a status not found generally in the society as a whole—or (b) a family or families in a position of disintegration and disruption, or (c) some combination of the foregoing categories. If the families concerned are found generally throughout the social system, that social system itself will be in a state of disintegration and disruption moving toward either a complete dissolution or some radically new and different social formulation.

ECONOMIC ALLOCATION IN KINSHIP STRUCTURE

Economic allocation in kinship structure has been defined above as the distribution of the goods and services making up the income of the units of the structure and of the goods and efforts making up the output of the units of the structure among the various members of the units. Economic activities and interrelations, insofar as their sphere is confined to kinship orientations, are best studied for present purposes as they operate within the family. There are, of course, all sorts of economic relations defined in the relational approach to kinship, but, changing as this does with every change of *ego,* description of the relations is confined to descriptions of *ego's* relations with other specific relatives, and any systematic operations of kinship groups fall from the picture. The functional basis for a substructure handling economic allocation is not difficult to find. The members of the familial and family groups must have food, shelter, clothing, and similar necessities if they are to survive physically. These requirements are not in the nature of free goods as that concept is defined by the economists, and even if they were, the problem of distribution would still arise in the social context to offset the effect of jealousies which might well arise no matter how homogeneous the articles concerned might be intrinsically, and so forth. To survive physically, the members of these groups must obtain and distribute these requirements. While it is theoretically possible that a particular concrete clan or family group might consume without producing at all, it is certainly not conceivable that this be true of more than a limited number of such groups in any particular society. This does not outlaw the possibility that in a particular society certain of these groups may exploit others and produce relatively little, but it does indicate that such groups, however strong they may become, can never become the characteristic groups in a given society unless that society is being extinguished.[26]

The degree to which the family substructures of economic allocation can break down for the society as a whole is, therefore, quite limited, but within a given society these substructures may and often do break down in particular cases. Then the functional necessity of such substructures emerges with sharp clarity. In China, for example, the failure of the male head of the family to carry out his productive role often results in the destruction of the family. This has been a frequent phenomenon in cases of opium addiction, and such extremes as starvation of the family, loss of status, sale of children, and even sale of wives have frequently resulted. The most spectacular result from the social point of view is apt to be that of forcing other members of the society into roles which violate the institutional patterns.[27] In the case of societies in which the males in the family play the predominant productive role this is particularly likely to result a compulsory redefinition of the status of women. Since other roles in other of the family substructures are intimately connected with those of economic allocation, changes in the economic roles are certain to have wide repercussions in the family.

The substructure of economic allocation is in a strategic position relative to the total society for another important reason. It is in this connection that the family has its primary interrelations with the structure of occupational roles for the society as a whole. The importance of this fact varies inversely with the degree to which the families in a society are self-sufficient economically. In the case of virtually complete economic

[26] Extinction is a limiting case, of course, but the possibility of its existence as an empirical process should not be overlooked. It may be noted simply that there exist, for example, in Kwantung, areas in which the exploitation of tenants by landlords and usurers is such that people are annually driven from the area. Concomitantly, the very land itself is being greatly and rapidly reduced in fertility. This is the result of a peculiar and complex social situation in the areas concerned, but there seems little doubt that the situation exists and that the process, if unchecked, will extinguish a considerable proportion of the family groups of that area by starvation in some cases, and the scattering of emigration in others, to mention only two of the possibilities.

[27] See Ida Pruitt, *A Daughter of the Han* (New Haven, 1945), pp. 55-75.

self-sufficiency, the structure of occupational roles for the society as a whole is virtually conterminous with that of the family, and the distinction, therefore, is of correspondingly little importance. On the other hand, industrialization must in all cases be incompatible with family economic self-sufficiency because of the extremes to which it inevitably carries the division of labor.[28] Whatever other factors may operate to impede or bolster such self-sufficiency, as the industrialization of a society increases, family self-sufficiency declines.

The link between the family groups and the larger economic aspects of the society as a whole has an additional importance since the status of the entire family in industrialized societies tends to be largely dependent upon the occupational role of the member or members upon whom the group depends for the bulk of its support.

The substructure of economic allocation may be divided for the purposes of analysis into two parts: the structure of production and the structure of consumption. The former includes all activities and sources from which goods and services accrue to the family group. The latter includes all activities and methods whereby these goods and services are allocated to the various members of the group and for the purposes of the group. In no known family system does each member consume exactly what he or she produces and no more or less. As was pointed out in the section above on role differentiation, some important family substructures crystallize along these lines. There is always, for example, some distinction in the family between women's work and men's work, between that of adults and that of children. Any changes in the society which disrupt these patterns will again have far-reaching social implications.

In connection with the productive structure, two considerations are of foremost importance here. One is the source of the income, and the other is the division of labor in its acquisition. As regards the former, it is of some importance to note whether the income is from the performance of functions by the family as a unit or by the integration of a member or members of the group into groups which are erected without reference to the family group, or whether the goods and services are produced and

[28] There are other reasons as well: *e.g.*, the premium placed by industrialization on locational utilization would make space for agricultural pursuits unavailable to the average industrial working family, even if there were surplus labor in the family for such work. The cause cited above would seem to be the main consideration, however.

consumed directly for and by the family or are produced for consumption outside the family and goods and services for the family bought with the proceeds of that transaction. Small-scale tenant or peasant ownership, agriculture and domestic industry are two of the commonest methods whereby the major economic efforts of the group concerned can be prevented from carrying its members outside the group to an important degree. Systems of hired agricultural labor and the factory system, particularly the latter, force the breakup of such patterns and force one or more of the members of the group into the primary roles of economic production.

The second question of the directness of the contribution to the family needs has as its limiting case the self-sufficient agricultural family. Here the family might produce all it consumed without reference to exchange for any purpose with individuals or groups outside the family. The situation of the modern industrial worker's family is at great variance with this since the overwhelming bulk of the income in this case is in the form of money wages—generalized purchasing power—earned for work having no necessary connection with the goods and services for which they are spent. It must, however, not be forgotten that even in this case a considerable portion of effort is always expended by the family members for direct consumption by the family. Under this heading are to be listed all those functions commonly called the "domestic duties," cleaning, cooking, serving, washing, caring for children and disabled members of the family, and the administration of the household itself. Even in the most highly urbanized apartment-dwelling families, some aspects of these functions must be met if the family is to continue. This residual core of family duties which are performed directly is important because the duties are so often integrally connected with the substructure of role differentiation in general and that of sex roles in particular.

This factor is also closely connected with the previous one in that, to the degree that the main income of the group is dependent upon the efforts of a member or members of the group working outside the family unit, some member or members of the family must be institutionally cast in this domestic role as their primary family productive role. The frequency with which these roles have fallen to women is certainly one of the more interesting uniformities of social history and one which cannot be entirely explained in terms of the position of women as the bearers of children, though this fact is no doubt of strategic importance here. Again one of the interesting facts about industrialization is that it affords job opportunities which are limited intrinsically only to a slight degree by the sex of the applicant, and not at all by any previously existing substructure of family economic roles. Furthermore, since the workers in modern industry receive generalized purchasing power for their efforts, and must do so if the society is to operate on any sizable scale, an industrial society offers the maximum opportunity of reducing these aspects of family economic production to a minimum by shifting them to the shoulders of specialists.

Some attention must be paid to the implications of the fact that the primary source of family income is not in work done by the family as a unit for home consumption. It has been mentioned above that the substructure of family economic allocation provides the single most important link between the family and the structure of occupational roles of the society as a whole. To the degree that the family is not self-sufficient the importance of this factor increases, because it increases the contact of the family with the productive structure of the society as a whole. There is still another aspect of this, however. Insofar as the family income is not directly consumed without the intermediation of exchange, the contact of the family with the society as a whole is further increased by the necessity of getting the goods and services it consumes from other sources. The changes in this direction brought about by the process of industrialization are also of great importance to the general structure of the family.

On the consumption side the ramifications are quite as numerous as on the production side. In the literature of social science there are frequent statements to the general effect that in well-integrated families the rule of economic allocation is roughly equivalent to the statement "from each according to his ability; to each according to his need"—a sort of family communism.[29] This statement may well be true, but, as is implicit in what has been said above, the definition of what constitutes "from each according to his ability" is always carefully institutionalized at least in part, and the same is true on the side of consumption. Despite the romantic tales of travelers and some social scientists, the income of the family is never simply dumped in a heap, as it were, and consumed willy-

[29] See Mai Hui-T'ing, *Problem of Chinese Family Reconstruction* (Shanghai, 1930), pp. 53ff.

nilly. Such ideas gained a firm hold on the imagination of Westerners with the romantic political interpretations of the noble savage which played so important a role in the intellectual life of the eighteenth and nineteenth centuries, and they recrudesce even now from time to time. It is quite safe to say that there is always some institutionalization of a substructure of consumption within the family, and there are at least three important considerations involved: (a) whether or not all income of all members goes into a common fund from which distribution is made, (b) how and by whom is the distribution controlled and, (c) to what purposes and to whom is it allocated for consumption.

It is not the function of this introduction to plumb at any great depth the general implications of these three considerations, but some of the more obvious aspects which the empirical sections of the study discuss may be mentioned here. If the income of the members of the family is pooled prior to distribution, this fact alone has implications for the system of distribution. It means that however and by whomever the common fund of the family is managed, individual expenditures must be cleared through the family as it were—either by the approval of a single member placed in a position of administration or a group of members so placed. This factor requires that all activities of family members which require the expenditure of goods and services subject to family supervision, however lenient that may be. In societies with a family structure in which this is not the case, the way is open for considerably greater freedom of action relative to the family. For example, in the United States the husband and father is held responsible for support of his wife and family, but his income over and above a certain level deemed commensurate with his status in the community does not necessarily go into any family fund at all. He may spend it as he sees fit, and unless he violates laws or shocks the community in other respects, neither legal nor institutional pressure will be brought to bear upon him. A change in these respects may have important effects in the direction of making the autonomy of individual members of the family possible.

The solution of the problem of how and by whom the distribution of the family income is controlled is perhaps the most important single link between the family substructure of economic allocation and that of political allocation. Authority over the economic resources of the family is important because with it goes some measure of authority over all other activities, at least insofar as these involve consumption. Empirically, there are many different solutions of the locus of this authority, and all sorts of combinations of control by one individual or by the consultation of several are possible. As regards the manner in which such decisions are made, it must be kept in mind that a certain amount of distribution of consumption is always institutionally defined, and however complete the authority of an individual over the family may be in these respects, his action will be frowned upon, even if not successfully resisted, if he transgresses certain limits. Questions such as the access of members of the family to the person or persons making these decisions, their ability to take issue with such decisions, and so on, are also of great importance, since they help define the range of action of the individual relative to his family.

Certain minimal purposes must always be served in the distribution of the family income, and there is always some social definition and enforcement of these requirements. On the other hand, beyond the minimum required by subsistence, all sorts of differences may arise. Custom may dictate expenditures on such things as weddings and funerals out of all proportion to such expenditures in other societies, and emotional attachments may dictate all sorts of "uneconomic" allocations.

The distribution of consumption among members may implement all sorts of considerations in the family. Role differentiation is one of the outstanding factors. Men may, for example, be permitted expenditures denied women, older persons those denied children, and so forth. A change in such patterns or a road whereby a family member may act independently of them will have effects reaching far afield.

POLITICAL ALLOCATION IN KINSHIP STRUCTURES

Political allocation in kinship structure has been defined for the purposes of this study as the distribution of power over and responsibility for the actions of the various members of the structural units involving on the one hand the institutionalized use of coercive sanctions of which force is the extreme form in one direction, and involving on the other accountability to the members of the group concerned or to other persons or groups in the society. The terms power and responsibility are of the essence of the term political as it is to be used in this study. Power here means the ability to exercise authority and control over the actions of others. Responsibility here means the accountability to other individuals or groups of an individual or individuals for his or their own acts or the acts of others. Power may be exercised in many ways and implemented variously. There must always be some specific institutionalization relative to the use of force, and if the system is to be stable in the face of the possible use of force by others to resist or overthrow it or in the face of the necessity of enforcing conformity with its values and requirements, there must be a socially defined and approved use of force with a socially defined and approved selection of personnel to wield it. The use of force to insure the carrying out of social action within certain limits is always an extreme, and in a sense it is the symbol of social frustration. Moreover, its effectiveness is predicated on its not being required in more than a limited number of cases. For should it become the major factor insuring uniformity with a given line of conduct widely generalized throughout the society, it would become necessary for so great a proportion of the society to become enforcement agents that the problem of *quis custodiet ipsos custodes* would inevitably arise.

The necessity of a family substructure of political allocation is implicit in what has been said above. Since the family operates as a unit in relation to many other aspects of the society, the questions of control of and responsibility for the actions of its members must be determined in a way generally known and generally to be expected throughout the society in question. In the absence of control and responsibility, there would be no way to insure the performance of necessary functions and no way to curb deviant activity. Both factors are required if for no other reason than the necessity of integrating new generations into the patterns of social life. Physical coercion need not play a large role. Cases of societies have been cited in which such forms of control play only minor roles. In fact, in the family as in the society at large, a widespread use of physical coercion is most frequently an indication of an extremely precarious institutional structure. Nevertheless, if the family is to function as a unit, it must be possible to see to it that certain requirements are met, by force if necessary, and it must be possible to take a definite person or persons to account if they fail to meet the requirements.

In any system of which power is an important part, the question of responsibility is sharply posed. Structures in which the locus of power is at variance with that of responsibility are inherently unstable. This instability lies in two directions. It is not practically effective in the long run to hold an individual responsible for circumstances or actions over which he lacks control, and possession of power unaccompanied by responsibility in the sphere of its exercise leaves the way open for its capricious and disruptive application. Either situation will in time compel a social reformulation.

There are in general two ways by which the balance of locus of power and responsibility can be maintained. The first of these is by the institutionalization of mutual power and mutual responsibility. In such a relation both parties (or all parties if more than two are involved) have, theoretically at least, equal powers and responsibilities. Friendship is an example of such a relation, and contractual relations in the modern business world are supposedly of this order. The second is by the institutionalization of a hierarchy in which power and responsibility vary inversely. In such a hierarchy the responsibility owed by a power wielder is not owed directly to the subject of his power but is owed to a third party or group or ideal. Military organizations are prominent examples of this type of balance, as are most administrative organizations of any complexity to a greater or lesser degree.

One of the most significant variables in this respect within the family structure is the varying aspect of the substructure of economic allocation. Changes in this respect may go hand in hand with radical changes in the distribution of power and so affect spheres of action far beyond economic considerations. The ability of an individual to find remunerative employment beyond the reach of family control or interference may well free him from such control or interference in all other spheres of his action. The last fifty years or so in the Orient has seen an increasing number of cases in which youths have utilized the increasing opportunities for economic independence of the family to implement independence on such scores as marriage, religion, residence, and the like. In growing recognition of this and other factors, there is an increasing tendency in China to give the youth an increased power in these and other respects. If this is not done voluntarily and with good grace, the issue is often forced.

In the case of both power and responsibility, three questions are crucial. The first is the question of locus: who possesses the power and/or responsibility. The second is that of definition: what range of action is covered by the power and/or responsibility. The third is a question of procedure: how are the applications of power and/or responsibility implemented. The solution of the locus of power and responsibility in the family is always important in understanding the general social structure of any society. It has already been pointed out above that if these two factors are not well balanced, far-reaching instability will result, but there are other implications of equal importance. Barring an equal distribution of power and responsibility, which is inherently impossible for the family as a whole,[30] the solution as to the locus of power and responsibility has important implications for questions of status. For example, if the power resides in the mother, the status of women cannot be inferior to that of men. A shift in the locus of power will always be accompanied by a change in the structure of role differentiation, though the change in both may result from some third variable. The locus of power and responsibility is also of importance relative to solidarity, for though the intensity of the solidarity may be relatively low, the strength of the solidarity between those over whom power is exercised and those by whom it is exercised must be great. Whether or not the power and responsibility devolve on one or more persons is another line of variation of some significance here.

The definition of power and responsibility has similar implications. Over some ranges of action, power and responsibility must be extended to all members of the family. In the classical definition of the patriarchal family, all ranges of action of all members were subjected to the control of one member, the patriarch, but this is an extreme case. In the multilineal conjugal family as exemplified in the United States, the range of action covered is, relatively speaking, quite limited, and the extent of control differs considerably among the members. Of some interest in this connection is the matter of what person or persons outside the family the responsible member or members are responsible to, and to what extent. This is again one of those major links between the family structure and the social structure at large, the connection here being with that of political allocation of the society in general. In many cases, the family head is held completely liable for the actions of any of the family members. In other cases, the entire family is held liable. In the United States, the head of the family cannot be held responsible for the criminal acts of family members,

---

[30] Again the necessity of training children is in point, but there is also the fact that complete equality in these respects would make it impossible to settle many cases of diametric opposition.

and he can be held economically responsible only within rather restricted limits.

In "traditional" China, all major political, economic, and other social relations were between the government or other organizations and the family, or between two or more families. An industrialized society, requiring, as it does, dealings with individuals and groups regardless of their family connections, tends to disrupt such a structure on the one hand and be retarded by it on the other. It has been pointed out above that if the family structure is a stable one, only in extreme and relatively infrequent cases can these factors be implemented by force.[31] In large part they depend upon the voluntary submission of the family members due to the inculcation of the value system of the society of which they are a part. There have been cases of sons who have even stood unrestrained and permitted themselves to be beaten nearly to death by their fathers for faults committed. Such extremes are unusual, but they indicate the lengths to which these matters carry. Other factors in the implementation of power and responsibility are the interrelations with other family substructures which bolster their exercise. It has already been pointed out above that the patterns of economic allocation, role differentiation, and solidarity are intensely important in these respects. This must not be taken to indicate any particular general causal priority of one of these elements over the others. Such may well be the case in a particular instance,

[31] In view of the high efficiency of limited applications of force for the attainment of specific ends, the inefficiency of the widespread use of force as a substitute for voluntary compliance would seem to be something of a paradox. The efficient use of widespread and continuous force as a stable social mechanism, however, would on the one hand require a level of social integration that would make it unnecessary, and is on the other hand incompatible with such a level. H. Goldhamer and E. A. Shils, in an article entitled "Types of Power and Status" in the *American Journal of Sociology* (XLV, 2, 171–183), have emphasized one aspect of this as follows:

> Large amounts of power cannot be exercised in a purely coercive fashion, for even though the mass of subordinated individuals do not recognize the power-holder as exercising legitimate power, the necessity of utilizing a large staff would introduce other than purely coercive power into the total power system; for the subordinate power-holders, who exercise dependent power and carry out sanctions for cases of non-conformity among the mass cannot themselves be controlled by coercion alone.

It was on propaganda and education in Nazi ideals that the Nazis depended for support at home and for considerable (and in the long run) lasting support abroad. Their system of force has proved easier to destroy than the attitudes and ideals they inculcated by other means.

but it must be borne in mind that the separation used here is solely an analytical tool. In any concrete case, some or all of them are apt to combine and no generalized *a priori* statement of causal priority can be made.

INTEGRATION AND EXPRESSION IN KINSHIP STRUCTURE

The category of integration and expression is unfortunately something more of a grab bag than the other four categories used here, and is in essence a residual category. It may be divided into two parts: (a) the distribution of the methods and techniques of socialization of children and of acclimatization of persons taken into the kinship units by marriage, adoption, and so on, and the general inculcation and maintenance in the members of the units of the values, attitudes, and procedures of the particular kinship structure, and (b) the distribution of the type and limits of reaction, symbolic or otherwise, on the part of the individual to the various aspects of the concrete structure with which he comes in contact. The most easily defined structure under this heading is that dealing with education. All societies have definite methods by means of which the children of the family are taught its ways of life and to a considerable degree those of the society at large, though many nonfamily structures may also play a role in the education of the new generation. Many of the things so taught are so commonplace as to escape ordinary notice, though modern anthropologists and psychologists increasingly focus upon such considerations. Such matters as the "proper" attitudes toward parents and others which are taught to children are obvious enough, perhaps, but more attention is now paid to such matters as the methods of teaching children to walk and to eat and the methods of their toilet training.

Education must play its role in the integration of the child in terms of all the other institutionalized patterns which have been previously discussed above. Here again is one of those major links between the family and the rest of society, for in the course of his family education, the child is always taught something of how to act outside the family. This must of necessity be so, if only to the degree that the child is taught to differentiate between family members and nonfamily members, and act in accordance with the differentiation. Commonly the matter goes a great deal further, of course, and a considerable portion of an individual's education in general social behavior as well as family behavior is carried on within the family.

The question of education in terms of family structure is an extremely broad and complex subject, and it is not proposed here to go into the matter extensively. Three factors are always of great importance in such educational structures. These are: (1) the content of the education, (2) the methods by which it is taught, and (3) the person or persons who carry out the teaching. There is a tendency to devote a larger proportion of one's concern to what is taught than to the other two categories. The methods used, the systems of rewards and punishments by which the learning process is bolstered, and the roles of the primary teachers are of equal importance.

The above remarks apply to family education in general and that of children raised from birth within the family in particular. Some special mention must also be made of the education of members brought into the family from outside at a more mature age. There are two major types of such individuals—those brought in by adoption and those brought in by marriage. The former may be brought in while quite young, and the earlier the age at which the adoption is made the more closely do the educational features of the case resemble those of the raising of other children. To the degree that the adopted person is mature, and always in the case of marriage,[32] there is the problem of introducing the new member to the specific family personalities and the particular family situation in which the new member will in future act. There is in all family systems a specifically institutionalized method of integration of new members, though the rigidity of the system and the sphere of action covered by it may vary enormously. In these respects, the introduction of new members via marriage is far more important than any other mode of their introduction. The other major mode, adoption, never occupies so strategic a role numerically or structually, since in every family there must be at least one such introduction by marriage, whereas adoption is not necessarily so ubiquitous in family systems.[33]

[32] In a great many societies, adoption and marriage may be combined, and the adoption in such a case may precede the marriage by many years. This is a phenomenon often observed in China and Japan, though of rather low prestige in both societies.

[33] The importance of adoption is not to be denied, of course. Adoption as used here means the acquisition of some person to fulfill at least in part a specific family

The type of consideration involved in the education of newly-married family members is closely bound up with the type of family structure concerned. If the family system is of a type in which one of the marriage partners moves into the family of orientation of the other and the unit of procreation so formed becomes a part of one partner's family of orientation [34] then the new member must be inducted into the functioning family by some member or members of the old family. Since, in such a situation, the new member must conform to the ways of the family or disrupt it, the new member must be placed for a time at least in a role of subordination in the structure, whatever the role of this new member may have been in his or her own family of orientation. The possibility of the development of a traumatic situation is not hard to imagine under conditions of this sort. If, on the other hand, after marriage a new family unit is formed independent of the families of orientation of either husband or wife, quite another order of problem is formed. In such a situation both partners must integrate to a new situation, and although the education is inevitably mutual, in part at least, the institutionalization may be such that the major burden of adjustment falls upon one or the other party, and with it almost certainly a corresponding degree of subordination.[35]

---

role ordinarily fulfilled by birth (in the case of "marriage by adoption" the person involved is always absorbed in some family role ordinarily filled by birth prior to the marriage). The person adopted may be a complete outsider or may be shifted from some other kinship role. This phenomenon is of great importance for social investigation, representing, as it does, the endowment of a person with some particular family role not previously held by him. Therefore, in the implementation of adoption, the various aspects institutionally appertaining to the role in question are apt to be highlighted. This is particularly so if the adoption is not made in infancy, due to the need of integrating an individual in a role different from his past one after the action institutionally appropriate to that past one has already been taught him at least in part. Since the process of adoption must throw special emphasis on matters which might otherwise be taken for granted, it may in many cases serve as a sort of "empirically underlined" example of the particular relation for which it substitutes. In some sense the role of an adopted member is always different from that of a member who acquires his role by birth, but if due recognition is given to this fact, its strategic value in analysis is not thereby diminished.

[34] This is the case in the classical formulation of patriarchal and matriarchal families.

[35] A comparison of the family systems of the United States and Germany is instructive in these respects. A far greater amount of adjustment and subordination is expected of the German wife as is reflected in the "hausfrau" role. The institu-

The second major category which will be discussed here under the heading of integration and expression is religion. Religion as the term is used here will be confined to action directly oriented to nonempirical ultimate ends.[36] Religious substructures frequently play highly important roles in family systems, though family systems in which little or no religious action is carried on in terms of the family system are certainly conceivable.[37] The primary function of such action, insofar as it will concern this study, lies in the degree to which it reinforces and maintains the generalized value orientation of the family in particular and the society in general. After the work of Durkheim,[38] and others, the general role of religion in these respects is hardly subject to question. It is by no means true, however, that the family everywhere operates as a religious unit. Certain religious systems, in fact, are specifically incompatible with such a state of affairs.[39] Insofar as the family is a religious unit, however, religion will fulfill such functions for the family, whether the faith inculcated be some specific religious system such as Christianity or Mohammedanism, or some less theologically elaborate faith such as grows up around familism or even individualism.

In the general area of expression the role played by education and religion may well be great, but the primary concerns roughly lumped under

---

tionally approved amount of adjustment and subordination of the female to the male in the family system of the United States is often underestimated due to a rather high emphasis on the factor of companionship in marriage and equality of the sexes. Despite the fact that the institutionalized roles are by no means equal, the difference in this direction as compared with the case in Germany is nevertheless significant.

[36] In a sense any action can be considered as oriented to nonempirical ultimate ends, i.e., nonempirical ends which are not means to further ends from the point of view of the individual involved. By the use here of this term plus the term "directly" it is meant to exclude not only the intermediary chains of logical action but also those of nonlogical action which are not consciously oriented to ends in themselves. It might be added here that in such action there must be a nonempirical content of the means as well, if it is only insofar as the means are viewed as capable of securing nonempirical ends.

[37] The United States family is one in which relatively little family religious activity is institutionalized, but even here the general community still holds the family responsible, however loosely, for a certain level of religious adherence by its members. At the opposite extreme in these respects, perhaps, are family systems of ancestor worship.

[38] Emile Durkheim, *Les Formes Elementaires de la Vie Religieuse* (Paris, 1925).

[39] *E.g.,* ascetic Buddhism.

this heading are amusement, artistic activities, and other emotional reactions of family members. Amusement here is meant to cover recreational activities, those activities viewed by the individuals concerned as furnishing relaxation and release from the usual duties and concerns of daily life. Games, gossip, dancing, drinking, feasts, and a variety of other phenomena fall under this rubric, though they may also enter significantly into other aspects of family and social action. Artistic activities are perhaps not often found highly developed along family lines for a society as a whole. Nevertheless, concern with the "beautiful" is never completely devoid of family influences whether in the field of plastic, graphic, musical, literary, or dramatic expression. What is taught a child in these respects within the family, either directly or indirectly, serves at least as the basis from which change must be made in future development.

Included in the category of "other emotional reactions" are such factors as anger, grief, pleasure, and love—imprecise terms all—which cannot be given greater precision here. Family systems must have some institutionalization of the mode and degree of expression of such emotions since the completely unrestricted display of almost any one of them might disrupt the organization. Some family systems repress emotional display to an extreme degree, and such systems must have as a component part highly formalized relations among family members and highly developed systems of interfamily symbolic activities.[40] Other systems permit a relatively wide range of such expression. Still other systems definitely prescribe a rather high level of expression along specific lines and by means of particular modes of expression.[41] This last type of system is apt to impress members of systems which institutionalize relatively free expression in such respects as hypocritical. This is due to the fact that in the last type as in the first, the action in such cases will have a highly formalized symbolic aspect.

[40] If emotional reactions are to be highly repressed, there must be a highly developed rigidly defined method of action in highly tinged affective situations. Insofar as the range and type of action is undefined, emotional expression can mount. Insofar as such formal definitions cannot account for the totality of possible concrete actions, the effort to close the system will result in some generalized or symbolic acts. Insofar as even this attempt to close the system fails to cover all cases, such a system will have elements of instability in that some undefined or unrepressed emotional displays will enter the system.

[41] E.g., the expression of grief at the death of a family member in China.

In any particular society, the family system may mix the three types mentioned above. It may, for example, repress anger, give relatively free rein to love, and enjoin considerable highly formalized expression of grief. Whatever the solution may be, there must be some solution. Variations in such solutions may be of extreme importance in cross-cultural· problems and analysis. In addition, such solutions may have rather far-reaching implications for other aspects of the family. Repression of patterns of romantic love, for example, must go hand in hand with systems of arranged marriages. If the father is to occupy a position of highly concentrated authority and respect in relation to his sons, anger on their part directed at his acts must be either greatly inhibited in its expression or channeled into harmless modes of expression lest the relationship suffer. Considerations of this sort are likely to figure prominently in changes of the family system within a society. Such changes are inevitable with developments, such as industrialization, which have far-reaching direct and indirect effects. An erroneous idea of the process of change may be given by choosing one act in the process and following its implications. Such a procedure may well result in the attribution of undue and independent causal significance to some particular event in what is actually a series of interdependent changes. Nevertheless, it cannot be too strongly emphasized that many of the factors of the type with which this study will be preoccupied are incompatible with a particular formulation of some of the other factors. In such cases, the introduction of one will always mean some change relative to the others. Expressive factors, being reactions to various aspects of the concrete system concerned, are not likely to take causal priority in the initiation of change, but they may be of extreme importance in the rate, direction, and integration of changes otherwise initiated.

One further observation may be made about the category of expression. It has here been separated in its treatment from that of integration but considered under a general heading with it. To a high degree the systems of expression are integrative as well. In fact, it is the underlying necessity of preventing malintegrative types of expression that furnishes the basis of the ubiquitous appearance of institutionalized structures of expression in the family system, if there is to be a family system. The obverse side of this relationship is the fact that the integrative activities are in themselves expressions of the generalized value orientation of the family. Again the distinction proves to be analytical, and extremely difficult even on those terms.

FOCI OF STRUCTURE IN KINSHIP SUBSTRUCTURE

Throughout the treatment of the five major categories of kinship substructures as outlined above, we have reiterated and illustrated the importance of variations in the type of the substructure and variations within similar substructures. Within a limited range, some of the more obvious implications of this sort of variation for other aspects of the structure have been mentioned. Social systems in general, however, vary not only by having a totally different content in certain institutional structures, but also by means of focusing on different aspects and with varying degrees of intensity upon structures otherwise quite similar. The plane of abstraction employed is of importance in these respects. A highly abstract consideration of all societies will indicate that all require a family system of some sort, but the importance given to the family system relative to other aspects of the social system, the degree of focus on the family system, leaves in and of itself room for the widest type of variation. A moment's consideration of the relative importance of the family system in T'ang China and the present-day United States is sufficient to substantiate this point. Therefore, in addition to the modes of variation discussed above, attention must also be given to those aspects of the social structure most emphasized by, and most strategic in, the social system, namely, to the foci of structure.

It is rather generally accepted by sociologists and social anthropologists that structures oriented to the fulfillment of these five requirements are to be found within all kinship structures as a matter of empirical fact. All modern studies which claim to handle the kinship aspect of a given society touch on these points and illustrate the concrete handling of these requirements in the particular society under scrutiny, though different terms and/or a different analytical approach may be and most frequently are used. Two aspects of this problem must be kept in mind, however. In the first place, the requirements may be performed by a structure which extends beyond the kinship structure itself, and over a considerable area this is commonly the case. For example, although such roles as the role of parents may be confined to the kinship structure, there is seldom a

[39]

distinction according to sex, generation, or age status which is not generalized in the social system far beyond the kinship structure itself. Even in societies like that of "traditional" China, in which the kinship structure covered a comparatively wide portion of the total social system, the generational, age, and sex distinctions apply beyond such limits. This point is important: (1) because the kinship experience of an individual is significant in determining and conditioning his experience and action in the society as a whole, and (2) because the relative generalization to the society as a whole of the substructures for handling these requirements of kinship structure is important in determining the relationship between the kinship structure and the remainder of the social system.[42]

In the second place, it is by no means true that there exists a perfect or even high correlation between these requisite functions and the devices which carry them out. For example, the father role is commonly a focus for the fulfillment of certain aspects of these requirements. It is important to keep this in mind, for failure to do so is one of the commonest sources of the "functional teleology" referred to above, and because in the concrete case, a one-to-one correlation between structure and function is rarely found, since these distinctions are, in the nature of the case, analytical.

---

[42] In the limiting case, the two might conceivably be conterminous, though the writer knows of no such concrete case.

CHAPTER TWO.

CONCRETE DISTINCTIONS

"TRADITIONAL" AND "TRANSITIONAL" CHINA

THE historical limits within which we shall try to analyze some of the more strategic and easily accessible aspects of kinship structure in China may be defined by dividing the study into two major parts: kinship structure in "traditional" China, and kinship structure in "transitional" China. The term "traditional" applies to those institutional patterns which for the most part trace their pedigree with remarkably slight change well back into Chinese history, sometimes going as far back as the Han emperors (206 B.C.–220 A.D.). Despite this general criterion, the particular formulations of institutional patterns given below as "traditional" will, as closely as possible, describe those formulations prevalent in the Ch'ing dynasty (1644 A.D.–1911 A.D.) which immediately preceded the present Republic of China.

The intention here is not to deny the importance of the many changes which occurred in Chinese institutional patterns during such periods as T'ang (618 A.D.–907 A.D.) and Sung (900 A.D.–1279 A.D.); the delineation of such changes and the analysis of their causes and their impact on Chinese society afford a fertile field for social scientists today. They are not, however, the primary concern of this study. The formulations present during the Ch'ing dynasty are taken because the Ch'ing dynasty at its height of power represents the last stable version of Chinese society from which the present "transitional" phase springs.

"Transitional" China is the China of the last seventy-five to one hundred years, and particularly of the last fifty years. The term "transitional" is used because it seems clear that in this period China has come into contact with and begun to absorb new ideas and techniques alien to her culture, and these ideas and techniques seem certain to destroy to a large extent patterns which have withstood not only the passage of many centuries but even the effects of long domination by foreign conquerors, some of whom strove to change them. Considerable evidence of present changes will be discussed in the course of this study, but the further point that the present situation cannot be stable and itself has a transitory character will also be discussed in the sections on "transitional" kinship structure and modernization..

Throughout the discussion of the "transitional" period it must be kept in mind that many of the "traditional" patterns persist. For the vast majority of Chinese the "traditional" patterns are anything but dead and gone, and in the case of a great many Chinese little change of any sort has taken place. Nevertheless there is slight room for doubt that the "traditional" patterns are doomed. The "transitional" period has its tone and nature set by the incursion of ideas, tools, and institutions from the West and the persistence and decay of the "traditional" patterns. A new and possibly stable pattern has begun to emerge. Whether or when it will win out is hard to say. At the present time the issue hangs in the balance. For this reason much of what is said of the "traditional" period holds true for the "transitional" one; and the sections on the "transitional" period, which attempts to define and analyze some of the dimensions and implications of the changes, will use the sections on the previous period as the base from which the change proceeds.

GENTRY AND PEASANTRY

In the discussion of both the "traditional" and the "transitional" phases of Chinese kinship structure it will be necessary to maintain a distinction which in the past has been overlooked to a considerable degree, though recent publications by outstanding Sinologists have done something to correct this situation. The distinction is that between the gentry of China and the people in general, the peasantry.[1] The gentry in China are characterized as a group by the following factors. First, their primary

[1] Professor Fei Hsiao-T'ung has done a great deal to call attention to these distinctions in his books *Peasant Life in China* (New York, 1939) and *Earthbound China,* written with Chang Chih-I, published by the University of Chicago Press (Chicago, 1945); and has published an article on the subject, "Peasantry and Gentry: An Interpretation of Chinese Social Structure and its Changes," in the July, 1946 issue of the *American Journal of Sociology.* Olga Lang in her Book, *Chinese Family and Society* (New Haven, 1946), has also kept the distinction in mind throughout her work (see especially pp. 147–153).

source of income is from land which they themselves do not cultivate. The other major sources of their income are government offices, intellectual and academic positions, and, more recently, certain forms of business (most notably banking and management of large industrial and commercial concerns). Perhaps the most important single factor relating to the income of the gentry is that it cannot, in institutionally approved cases, come from physical labor in any form.[2] Second, the gentry are primarily identified with the intellectual aspects of China. Despite the presumed free examination system of China, entrance to the examinations was to a large degree monopolized by sons of gentry families, and success in the examination system carried with it gentry status. In fact, the examination system furnished the major path for social ascent in social status in "traditional" China.[3] Third, through their monopoly of learning and the fact that the distribution of state positions was determined on the basis of success in the mastery of this system of learning, the gentry for more than two thousand years manned and controlled the administrative, judicial, and legislative systems of the state. Simultaneously, they controlled its economy by their position as absentee landlords and its intellectual life by their monopoly of learning. Here again, in the cases in which people of other than gentry background entered these positions (usually by military conquest), such intruders were absorbed into the gentry category. Fourth, the institutional patterns which characterized the gentry group were further institutionalized as the ideal patterns toward which the nongentry strove.

Of the remainder of the population, the nongentry group of overwhelming importance in both "traditional" and "transitional" China is the peasantry. The peasants cultivate the land. Economically speaking,

[2] Mr. Shih Kuo-Heng in his book, *China Enters the Machine Age* (Cambridge, 1944), cites a case in the plants of Kunming. Industrial workers and foremen occupied a position of lower prestige than office clerks. The clerks had no contact with physical labor, and hence were at least tentatively identified with the gentry. The fact that the industrial workers and foremen were far more important to the functioning of the concern did not alter the situation but increased the resentment of the industrial workers and foremen. See pp. 116–123.

[3] This went so far that, according to informants, relatives of a successful examinations candidate would sometimes erect signs announcing his achievement and stating their family relationship to him. These signs would be kept in order in the local villages, perhaps for many generations. See also J. D. Ball, *Things Chinese* (New York, 1906), p. 266.

the peasantry includes: farmers who own and cultivate their own land, several types of tenants, and hired nonlandowning agricultural laborers. The distinctions between ownership, tenancy, and laborer status are crucial for many purposes, but all people in these categories and their families are members of the peasantry at least so long as they work the land. Even today the estimates of social scientists place the percentage of Chinese in peasant status at as much as eighty per cent or more of the Chinese population.[4]

Aside from the peasantry [5] the following groups can be distinguished: (1) handicraftsmen, (2) merchants (especially small merchants), (3) servants, (4) soldiers, and (5) miscellaneous (for instance, priests, entertainers, and the like). The "transitional" period has brought with it to an increasing degree (6) domestic industry workers, and (7) factory industry workers.[6] In terms of relative numbers, none of these groups has ever risen to power in the last two thousand years of Chinese history, although they have been of great importance from other points of view.

Another reason for the maintenance here of the basic gentry-peasantry dichotomy lies in the fact that for the majority of matters touched on, the groups mentioned above tend to follow the social patterns of the peasantry if the individuals concerned are low in economic status and of the gentry if and to the degree that their economic status makes this possible.[7] Such groups as priests, of course, lead radically different lives, regardless of income, but this factor, though strategic for many purposes, does not bear importantly on the line of argument followed

[4] See e.g., R. H. Tawney, *Land and Labor in China* (New York, 1932), p. 26, and J. L. Buck, *Land Utilization in China* (Chicago, 1937), p. 363.

[5] It must be kept in mind that this study generally does not focus attention on the differences which arise from the fact that through China one comes in contact with many remnants of culture groups overrun by the Chinese. These groups vary considerably in the degree to which they have maintained their own distinctive ways. Research on south and southwestern China promises to reveal interesting comparative perspectives on Chinese society. It is regrettable that the preliminary analysis of the main stream is of such complexity as to preclude the careful consideration here of such interesting variations.

[6] The appearance of professional men in the Western sense, of doctors, lawyers, engineers, and the like, does not add to this list. From the Chinese point of view, rightly or wrongly, these men fall into the gentry group of modern China.

[7] This tendency of the Chinese to assume as many of the gentry patterns as possible in accordance with betterment of their general income status, is taken up from time to time throughout this study.

here. On the other hand, as attention is switched from the "traditional" to the "transitional" periods, subsidiary distinctions are of greater significance. The differences between the peasantry and the gentry and such groups as craft, domestic, and factory workers and merchants become more and more important in the "transitional" period because the degree and type of pressure exerted upon persons who are completely or partially in such groups comes to differ appreciably from that upon the gentry and the peasantry.

The fact that the distinction between the gentry and the peasantry has been slighted, if not ignored, by the great majority of Western writers on China may well account for a considerable part of the hazy understanding of China which persists today. By and large, the picture of the gentry is taken to represent China as a whole in the vast majority of both literary and academic works. When the peasants are mentioned, gentry ways are often attributed to them. Even Chinese writers have done so frequently.[8] The confusion is understandable. While the gentry patterns were exemplified in actuality only by a small percentage of the total population of "traditional" China, there seems to be little room for doubt that their patterns were considered the ideal patterns by almost the entire society. The vast majority of the people did not live in gentry style, nor could they have been optimistic about the possibility of achieving it during their lifetimes. But the same vast majority longed to be able to put such practices into effect and live their lives by such rules. An ideal with so little hope of fulfillment must have contained the elements of quite severe and widespread frustration, held in check, presumably, by other integrative features of the society in stable times, but forming a reservoir of unrest easily kindled if the integration failed. It must be added, further, that, however small the chances, the possibility of an individual peasant's transforming his role in either his or his son's generation did in fact exist, and was in fact realized in a sufficient number of cases to furnish one of the most important factors differentiating the social structure of China from a truly feudal social structure.

So strategic a place did the gentry occupy in Chinese society as a

[8] Lin Yutang, who is widely accepted by the Western public, particularly in the United States, as presenting an authoritative picture of China, with high consistency presents the gentry patterns as those of the average Chinese. See his book, *My Country and My People* (New York, 1939).

whole that it is hardly surprising that they set their stamp so firmly upon it. It is also interesting to note that certainly since the end of the Chou Dynasty and the beginning of the Ch'in Dynasty in the third century before the Christian Era, force has not been the primary method by which the supremacy of the gentry patterns has been maintained or inculcated. Apparently from that time until the last century, the main outline of these patterns has been accepted as good and right. There have been many changing dynasties, various agrarian reform movements directed against the landlords and so against the gentry, and the sometimes radical social reforms of the government. But until the last century of history there has not been any major movement which seriously threatened to destroy forever or even to attack the status of the gentry patterns as ideal patterns.[9] The close alignment of the gentry with all the artistic, intellectual, political, and economic development of Chinese culture was such that they came to exemplify the Chinese patterns not only for foreigners, whose close contacts were apt to be largely with the gentry, but for Chinese in general as well.[10] It is no wonder that the West has generally accepted this pattern

[9] See Lang, *op. cit.*, pp. 5–8.
[10] The fact that these patterns are considered *the Chinese way* by the Chinese themselves often make research in this field a tricky matter. This is well exemplified by the problem of the remarriage of widows. Any casual investigation of the problem will bring out the fact that the remarriage of widows was forbidden in "traditional" China, if not today. Closer investigation and careful questioning reveals, however, that actually the remarriage of widows among the peasants was not only a frequent occurrence but that little or nothing was made of it among the peasants. If the question is followed further, it develops that not only was such remarriage frequent, but, if the widow were young and lacked grown sons, her remarriage was almost inevitable. On the other hand, such remarriage by widows of the gentry was and is most strongly inhibited and frowned upon. When it did take place, face was lost not only by the parties of the new marriage but by all their relatives. The remarriage of gentry widows in "transitional" China is infrequent perhaps, but it is becoming less so. In "traditional" China it happened quite rarely indeed.

So much more "real" are the ideal patterns than the actual ones from the point of view of the Chinese themselves that the question of the permission of the remarriage of widows is raised in many discussions by Chinese sociologists of Chinese family reform (*e.g.*, Mai Hui-T'ing: *Problems of Chinese Family Reconstruction* (Shanghai, 1930), pp. 300–312). The necessity of permitting this is stated as a necessary reform, but it seems always to have been permitted with little or no comment among the peasantry, whether or not it was considered a variation from the ideal. Extreme care is required in interviews and in research on written materials if one is to separate the idealizations from the empirically valid descriptions of Chinese society.

as empirically valid for the society as a whole instead of a small minority.

The analysis which follows will attempt to differentiate these two major groups in the various aspects to be discussed. The gentry picture offers relatively little difficulty, but the peasantry picture is less simple. There are two main reasons for this. In the first place, as pointed out above, most of the available material in the field is stated in gentry terms, and extreme care is required to ascertain the actual peasantry conditions. In the second place, the range of variation of peasantry patterns is considerably greater than that of the gentry. Given the vastly more elaborate ritual activities and wider social contacts and experiences of the gentry, this second factor would seem to be a contradiction in terms. The paradox, however, is only superficial. It is resolved at once if the status of gentry patterns as ideals are kept in mind. There are in a sense no ideal peasantry patterns in the Chinese culture.[11] Peasantry patterns differ from gentry patterns only because peasants lack the means, most notably the economic means, to fulfill the gentry patterns.[12] Therefore the scale of variation of peasantry patterns is, relatively speaking, great, and subject to fine gradation. The gentry patterns themselves, however, are carefully and minutely worked out. What is institutionally required of a member of the gentry is well known for almost any given situation, and if an individual is of gentry status, he must conform or lose face for himself and his family. The range of *ad hoc* variation which characterizes peasantry patterns does not characterize gentry patterns. This raises an interesting point, for despite the fact that in the vast majority of China's myriad of villages the peasants in "traditional" times did things "just as had their fathers before them," there existed always a potential change. At any time that his material circumstances permitted, a given peasant and his family would begin to follow patterns more and more closely in accord with those of a

[11] The Chinese differ significantly from the Japanese in this respect. Status is measured along a continuum with the gentry at the top, setting the standards for all, regardless of whether the standards are attained wholly or in part. Japanese status structure in these respects is discontinuous. A peasant in modern Japan does not see the patterns of the "New Nobility" as ideal patterns for himself, any more than the peasant of Tokugawa Japan took the *samurai* or *daimyo* patterns as an ideal.

[12] Many of the gentry patterns require considerable training; hence the mere acquisition of means will not be automatically accompanied by conformity with gentry patterns. When the economic basis is present, however, the patterns will be conformed with as soon and as completely as possible, though the process may require more than one generation.

highly restricted number of persons in his area, that is, the gentry, and less closely in accord with those of his other neighbors. This potential change was held in check by the fact that in the main the economic and social opportunities or talents necessary were lacking, and so the peasant and his family continued to do the same thing as the generations before them.

THE FAMILY UNIT

The "traditional" Chinese gentry family had its foundations deep in the classical injunctions of Confucius and Mencius in general, and more specifically in the Sung Dynasty interpretation of those formulations. The "traditional" gentry family was patrilineal, patrilocal, and patriarchal. It included a father and a mother, all their sons, their unmarried daughters, their sons' wives and children, the sons of their sons, the wives and children of the sons of their sons, and so on for as many generations as possible. The male line of descent stayed in the family unit, and the females who were members by birth married out of the unit and were lost to it. Other females entered the unit in the status of wives. Of course any given gentry family might contain more or fewer members, and the generations therein might be represented more or less fully, depending upon the prosperity, health, and longevity of the family members, and upon their decision and ability to stay together as a unit. When such families were divided, the brothers of a given generation separated their direct descendants and their wives and children from the former aggregate and erected a new household for them. Such division was not considered fortunate, and all effort was made to prevent it or stave it off as long as possible. The ultimate ideal in these respects was that the family contain six generations living together as a unit forming a single household, or continue for nine generations without a division of property.[13] The com-

---

[13] One of the most frequently told tales in this regard is that of Chang Kung-I who lived under the T'ang dynasty in what is now the province of Shantung. Chang Kung-I had achieved the remarkable feat of keeping his family of many branches and many generations together. This fact was noted and applauded by the T'ang emperor who called him to court to pay him honor for his feat. At their interview the emperor asked him how he had managed to accomplish this ideal, whereupon Chang Kung-I took a writing brush and wrote the characters *jen-nai*, the word for "forbearance," a hundred times. This tale is noteworthy not only for its implications as to the qualities needed to keep so large a family together, but also because it illustrates the extreme honor attached to such a feat. See Lang, *op. cit.*, p. 31.

plexity attendant upon such an aggregation and the economic resources required for its maintenance were so great that, needless to say, even among the wealthiest gentry such an extreme was unusual. Patrilineal families of three and four generations probably formed the great bulk of "traditional" gentry families.

It is necessary in considering the Chinese family unit to distinguish between the term as used here and terms referring to units such as the Chinese clan or *tsu*, the subclan or *fang*, and similar units. The term "family" as used here has been defined above.[14] In the "traditional" gentry pattern the unit which generally has been referred to in Chinese as the *chia-t'ing* was such a unit. In recent years, as the need to distinguish this large unit from a smaller one has grown, the terms *ta-chia chih-tu*, or "large family system" and *hsiao-chia chih-tu* or "small family system" have come into widespread use. The term *ta-chia chih-tu* or "large family system" refers to the "traditional" gentry family now under discussion.

The Chinese clan or *tsu*[15] is a radically different type of unit from the *chia-t'ing*. The *tsu* includes all persons of a single surname who can trace their descent from a common ancestor. The *tsu* includes people of many and varied statuses from the highest gentry status through those of agricultural laborers, servants, and even soldiers.[16] The *tsu* holds property as an organization, exercises quite broad judicial functions (on an extralegal basis in modern China), arranges for ancestor worship at the proper times, and performs many other functions as an organization. It is also a membership unit. It is not, however, the smallest such unit treated as a unit for generalized purposes by other parts of the society and by other parts of the kinship structure. The *tsu* ordinarily has a great many members, sometimes as many as several thousands. The center of the strongly developed

---

[14] See p. 5.

[15] Mrs. Y. C. Wang (Hu Hsin-Chin) in a still unpublished doctoral dissertation entitled *The Common Descent Group in China and its Functions* has contributed immeasurably to the understanding of the *tsu*. This study goes farther into the problem of the clan in China than any work in a Western language known to the author. Material used here on the *tsu* is based on this work as well as on my own research.

[16] Soldiers have for centuries been considered the lowest rung of Chinese society. The present Chinese government has been at some pains to change this conception, as have the Chinese Communist groups. The latter seem to have had the more success along these lines, but by and large the Chinese still aver that "good iron is not used for nails; good men do not become soldiers."

tsu today is in Central and Southern China—the Yangtze Valley in general and the provinces of Fukien and Kwantung. According to Mrs. Wang: "Here many villages are completely inhabited or predominantly by people of a single surname, recognizing a relationship among themselves."[17] These villages usually contain only a part of the total *tsu.* Even in villages composed entirely of members of a single *tsu,* however, the *chia-t'ing* distinctions are clearly drawn. Mrs. Wang observes that the *chia* is ". . . the relationship group holding property in common and maintaining a common household."[18]

The *tsu* is quite often subdivided, especially when it reaches large proportions. The terms used for such subdivisions vary somewhat with local usage. One of the commonest is the *fang* mentioned above. Where such subdivisions exist, they are always segmented replicas of the *tsu* and are never merely enlarged *chia-t'ing.* It is important that the distinctions between the *tsu* and its subdivisions on the one hand and the *chia-t'ing* on the other be maintained. It is the *tsu,* or subdivision thereof, and not the family, which maintains large relief and educational funds, representatives and lodgings in distant places frequented by the members, and so forth. Many major courses of action are conditioned by the *tsu* organization where it exists. Its importance should not be minimized,[19] although the focus of authority, responsibility, and decision in the overwhelming majority of matters of ordinary living is not the *tsu* but the *chia-t'ing.*

As pointed out above, the *tsu* and its subdivisions cut across the lines of distinction between peasantry and gentry. According to Mrs. Wang, although the gentry generally forms the core of its control, there is no thought of denying membership in the *tsu* to a poor peasant, provided he has not committed some specific offense which carries with it the penalty of being stricken from the *tsu* genealogical tables. It is also possible for peasants to rise to positions of influence.[20] Once again there is a vital dif-

[17] *Op. cit.,* p. 107.

[18] *Op. cit.,* p. 22.

[19] See Akira Nagano, *Chinese Social Organization* (*Chung Kuo She-Hui Tsu-Chih*), pp. 1–48. This book was translated into Chinese by Mr. Chu Chia-Ch'ing and published by Kuang Ming Shu Tien (Shanghai, 1932).

[20] "Thus, while wealth and social standing do determine to a large extent the influence a man wields in this group of informal leaders (of the *tsu,* M.J.L.), an influence shared by his extended family, it is by no means impossible for a man of strong personality to gain the ascendancy with only a limited amount of the two mentioned assets." Wang, *op. cit.,* p. 128.

ference in regard to the *chia-t'ing*. In "traditional" formulations the members of a *chia-t'ing* all share a common social status. There is a complication in the case of a family whose son had newly entered the gentry and continued to live with his peasant parents. By and large circumstances did not permit this, however, and the son either set up a new *chia-t'ing*, or, if he stayed in his former one, its other members conformed as closely as possible to gentry patterns.

Although the term *chia-t'ing* means simply "family," its connotation has always been that of the "traditional" gentry patrilineal family described above. As a description of the ideal pattern of the society this has not been erroneous. As a picture of actual conditions, however, there can be no doubt whatever that such a family does not exist today among the vast majority of the Chinese, and there is every reason to doubt that it ever did. Such a family unit, consisting of three or four generations, including wives and children, might well be expected to average upwards of nine members as a minimum. Such figures as are available, however, reflect no such situation, as Miss Olga Lang in her outstanding contribution to Western knowledge of China points out:

Historical records, such as official census taken to determine the number of taxpayers, indicate that the average size of the household, which coincided with the family for the overwhelming majority of the Chinese, was relatively small. In the early imperial period (Han Dynasty) the average family comprised from five to six persons, and under the Yüan and Ming dynasties (thirteenth to seventeenth centuries) the average was under six. As the census taken for taxation did not include infants, the real size of the family was somewhat larger, but it would not have exceeded six to eight persons—the average size of a conjugal or of a stem family.[21]

[21] *Op. cit.,* p. 16. It is to be noted that Miss Lang distinguishes between the terms "household," *hu,* and "family," *chia-t'ing*. On page 13 of her work she states:

The term "family" or "family unit" is used in this book in accordance with the current Chinese concept of the family (*chia* or *chia-t'ing*) which was also prevalent in imperial times and refers to the economic family, i.e., a unit consisting of members related to each other by blood, marriage, or adoption, and having a common budget and common property. Both the persons staying together and those temporarily absent are included. The family often coincides with the household (*hu*)—in the lower classes for example—but the two terms are not identical. Thus slaves, servants, boarders, even relatives staying temporarily with the family are members of the household but not of the family.

Many aspects of traditional China militated against the possibility that the majority of the people could live up to the standard of the large patriarchal family. Most noteworthy is the fact that an appreciable economic base is required to support such a unit under any economic conditions. The economic structure of China was (and is) such that there was an inevitable tendency for family fortunes based solely on land to degenerate. The only way to offset this was to gain an initial start in accumulation, not from frugal cultivation, but from some source outside the reach of ordinary peasant life such as banditry, the accepted graft involved in government office, acumen in trade, or the like. Once such a start was gained it had to be kept expanding by similar "outside" methods or careful reinvestment of the income of land, because all the sons inherited the property equally.

Although ideally the brothers were expected to stay together in the family, making the eldest one among them the family head or *chia-chang,* in actuality the pressure pushing them toward division was strong indeed.[22] If a gentry family's holdings did not continue to increase, the families of succeeding generations were sure to break up the holdings bit by bit until the separate families' resources were reduced to such a point that the members would be forced to do their own work or be pushed to the wall. The relentlessness of the usurers was such that once a family was on the downgrade the rate of acceleration was rapid, particularly if an attempt was made to continue the complex and expensive ceremonials that surrounded so many events in Chinese life. The ordinary peasant family never held land to a much greater extent than its subsistence minimum. Whenever there was more than one son, it was necessary that the others leave or that most or all of them forego marriage.[23] The best available

---

After family division brothers and other relatives cease to be members of the same family.

The distinction between *hu* and *chia-t'ing* is important to observe and will be referred to again. The difference between the definition of the family used by Miss Lang and that used here is largely a matter of generalization. For wider sociological purposes than the study of China, the more generalized definition employed here is believed preferable.

[22] The various stresses and strains within the family structure are taken up below. See *e.g.,* sections on "political" and "economic" substructures.

[23] These excess sons sometimes left the family only temporarily and sent their wages home for the economic betterment of the family. The break was not desired,

solution for the excess sons was to become tenants or to marry the daughter of some peasant who was without sons and thus become the son and land inheritor of that family.[24] But tenancy usually required setting up a new household and family elsewhere, and marriage into a family without male heirs involved becoming a member of another family already established. The alternative possibility, if a man were to continue agricultural life, was to become an agricultural laborer. But this too was disruptive to large families because such laborers often lived on the place of the people for whom they worked and became parts of their household. Also, so low was the status of these laborers that it was extremely difficult for them to find wives and so continue their part of a particular family.

In "traditional" China, if the excess sons did not attempt to stay in the agricultural field, they had little occupational choice, and that unfavorable. Education was out of the question for them because their families could not afford to support them in the economic unproductiveness that such a course would require. Many boys were apprenticed to tradesmen or craftsmen, but they were not likely to go far, since careful training and advancement tended to go to the master's sons or relatives. Peasants' sons so apprenticed were not likely to rise above the category of relatively unskilled labor, or, if they did, they were not likely to rise above the category of journeymen or clerks. The religious life could and did absorb some of these people but not many. The ascetic religious life did not ordinarily have a wide appeal in China. Many excess sons were absorbed into the households and businesses of the wealthy as servants, and others became soldiers. Some became bandits, of course, but this was only another symptom that affairs had reached an absolute impasse such as characterized the rise and fall of dynasties. At any rate, all these alternatives tended to take the men concerned out of the families in which they grew up. Sometimes they then became the heads of new families, but often they were unable to set up new families at all.

When the disruptive principle of equal division among male descend-

---

but, despite the fact that spiritual allegiance was maintained, the excess sons were usually cut off from the family for life unless the son who remained at home died. Such sons were at best only peripheral family members.

[24] Such marriage was not highly esteemed, however, and was avoided wherever possible.

ants is coupled with the fact that in the wealthier families the chances of survival increased, and hence the average number of sons reaching maturity increased, it is not difficult to see that the situation was such that any unchecked slackening of the rate of accumulation, would inevitably reduce the family units to a small size again. Given the additional intra-family strains, which would tend to precipitate the call for division, it is no wonder that only a small minority of families was able to survive and was able to maintain the economic basis for the "traditional" gentry family.

There is no adequate statistical proof of the relative absence of these large family units. From the modern statistical point of view the classical Chinese historical documents are imprecise and untrustworthy.[25] Nevertheless, there are strong reasons for granting the validity of this hypothesis. In the first place, there is the play of the factors mentioned above, but, in addition, analysis may be of some use in this connection. In "transitional" China, statistical studies are in a rudimentary stage, but one thing does emerge fairly clearly from them, and that is that the large patriarchal family certainly does not exist in China now save in a very small segment of the population. The figures gathered in recent years are consistent at least in this respect and place the number of members of the average Chinese family between four and six members, a far cry from the large numbers involved in the "traditional" gentry description usually given.[26] Now if this is a recent change, then one would expect to find that in the Ch'ing Dynasty the "traditional" gentry family was the average size family. If this were true in the Ch'ing at its height of stability under the Emperor Ch'ien Lung throughout the middle and the better part of the latter half of the eighteenth century, then between the early eighteen hundreds and the first part of the twentieth century an extremely dramatic decrease occurred in the size of the Chinese family at a time when the

[25] The reasons for this are no doubt significant. They are probably to be found in the character and orientation of the mandarins who made such censuses. The censuses themselves were largely taken as a basis for tax collection, as noted above by Miss Lang, and this factor accounts in part for their nature. Nothing like a modern census has ever been taken for China as a whole, and even the recent attempts such as those Mr. Chen Ta has reported in his "Population of China," *Supplement to The American Journal of Sociology*, Vol. 52, No. 1, are only fair approximations, at best.

[26] J. L. Buck's *Land Utilization in China* is the most comprehensive of these efforts and it coincides with this finding. See pp. 368–370.

Chinese population was increasing at a rapid rate.[27] Such a change after nearly two millennia would be striking indeed and might well be expected to have left its mark deep on the Chinese who experienced it and upon their descendants. In the last hundred years and particularly in the last fifty years, as will be brought out below, many changes have begun and progressed in the Chinese family, but there is nothing to indicate that so radical a change occurred in the size of the average Chinese family.[28] Not only is there nothing to indicate any such occurrence during late Ch'ing, but no evidence has been forthcoming to indicate that the Ming Dynasty (1368–1644) or the Yüan Dynasty (1280–1368) or the Sung Dynasty or the T'ang Dynasty saw such changes, and it is the personal belief of the author that its occurrence at any time subsequent to the Ch'in Dynasty (255–206 B.C.) is unlikely. So great a change at any period along this line would certainly have been cause for comment by the great Chinese historical writers. Their failure to comment on any such event is perhaps reason enough to doubt its occurrence. Therefore until positive evidence to the contrary is adduced it seems legitimate to assume that a family of the size of the "traditional" gentry *chia-t'ing* has not been characteristic of any but a small, albeit strategic, portion of Chinese society for at least the last several hundred years, if not the last two thousand years. Its existence for the gentry and as an ideal for the whole society was real enough, but its existence as a "typical" Chinese family, if by that term is meant the type of family in which the average Chinese lived, is not more than a charming though misleading myth.

The type of family in which the average Chinese lived during the "traditional" period must in fact have been the *famille souche* or "stem family." The classical formulation of the *famille souche*[29] is that of a family in which one of the sons marries and continues to live with the parents, while the other sons and daughters marry and go out of the

[27] See W. F. Wilcox, "A Westerner's Effort to Estimate the Population of China and Its Increase since 1650," *Journal of the American Statistical Association*, XXV, New Series No. 171, 266.

[28] The memory of living men and their recollection of their immediate ancestors, whose lives extend well back into the Ch'ing Dynasty is available today. This source, as far as is known to the writer, has produced no evidence to substantiate a change of this sort or of this magnitude. Interviews with elderly Chinese in Szechuan province during 1943–44, while indicative of many changes, brought out no alterations of the magnitude referred to here.

[29] F. Le Play, *Les Ouvriers Europeens* (Tours, 1879), I, 457.

family unit. This family is an intermediate stage, as far as size is concerned, between the patriarchal family ascribed to the "traditional" gentry group of China and the simple conjugal family—a family consisting of husband, wife, and unmarried children—which characterizes the United States in particular and the urban sections of all of the industrialized West in general. Such an intermediate stage as the *famille souche* is more likely to have been the actual family of the majority of Chinese during the "traditional" period, than the simple conjugal type of family. Although the large "joint" or "extended" family apparently was not in the majority, it is equally unlikely, perhaps, that the conjugal family was the statistical average. There were several reasons for this. Chief among these was the fact that the existence of the "extended" family as an ideal to be striven for seems unquestionable. The attainment of this goal was almost inevitably frustrated, but in falling short of the gentry family goal, the *famille souche* was the next step. In addition, the patterns of filial piety and ancestor worship were too deeply ingrained for parents to be cut loose by sons, and the cultural emphasis on posterity and the necessity of continuance of the family line was too great to allow the possibility of parental rejection of all the sons. Thus, though economic conditions might force some of the sons to leave the families in which they were born and set up their own family units, the heavy forces of cultural discipline and habituation would lead parents to lay strong claims on at least one son and would make that son susceptible to their claims. Thirdly, there was the question of such property as was owned or habitually farmed in tenancy by the family. While too small to support a "joint" family, such assets were apt to be sufficient to support a *famille souche* when supplemented by spare time domestic labor (for example, basketmaking) of the family. While all sons had a right to inherit equally, the right could not have been meaningful to peasants living in areas where the average family's land was just sufficient to support life.[80] Under such circum-

---

[80] Part of the pressure as regards land was, of course, the result of the fact that alternative land for cultivation was not generally available. At times hostile barbarians limited the possibility of opening up frontier lands, and at all times the patrilocal emphasis limited the frontier spirit. Whatever the causes of the limitation on alternative land, no one seems to challenge the fact. Like Europe, China appears to have lacked for centuries land to be had simply for the taking. The frontier theories of history developed in treatment of the United States may overstate their case, but a similar frontier would in all probability have made a great difference in China.

stances, since equal division between two or more sons meant starvation for all, only one son could feasibly remain. Whether given a cash settlement or not, the other sons had to go elsewhere or find alternative employment[31] in the locality if all were not to be reduced to starvation.[32] At any rate, succession to such property as existed had to be undertaken in the ordinary case not later than the time that the parents grew too old or feeble to work any longer. Taking over the property carried with it the responsibility of caring for the parents. When such holdings had reached a bare subsistence level, the assumption by one son of the total responsibility for the support of the parents in their old age would often be accepted by the other sons as adequate reimbursement to them for the inheritance of the total holding by the son assuming the responsibility.

Finally, the fact of increased mortality among the lower income groups contributed to the limitation of family size. Miss Lang focuses on this factor as the major cause of failure to attain the ideal type "joint" family:

It seems that in imperial China the large joint family was universally accepted as an ideal. The poor, however, were prevented from carrying it into practice, mainly because the high mortality rate struck them more heavily than the well-to-do people. More of their children died; fewer adults lived to old age and became grandparents and great-grandparents. As a matter of fact, the old people so highly appreciated in Old China were relatively rare there.[33]

Whether or not the high death rate constituted the main reason for the general lack of "joint" families during the imperial period would be difficult to determine in any definitive fashion without far more precise statistics than are available. It would require as a minimum, knowledge as to how many persons living in small families had lost through early death the relatives who would otherwise have been found in large patriarchal families. Certainly it can hardly be denied that this factor

[31] The importance of alternative employment is so great in the Chinese situation that it cannot rightly be ignored. This matter is dealt with extensively in later sections of the study.

[32] See Fei Hsiao-T'ung and others *Earthbound China* for a graphic description of the process of persons being reduced to destitution in China. This is a picture of the "transitional" period, but this aspect of it must have been a frequent and continuous feature of the "traditional" scene as well.

[33] *Op. cit.,* p. 16.

played a major role in the frustration of the large family goal and, in conjunction with the factors above mentioned, offered obstacles aplenty to that goal.

The interdependence of the reasons given above is obvious enough, since they represent little more than different aspects of the same process. There is, however, another aspect of this process which has not been stressed and indeed has seldom if ever been mentioned in treatises on the Chinese family. It has been suggested above that the *famille souche* rather than the simple conjugal family was in all likelihood the type of family in which the average Chinese lived during the "traditional" period. Unlike the patriarchal family or the conjugal family, the *famille souche,* wherever it is institutionalized, always forces a number of persons to live in family units other than the predominant type. Ordinarily these persons will be forced into conjugal family units. This arises from the fact that the sons who leave their family of orientation and set up new families must live in simple conjugal units at least until they have an adult married son. Of course some sons may marry daughters of men having no male heirs and be taken into their families as adopted sons. Adopted sons are not left outside *famille souche* patterns even temporarily, but the distribution of children would have to be singular indeed if this type of arrangement were to cover more than a small portion of the displaced sons. Even if the period of conjugal family life is only a temporary affair, there would have to be a considerable portion of the members of the society spending a period of from fifteen to twenty or more years outside of the type of family considered normal in the society in which they live. This cannot be without its effect on the integration of the society.

Apart from the portion of the society affected by the peculiar discipline of the *famille souche* there are others who are forced into conjugal families by the fact that the means at their disposal are not sufficient to support even the *famille souche* pattern. In addition there are still others, as mentioned above, who are forced to live outside of families entirely. The proportion of persons in this category could not remain large for any extended period of time, for such a predicament on their part forces the violation of nearly all the patterns held right and good in such matters by their society. There is reason to believe, however, that at periods of great stress in the history of China the proportion of people in such a predicament reached alarming heights. Such periods were characterized by extreme unrest and depression of the society and most often ended with the overthrow of dynasties and/or radical reforms which restored the balance of the society and reduced to more normal proportions the number of persons forced into the position of marginal unfortunates.

In summation the following remarks may be made about the "traditional" Chinese family as regards its size and composition. In the first place the patriarchal or "joint" family widely ascribed to Chinese society was the pattern of living for the gentry class of the "traditional" period. This was certainly true during the Ch'ing Dynasty and was probably true as far back as the T'ang Dynasty or further.[34] Not only did the "joint" family set the pattern of living for the highly influential gentry segment of Chinese society, but it was the ideal family pattern for the society as a whole. Although it was realized by the gentry class, this family pattern was not attained by the people in general, however much they tried to achieve it. In this factor an inherent social element of frustration was to be found. Although the "joint" families of the gentry contained many members, say nine as a minimum and considerably more as a maximum, the average Chinese family in all probability did not have in excess of six members. Due to circumstances beyond his control the average Chinese was forced to live in a *famille souche* type of family rather than in the ideal "joint" type. As a further complication because of the peculiar discipline of the *famille souche* many persons were forced to live at least temporarily in simple conjugal families for periods of from fifteen to twenty or more years. In addition the same factors of inheritance patterns, economic conditions, mortality and so on which frustrated the average Chinese desire to live in a joint family and reduced him to a *famille souche* pattern, often reduced him even further to living in a simple conjugal family or left him completely destitute and forced him to live outside a family altogether. The further frustration involved in

[34] Miss Lang notes that the end of the Chou Dynasty brought with it the disintegration of the "joint" family. She further adds that for agricultural and colonization purposes the Ch'in Dynasty and the early imperial dynasties attempted to force the peasant to live in conjugal families and to break up the noble "joint" families as political insulation against them. It is interesting to note that the Ch'in Dynasty should have started such a move. As will be noted below, the conjugal family is considerably more efficient for certain pragmatic ends, and the Ch'in era like the present one, laid a new stress on such matters. There is, however, no mistaking the self-conscious imperial encouragement given to the "joint" family from T'ang times until the overthrow of the dynastic system in 1911 (see footnote 13, Chapter II).

this process is obvious enough and at severe periods reached potent enough proportions to serve as one factor in the overthrow of dynasties.

Finally, in the study of the "traditional" Chinese peasant family, as opposed to the "traditional" gentry family, it must be kept in mind that altogether the unit being studied represents a compromise with fate from the point of view of the actors, the fact that no ideal type family other than the gentry family exists is closely and intimately connected with the fact that social mobility in China, though difficult, is not impossible, that Chinese society is not a feudal society of closed classes and has not been so for at least several centuries.

PART TWO

"TRADITIONAL" FAMILY STRUCTURE

CHAPTER THREE

THE KINSHIP SUBSTRUCTURE OF ROLE DIFFERENTIATION

IN the general discussion of kinship structure in Chapter I the term role differentiation was defined as the differential arrangement of the members of the structure. Of the various possible terms in which such differentiation might be made, five have been suggested as functional prerequisites for any kinship structure. These five are age, generation, sex, "economic" position, and "political" position. Study of the differentiation of age roles affords an easy entrée into the kinship role substructure because the "traditional" picture for this aspect of both gentry and peasantry patterns is relatively clear and uniform. Since Chinese society in general has placed strong emphasis on age considerations as well as those of kinship, it is not odd that age considerations play a considerable part in role differentiation within the family. Even the most cursory examination of the available material strongly emphasizes this aspect of Chinese life.

AGE DIFFERENTIATION

In the generalized treatment of kinship structure in the introductory chapter, we noted two distinctions in age differentiation. There may be differentiation on the basis of "absolute" age groupings, and there may be differentiation on the basis of "relative" age. During the "traditional" period, Chinese society characteristically emphasized both types of distinction. Chinese society's orientation to age is one which invests increasing age with increasingly higher status. This is in marked contrast with the pattern prevalent in the industrialized West. By contrast the industrialized West, especially as epitomized by the United States, is overwhelmingly a youth culture. It is true that the West does honor to increasing age in one sense, and particularly great age, but by contrast with the Chinese pattern in these respects, it is largely a matter of sentimentality. This is not to say that the Chinese do not recognize and cope with the facts of senility, but in China extreme age lends to judgment a weight of validity that is lacking in the West.

In general the Chinese peasantry are less in a position to cater to old age than are the gentry. As Miss Lang points out in the quotation above,[1] there were not many old persons in imperial China. It is reasonable also to assume within limits that the incidence of such persons among the peasantry was not so great as that among the gentry. This might not follow if the average peasant family lived reasonably well above the subsistence level, but given the extremely small margin by which the average peasant family seems to have fended off disaster even in the best of times, the point is probably sound. The better economic position of the gentry meant crucial differences in food, clothing, medical care,[2] and sanitation. By modern Western standards much may have been left to be desired, but even today in areas where modern sanitation and modern ideas of health requirements have not penetrated, reports of observers show that the economic equivalent of gentry status or approach to it inevitably increases the life-span of family members.[3]

Besides the fact that there were few really aged people to cope with, the margin of subsistence which always pressed on the peasant family did not permit the attention, care, and reverence of old age that could be

[1] *Supra*, p. 57.

[2] At least in sickness the gentry had an advantage in the sense of nursing, rest, and better food. The remedies actually used, while sometimes containing efficacious ingredients, were oftentimes an awesome concoction. In cases where the sick were unable to purchase medicines they may often have actually benefited thereby. In many cases of extreme illness, however, the peasants must have been driven to extreme measures such as borrowing, in order to enjoy the drawbacks of attention by the Chinese pharmacists.

[3] See in general Dr. Fei Hsiao-T'ung's book *Earthbound China*. On pages 86 and 250–253 Dr. Fei gives examples showing increase in family size with economic betterment. See also Olga Lang, *op. cit.*, Chapter III. These figures are not conclusive. They might have been offset in both imperial and modern times by the greater opportunity for dissipation by the groups which were more prosperous. The general position, however, does not seem to be challenged by any of the research available. While such figures positively correlating increase in survival of family members and family size with improved economic position are not definitive in the sense applied to statistical results by modern statisticians, they are not challenged and hence may be presumed to carry some force until refuted.

supported by the gentry. In the case, for example, of parents too old to work in a peasant family, the burden was clear. As the old parents retired from work, their economic contribution to the family ceased, but their claims on the family by no means diminished proportionately. The general poverty of the family and the unproductiveness of the aged made it rarely possible to increase the material comforts of the aged when they were no longer productive. Moreover, with the pressure of subsistence as great a problem as it was in the average peasant home, the peasant was forced to take a more objective view of an old person's injunctions. This was particularly so with regard to decisions within the economic realm. In a peasant family the whim of an old man might mean the difference between the continued existence of the family and complete economic ruin. In families in which the economic margin was greater, such a result was proportionately less likely. So it was that among the peasantry one was more likely to find the attitude of deference to the aged family member accompanied by tactful disregard of his wishes, in case they countered the judgment of the person in the family upon whom actual economic responsibility rested.

Despite the fact that the peasantry in the "traditional" period may not have accorded the old family members the true advantages and authority symbolized by the position of Chia Pao Yü's grandmother in the novel, *Dream of the Red Chamber,*[4] there can be no denying the respect and deference shown to the old people. There was no possibility of abandoning them, nor did the thought arise. Neither peasantry nor gentry

[4] This famous novel of Chinese family life has been widely and justifiably quoted by both Chinese and Westerners to illustrate various aspects of life in the "traditional" family. The novel is a gold mine of information and insight in this respect. A word of caution is, however, in order in the use of this novel. The novel is highly romantic. While the family described might well have existed, the position of the hero, Chia Pao Yü, was by no means the normal one for a boy of his social status. With rare exceptions, Pao Yü is able to escape all the more obvious strains ordinarily involved in the role of a boy his age. Thousands of boys found escape from the frustrations of their daily life by vicarious participation in Pao Yü's life. There are other romantic aspects to the novel, and in using it social scientists should be sure they are citing its realistic passages rather than its romantic ones.

The translation, *Dream of the Red Chamber,* used by this study was made by Wang Chi-Chen and published by George Routledge & Sons, Ltd., London, n.d. The Chinese title is, of course, *Hung Lou Meng* and the author is Tsao Hsüeh-Chin.

of the "traditional" period of China would have been able to understand the isolated position of the aged in the United States today. The situation has changed considerably in China, but it is perhaps not too much to say that the average Chinese would regard the situation of the aged in the United States as an example of unintelligible barbarism and lack of "human feeling."

ABSOLUTE AGE GROUPS

There is a marked distinction between "absolute" age groups in the patterns of the Chinese family. These age groups are not "absolute" in the sense that they always have a sharp temporal line drawn between them, but are "absolute" in the sense that a given individual is classed in one and only one of them at a time and is classed in this category regardless of his age relative to another person. The line is anything but "absolute" so far as temporal demarcation is concerned. For example, as will be shown below, the actual time at which a child is considered to have emerged from the infant class depends to some degree on whether or not a younger sibling has been born. In the classification of absolute age groups, we will use terms which were widely used in the "traditional" period and are in use today. This is not to say that only these terms were used and only these distinctions were made. China was and is extremely complex so far as cultural and linguistic variation is concerned. There may be many places in China where different terms were used for the periods of age given here, or even where different periods were distinguished. Those distinguished here, however, would appear to be generally typical of the society.

The Ying-erh Shih-ch'i. In the main, five periods are to be distinguished. The first of these is the *ying-erh shih-ch'i,* literally, the "infant period." At this stage, as at all other stages in the life of the "traditional" Chinese family, a distinction was drawn between the treatment of the boys and the girls, although sometimes the distinction has been exaggerated.[5] The birth of a child was a great event in the Chinese family. Through the nine months of pregnancy the mother was referred to as having "happiness in her body." Children were always welcome, subject only to the economic limitations of the family. Everyone looked forward

[5] These distinctions will be further elaborated in the section on sex role differentiation.

primarily to the birth of a son. In cases of direct poverty sons were as well received as circumstances permitted.[6] Even girls were welcome in families where there was no economic problem. Mr. Martin Yang, in writing of the reception of a birth, describes the occasion as follows:

The third day after the birth is called *kuo-san-jih* and is ceremonially celebrated. The child is bathed and clothed in its first garment, a little jacket made of a single piece of red cloth. He is then presented to his grandparents. The family has a feast on this day, but not an elaborate one. The main dish on this occasion is a special kind of noodles made of flour, eggs and the powder of sesame seeds and soaked without salt or sauce. It is believed that these noodles are good for the mother's milk and speed her recovery. Food is also distributed to neighbors and clan members so that they may share the family's joy in the newborn child. Upper class families take this occasion to thank their ancestors for the birth of the child and to pray for the safety of the new life. Congratulations and gifts from neighbors and clan members are received. Neighboring families usually offer . . . foods . . . thought to be the most nourishing for the mother. The gifts come in a fine basket covered with a piece of red cloth and are presented by the mother of the donor's family. She sees the child when presenting her family's gift and praises it and the mother. All gifts must be rewarded or at least the givers' names must be remembered, so that similar congratulatory offerings may be made on the birth of a child in the donor's family. These reciprocal presentations go on for many generations.[7]

The initiation of the child into the family, its treatment during the *ying-erh shih-ch'i,* and its subsequent development are strikingly conditioned by the child's symbolic importance. One of the most important processes which continues throughout life is the differential treatment of the child on the basis of sex.[8] The status of females relative to males in the society and in the family has its beginning in infancy—particularly in the "traditional" period. Interestingly enough, this pattern is one of the few "traditional" patterns which was apparently more sharply observed by the peasantry than the gentry. The restricted means of the peasants eliminated much of the ceremony observed by the gentry, but at the same time it

[6] In cases in which infanticide was practiced it was inevitably girls who suffered this fate. The author knows of no case of male infanticide because of the pressure of subsistence, though there may have been such cases.

[7] Martin C. Yang, *A Chinese Village* (New York, 1946), pp. 123–124.

[8] This differential treatment and its implications for the mother's status will be discussed below.

forced a closer observance of sex distinction in infancy. In peasant families the distinction sometimes determined survival.

In general, however, the Chinese attitude toward children is a very tender one. The fact that much of the scientific knowledge about child care which has become a part of the outlook of Western parents in particular often leads them to the conclusion that the Chinese are frightfully callous about their children. Such is not the case, if the emotions of the parents rather than the actual physical treatment of the child are considered. So deep is this factor based in Chinese society that Mencius, in demonstrating his principle of the inherent goodness of man, points out that no person, however evil or debased, will stand idly by and permit a small child to stumble blindly into a well. Apart from the philosophical position which Mencius supports upon this fact, there is no denying its implication about the position of helpless children and the minimal attitude with which their well-being must be considered by even the wickedest stranger.[9]

Miss Lang has put the matter very well as follows:

Wherever Chinese babies are said to come from—whether they are found on the city wall, or hidden inside a yellow pumpkin, or in the flowing skirts of the Goddess of Mercy—they are all welcome in every family that can feed them. Modernization has not diminished the desire of the Chinese for children or their pride in them.

This pride is shown by fathers and mothers alike. On her second day in China the author saw a coolie in the Market of the Heavenly Bridge in Peiping. He carried in his arms a lively handful of a baby in scarlet gown and a yellow and black tiger cap; his older boy, a child of about three, clung to his father's right hand. The boy's eyes sparkled like black cherries under the red-ribboned tuft of hair left on his clean shaven head; his little buttock protruded from a

[9] Further strength is added to this point when one considers that Mencius posits a person who has no particularistic relation to the child, one who is a stranger to it. In Chinese society a stranger is exempted from concern over the welfare of others (as long as he is not actively the cause of their ills) to an extent that the West does not recognize as fitting. The lack of concern of the Chinese in these respects was a continual shock to Americans stationed in China during the war. It was a factor always mentioned in "bull sessions" about the Chinese. Equally interesting was the surprise and gratitude shown by the Chinese when foreigners showed strangers in pain or in trouble any consideration at all, even if the level of consideration was below that which would have been expected of them in the ordinary course of everyday life at home.

split in his pants; and in his right hand he held a newly acquired treasure—a straw cage with a huge cricket inside. The father's face shone with a pride in his offspring. No less proud was the bespectacled face of a university professor whom I saw walking on the campus of a missionary university with his graceful little boy and girl dressed in modern style white clothes. Many such fathers crossed my path in towns and villages in the north and in the south.

In feudal China and under the empire the eldest son was supposed to enjoy a privileged position in the family as the future family head and officiator in ancestor worship. His younger brothers and sisters owed him respect and obedience. Respect for the elder brother has been preserved, but he certainly enjoys no preference as far as his parents' affection is concerned. The smallest child—boy or girl—is the pet of the family.[10]

It was (and is) in the peasant families that the question of ability to "feed them" of which Miss Lang speaks came up with great frequency and great force. If the situation were acute, recourse to female infanticide or the sale of female children would not be unusual. This, however, eliminated only girls. When there was a chronic shortage not sufficient to drive the parents to the length of infanticide or sale of female infants, then the differential treatment of children during the *ying-erh shih-ch'i* appeared in force. The sons were, after all, of overwhelming importance to the family in all major spheres: economically and religiously, symbolically and actually. In a society where sons are of such importance it is not hard to understand their preferential treatment over daughters in any threatening circumstance. In the gentry families economic pressure did not enter into the situation. In the first year or two of the *ying-erh chich-ch'i,* at least, actual differential treatment of children on a sex basis was less likely than in peasant families in difficult economic straits.

The *ying-erh shih-ch'i* was a stage of freedom and indulgence for the Chinese child. For the first two years of its life the child was petted and played with by all the family members. In peasant families and in old gentry families where the rules of reserve were strongly observed, the child's needs were catered to and attention was given the child by the women of the family and the servants, even though the fathers maintained some aloofness before other persons. During the period of infancy no systematic training or discipline of the child was attempted at all. Only

[10] *Op. cit.,* p. 238.

in the latter part of the *ying-erh shih-ch'i* were such factors introduced. During this period the child was constantly watched and tended by the mother. Whenever the child seemed to desire food the mother nursed him. The child was always placated when aroused, and it was generally felt that anything should be done to prevent a child's crying. Arthur H. Smith points out that infants "must not be allowed to cry continuously. In this respect, at least, it does not appear that there is much distinction between the treatment of boys and girls." [11] Although the mother was the constant attendant of the child during this period of its life, the child received general attention from the male parent as well. [12]

The general position of the child during the *ying-erh shih-ch'i* demanded kindly attention and care. [13] This position holds apparently

[11] Arthur H. Smith, *Village Life in China* (New York, 1899), p. 238.

[12] Dr. Martin C. Yang in his volume on the Chinese village of Taitou does not find this so. He states (*op. cit.,* pp. 126–127):

> The young father shows no interest in his child; on the contrary, he is angry if it disturbs him by crying at night. Occasionally a father hates the very existence of his child. He will not touch it for any reason. He is embarrassed when a relative asks him about it; and to be seen actually holding the baby is a disgrace. He believes that he has helped in "making the child" and that this in itself was shameful to him. He won't do anything to help because he believes that baby-tending is entirely a woman's job.

The point of view expressed here by Dr. Yang is unusual. It may well be that Dr. Yang's village was quite different in these respects from the general Chinese scene. It was apparently true, as Dr. Yang observes, that a sharp line was drawn between father and mother so far as the care and responsibility for the health, cleanliness, feeding, and clothing of the infant was concerned, and it is hardly to be doubted that the father would be careful not to give the impression that such "woman's work" devolved upon him, but it has not been the personal experience of the author or apparently of other researchers that the young father lacks interest in the child. Furthermore, cases of young fathers' hating their children and especially cases of their feeling shame at having fathered them have been a great deal rarer for other researchers than for Dr. Yang at Taitou. Until considerably more evidence is assembled to contradict the prevailing views, it would seem safer to assume that the Chinese father does not ignore his infants nor is he at all ashamed of his fathering of them. This latter is particularly true. It would be hard indeed to comprehend the two-thousand-year stability of Chinese family patterns on the basis of a reconciliation of the undoubtedly strong urge to have children, and many of them, and a sense of shame in fatherhood. It is hard to see how the tensions so created could have been kept from breaking loose in such a fashion as to change the pattern radically.

[13] As regards the attention given children by their grandparents, especially their grandfathers, some insight may be gained by consideration of a form of congratu-

for gentry and peasantry of the "traditional" and "transitional" periods alike. The general security of the child was not seriously infringed upon at any point. It has been noted above that the child was fed whenever it was hungry, day or night. It is also to be noted that there was no severity of toilet training discipline during this period either. If the mother noticed the child's need in time, she might take him outside the house, but, if she failed to do so, nothing was said, and the refuse was either removed or, in many cases among peasant families living in houses with dirt floors, simply left where it was. Actual toilet training was not even mentioned until the child began to walk or was weaned. Later, when discipline occurred, it took the form of light ridicule and perhaps even mild chastisement, but no such thing as a severe spanking, pinching, or great embarrassment was inflicted upon the child then or ever in the course of toilet training. Furthermore, no distinction was drawn between children on the basis of sex for these purposes for at least the first three or four years.[14]

Prior to the age of one year the child showed no sphincter control whatever. Between the ages of one and two the child might call the attention of its mother to its need in time to prevent soiling itself, but lapses of control were more often the rule and were not visited by reprimand. Between the ages of two and three growing control was evidenced and lapses were apt to be met with mild ridicule or reprimand. After the age of three the child generally controlled these natural functions, but lapses still occurred. If a child wet the bed at night, it was asked to call its mother next time it felt the need to relieve itself, but all in all little or no notice was taken of the incident.

At the age of three or four or shortly thereafter parents placed some restrictions on the place of relief and began to make a differentiation on the basis of sex. Here the discipline, although it was quite mild, fell with greater force upon girls. Girls were expected to absent themselves from the presence of others, particularly from the presence of men, at such

---

lation frequently paid to grandparents (especially grandfathers). This is found in the statement: "Congratulations (on having) the happiness of holding sweets in (your) mouth and of playing with (your) grandchild (especially 'grandson') (*kung ho han i lung sun chih lo*)."

[14] Throughout this study age is reckoned on the Western basis of chronology dating from the actual birth of the child. The Chinese system of age reckoning is never used without specific mention.

times. There was very much less restriction upon boys, particularly as regards micturition. By the age of four, however, children had begun to repair for defecation to the jars or pots used to collect excrement for spreading as fertilizer on the fields.

In the matter of toilet training, however, there was a noticeable difference observed between peasants and gentry. The gentry observed a more marked reserve in their conduct in general than did the peasants, and their reserve was reflected in this sphere of action. In gentry families the boys as well as the girls were trained to seek a certain degree of privacy in their performance of natural functions. The gentry took no more notice than anyone else of the public performance of the peasants in such matters, but they reprimanded their sons for similar lack of concern and reminded them that such conduct was not fitting for persons of their status.

Another factor to be kept in mind is the relationship between weaning and toilet training and the relevance of both to the upper limit of the *ying-erh shih-ch'i.* As remarked above, the temporal demarcation of the "absolute" age groups was not fixed. The period might be more or less prolonged. The most important factor in determining the length of infancy was the birth of the succeeding child, if there were a succeeding child. After the arrival of a succeeding child the earlier child received much less attention. This was less true of gentry families where nurses and servants lessened the need for a withdrawal of attention. The older child among the peasants was weaned at this time, although the weaning was not necessarily complete. If there were sufficient milk after the new infant was fed, the cries of the older child for nursing were heeded. Nevertheless, the older child was ignored in favor of the younger child to a marked degree. Dr. Yang observes on this score, and in this he is corroborated by other Chinese,[15] that:

When the second child is born, the mother will have to shift her attention from the first one. From this time on, the older child begins to sleep with his father instead of with his mother. The small family sleeps in the same bed, it is true, but it is a very broad one, and the parents sleep at opposite ends of it. The baby sleeps beside the mother, and the older child then moves to the father's side. When this change occurs, the father begins to dress the child, too. When the father is busy in the field, the boy is taken care of by his grandmother or

[15] Much of this material has been obtained by interviews with Chinese students and social scientists.

by an older sibling, either his own, or the elder child of one of his father's brothers. The only chance he now has for being with his mother is on the rare occasions when the new baby is sleeping . . . the separation is not too keenly felt because his mother is still much in evidence even though she is not directing her attention to him, and his new companions are people to whom he is already accustomed.[16]

There was a distinction between gentry and peasant families in the weaning process. Among the gentry wet nurses were commonly employed for children. When the weaning time was reached, generally sometime between the first and second years, the wet nurse was sent away and the weaning was thus abrupt and complete. The trauma to the child was somewhat softened by the fact that within a few months, when the weaning had been satisfactorily accomplished, the wet nurse was recalled and, while she did not nurse the child, continued to serve and care for him, thereby continuing his contact with a loved and attentive person. While in the peasant families, as pointed out above, the weaning process was not so abrupt, the change in attention was more marked then in the gentry families.

If the birth of a succeeding child did not follow quickly or take place at all, the period prior to weaning might be prolonged. Nursing children of two, three, and even four years of age sometimes occurred among peasant families. If the time at which weaning took place were more or less late, toilet training was likely to be similarly delayed. The discipline was, as remarked, at no time severe, but particularly in peasant families, the advent of a younger child hastened the development of the older child in all respects. This was of necessity so if the child lacked elder siblings or other relatives besides his mother who could care for him. In recognition of these factors there was a tendency to consider that a child who was quickly followed by younger siblings reached the *yu-nien* stage at an earlier chronological age than a child not so closely followed by younger siblings. A child of three or three and a half years of age with a younger brother of one or two might be considered a *yu-nien,* whereas a child of four or four and a half lacking younger siblings might continue to be considered in the *ying-erh shih-ch'i.*

In gentry families the length of the *ying-erh shih-ch'i* had greater uniformity, since the advent of a succeeding infant did not alter the

[16] *Op. cit.,* p. 127.

amount of attention available for the older child. In general the period lasted about four years. During the earlier part of the period, roughly for the first two years, it has been no..d above that the child was relatively free from restraint and attempts at education. After this, however, discipline and teaching did begin. From the age of two to the age of four discipline remained very mild.

Some slight ridicule was used, for example, in toilet training, and some recourse to light chastisement was noticeable in correcting general conduct. Excessive punishment of the type often inflicted on older persons was altogether absent, even on a relative basis. The education of this period of a child's life was oriented to teaching proper respect for others, industriousness, and the like. Miss Lang points out:

As of old the main aim of education is to raise obedient children, devoted to their family, working hard at school or in the house, and living peacefully with their sisters and brothers and with the neighboring children. The old Chinese virtues of filial piety, forbearance, and good manners are still highly appreciated.[17]

In peasant families children were likely at this time to be told stories by their grandparents, particularly the grandmother, and in gentry families they were even read to. The stories were often highly fanciful and usually of a didactic nature. One of the most frequently used sources of such tales for children was a collection called *The Twenty-Four Examples of Filial Piety*.[18] This group of tales was used for children of the next age group as well, but its use was often begun at this point. Although the great mass of persons in China were illiterate, the tales were not lost to the peasants. China was a nation of storytellers, and these tales were known to all regardless of literacy. This collection of tales cites examples of exceptional sacrifices made by children for their parents. One of the stories may be quoted briefly:

He fanned the pillow and warmed the coverlet. During the Han Dynasty, Hwang Hsang at nine years of age lost his mother. His mind was so constantly and so intensely occupied in thinking of her that the neighbors praised him as very filial. Employing himself in assiduous and fatiguing work, he served his

[17] *Op. cit.,* p. 239.
[18] Twelve of these tales are reproduced by the Rev. Justus Doolittle in his work *Social Life of the Chinese* (New York, 1867). See Vol. 1 of that work, pp. 453–459.

father with perfect obedience. In summer, when the weather was hot, with his fan he cooled his father's pillow and bed. In winter when the weather was cold, with his own body he warmed his father's coverlet and mat. The prefect Tein presented him with a banner as a token of distinction.[19]

In addition to obedience and filial piety a child near the age of four began to learn the social practices and distinctions he had to know in later life. Children were taught that they must recognize the authority not only of their parents and grandparents but of their older siblings as well. They were taught proper greetings and the like. In these respects the instruction which began toward the end of the *ying-erh shih-ch'i* was vastly more elaborate and complex in gentry families than in peasant families.

The Chinese child was not permitted to play with the same carefree physical abandon characteristic of Western children. The rather strenuous physical games and exercises such as tree-climbing, fighting, and football were not part of the lives of Chinese children. This factor exerted its real force in later periods of the child's development, but it was during this period that the child began to learn that his person was primarily the property of the ancestors, that it was to be carefully guarded to serve the interests of the family, and that no undue chances were to be taken with it.

The Yu-nien Shih-ch'i. The next age group distinguished in Chinese kinship structure was that of the *yu-nien*. The *yu-nien* stage picked up where the *ying-erh shih-ch'i* left off. The term *yu-nien* seems to have referred primarily to the immaturity and inexperience of the person in its category. An oft-quoted Chinese phrase contains this idea: *nien yu wu chih,* which translated literally means "young in years and without knowledge." *Yu-nien* ranged in age from four years or earlier to fifteen or sixteen. During this period the real discipline of Chinese life made itself felt upon the children. In the "traditional" era of China one of the most striking features of the period was the fact that role differentiation on the basis of sex was genuinely imposed upon the lives of the children and was never thereafter absent from their lives.

In the gentry family this was strikingly symbolized by the fact that the male *yu-nien* was sent to live in his father's section of the house. Nurses and servants continued to care for him, but his father took over

---

[19] Quoted from J. Doolittle's translation, *op. cit.,* p. 457.

his immediate supervision. His mother was a person to whom he could appeal for protection against his father's wrath, but she had no real power to protect him, and the very necessity of his appeal was evidence of his removal from her sphere of supervision and control.

The girl of this age group in "traditional" families remained under the supervision and direction of her mother. Her training took the form of preparation for the roles she would assume in the future as a wife and mother. At this period in some gentry families an indulgence was begun that was apt to prove frustrating in the extreme to the girl in later life. An intelligent daughter frequently became a favorite of her father, and he personally instructed her in the art of reading and in the study of the classics, or had her tutored. Any interests she cultivated on this score were almost certain to be doomed by her marriage later.

The boys of gentry families began to go to school during the early part of the *yu-nien* period. They sometimes had private tutors if the family could afford it, but they were more likely to be educated in village or clan schools, or schools provided by a small group of gentry families. The entry into school marked the beginning of severe and arduous discipline, both intellectually and physically. It is interesting to note that schooling constituted the boy's first real discipline from an outside source. At the same time, severer forms of discipline began for the child at home. Spanking began in the early part of this period. At first it probably was not too severe, but as the years wore on it became more so. There were no *de facto* limitations on punishment by the father, whatever the *de jure* ones may have been. Cases of severe beatings were frequent, and there have even been cases of sons beaten to death by their fathers. Such an extreme was unusual, however, not only because of the usual paternal attachment of father to son, but also because of the extreme importance of the son as the inheritor of the family line with its ceremonial obligations to the ancestors.

Girls were sometimes beaten, but mothers did not ordinarily go beyond slaps and severe scolding. There were, of course, children of both sexes who grew up without experiencing beatings or any severe corporal punishment, but most of the children received at least a taste of such discipline. The father was the "terrible one" from the point of view of the children, and, although he regularly attended to the sons, he sometimes took over the discipline of daughters also. The discipline suffered in this age group by a girl was, however, lightened if she became her father's favorite.[20] This phenomenon was most noticeable in gentry families and was relatively rare in peasant families, but when it occurred the *yu-nien* stage of the girl's life was usually a pleasant one indeed.[21]

But the severest discipline met by the sons of the gentry families during this stage of their lives came in their schooling. Their teachers were their absolute masters. Such was the prestige of the scholar that it was almost inconceivable that a father take the side of a son against his teacher, and so well known was this fact that cases of complaints by sons must have been extremely rare. The teacher could and did inflict corporal punishment whenever he felt it necessary. Since the teachers were always men who had been through such training themselves and since they were often men whose own scholarly careers had been frustrated and who had been left with no alternative way to earn their living, there may well have been a considerable component of sadism in their treatment of their pupils. The learning process itself was one that was almost certainly ill-suited to young active children. It was based almost entirely on learning by rote. A young student would learn to recite the classics perfectly without having the vaguest inkling of the meaning of the material he had committed to memory. There was a definite ascetic attitude toward study. Schoolrooms were ill-heated, if heated at all. Lighting was bad. In winter the long hours at the uncomfortable tables in the cold rooms must have been hard to bear. The writing process was a further hurdle requiring long tedious hours of tracing strokes and the ceaseless writing of characters which the child did not even understand.

In the peasant families there were some marked differences from gentry practices in the treatment of the *yu-nien*. Differentiation on the basis of sex occurred earlier among the peasants. This was largely due to the fact that the division of labor began earlier in peasant than in gentry families. It would perhaps be fair to say that gentry families made formal observance of these distinctions at an earlier time, but peasant families were earlier in their practical observance of them. The girls were inducted into women's tasks and the boys into men's tasks. Their briefer leisure gave them considerably less time for joint play than gentry chil-

---

[20] This matter is taken up specifically in the sections devoted to kinship solidarity.

[21] There is some evidence to show that the *yu-nien* period of a girl's life was and is regarded by her as the happiest and most carefree period of her life.

dren had. Joint play of boys and girls was permitted by both gentry and peasantry families, but after the age of ten years such joint play as existed was carried on under adult scrutiny, and all joint play ended at the beginning or shortly after the beginning of the teens. At the same time ceremonial practices and etiquette were far less elaborated and observed among the peasants so that there was relatively less differentiation among peasant boys and girls as ceremonial performers. In peasant as well as gentry families, however, the boys were eventually to handle the rites of ancestor worship, and they began to learn such matters while *yu-nien*.

At the age of five or six the peasant boy began to accompany his father to the fields. At first he was given light tasks: fetching tools, providing drinking water, watching the farm animals, if there were any, and the like. Though they were light tasks as farm work went in China, the jobs were quite heavy for children so young. Even today it is not unusual to see a small Chinese boy carrying heavy loads of water on a balance pole. The boys also learned weeding and use of the Chinese hoe, which was not light work. They remained with their fathers and brothers in the fields all day during the working seasons.

The peasant girls appeared in the fields only during periods of great activity, such as planting and harvest. At times when extra help was needed, both wives and daughters went to help the men. The peasant girl *yu-nien* [22] had plenty of work to do at home. She learned to tend the fire, to cook, to wash, clean, and sew. The women in the average Chinese peasant household made all the clothes for its members, including shoes, which were not made of leather but of layers of old cloth sewn together for a sole, with uppers sewn on. Gentry girls were taught this art as well, but for the gentry girls shoemaking assumed more symbolic than actual economic importance. A gentry girl was expected to make all the shoes for her husband's family during her first year in it, but the functional importance of this in all probability lay largely in her symbolic subjection to and production for her new family. [23]

At this stage of development in peasant families the relative lack of significance of the girl was first brought home to her. The *yu-nien* girl

[22] Female *yu-nien* may be called *yu-nü*. Male *yu-nien* may be called simply by that title or by the title *yu t'ung*.

[23] This matter is mentioned again briefly under the age group of young married women, and is also considered as part of the setting of role differentiation on the basis of sex.

was increasingly made aware that she was destined to marry out of the family and that care and money spent upon her was in a sense a waste of the family resources. Furthermore, when time for her marriage was reached, a cash outlay for her dowry would be necessary, unless the social and economic position of her family was such that they would simply sell her outright to her husband's family. The feeling of impermanence was more strongly brought home to peasant girls than to gentry girls. It is true that both were prepared to leave their families, but in gentry families the girl did not feel herself such an economic burden.[24]

In "traditional" China, as this stage of *yu-nien* went on, the girls of both peasantry and gentry families were more and more withdrawn from contacts with outsiders. This was, of course, particularly marked by contrast with the treatment of the boys in these respects. The segregation was part of the general taboo on the intermingling of the sexes. Chinese women in general were confined to their homes. Visiting by women was relatively restricted. In the large gentry family most of a woman's contacts were with the women of her husband's family. She retained some contact with her own family of orientation through visits, and some slight contact with female friends, but the latter was slight, particularly among the more straight-laced gentry.[25] The increasing isolation of the sexes for the *yu-nien* girl meant increasing isolation from all save the women of her own family. Boys, on the other hand, were free to go outside the walls of the family compound, and their nonfamily contacts broadened greatly during this period. In fact, for the gentry boys some of the firmest outside associations they were to form were made in this

[24] In the course of this paper the position of women as one of the greatest foci of insecurity in Chinese kinship structure if not in all Chinese society will be examined at some length. The factor mentioned here is one of the aspects of this whole question.

[25] This factor may not have been so noticeable prior to the Sung Dynasty, at which time there was a general reinterpretation of the Confucian doctrines. See C. P. Fitzgerald, *China, a Short Cultural History* (New York, 1938), pp. 404-417; also A. Waley in his introduction to an English translation of *Chin P'ing Mei* (New York, 1940), p. xv, states: "But Confucianism was, especially since the Sung dynasty, a Puritanical and ascetic creed . . ." The views of informants, along with the spread of foot-binding at that time, lead the author to believe that a much stricter interpretation was placed on the roles and status of women. See also Hu Shih, "The Indianization of China: A Case Study in Cultural Borrowing," *Independence, Convergence, and Borrowing* (Cambridge, 1937), pp. 219-247, esp. pp. 241-246.

period, associations based on attendance of a common school or work under a common master.

There was some difference between the traditional peasantry and gentry families on this score. The peasant *yu-nien* girls were less withdrawn from outside contact than were the gentry *yu-nien* girls. This difference in treatment was largely a function of the difference in living standards. In the first place, gentry houses were usually large rambling aggregations of interconnected units and halls surrounded by high outside walls. Inside the walls the family made up a unit which could operate with little or no outside contact on the part of the women. Food and other requirements were brought into the grounds by tradesmen or by servants sent out to purchase supplies. The family business was conducted by the men. Entertaining of nonkin outsiders was relatively rare, and, when it occurred, it was conducted by the men with the women as much out of sight as possible. The main contact with nonkin persons open to gentry *yu-nien* girls was that with servants and the tradesmen who came into the courts, except in the rare cases in which the *yu-nien* girls studied at school. Servants, however, were "household" members, although not family members, and thus relations with them represented no new contacts.

The peasants lived in small separate houses, or sometimes several families shared one of the old gentry houses. In any case, their living quarters afforded them much less seclusion than was afforded gentry families. Light inside their houses was poor, and peasant women frequently sat on their doorsteps or along the street to do sewing and similar jobs. They did their washing along the banks of the local streams or canals, and several groups of women were generally busy with their work at the same time.[26] Since they had no servants to shop and market for them, the peasant women and their daughters who accompanied them came into more contact with local shopkeepers and peddlers than did their gentry counterparts.

Furthermore peasant women and their daughters had more contact with the men of the family in their occupational roles than did gentry women. It is true that the women did not commonly labor in the fields,

[26] These groups of women are still a prominent feature of the Chinese landscape. There is every reason to believe that despite the arduous labor the accompanying social contacts gave this work a decidedly pleasurable aspect.

but when the fields required little attention they were in contact with the men of the family around the house, helping the men in some household tasks or watching them while away their time. Chinese land division was such that in the field work that they did, peasant women could not fail to come in contact with both the men and women working on neighboring plots of land, and since the pieces of land tended by one family were usually scattered about, they came in contact with various groups.

Between the work of peasantry and gentry *yu-nien* there was one overwhelming distinction, however. The peasant boy went to work in the fields or as an apprentice under some craftsman or merchant, whereas the gentry *yu-nien* went to school. In some cases peasant *yu-nien* did attend school. Sometimes an alert peasant boy would be educated by means of *tsu* funds, or the village might contribute to the schooling of an exceptionally promising young lad. If the boy were at all promising and if his family could possibly afford the expense, they would send him to school, but under ordinary circumstances the peasant boy's chances for schooling were slim. In the average case not only was there a dearth of funds to pay for his tuition, but also his labor was sorely needed to keep up the family economic position to a subsistence level or one slightly above that, and funds were lacking to replace his labor if he went to school. If he did go to school, he was relieved of the discipline of his father when he was in school,[27] but he had in its place the discipline of Confucian schooling which, if anything, was apt to exceed paternal discipline in severity.

Another form of work for the male *yu-nien* was in apprenticeships. While the craftsmen of China were not numerous relative to the general population, they were important for many purposes. Apprentices were recruited largely from the sons of the master craftsmen or sons of their kinsmen outside the family or of friends. It was not unusual, however, for peasant boys to be recruited for this work. While boys were seldom if ever sold or killed in difficult times as female *yu-nien* or female infants were, if there were more than one son and if the land held were inadequate to support more than one married son and his children, one or more of the other boys might be put in apprenticeship to a craftsman or a mer-

[27] When a peasant boy went to school, he sometimes boarded there away from home. If he attended a local school, he was relieved of arduous field work and the like and given only light tasks about the house.

chant. Whether the boy were the son of the master concerned or of a peasant,[28] his lot was a hard one by present child labor standards, though it was probably no worse than that of the European apprentice of the craft era. He worked extremely hard at first on menial tasks—cleaning up, fetching and carrying for the master, doing the bidding of the journeymen of the shop or of the family. His quarters were neither private nor comfortable. If he got wages at all, they went to his parents. His master was free to beat him if he chose to do so. After the relatively unfettered days of the *ying-erh shih-ch'i,* this experience was a hard and bitter change.

Structurally speaking, the severity of the *yu-t'ung's* discipline was of the utmost importance in the Chinese family. The Chinese son was not placed in the same type of competitive position with his father that seems to have overshadowed the development of the sons of outstanding men in the West. There was no question in the mind of the boy that he too would one day have the power and position in the family represented by his father. Not only would he have it, but he would have it as often as possible in terms of power and status in a continuation of the same group controlled by his father. Hostility and feelings of inferiority on this plane, therefore, were to some extent mitigated, but the severe discipline without doubt placed a great burden on the solidarity of the relationship between father and son. It forced the relationship into a pattern of avoidance, respect, and fear rather than the pattern of love and intimacy which is accented, however unsuccessfully, in the United States. Structurally speaking, the discipline had the effect of emphasizing the status of the head of the family, and the preparation of the son to take over his position.[29]

However important the institutionalization of this relationship between father and son may have been for the preservation of the family structure of China, it certainly placed considerable strain on the relation between the participants as individuals. In the stable "traditional" periods, the strain was offset by other aspects of the social structure which bolstered the whole position of the family. The removal of these factors has thrown some light on the strain involved.[30] It was during the *yu-nien* period that

[28] A son of a master would be better treated and would be taught more.

[29] This whole matter is considered at greater length in the succeeding section on solidarity. See Chapter IV, pp. 166–175. It is interesting to note that this was not necessarily the case in the relations between father and daughter. See Chapter IV, pp. 179–181.

[30] This matter is taken up in the discussion of the "transitional" family.

this pattern was first impressed upon the boys. By the end of this period the boy had either become used and submissive to the pattern or he had been made a more or less frustrated rebel for life. The "traditional" family period was sufficiently well integrated to habituate most of the *yu-t'ung* peacefully to the structure and to frustrate the rebellion of most of the rest until they could succeed their fathers in the normal and accepted fashion.

Some, of course, followed deviating patterns, but they could not have comprised a significant number save in periods of extreme political and economic strife. Even then it is unlikely that they amounted to a large or strategic group because prior to the twentieth century all such upheavals resulted in a renovation of the old society, an eradication of the excesses and corruption to which the society tended. Relatively little reform of the basic structural features of the society, however, was attempted or advocated. Had the proportion of true rebels been high enough in one of these periods of disintegration, it is not unlikely that the whole pattern might have been swept away.

The difficulty of the *yu-nien* period for Chinese males was further accentuated by the fact that in the succeeding periods discipline was sharply diminished, and ultimately, of course, the boy graduated from the receiving end of paternal discipline to become the source of its administration. The "traditional" family in China did not institutionalize a carefree existence for children in this age group as is done in the United States. This was true of gentry and peasantry families alike. Of course gentry sons, unlike peasant sons, had an economic basis for evading productive labor. Gentry sons could afford to be idle, but if the gentry son were seriously enlisted in academic work, and most of them were, there was little chance for frivolity. Such carefree existence as Chinese males experienced was confined to the *ying-erh-shih-ch'i* and extreme old age, with indulgence in proportion to economic resources in the period of adult maturity.[31] Actually it was not until the stage of *lao-nien*, old age,

[31] It was during the period of early adult maturity that gambling and extra-familial sexual indulgence was apt to take place. In later life the responsibilities placed on the man usually interfered with this sort of indulgence. In the case of the extremely wealthy, such indulgence would, of course, be sustained from early manhood until financial or physical breakdown or both. It must also be kept in mind that in "traditional" China, as in other societies, there were individuals characterized as worthless by the society who managed to make a career of gambling, drinking, and

that the male Chinese was institutionally expected to relax his serious application to the complex business of living and superintending the living of others. In between the *ying-erh shih-ch'i* and the *lao-nien shih-ch'i* a serious and industrious attitude toward life was expected.

Despite this rather strict view of things, however, there was a definite relaxation of discipline after the *yu-nien* period. The father's control remained absolute, but he was expected to treat his son much more nearly as an equal. If he decided to beat his son after the son was past the *yu-nien* stage, no one would interfere, but his conduct would be regarded as either unduly stern or as the result of an unbridled temper and a loss of self-control. The general view was that if he had been successful as a father such discipline would no longer be necessary to gain respect and obedience from his son.

Ch'ing-nien Shih-ch'i. The next age group recognized in Chinese society and in the Chinese family structure is that of the *ch'ing-nien*. The term *ch'ing-nien* in "traditional" China covered in general the years between sixteen or seventeen and thirty in the case of males, and started and ended somewhat earlier in the case of females, when it was applied to them. The term, however, was very much more limited in its applicability than those which have gone before. In the first place, during the movement leading up to the overthrow of the Ch'ing Dynasty and in the subsequent history of the Republic this term came to have a very different meaning from that which it had during the "traditional" period. In the "transitional" period the term took on a decided political tinge and became less strictly an age group designation than it had been formerly.[32]

In the second place, the use of this term was to a large degree confined to the gentry and wealthy merchant groups in the "traditional" period and was relatively little used among the peasantry. Thirdly, the term was one used generally in town or city environments rather than in the rural districts. In the fourth place, the *ch'ing-nien* period was a highly interstitial

---

wenching, regardless of whether they came from peasant or gentry backgrounds.

In the Chinese language there are special terms for the activities of such persons. One of these terms is made up of the characters for prostitutes and gambling; the term used for a person indulging in such activity is often *pu ch'eng ch'ang,* which has the literal meaning of "not achieve the normal."

[32] For discussion of this point see the treatment of the "transitional" kinship structure.

one: in the ordinary case it was a short period in "traditional" China, a gap between boyhood and manhood. In the fifth place, in the "traditional" period, at least, membership in this age group terminated with marriage. Finally, it was a term which by and large was not applied to females during the "traditional" period.[33] The term *ch'ing-nien* may be said roughly to cover the period during which an individual can no longer be treated as a *yu-nien* or child for most purposes and yet is not a full-fledged adult member of the society.

The male *ch'ing-nien* of the "traditional" period was not under great strain. The period must have been a relatively easy one by comparison with that which preceded it. By this time in his life the worst of his discipline was over. He was habituated to most of the things that went on about him and what was expected of him. Paternal discipline was considerably slackened, not only because he had by now learned most of the things necessary, but also because, as pointed out above, his father was no longer expected to treat him as a child and beat him for his mistakes. The emphasis of the father's discipline now lay rather in the supervision of the boy's judgment in applying the patterns he had learned. His views on various matters were more often sought than formerly, whether or not they were authoritative.

If the *ch'ing-nien* were in academic training, as was often the case, the period was still a relief after what had gone before. The most difficult schooling was over, for the *ch'ing-nien* with an academic background was now literate. During this period he took or at least prepared to take the initial examinations. If he failed them, he went back to work on his studies; if he passed them, he continued his studies, but he also received considerable recognition of a most pleasing sort. Even if he failed, he had already achieved honorific status, for he had achieved literacy in an almost totally illiterate society which gave to literacy and learning the highest esteem it could bestow.

The male *ch'ing-nien* had more autonomy of action than he had ever had before. To a certain extent he was able to indulge himself, for by now he could apportion his work, make time for other things, and seek new experience. During his *yu-nien* period the youth had met other youths outside his family, particularly at school. Now he saw a great deal of these

---

[33] By and large, age group designations particularly after the *yu-nien* period were much vaguer in their application to females in China than to males.

outsiders, with whom a considerable part of his vital everyday experience now lay.

In general the *ch'ing-nien* period (or late *yu-nien* period if the boy did not pass through *ch'ing-nien* status) was one in which the boy first indulged in heterosexual intercourse. Previously the *ch'ing-nien* had had relatively little contact with girls and women since his early years as a *yu-nien*. Now, both by himself and with his friends, he sought out the companionship of women. This of necessity plunged him into some rather specialized aspects of Chinese society and in a sense took him out of his family or made him a problem for the family. There were two major sources to which the *ch'ing-nien* could look for sexual gratification. One was to the servant girls of his own family's household. Sexual relations with the female members of his own family were ruled out by a strict incest taboo, and he was not ordinarily permitted to be alone with female relatives of his own age. The servant girls, however, were accessible to him. It was common practice in gentry families for one or more of the servant girls of the household to be assigned to serve him and care for his quarters. It was by no means infrequent for sexual relationships to be carried on between the *ch'ing-nien* and these servant girls. Such conduct, however, was somewhat limited by the fact that the relationships were disruptive of the household, and discovery of them might bring parental displeasure and punishment.

The other avenue of heterosexual gratification open to the *ch'ing-nien* was afforded by prostitutes. It was common for Chinese of the gentry class to have their first contact with prostitutes while they were *ch'ing-nien*. Exploration of the possibilities of this type of experience was usually shared with one's schoolmates and friends. The complicated feature of this path of gratification lay in the fact that it exposed the *ch'ing-nien* to the practices of gambling and drinking at the same time. It was certainly not true that there was no opportunity to indulge in these latter two activities apart from sexual activities, but the three were often found together, and upon experiencing one of them, the *ch'ing-nien* was likely to find his early taste of the other two as well.

Access to these pleasures was possible because as a young adult the *ch'ing-nien*, unlike the *yu-nien*, was given a certain amount of spending money to care for his needs. As a *yu-nien*, he had seen gambling going on about him, for gambling in one form or another was nearly ubiquitous in China,[34] but as a *yu-nien* his lack of spending money and the consequent unwillingness of gamblers to grant him credit kept him from any genuine involvement.

The greater freedom of the *ch'ing-nien,* coupled with the maturing physical desires which he now more insistently felt, tended to draw the *ch'ing-nien* into activities disruptive to the accepted family pattern. This was particularly so since youths who in the "traditional" period came under the rubric *ch'ing-nien* were by and large city or town dwelling youths, and when they were rural residents, they usually attended schools at larger population centers or had available the means to travel there. At any rate the accessibility of the larger population centers meant greater opportunity for indulgence of all sorts. The parents of the *ch'ing-nien* were therefore under some compulsion for the sake of family stability to procure a wife for the boy and see him safely married and assuming a more stable role.

The factor of marriage was a major one in the life of the *ch'ing-nien* boy. He did not, however, play any prominent role in the decision. His wife was chosen for him by his parents. Usually his mother played a major role in this matter of choice, since it was she who would have, at least during the early years of the marriage, a relationship with their daughter-in-law that would overshadow that between the newly-married husband and wife. Though the father played a supervisory role and could alter or even veto his wife's decision in such matters if he chose, he did not usually do so. Sometimes even in the "traditional" period, the son's opinion might be asked, but consultation with him was not the usual procedure. Ordinarily the boy neither met nor saw his bride before the engagement. Custom, in fact, decreed that his first glimpse of his wife come on the day the marriage ceremony took place.

Although he was not seriously consulted in the matter of his marriage, the *ch'ing-nien* could not have failed to have derived a certain satisfaction from the attention which he received at this time. Marriage meant adulthood, and the buzz of gossip, conjecture, and concern that surrounded so important a family matter could hardly fail to come to his attention, even though he might be told nothing definite until his parents summoned him

---

[34] Even candy vendors have wheels at which the purchaser may try his luck. For a given sum, the sport may spin the wheel; the amount or the type of candy received by him is determined by its stopping place. In gambling, China has nothing whatever to learn from the West.

to announce the date of his marriage. In a sense which had never been true of him since infancy, unless he had distinguished himself in the examinations or in some other fashion, he was the center of attention.

Marriage, however, was not without its drawbacks. One of the age-old sources of frustration in China might appear at this time: frustration over the choice of a wife. Despite all the precautions taken against the *ch'ing-nien's* having contact with young women of his own class, he sometimes did arrange contact with them. If this happened and an emotional bond grew between them, the bond was almost inevitably shattered by the marriage of the principals to other people. One of the most frequent sources of difficulty of this sort arose from contact between cousins of different or even the same surname. Sexual relations and marriage between cousins of the same surname were always ruled out by the incest taboo. Cross-cousin marriages were sometimes institutionally approved or even considered highly desirable in certain areas.[35] Much more contact between cousins of different sexes of a marriageable age took place than was ordinarily possible between nonrelated members of the same class. This was particularly true of first cousins of the same surname who were sometimes members of a single family, but it was also true of cross-cousins who were brought into the family.

Accounts of such attachments may be read in the famous Chinese novel of the eighteenth century, *Dream of the Red Chamber,* and in the twentieth-century novel by Lin Yu-Tang entitled *Moment in Peking.*[36] In the former, the hero, Chia Pao-yü, is very much involved in just this problem, and a character of the latter is not only similarly involved but keeps referring to Chia Pao-Yü's situation into the bargain.[37] Since premarital romantic attachments never occurred in theory and were institutionally disapproved, they were not likely to be taken into consideration by parents in selecting a wife for their son, nor were they likely to be considered by parents seeking a husband for their daughter. If the attachment were with someone below the social class of the *ch'ing-nien,* the relation was broken upon discovery, and discovery in this case as in the other was a signal for measures to be taken to arrange a suitable mar-

[35] See Francis L. K. Hsu's article, "Observations on Cross-Cousin Marriage in China," *American Anthropologist;* 47, 1, 83–103.

[36] New York, 1939.

[37] Miss Lang in illustrating much this same point discusses the case of Chia Pao-Yu at somewhat greater length than is done here. *Op. cit.,* pp. 33ff.

riage with someone else.[38] The forced rupture of such relationships undoubtedly placed some strain upon the relationship between the *ch'ing-nien* and his parents, but all in all, the successful revolts against such treatment were few and far between.[39] Usually the parents had their way, most frequently without even a remonstrance from the frustrated son or daughter. At the same time, the apparent ease of the victory should not conceal the seriousness of the conflict. One of the factors which emerges most clearly as a disruptive factor in the families of the "traditional" period is the lack of participation by the *ch'ing-nien* in this vital decision. It was to be the *ch'ing-nien* who formed the most explosive age group in the "transitional" period, and one of their major concerns and most frequent battle cries was that of revolt against the parental choice of their mates.

Our discussion of the *ch'ing-nien* has proceeded in terms of male *ch'ing-nien* only. This has been necessary because the term was not generally applied to girls at all during the "traditional" period. The age groups of females tended to be rather more vague than those of males in all categories. For the girl in China, marriage was the great pivot of her development, as we shall observe later. Coupled with the fact that marriage for girls in "traditional" China was generally carried out at an early age and that the average girl married at an age from one to several years younger than that generally accepted as the proper marriage age for the males of her own class, this tended to cancel out the period which *ch'ing-nien* covered. Even among the town and city gentry, daughters were not likely to be called *ch'ing-nien*. Marriage, of course, really marked the end of the *ch'ing-nien* period, for then one assumed a full role as an adult, and marriage was not delayed much past the point at which a girl was physically mature. Long before she matured physically, a girl's marriage

[38] Attachments of all degrees between gentry sons and female servants were not uncommon, and attachments between gentry daughters and male servants, going even so far as sexual intercourse were not unknown. The latter, in particular, was a subject of grave concern.

[39] One of the very rare cases of successfully concluded romantic love is that from a story by Ch'en Hsuan of the T'ang Dynasty. This instance involves catalepsy and certain supernatural manifestations in the achievement of its end. It is the only tale of a happy conclusion to such a romance dating from any but the modern period that the author can recall. There are others, no doubt, but they are not frequent. This story is translated by Wang Chi-Chen in a volume entitled *Traditional Chinese Tales* (New York, 1944). See pp. 17-20.

was under consideration, and the period between physical maturity and marriage was not prolonged unless she was a special favorite of her parents. The bond formed between daughter and father would sometimes be permitted to delay the marriage, particularly in the families of scholars. In such cases an interstitial stage for girls was sometimes approximated and in this situation the term *ch'ing-nien* or some equivalent might have been used. The usage was not general enough to characterize the society, however, or even the gentry group as a whole.

The peasantry have not entered into the description of the *ch'ing-nien* stage in the "traditional" period any more than have the girls of gentry families. Apparently the term was not well known or much in use among them at that time. In fact the propriety of considering *ch'ing-nien* to be an age group at all in the kinship structure of the "traditional" period may well be raised. The validity of the question is borne out by the fact that during the "traditional" period the tendency was not to refer to *ch'ing-nien* as an age group into which one normally progressed but rather to refer to *ch'ing-nien-jen* literally, "green years men." [40] The term as used in China today generally leaves off the final character, *jen*. The net effect of the use of the term seems to have been to focus attention not upon an age group, but upon a particular individual. This distinction in usage between the "traditional" and "transitional" periods fits in well with what has been said above. It is hardly likely that a term so restricted in its usage could denote a genuine age group. It is treated here more or less as such, however, because its usage at that time clearly underlies its present usage, and there can be no underestimating its distinctness or importance today.

The question may well be raised as to why no transitional stage between the *yu-nien* period and the *chuang-nien* period grew up at all for the peasantry and for women in general. It has been pointed out above that during this period the term was applied to youths too old to be considered *yu-nien* and yet not advanced enough to have assumed the full responsibilities of the adult roles. Such a transitory position was in the nature of the case ruled out for virtually all sons of the peasantry. The primary reason probably lay in the fact that in the development of the peasantry there was no noticeable break between *yu-nien* status and

---

[40] I am indebted to Mr. Shih Huo-Heng for this point about usage. Mr. Shih has been good enough to criticize and make suggestions in general throughout this section.

marriage. The discipline and roles of the peasant boy changed slowly and gradually. In his early *yu-nien* days he was given field work and though much of it was heavy by modern Western standards of child labor, it was relatively light by Chinese field standards. The boy did some hoeing, water carrying, and the like, but he also watched over the grazing water buffaloes or other animals, if such there were, and he gathered fuel from the hills and so forth. These latter tasks were relatively simpler, easier and, above all, freer of immediate parental or adult supervision than the former tasks. As the *yu-nien* period progressed, the boy was given heavier and heavier tasks in accordance with his growing physical ability to bear them and in accordance with his training and skill. The process was paralleled by the boy's gradually increasing induction into more adult functions, such as representing the family by carrying messages of a more formal or ceremonial sort for the father, messages to the landlord.

Even marriage meant less of a break in the peasantry class than it did among the gentry. Marriage among peasants occasioned even less abrupt change in the case of peasants who adopted girls to become wives for their sons. The girls [41] were adopted when quite young and raised in the households in which they were to become daughters-in-law. In marriages of this sort no new woman was introduced to the family at the time of the marriage ceremony. Such marriages were considered inferior to ordinary ones, but they were cheaper and were often resorted to.

For the gentry boy development was not so gradual as for the peasant. In the first place, his school discipline changed. He passed the point where he learned by rote, and was expected now to understand as well as to repeat. The advent of the examinations marked a change. Whether successful or no, the gentry boy in his teens reached a stage of study at which he had to go away to study, or study more by himself at home, either of which required more freedom and initiative of him. Although his interests lay more outside the family than formerly, especially if he went away to the cities and towns, his marriage brought him back into the family in a sense. Unlike the peasant boy he did not merely continue familiar duties: he took up duties and responsibilities which he had seen fulfilled but had not carried out himself.

[41] These girls were sometimes called *hsiao-hsi*. This type of marriage is discussed by Fei Hsiao-T'ung in *Peasant Life in China,* pp. 33–35. Informants point out that the term *t'ang yang hsi* was more commonly used to refer to such girls.

The only use of the term *ch'ing-nien* among the peasantry in "traditional" times would seem to have been confined to those few peasants' sons who got a chance for education. Where they had such an opportunity, they were absorbed more and more into the gentry pattern, even though their position was economically more difficult. A peasant boy who showed talent might continue his academic development with funds provided by his village, by his *tsu,* or by his own family if they were unusually well-to-do. In any case, after he passed a moderately elementary level in his studies, he would have to leave his village in order to continue. Usually this meant going to some larger center of population in which opportunities for more advanced study were available. Furthermore the discipline of the academic process was the same for sons of peasants and sons of gentry. By the time they were well into the second half of their teens, the type of work required was altered. If they returned home, they did not fit into the ordinary picture of development, nor did they if they stayed away. Like gentry sons at a similar stage of development, they had to be given greater scope for self-reliance than did *yu-nien.*[42]

For the girls there was in general no such break, though there may have been isolated cases among gentry daughters of the type mentioned above. The advent of the menstrual period, certainly the most dramatic physical development of the female *yu-nien* stage, does not seem to have been the occasion for any particular *rite de passage* as it often is in other societies. In the course of this study it has not been possible to unearth any particular data on the menarche for the Ch'ing Dynasty period. It is highly probable, however, that much the same attitudes and practices were observed then as are observed now in the more "traditional" families. If this be true, then it can be said that little was made of the factor. Long before it took place, girls had been separated from males of other families and to a considerable extent from those of their own family as well, save when under parental or adult scrutiny. No other significant change seems to have demarcated this period prior to marriage. The girl was gradually taught the skills and duties appropriate to women of her status. Toward the end of the *yu-nien* period she did not take on new family responsibilities because she was destined to marry out of the family. There was

[42] This factor of relatively greater self-reliance emerges with great clarity among the *ch'ing-nien* both male and female, peasantry and gentry, of the "transitional" period.

no period in the latter or middle teens which could be distinguished from what went before by greater independence and self-reliance, because the more mature she became prior to her marriage the more she had to be kept from possible male contamination. As Miss Lang has pointed out [43] clandestine contact usually resulted in sexual intercourse. Premarital intercourse for girls was an extremely serious thing in "traditional" China. In the gentry class it almost certainly obviated the possibility of a suitable marriage, and in the peasant class it usually placed the girl's parents in a less advantageous bargaining position. Therefore at this time the girls were, if anything, less free than they had been earlier. And after they married, the severest discipline for women set in. Certainly nothing corresponding to the *ch'ing-nien* period, which later became so important, was to be found.

Chuang-nien Shih-ch'i and Chung-nien Shih-ch'i. For the vast majority of the population of China during the Ch'ing Dynasty the age group following the *yu-nien* period was that of the *chuang-nien*. The word *chuang* is applied variously in Chinese in a complex of terms centering around such meanings as "strong," "ablebodied," "vigorous," "healthy," "fertile," and "flourishing." When combined with the character *nien* it takes on the meaning of the vigorous period of life as a full-fledged adult. The age group here represented by this term generally covered the years from marriage to an age between thirty and forty years during the "traditional" period. Since there is no evidence of any truly decisive break between this age group and that which succeeds it, the *chung-nein* or middle-aged group which extends from sometime between thirty or forty to the period of old age, *lao-nien,* it might be well to consider both *chuang-nien* and *chung-nien* as representing the former and latter halves of a more general age status, that of "adult," *ch'eng-jen,* literally a "complete" or "finished" person. Both *chuang-nien* and *chung-nien* were and are considered *ch'eng-jen.* A *lao-nien* in both "traditional" and "transitional" China is something more than a *ch'eng-jen.*

The beginning of the *chuang-nien* period was marked more by marriage than by the attainment of a definite age.[44] Few things were as im-

[43] *Op. cit.,* p. 34.
[44] Sometimes in poor peasant families in which the marriage of a son to a girl adopted for the purpose took place, the birth of the first child, preferably a son, probably demarcated the beginning of this period rather than the actual marriage, which under these circumstances was apt to be minimized in importance.

portant in the life of a Chinese as his marriage. The importance of the event was greater in some groups than in others, but marriage was central to all families without exception and was central to a degree not generally equaled in the West at the present time. In the first place, no Chinese could live a complete life without marriage. There were groups in China which eschewed marriage. There were, for example, the various ascetic groups of monks and nuns, for the most part tied to the Buddhist and Taoist priestly groups, but apart from these groups unmarried adults never existed save as the marginal unfortunates mentioned in Chapter II. A person outside an ascetic organization who followed a celibate life by choice would have been regarded as the ultimate in perversity. Marriage was buttressed by the religious practices common to virtually all Chinese: ancestor worship. Though adopted children could continue a line, if necessary, they were considered a poor second to one's own children in carrying on these functions. Failure to maintain the line through one's own efforts or through adoption meant not only the negation of one's own life but of all one's ancestors in the bargain.

Professor Mai Hui-T'ing in his book on Chinese family problems characterizes the "traditional" Chinese attitude by quotations, well known to most or all Chinese, which bear on this problem.[45] One is Mencius' famous injunction: "there are three unfilial (acts); (of these) lack of posterity is the greatest (*Pu hsiao yu san wu hou wei ta*).[46] The other is a frequently used form of well wishing which has been roughly translated by R. H. Mathews as "May your children be as numerous as grasshoppers (Chung ssu yen ch'ing)."[47] No person unmarried was really a *ch'eng-jen* —a "finished person." Therefore marriage marked entrance into full adult status. This gave rise to the second consideration. Once married a person had to be accepted as an adult although in a sense his or her status as such might not be considered truly complete until children resulted from the union. At any rate, with marriage the full responsibilities of the family and the society descended upon the individual. His age was no longer a protection against responsibility. If he was old enough for marriage, he was old enough to behave as an adult.

[45] *Op. cit.,* p. 350.

[46] So preoccupied was Mencius with the heinousness of this offense that he neglected to state the other two unfilial acts, and what he had in mind at the time has thereby remained one of the minor textual problems of Chinese literature.

[47] See R. H. Mathews, *Chinese-English Dictionary* (Cambridge, 1945), p. 213.

When a man married in China, if his father or older brother were not living or if he were not living with them or some other older male in his direct line of descent, he became the institutionally approved head of his family. If his mother were living, he might well defer to her wishes and be ruled by her in all things, but it was he and he alone who was ideally considered to have the authority of the family and complete responsibility for it, both as regards its welfare and its conduct in the society.[48] If after marriage he lived with some older male member of his direct line of descent, he was subordinate to the older member but in the ordinary case physical punishment would not be administered to him now. Whereas before his opinion might have been asked on matters in order to train his judgment, now he was more nearly a full partner in the family. His opinion might still be overruled, but on matters of importance he could expect to be consulted. Consistent failure of a father or mother or elder brother to consult such a son would be regarded as undue domination and in the end would harm the family by increasing the inability of one of its strategic members to take over a role which would more or less inevitably come to him.

Not only could the married son expect to be consulted, but also he could now represent the family. As a *yu-nien* or *ch'ing-nien* he might be sent with messages for the family or the like, but as a married man—a responsible husband and possibly a father—he could fully represent his family in ceremonial and legal functions. If he were the head of his own family, he would have to do so, of course, but, even if he did not become its head upon marriage, he became fully qualified to represent it in lieu of the true head if circumstances required it.

The peasants were forced to deviate somewhat from the gentry patterns in these respects. Most notable among these differences was the fact that some peasant youths had to delay marriage for economic reasons. In China the bridegroom's parents were supposed to give the bride's family a gift upon the conclusion of the engagement, and the bride's family was expected to provide a dowry. Among the gentry it was expected that the gift of the bridegroom's family would be used toward the dowry of the bride. There was great prestige in a family's providing as lavish a dowry as possible. Among the peasantry, however, the girl represented a net

[48] The degree to which a widowed mother actually took over power and was approved in so doing is discussed below.

economic loss to her parents for care and feeding. If her family were well off, a dowry would be provided. Most of the peasants were not at all well off, however, and the gift of the bridegroom's family was necessary if the bride were to be outfitted at all. There was considerable social pressure on the bride's family to use this gift to provide her with a trousseau, but economic pressure was also great, and it was more important for a man to keep his own family above water and provide wives for his sons than to send his daughter off in style. As a result, the gift of the bridegroom's family often amounted to the actual purchase of a wife.

In peasant families which lacked the funds to purchase brides for their sons, marriage had to be delayed. It has been pointed out above that adoption of a young girl was one expedient used by the very poor to provide wives for their sons. There were other alternatives. It was sometimes possible to arrange a marriage with a girl who for some reason was older than the normal age for marriage. Marriage with a widow might also be arranged; both of these arrangements were less expensive than the customary marriages.[49]

In ordinary circumstances more was in question than simply the purchase price of a bride. Economic pressure could and very often did produce a situation in which the family was solely concerned with getting the daughter married at an advantageous figure at the minimum compliance with the institutional requirements which fixed the necessity of parents arranging marriages for their children. When pressure was not so great, however, parents gave thought to the future security of the daughter and the advantage of the match in relating the family with some new family. The latter factor counted more among the gentry, where such alliances could operate with great effect since the parties to it controlled numerous sources of advantage. Peasants usually married other peasants in roughly similar economic circumstances so that they had

[49] Informants point out that the cash payment for such marriages may actually have been higher than for ordinary marriages because the woman could be married at once and there was no risk of her death during a long engagement. In the case of the widows the matter was further complicated by the fact that the people who controlled her usually cared little for her future welfare and demanded as much cash as could be gotten for her immediately. Despite the greater initial expense, such marriages were less expensive in the long run because they did not require that the husband or his family have any resources over and above the purchase price of the bride.

less to hope for from the establishment of some new interfamily connection.

The peasants were, often as not, more concerned that the marriage not get them unduly involved with new relatives than they were with possible advantages in these matters. The peasantry, more than the gentry, had to depend on their *tsu* organizations for such advantages. Concern over the daughter's future security was not completely omitted, however. Some extra consideration had to be given, even in situations of economic pressure, because if her new family were intolerable or if she were deserted by her husband, she might be forced back into her own family. If she came back, she could not well be turned away, but her return might upset the family balance and increase the economic problem. Furthermore, if for some reason she had to return, it was more difficult to arrange a new match for her. She might be forced to remain a useless appendage to the family until her death.

Marriage was arranged by a go-between who had intimate knowledge of the conditions of the families concerned. The likelihood of a boy's family putting up a deceptive front was small. The boy's marriage required not only sufficient money for the "gift" to the bride's family, but also sufficient assurance as to her future. The primary basis of such assurance was the possession of land. Families with daughters were extremely reluctant to marry them to the sons of families who had neither land of their own nor a firm tenant position. Thus the marginal economic members of the Chinese population were marginal in more senses than the economic one, for their marriages were delayed or prevented, and they were forced to continue in an immature role past the usual period.

The situation was further complicated by the fact that there were means of disposing of daughters other than marriage. The means most commonly known in the West was that of outright sale of daughters into prostitution. There were procurers who regularly went about the country purchasing girls from families in economic difficulties. Kidnapping of girls for sale to the brothel keepers was also common in bandit-infested areas. Whatever the status of such a trade from the moral point of view, from the point of view of the functioning of society the trade of prostitution competed with the poorer families seeking wives for their sons.

Another major force drawing daughters away from marriage in the local villages was the practice of concubinage. Concubinage has sometimes been presented as having been the ordinary practice of families through-out China. This was never the case.[50] Concubinage was extremely common throughout the gentry class of China, and many women were absorbed by the practice, but it was not common among the peasantry. Concubines might be taken at the wife's request as well as at the husband's desire and was particularly likely in the case of a failure of the first wife to produce a male heir. In such cases the husband might even be ordered by his father to take a concubine. Since the children of concubines were fully legitimate, concubinage could be used to maintain the line of descent. Pure pleasure and self-indulgence also played a large role in concubinage, and some informants hold that the taking of concubines was often rather in the nature of what Thorstein Veblen would have called competitively con-spicuous consumption on the part of the leisure class. At any rate concu-bines were usually purchased from peasant stock. Go-betweens were used as in virtually all relations of Chinese with outsiders, but taking a con-cubine was a much less formalized matter than taking a wife, and the element of purchase was considerably less subtle. Gentry families were extremely reluctant to let their daughters become concubines unless their future master held a position of unusual prestige or wealth.[51]

Concubinage and prostitution, with the closely allied professions of acting, dancing, and the like, combined with female infanticide as the three major factors tending to complicate the matter of wife-getting for the average peasant. In particularly hard times the problem must have reached sizable proportions because, the harder the lot of the peasant, the more likely it was that his daughters would be drained away from peasant marriages.

The gentry were limited in number, and even their profuse use of con-cubines could not have made a sizable dent in the quantity of peasant daughters available for marriage. Prostitution, on the other hand, was prodigal in its use of female life, and the life expectancy of the average

---

[50] See A. H. Smith, *op. cit.,* p. 297.

[51] Situations in which a man married one girl and took her sister as a concu-bine were not, however, unusual. A wife ordinarily preferred such an arrangement and often suggested it when the advent of a concubine seemed likely, because it was easier to integrate her sister into the family than to handle an outsider bound to her by no previous ties. The position of a concubine held considerably less prestige than did that of wife; so under ordinary circumstances the gentry families tried to avoid such a status for their daughters.

peasant daughter sold to be a prostitute could not have been great. There are indications quite otherwise.[52]

There is probably no really sound basis for conjecture about female infanticide. In time of famine, drought, high taxes, and the like, it probably reached large proportions, thereby preventing the marriage of some peasants, and delaying that of others. Men who were cut off from normal family life by their inability to obtain wives were a source of unrest in the community. Without family ties to hold them back, there was little else to restrain them. Some of them became bandits, in which role they had everything to gain and little to lose. If they gained wealth through banditry they could go elsewhere, purchase land, marry, reëstablish family continuity, and once again enter respectable roles in the society.

The marriage ceremony was perhaps the most important event of the *chuang-nien* period for the members of both sexes and of the gentry and peasantry alike. In the case of the women the birth of their first son was of nearly equal importance, perhaps, but in a sense this could be viewed rather as a crucially important step in the completion of the marriage. The literature in China abounds with descriptions of Chinese weddings.[53] The marriage rituals when fully carried out in the "traditional" fashion were vivid and picturesque and never failed to catch the eye of travelers and scholars. Actual practices no doubt varied considerably throughout China, even during the "traditional" period. By local custom two neighboring communities might differ in marriage procedure. Variations in the ritual and inclusions or exclusions which differed from the "traditional" patterns as stipulated in the great canons of ritual conduct such as the *Li Chi (The Book of Rites)* were common.[54]

At this point the distinction between peasantry and gentry must be reaffirmed. While the marriage procedure will not be described in detail here, some of its structural components should be noted, using the gentry patterns as a model. As in so many other parts of the analysis this procedure is necessary because the peasants attempted to conform to the patterns of the gentry even though their economic situation seldom permitted full conformity. The fact that the ordinary run of the population

[52] See Hendrik de Leeuw, *Cities of Sin* (New York, 1938), pp. 39–68.

[53] See A. H. Smith, *op. cit.,* Chapter XVIII; and J. Doolittle, *op. cit.,* Chapters II and III.

[54] See *infra* footnote 53, Chapter III.

would not be able to follow all the rites was understood far back in Chinese history, though the point has often been overlooked by both modern Western scholars and modern Chinese students in the field. In James Legge's translation of the *Li Chi* one finds the following quotation on this point: "The rules of ceremony do not go down to the common people" (*Li pu hsia shu jen*). At this point the translator has inserted an interpretative note to the following effect: "Not that the common people are altogether freed from the rules. But their occupations are engrossing, and their means small. Much cannot be expected of them." [55] There is little room for doubt that, whatever the authentic dating of this portion of the text may be,[56] Dr. Legge in his note on the passage has correctly stated what has been the orthodox attitude in these matters for the past several hundred years.

In the first place it must be noted that while marriage played a tremendous role in the lives of the two persons immediately concerned, in "traditional" China it was not primarily concerned with the immediate participants. Marriage was the concern of the whole family, not merely of the bride and groom, and the interests of the marital pair were subordinated to those of the family. In all save a few institutionally unapproved cases, marriage was the result of negotiations between two families. Because of the nature of Chinese society, an agent had to be employed.[57] This was done by peasant and gentry families alike, though

[55] The Legge translation of the *Li Chi* is to be found in volumes twenty-seven and twenty-eight of F. Max Muller's series *The Sacred Books of the East* (Oxford, 1885). This quotation is to be found in Vol. 27, p. 90. Dr. Legge's interpretation is confirmed by informants.

[56] The *Li Chi* text is presumably one of the older Chinese texts. The exact dating of such texts and their various portions is a matter of great complexity. This portion of the *Li Chi* is apparently authentically ancient.

[57] The go-between was used in virtually all negotiations between two persons not of the same family. Marriage was only a special case of this use. One of the major functional bases for the go-between as used in marriage arrangements was undoubtedly the intimate nature of the questions of interest to the parties concerned. No ordinary stranger could have put such questions to members of another family and have remained in close relations with them. The question of loss of face was involved on the one hand, but more importantly that of objectivity was involved on the other. In the choice of a daughter-in-law or a husband for their children, Chinese parents looked for specific qualities in the person concerned, and in his or her family. Furthermore, these facts had to be weighed against other possible choices. The relations between friends in China or between future in-laws had to be of a subjective nature. Only through a third person could the necessary objectivity be ob-

the remuneration and ritual differed widely. Chinese marriage was not merely the performance of a single ritual on a particular day. It was a process which began with the selection of a go-between. The complete ritual called for full investigation of the parties concerned—both the individuals and their families—and several exchanges of gifts and information. Of these six were ordinarily distinguished.[58] It was in such matters as these that peasantry and gentry practices diverged. The gentry actually followed the prescriptions; the peasants ignored some of them, at least. The importance of the preliminary visits and exchanges did not lie in any contact between the prospective bridal pair. Ordinarily such contact did not take place until the day on which they were to begin their life together. The negotiations permitted the arrangement of a new solidarity and relationship between two otherwise separate and distinct families.[59]

On the day the two principals were to begin life together, the bride was sent to the house of her husband. She was clothed in red when she arrived at her husband's home. The color indicated her ritual birth in her

---

tained. So important did the go-between become in marriage arrangements that an old Chinese proverb held, in speaking of marriage, that it could not be achieved without "the order of the parents and the word of the go-between (*Fu mu chih ming mei cho chih yen*). See Mai Hui-T'ing, *op. cit.*, p. 63. This proverb attributed to the go-between a position in marriage arrangement of equal importance with parents. Neither of the immediate parties to the marriage was considered so important.

[58] These six were as follows: (1) *Na-ts'ai:* the boy's family received a go-between and through the go-between asked the girl's family for a marriage; (2) *Wen-ming:* through a go-between the families of the boy and girl exchanged cards with the names of the couple and their birthdays; (3) *Na-chi:* this was the astrological interpretation of the characters of the names and birthdates and the presentations of them to the ancestors in the ancestral shrines; (4) *Na-cheng:* after the names and birthdates had been presented to the ancestors (if they were approved) the boy's family sent a present to the girl's family and the negotiations over the marriage contract were begun; (5) *Ch'ing-ch'i:* the boy's family asked the girl's family through the go-between to set the date for the wedding after the marriage contract had been set; (6) *Ch'in-ying:* on the wedding day the bride left her old home and was formally welcomed and received at her husband's home. These ceremonies were all attended by different kinds of gift exchange. See Mai Hui-T'ing, *op. cit.*, pp. 192–193. See also Sun Pen-Wen *Modern Chinese Social Problems (Hsien-Tai Chung-Kuo She-Hui Wen-T'i)*, 3 vols. (Chungking, 1942), I, 121–122.

[59] In the case of a cross-cousin marriage or the marriage of a second daughter of a given family to a second son of the same family into which her sister had married, this was, of course, not true, but even in these cases it meant a special reaffirmation or strengthening of old bonds.

husband's family. Here again the ritual was often observed in a merely perfunctory fashion by the peasants. The gentry, however, observed it elaborately. It often included lavish processional displays of the bride's dowry, rich costumes, and the like. Even the peasants, wherever possible, had their brides brought in a sedan chair sealed with red paper. At the home of the groom there were ceremonies for the reception of the bride. She was met for the first time by her husband, presented to his family, and inducted into the worship of his ancestors. Bride and groom were introduced to family friends, relatives, and neighbors at a feast. That evening they slept together as man and wife. At one time the bride's worship of the bridegroom's ancestors, a ceremony known as *miao chien,* took place some three months after their marriage night. This may have been a remnant of a custom permitting dissolution of a marriage which had not resulted in pregnancy within a stated length of time. By late Ch'ing times, the *miao-chien* seems to have been performed on the day the bride arrived at the home of her new family.

In these bare ritual bones of the process, the main factors involved and their relation to the family can be seen, even though the peasantry and gentry may have differed widely in their ritual implementation of these factors. In the first place, after the marriage day the bride was cut off from her family of orientation. This did not mean that the members of her family had no further contact with her. They often did, and, as will be seen later, often served as her sole bulwark against mistreatment, but she ceased to be considered a member of her biological father's family. She became a member of her husband's family. This interpretation is abundantly borne out by the fact that an examination of Chinese genealogical tables shows that daughters were not entered by name but by the symbol for female, *nü.* In a country where names and descent were so important, the names of daughters were not preserved in the genealogical tables of their families of orientation. It was upon her death and the entry of her ancestor tablet alongside that of her husband that her name reentered a family, but then it was in the family which she had shared with her husband, and the name which was entered was her father's surname plus an honorific title.[60]

[60] Alongside her husband's name on the ancestor tablet was entered her biological father's surname followed by the term *lao-ju-jen* which has the literal meaning of "aged (or venerable) dependent person."

The bride's ritual birth into her husband's family was sometimes per-functory in peasant families, particularly in a case of remarriage. Of course if it were a case of marriage of a son to a "daughter" adopted quite some time before for this purpose, then both her leave-taking of her former family and her induction into the new were more or less ignored at the time of marriage. Despite these exceptions, in the ordinary case the func-tion of the new bride's introduction to her new family and the delinea-tion of her status were accomplished by these rituals. At the same time the presence of friends, neighbors, and relatives outside the family unit signified her introduction in her new status relative to people who main-tained important relations with her new family.

Wherever possible, even among the peasants, a feast of some propor-tions was held on this occasion. Its importance was such that Chinese of all economic levels made great sacrifices if necessary to signalize the event. The peasants' outlay was more limited than the gentry's, but even so their efforts were such that the expenses involved in marriage celebrations to-gether with those involved in funeral observances formed one of the major factors leading them to borrow money and hence involve them-selves in a hopeless economic morass.

Introduction to relatives, friends, and neighbors of the family unit was of great importance to the family. Meeting friends and neighbors of the husband's family was, perhaps, particularly significant in the case of the peasants because peasant women came more frequently in contact with persons outside the family unit than did the gentry women of the "traditional" period. In theory, at least, the gentry women kept rather close to home. But here it must be noted that the function of introduction was not unilateral. The ceremonies also served to introduce the son in his new status as an adult. This factor was probably more important socially and economically among the gentry families than among peasant families.

In the course of the introduction the status of the new pair relative to those present was symbolically reinforced. Unlike weddings of the modern United States, the convenience and happiness of the bridal pair were not emphasized. Quite the contrary, the bride and groom, and espe-cially the bride, were kept busy with the ceremonial serving of their family members and guests. In gentry families, of course, the bulk of the actual food was brought out by servants, but the bride and groom had to be in constant attendance on the needs of the persons present, and the bride offered each guest in the order of precedence some wine or tea or some of the various delicacies provided. The bridal pair also made offerings to the ancestors and to the husband's parents. The attention and subservience of the bride to her new parents was, of course, particularly important.

It is interesting to observe that the adult name for the man was given its first ceremonial usage at the marriage and became the name he bore throughout the remainder of his life, and no one save those on terms of great intimacy with him would use his earlier names either in reference to him or in conversations with him. Even his intimates would no longer use his childish or clan names publicly or on formal occasions.[61] The groom's use of his adult name was of obvious significance. With his marriage he attained a new status. In China where names were so important this was a suitable mode of recognizing that fact. It is of importance to note, however, that from this time on the status of the man in his family changed only in terms of the gradual accretion of authority, responsibility, and prestige as the years accumulated, except for its change at the death or retirement of his father. The birth of his sons was important to him and his position, but even without sons his status would continue to change gradually. The death or retirement of his father was of great importance to him, especially if he were an eldest son; it meant simply a wider sway for powers to which he was already well accustomed on a smaller scale. Marriage was his last great change in the family unit. His wife, however, experienced at least two others of similar

[61] The matter of names in China requires a special study in itself. The confusion of various different names for the same individual constitutes one of the truly difficult problems in the translation of the old texts. As a small infant, a boy was given a baby name, often a term of endearment or a derogatory term to mislead evil spirits. With the passage to *yu-nien* status this name was dropped, and a clan name was given him. His adult name was given him before his marriage either in late *yu-nien* period or in *ch'ing-nien* period, and its first ceremonial usage other than its giving was its inscription on the cards exchanged during the marriage negotiations. Although a boy might be called by his adult name before his marriage, he was supposed to be called by it after his marriage. It is interesting that the desire for the assumption of one's adult name should have been so strong prior to its first important ceremonial usage. In China the premium placed on adult status was high, and this was no doubt a factor in the matter. The desire to assume adult status as soon as possible is interesting by contrast with the "youth" culture of the United States where the desire for privilege and freedom is marked, but the early desire to assume adult roles is not noticeably strong.

importance to her: the birth of her first son and the death or retirement of her mother-in-law.

The presentation of the new daughter to the ancestors of her husband's family was of unusual significance for the bride in both peasant and gentry families. It symbolized the beginning of a new process for her—her incorporation into a new family and a new family line. She had left her old home, and she was now presented, with proper subservience, to the ancestors of her new one. In a sense the incorporation was begun with this introduction, cemented by the birth and presentation to the ancestors of her first son, and sealed by her death and the inclusion of her ancestral tablet in the ancestral shrine. The presentation to ancestors with more or less ceremony was a feature of marriage in all classes. In the kinship structure of China the bride's relation to the dead was as important as her relation to the living.

If the Chinese marriage is viewed as a process rather than a day's ceremony, then two other factors should be considered as part of it. The first is the bride's first performance of what were to become her daily duties, and the second is her initial pregnancy and childbirth, which has been mentioned before. The completion of the marriage day's ceremonies might be said to have taken place the following morning. At that time the new bride arose early and went to the rooms of her new parents. She took them morning tea and breakfast and waited upon her mother-in-law that she might comb her mother-in-law's hair and do her bidding. This performance in a sense marked the true conclusion of the marriage ceremony and the beginning of her normal career as daughter-in-law. Her conception and pregnancy might be included by considering them a legitimate extension of the marital night. Strength is lent this view by the fact that barrenness was one of the seven accepted grounds of divorce in China. The subservience of the daughter-in-law to her new parents and the importance of her first pregnancy were recognized and honored by peasantry and gentry alike, though, as one might expect, with considerably less formality and ceremony on the part of the former.

Although the importance of marriage as marking the beginning of *chuang-nien* status for both men and women was roughly equivalent, the importance in their respective family lives of the *chuang-nien* period was radically different. The *chuang-nien* period may be viewed as extending roughly from marriage to the period of the late thirties at which time the *chung-nien* period begins. If this view is followed, it may be stated quite unequivocally that, just as the *yu-nien* period loomed as the most difficult period for Chinese males of both gentry and peasantry groups, the *chuang-nien* period was of overwhelming importance in the life of a Chinese female. The factors involved can be listed under four major headings: (1) a Chinese female now entered a new family environment; (2) she came under the supervision and discipline of her mother-in-law; (3) she began her experience of approved heterosexual intercourse; and (4) she began and carried out the bearing and rearing of her children.

The symbolic recognition of the entrance of the Chinese girl into a new family at her marriage has been mentioned above. It was symbolized by her representation in her own family's genealogical tables as a nameless *nü,* by the red clothes she wore when she entered her husband's home, and finally by her appearance at death on the ancestral tablet of her husband at which time her own father's surname appeared followed by the term *lao-ju-jen.* Thus came the final recognition by her husband's family of the incorporation of a person of a different surname. Structurally this was of importance both as regards role differentiation on an age group basis and as regards differentiation on the basis of sex. The aspect of importance for the former was that the Chinese female now made a change of environment of major proportions and of a type not made by men at any time during their lives. It has been pointed out above that although her status in the family was no doubt lower than that of her brothers during her *yu-nien* period, the discipline of the Chinese girl was in all probability considerably lighter. A Chinese mother may not have esteemed her daughter as highly as she did her sons, but ordinarily the discipline which she enforced was less severe than that enforced by her husband under whose supervision her sons fell. Now the tables were turned. The daughter entered an unfamiliar family, and from the point of view of her new family, she posed the problem of the integration of a stranger into a tightly knit disciplined group.

The job of her supervision fell not to her husband but to her mother-in-law, as will be brought out below. From her own point of view the wife was faced with a situation shared in a sense by all strangers entering highly personalized situations. In important respects her period as a *yu-nien* under the supervision of her mother had been devoted to training her to assume in general the duties which were to be required of her when she started her next stage of life, but she could, however, have no preparation for the individual idiosyncrasies of the various persons with whom she later came in contact. There was no gradual preparation for this nor any gradual introduction to it. From the outset she was expected not only to fulfill certain domestic obligations, but also to cater to the idiosyncrasies of those strange to her.

Furthermore she entered her new family with very low status indeed. Technically the younger siblings of her husband were to treat her with respect, but she could not count even on this. The siblings were already firmly established in a set of particularistic relations with the other family members. If there were warmth and affection, they and not she would receive it, and so any situation in which she came into conflict with them was biased in their favor. She had no one in her new family to stand by her now in case of unfair treatment. As has been emphasized above, her relationship to her new family superseded her relationship to her husband, and in case of conflict she could not institutionally have expected his support. She might in fact have so intoxicated and entranced him by her personal attractions that she gained a certain ascendancy and dominance over him; but if she did, her position only became more difficult under the conditions which ordinarily prevailed. Her husband was institutionally expected to side with his family rather than with her, save in case of extreme provocation such as attempted incest on the part of her father-in-law. If, instead, he sided with his wife, he violated thereby the delicate balance of arrangements of the whole family and set into operation tensions and aggressions not only toward himself but especially toward her.

The isolation of the new wife in a strange situation among strangers was not completely unrecognized by society. It was a lonesome period for her, completely absorbed as she was in so foreign an environment. The strongest bond of affection which she knew was ordinarily that with her own mother and her sisters. In gentry families she sometimes had very strong bonds of affection with her own father, but this was rarely the case among the peasants. At any rate, although little or no allowance was made for her lack of familiarity in her new environment, some outside release was granted to her. There were institutionally approved visits to her former family. The visits were usually made during her pregnancies, and her solidarity with her own mother was reaffirmed at such times.

It is, however, necessary to add that opportunity for such visits were greater among the gentry families than among peasant ones. This was, no doubt, largely due to three factors. If travel of any proportions was involved, peasant families seldom had the necessary funds. Secondly, it was more difficult to spare the services of a peasant wife. Lastly, the economic condition of her family of orientation was often such that her appearance would have placed an undue and unwanted burden upon them, and, in general, conditions there were often such as to make a visit of little comfort to a returning daughter. The new wife's isolation was further recognized and to a degree assuaged by the fact that when she was to be delivered of her children, her mother would if possible be brought to see her through this ordeal. This, however, was also more common among gentry families than among the peasantry.

The second factor of importance in this rather trying stage of the Chinese woman's life was the fact that she was placed under the supervision and discipline of her mother-in-law. In gentry families the new wife was almost inevitably placed under her mother-in-law's domination. In peasant families she might escape the domination due to the fact that the majority of peasants lived perforce under the *famille souche* patterns, and hence the mother-in-law sometimes lived in a separate household. The exemption was not complete, however, for the mother-in-law might pay visits of some length to her son's household.[62]

From the functional point of view the husband's mother was charged with the integration of the bride into the family unit. Structurally speaking, this meant that the bride was placed in a position of subordination to her mother-in-law. It is not unimportant to keep in mind the fact that the bride's integration was not given over to the person with whom she was most likely to have a warm personal relationship—her husband. From the point of view of preservation of solidarity between husband and wife, perhaps that was fortunate. The integration of the wife in a subservient position among strangers was bound to be a trying process at best from her point of view, and to place the responsibility upon her husband might have placed undue strain on their relationship, much as

[62] Miss Yao T'su Ai cites some cases of this in her article entitled "The Principal Sources of Mother-in-law–Daughter-in-law Conflicts (*P'o Hsi Ch'ung-t'u ti Chu-yao Yuan-yin*)" in the *Sociological World* (*She-hui Hsüeh Chieh*), VI (June, 1933), 259–270.

giving over the actual classical education of sons to their fathers might have placed undue strain on that relationship. There were other functional reasons for the dominance of the mother-in-law, however. The daughter had to be integrated primarily into a female role in the family, and her husband was hardly the appropriate person to do this.

In terms of the power structure, the Chinese family during the "traditional" period was under the control of the eldest male of the earliest generation included in the unit. He was the *chia-chang*. Technically speaking, all family activities were subject to his will and whim. Actually, however, the supervision of his *hu* (household) fell to the wife. If his mother were still surviving, she might continue to hold sway, or she might, as was often the case, go into semiretirement, retaining only a general consultative position with more or less honorific supervisory status. The wife of the *chia-chang* or his mother could be overruled by the *chia-chang* himself, but in the common run of everyday matters she seldom was. The *chia-chang's* wife therefore controlled *hu* expenditures, *hu* servants, and the general domestic conduct of all *hu* members. The new bride had to be readied to assume her future share of such tasks. In whole or in part (depending on whether or not her husband had elder married brothers living within the family) she would eventually succeed to her mother-in-law's position.

Now one thing emerges quite clearly from a study of the relationship between mother-in-law and daughter-in-law both in the "traditional" and "transitional" periods. It was normally a severely trying relationship from the point of view of the daughter-in-law. Ordinarily the discipline involved was stringent, and it was administered by a person who had no close and warm intimacy with the subject. The daughter was familiar with a person who supervised a household. She had been in close contact with her mother. She had performed household functions before, but she had not done so under a person who held no particular affection for her. As a married woman she had to face a situation where she could at best expect just treatment from her mother-in-law. Warmth and consideration might be hers into the bargain, but, if so, they came as a sort of institutionally "unearned increment."

The mother-in-law's treatment of her subject daughter-in-law was likely to be unfeeling and domineering and was quite frequently harsh, vindictive, and unjust. Her power over her daughter-in-law was well-nigh absolute. She could even force her daughter-in-law's divorce if she liked, and there were many cases of a daughter-in-law forced out of the family because she had incurred the disapproval of her mother-in-law. Again, the wishes of the husband were not taken into consideration. Often harsh treatment was further reinforced by extreme jealousy on the part of the mother-in-law. She had warm relations with her son, and she was likely to react sharply to the entrance of another woman in his life, especially if the son were unusually attentive to his wife. What would in the West have been considered ordinary feeling and sympathy for the new wife in her strange environment was likely to be lacking for reasons not confined to this particular relationship. Throughout Chinese society the consideration of feelings went in one direction—from children to parents, from youth to their elders. One did not concern oneself with the son's happiness; his father's happiness was what mattered. Of course, the treatment of one's own children was tempered because, despite the fact that the emphasis remained as stated, parents had warm affection for their children. While children were expected to comply with the practices of filial piety, they had passed through a period of warm if not lavish affection. Such particularistic considerations tempered relations with their parents. The daughter-in-law, on the other hand, was a stranger expected to devote her efforts to the cares and desires of others. There were no previous ties to temper the treatment she received.

The Chinese man came under no such discipline at any time in his life. The discipline administered to him by his father was severe, but his father, however awe-inspiring, was not a stranger to him. The best analogy in male life was the case of the teacher's discipline of his pupils or the master craftsman's discipline of a nonrelated apprentice. Of these the latter is the closer approximation, since the apprentice was in a menial position, forced to cater to everyone, and lived in such an environment all the time. The student often had time away from the school. Both the student and the apprentice, however, were at least in theory learning something and moving toward occupational competency. In the case of the student, the harshness of the discipline was further tempered by the fact that he was entering the road to high status in China.

One might think that, since mothers-in-law had once been daughters-in-law, they might have been sympathetic taskmasters. But on the contrary, there seems to have been in operation a process like that found in schools in which hazing is institutionalized. Those who have endured and hated the hazing when freshmen are quite likely to turn into ardent hazers the following year and staunchly support and defend the practice. Mothers-in-law seemed to have acted in just such a fashion.

The third radically new feature of this period of a Chinese woman's life was her initial experience of heterosexual intercourse. Chastity held a high place on the list of virtues for women in China. The tales of exemplary women's lives are full of anecdotes of vigorous defense and maintenance of chastity which went to extremes unequalled outside the hagiography of the West. Even a cynic of the proportions of Remy de Gourmont would be satisfied by the measures taken in these tales.[63] At the time of her marriage the young girl was commonly lacking not only in actual experience of sexual intercourse, but also in the type of preliminary sex play which has become an accepted part of experience in the modern industrialized West. Of course such lack of experience was by no means always found. Among peasant girls and among servant girls in the gentry households some premarital experience was not uncommon, though certainly frowned upon. The methods of preventing such contact were isolation and chaperonage, both of which, in the "traditional" picture, were more likely to break down in the two cases named than elsewhere. Preventive measures and early marriage tended to avoid the danger by either allowing women to have institutionally approved sexual contacts when their sexual desires became urgent or preventing contact if marriage should be delayed. The type of prudery which has dominated the Western approach to the problem played no such role in "traditional" China. Responsibility lay primarily with the family rather than with the individual; thus when unapproved meetings took place, the couple involved were likely to carry out their physical inclinations fully and completely.[64]

In the ordinary case then, the girl was largely ignorant of sex save for her own observation of the processes of nature and the explanation given her by her own mother just prior to her wedding day. The adjustment to such intimate experience with a strange man not of her own

[63] See Florence Ayscough's book, *Chinese Women* (Boston, 1937), pp. 271–273.

[64] See Olga Lang, *op. cit.*, p. 34. The writer has, however, only heard of one area in which there seems to have existed, at least among the peasants, a tacit approval of premarital intercourse. The peasants in some parts of the Province of Shanshi are said to express a preference for wives who have already had sexual experience.

choosing probably offered some difficulties at best, and was certainly complicated by her entry into a strange environment and her initiation to the
strict discipline imposed by her mother-in-law. Gentry girls were rather
less prepared than peasant girls. The latter were not only more intimately
acquainted with these matters from their observation of animals in the
rural setting, but also, due to the crowded conditions of their living
quarters, they had had ample opportunity to observe the sexual activities of their parents.

It is not intended here to argue that the induction of the average
Chinese woman into marital sexual relations was severely traumatic. It is
probable that the Chinese safeguards against premarital intercourse have
not on the whole produced effects like those which psychoanalysts point
to as the products of the prudery and ignorance of the West. The physical
acts themselves carry none of the moral taint or the aura of brutishness
which so often accompanies them in the West. In China stigma was only
attached to women who had sex relations outside an institutionally approved familial setting, and, of course, few restrictions save the incest
taboos were placed on the conduct of men in these respects. Empirical data
on the incidence of frigidity among Chinese women at the height of the
Ch'ing period or later in the Ch'ing period are lacking, but the internal
evidence of the family life does not in general suggest that sex posed anything like the problem it did in the areas of the West dominated by what
has been loosely stigmatized as the Victorian code.

Nevertheless, traumatic or no, the new experience of sexual relations
could not have been unimportant in the life of the Chinese woman, and
without a doubt it required some special adjustment on her part. In many
areas at various times the phenomenon of the "honeymoon" has been
institutionalized. Whatever other functions the practice may have served,
it has certainly been important for its isolation of the bridal couple during
the initial period of physical and emotional adjustment. The effect has
been to cut down the number of other factors to which the couple must
adjust just at the time when the incidence of physical and emotional
adjustment is likely to be greatest—particularly in societies in which premarital intercourse is institutionally unacceptable. In the Chinese case,
however, there was really nothing comparable to the "honeymoon."
Sexual adjustment had to be carried out by the young wife at the same
time that she had to carry out drastic adjustments in other spheres. The

emphasis was not on her being alone with her husband but upon her taking up life in his family.

The deëmphasizing of the sexual life of the couple concerned was symbolized by the Chinese saying which may be roughly translated: "(when you) ascend the bed (act like) husband and wife; descend to the ground (and act like) *Chün tzu* (i.e., the Confucian ideal of persons of reserved, dignified, superior conduct) (*Shang ch'uang fu fu lo ti chün tzu*)." [65] That is to say only in the privacy of the marital bed was intimacy between the couple to be expressed. The fact that the sexual life of the couple was deëmphasized did not remove the wife's needs for sexual adjustment, nor did it make the adjustment easier. The problem was less acute among the men for several reasons. In a great many cases they had had premarital experience, and the sexual aspect of marital life was less novel to them. In addition, the men were in a position to absent themselves if they chose, but their wives could not. Finally the men were in the midst of people familiar to them and so required less adjustment.

Closely connected with the above is the fourth factor of major importance to women in the first years of married life. They now began to bear and rear their children. The bearing of children often continued into the *chung-nien* period, but the first experience and perhaps the majority of such experiences were concentrated in the *chuang-nien* period. It has already been mentioned that great emphasis was placed on childbearing and that the sooner pregnancy resulted from a marriage the more fortunate it was deemed. Pregnancy and childbirth, however, pose special discomforts even in relatively uncomplicated cases. The complex physiological and psychological changes that take place in a woman during this experience are even now incompletely understood, but their importance and requirements for special adjustment are certainly beyond question. The fact that this experience also came to the Chinese woman at that period when her life was so complicated by the abovementioned factors must have added its weight to her problem, and after childbirth came the difficulties attendant upon the rearing of the child. It might be expected that by this time the problems of adjustment were less, but this was not entirely true—especially as regards the relation of the wife with her mother-in-law. This relationship, unless especially felicitous, might even become worse through conflict

[65] The quotation through its choice of words places emphasis on the conduct of the men.

over the care of the child.[66] In addition, not one but many children were desired, and one pregnancy and delivery was likely to be followed as quickly as possible by another. The exhaustion of Chinese women by such reiterated childbearing reached high proportions. Death in childbirth of both mother and child was frequent, to say nothing of the debilitating effect on those who survived. Certainly such an arduous physical experience so often repeated must have greatly increased the general discomfort of women.

Childbearing, however, was not an entirely black picture. There were major compensations involved. The woman with "happiness in her body," especially during her first pregnancy, usually received special consideration, and if her child were a son, her status was immensely improved. A wife who had borne a son had gone a long way toward her complete incorporation in the family, for she had produced the means of its continuance. On the other hand her failure to bear sons or to bear at all made her lot worse. Her failure was blamed on herself, regardless of justice. Her relations with her husband were strained, but above all there was a strain upon her relations with her mother-in-law, the jealous guardian of the family. A mother-in-law was unlikely to blame her son for that most unfilial sin, the failure to continue the line.

The burdens of childbearing and rearing were less for gentry women than for peasant women, though they probably bore at least as many children as did women of the peasantry group. Birth control does not seem to have been well-understood in China then or now, though there were undoubtedly "folk" medicines. Even so, the desire for progeny was so great that the individual would have had to be unusual or the situation extreme for such measures to be taken. Gentry women, however, were considerably better fed than peasantry women. They had greater leisure, and less exacting tasks were demanded of them. The domination of mothers-in-law did not mean that young gentry wives performed tasks which were physically exhausting, as peasant women did. Their subordination was as great, but the weight of actual execution of household tasks fell upon the servants in a gentry household.

It is not improbable that the generally better health situation of the gentry women resulted in their having a higher fertility rate. Just what the correlation in these respects can be or what it actually was is not

[66] Yao T'su-Ai, *op. cit.*, pp. 268–270.

known, but it seems reasonable that the fertility rate increased with distance from the bare subsistence level. It is certainly true that the chances of the children surviving to reach maturity were greater among the gentry than among the peasantry. The sanitation even in a gentry household was appalling from the modern point of view, but it was vastly superior to that in the peasants' households. Diseases were and are endemic in China on a scale at present felt scandalous in the West. Epidemics were frequent, and, while the gentry were certainly not invulnerable to these factors, their greater isolation, sanitation, and the like gave them some advantage over the peasants. Furthermore, the burden of arduous physical labor, usually under adverse health conditions, no doubt served to shorten the life expectancy of peasants and made such life as there was more difficult to bear.

The gentry wife also ordinarily had servants at her disposal. A considerable part of her obligations other than childbearing were such as servants could perform. Among gentry women, for example, it was common for wet nurses to be hired to suckle the infants. This indulgence was not ordinarily available to peasant mothers. In extreme cases when a peasant wife was unable to nurse her own child, the wife of a relative or even of a neighbor might be found who could take over this task, but it was not at all unlikely that in such a situation the child would simply fail to survive.

The hiring of a wet nurse relieved the young mother not only of the task of feeding her child but commonly of the general care of the child as well. Gentry mothers were, however, attentive to and much concerned about their children. But much of their attention was in the form of the pleasures derived from playing with the children and the like. There were countless maternal details which the gentry mother might well handle herself in any specific instance, but the important distinction between the gentry mother and the peasant mother was that the latter could not shift the burden of these functions to a servant if they became irksome or if she desired to occupy her time otherwise.

Another distinction between peasantry and gentry may be noted here. It has been stated above that the burdens of the gentry women were less than those of the peasantry. In addition, greater concessions were made to young gentry mothers. Since the family was not economically dependent upon her for any activities, she could be relieved of some duties when she became pregnant or had children to supervise. Whatever a mother-in-law might think of a daughter-in-law, she would give a second thought to her treatment while pregnant, lest she jeopardize the son for whom the family hoped.

Peasant women did not receive these concessions. This was not because the peasants would not have liked to have made them. Probably even in peasant families a pregnant daughter-in-law was better treated by her husband's mother than otherwise would have been the case. Nevertheless, she could not be relieved of her duties to any great extent. Her work had its symbolic context just as did that of the gentry women, but it was also of great economic importance. Without her help the family would have had to obtain someone else to do her work, and that was beyond their means. During brief illnesses or confinement a relative or a neighbor might help out, but over a long period the peasant mother could not be relieved of her duties, nor could she relegate the care of her children to others. When some of the children had grown up a bit, the peasant mother could have them care for their younger siblings. This duty was typically assigned to girls though sometimes boys did it too. That was a peasant mother's only relief. Children, however much wanted, added greatly to the burden of the peasant woman's life.

Childbearing and the raising of children were in and of themselves desirable, since there was important prestige in the successful bearing and rearing of children. Nevertheless, especially in the case of the peasantry, other factors of the kinship structure were such that these activities fell in the period of the most extreme insecurity, uncertainty, and difficulty in the life of the Chinese woman. The prestige and recompense involved in childbearing, for the Chinese peasant woman at least, could hardly have overcome these other factors, with the discomforts of pregnancy and the responsibilities of child care added to them. The result was a genuine core of unrest in the kinship structure. The particular conjunction of strains which was present for the young wife in the family system of "traditional" China has played a major role in exciting the concern of Chinese women for family reform and reform in general.

In extreme cases of mistreatment another force operated, especially among peasant families. If the wife came from reasonably nearby and word of unusual mistreatment reached her family, her brothers and her father might be moved to action. Writing in the late nineteenth century,

Dr. Arthur H. Smith pointed out that, while the daughter-in-law lacked anything like institutionalized protection, her family of orientation some-times secured better treatment of her by the threat or use of force.[67]

Other than intervention by members of her own family of orientation, virtually the sole way out left to her was suicide or attempted suicide. The matter of suicide in China will be taken up again later in this study, but here some of the tentatively held facts may be briefly mentioned.[68] Suicide in China was relatively rare. The further back ones goes in the last two centuries of China, the rarer it seems to have been. The sex ratio of the suicides which did occur was considerably different from that of the West. In China far more women than men committed suicide. Furthermore, almost no suicides appeared below the age of fifteen to seventeen and very few appeared after the age of thirty-five to forty. Thus, roughly, the majority of suicides occurred among women in the age group under discussion here. Another "fact" may be added to this. There is some reason to believe that in China there was an unusual proportion of un-successful suicide attempts. Suicide in China did not symbolize primarily the taking of responsibility as it did in Japan. In China suicide was the protest par excellence against existing conditions. A suicide had theo-retically always to be investigated by the district magistrate and a report thereof sent directly to the top of the bureaucracy. The occurrence of a suicide connoted something most seriously awry and raised in miniature at least the question as to whether the ruler had not violated the "mandate of heaven" and so lost his real claim to authority. Attempted suicide was something which could not be ignored. The number of unsuccessful suicide attempts in such a situation seriously argues for an interpretation that attempted suicide was used as a last resort for the redress of wrongs. Whether or not the attempt was deliberately unsuccessful, it sufficed to play such a role.

Aside from the general ethical concern aroused in China by an at-tempted or successful suicide, a further consideration reinforced the

[67] *Op. cit.,* pp. 277–278.

[68] The term "tentatively" is here used because nothing like adequate statistical facts exist to bolster the point. Interview materials agree so overwhelmingly, and the picture presented by information gathered in this manner along with mentions of such incidents in literature and the like, tally so well with the stresses and strains involved in the general structural picture that the material is here presented as "at least the most plausible picture until evidence to the contrary turns up."

efficacy of suicide attempts as protests. For the peasants, wives were not too easily come by. The son's wife was important for the family's economic structure as well as for its continuation. She had to be replaced in some way or the family would suffer greatly. In gentry families the economic aspect was, perhaps, not a major factor, but the "suicide protest" was nevertheless effective. It was not difficult for a gentry family to find another wife for its son, but there would be extreme difficulty in finding another wife of good family and in finding wives of good family for subsequent sons. The possibility of securing advantageous marriages for the family's daughters was also affected. The implication of a suicide in a Chinese family was that the *li,* the rules of right conduct, were being seriously ignored.

The young wife was not therefore completely devoid of means to strike back, but the only means at her disposal were extreme ones. Her own family would not interfere unless her abuse was extreme and could not be counted on to do so even then. Suicide attempts would almost certainly bring about redress, but the stigma attached to suicide in China and the strong desire to live out one's full life in this world were deterrents to sincere suicide attempts, whether successful or unsuccessful: and the possibility of miscalculation, along with these other factors, was a deterrent to calculated unsuccessful attempts. Within a wide range of misery, therefore, the Chinese woman at this stage of her life, in gentry and in peasantry families, had little real hope of gaining amelioration of her condition or redress of her wrongs.

The life of the male of *chuang-nien* classification during the "traditional" period has been touched on previously and may be pulled together at this point. The importance of his marriage was, of course, great to him and to his family. His marriage and the birth of his first child, more especially of his first son, were the great events in his life during this stage unless his father happened to die at this time. If his father or his father and older brother did die or had died previously, a new dimension was introduced in his taking over leadership of the family. This was not, however, characteristic only of this age group, but might fall equally well in one of the subsequent periods of his life. If the deaths had occurred earlier, he would not as a nonadult have succeeded to control prior to this time. The facts of life expectancy were such, however, that there must actually have been a considerable coincidence between the man's participation in this age group and his accession to headship of his family. This was particularly likely to be true among the peasants, where life expectancy was probably shorter than among the gentry. Another factor operated here too. Peasants forced into conjugal family status by the *famille souche* patterns and economic pressures had to set up new families at the time of marriage. They then became *chia-chang* as well as husbands.

It was now that the Chinese male accepted the full responsibilities of an adult. Though his training period was not entirely over, it was largely finished, especially for scholars. He was expected to go to work as a full-fledged ablebodied man bearing the same economic burdens as other older men. If he were in a gentry family, he might not go to work. He might continue his studies or even idle away his time if there were funds available and parental discipline were lax. Ordinarily, however, even among the gentry, his career began now. He held less responsibility than his father, who was family head, but this too would come to him, and he was expected to be capable of assuming the additional burden when it came.

He gained further prestige in the family and with his father by the birth of his children, especially if they were boys. This was true of gentry and peasantry alike, though probably there was a difference of degree in favor of the gentry. The gain of prestige was accompanied by another factor which probably operated with considerably greater force among the gentry than among the peasantry. In gentry families, especially, son and father were not usually on warm intimate terms after the *ying-erh shih-ch'i*. The pattern was one of respect, awe, and avoidance. It always remained so to some degree, but as the son assumed adult roles and had children, the barrier of reserve between him and his father tended to become less rigid. The weakening of the barrier served to ease the pressure between the two key members of the family.

This factor was less significant among the peasantry than among the gentry groups. From the time in the *yu-nien* period at which the boys began field work, they came into much closer contact with their fathers than did the gentry boys. The tasks performed by the peasantry males were such that an aloof, reserved relationship could not well be maintained. Another factor tending away from avoidance and toward intimacy between peasant father and son was their daily sharing of the same work, even during the son's early years. By the time a gentry son experienced the rigors of scholastic training his father was comfortably past the scholastic training, and his distance from it dimmed his insight into the difficulties and the rewards of the experience from his son's point of view. Similarly, the gentry son lacked understanding of the various trials and tribulations of his father's life. Among the peasants father and son shared a mutual insight into one another's lives which did not begin among the gentry until much later in life.

There was also, however, a growth of intimacy between peasant fathers and sons during the *chuang-nien* period. During the *yu-nien* period the peasant boy met his father at work primarily as a pupil. The father had to teach him the performance of these tasks and guide him in his growing command over techniques. When he reached *chuang-nien* status he was no longer a pupil. With his marriage he was faced with problems hitherto new to him, and so he gained insight into a part of his father's life he had not previously known.

What has here been said of the relations between peasant fathers and sons was also true to a great extent of artisan, shopkeeper, and small merchant families. In all of these cases the *yu-nien* boy was his father's student, and the gradual process of becoming a junior partner and then going on toward greater intimacy was a prominent factor in his life. The craftsmen group was most noteworthy in these respects. The complexity and skill required by some of the crafts was such that the difficulty in teaching them and the task of learning them must have approached formidable proportions. Unlike the scholastic learning of the gentry, schooling was not necessarily conducted by an outsider. The discipline involved must have placed some strain on the relations of father and son. It is perhaps not going too far to suggest that the greater intimacy between father and son in general respects here served to diminish the effect of this strain.

Another factor may be brought out concerning men during the *chuang-nien* period. Here again the effect of the factor concerned is not confined to the *chuang-nien* stage but extended to the *chung-nien* period and afterward. Ordinarily in the *chuang-nien* period of life a man not only saw the birth of his first children, but he also saw some of them continue well beyond the *ying-erh shih-ch'i*. If he had any sons, that meant that he took up the supervision of their growth and socialization. His father had the power and authority to interfere in the training of the grandchildren if he so desired, but even when he did so it was customary for him to exercise his prerogative by orders to his children regarding the proper upbringing of his grandchildren. When children were past the *ying-erh shih-ch'i,* the actual supervision of the sons fell upon their fathers and that of the girls upon their mothers. Thus the man assumed the role of leader or disciplinarian to some extent. This might not have been entirely new to him if he had had younger siblings, because in that case he had already had some such role. It did, however, represent the assumption on his part of a more complete responsibility for others than he had had before. This was true of gentry and peasantry families alike.

Membership in the *chuang-nien* age group gave way to membership in the *chung-nien* group without a sharp line of demarcation. In general the *chung-nien* period began when an individual reached the age of between thirty-five and forty years. Forty seems to have been the upper limit for the beginning of this period of life. The end of the period was also subject to variation. Roughly speaking the age of fifty-five or so was the time at which people passed into *lao-nien* status. *Chung-nien* status was a comfortable one in "traditional" China for both sexes, but the contrast was more marked from the woman's point of view. Actually it would not be going too far to point out that there were three age groups in traditional China in which strains on the individuals of both sexes were at a minimum. These were the *ying-erh, chung-nien*, and *lao-nien* groups. The *chung-nien* status was not, perhaps, quite so secure as the other two, but by contrast with earlier periods the tenor of life was smooth and unruffled.

The relative lack of strain of this period was clearest for women to whom the preceding period had been so keenly arduous. There were several factors at work here. In the first place, habituation had by now played its role. Such burdens of her position as had not been lifted, she had become accustomed to bear. Ordinarily her mother-in-law was now either dead or retired. By this time she knew the personal idiosyncracies of her husband's family (which was now hers too) as well, if not better, than he did. She had learned when she had to yield to other family members and when she could safely ignore or even defy them. Now, either she had learned to manage her home properly or she was never likely to learn to do so. At any rate, the period of tutelage was over. If she were inept, someone else had already taken over her functions, or else the family was beginning to suffer for the lack of performance of these functions. Her childbearing was by and large completed by this time. The rearing of her children was a process either well in hand or abandoned. By this time her older children were able to take over a considerable amount of the labor involved in child care. The worry over her children occasioned by her lack of familiarity with childhood diseases and child development were largely a thing of the past. In every aspect of her life, by the time she had reached this age, the Chinese woman of both peasantry and gentry families in the "traditional" period knew exactly what to expect from her friends, relatives, and neighbors, and exactly how to react. A calamity such as a war or a flood might upset the pattern and throw her out of the ways in which she was so well accustomed to act, but such dislocation would be distributed regardless of age group status. Lastly, her family had become used to her. With the birth of her children she became more and more an integral part of the family on the ceremonial level. The sons whom she had borne assured the family of its continuity and of the proper worship and respect of the line which had gone before. On the pragmatic level she had become a family fixture; everyone knew her and her idiosyncrasies. Furthermore, there was in the family by that time a new generation whose members knew no time at which she had not been a family member. They had not even a memory of her former position as an outsider.

By all odds the most important factor of alleviation which the Chinese woman experienced now was the change in her status relative to her mother-in-law. During the time in which she was a *chung-nien,* if not before, her mother-in-law either died or became old and had to retire *de facto* if not *de jure.* The effective removal of the mother-in-law was of great importance to the Chinese woman. In the first place, it meant release from whatever remained of a difficult relationship. In the second place, it meant that she now took over the household into which she had at one time come as an outsider in a position of very low status and prestige. Now she had risen to the effective headship of the female hierarchy of the family. If her mother-in-law were dead, the outstanding symbol of her past position as an outsider and a lowly subordinate was removed. The death of her mother-in-law brought the Chinese woman into her own.

The *chung-nien* woman ordinarily became a mother-in-law herself. It is interesting to note that her position as "mother-in-law" to her daughters' husbands was hardly important in any respect. When her son married, she was in a position to assume a role which formerly had been a source of discomfort to herself. The question may again be raised at this point as to why the Chinese woman, who had just been released from the daughter-in-law position, should have been so harsh with her sons' wives. The necessity of training her daughter-in-law has been cited and with it her lack of affectionate bonds with the newcomer and the presence of such bonds with the other family members. Another aspect of the pattern lay in the fact that by her treatment of the newcomer she accentuated the fact that she herself was no longer an outsider. She had served her time, as it were. Her days as an outsider were not forgotten, but the presence of the new daughter-in-law gave her the opportunity to show that here was the only legitimate object of such outsider feelings. The supposition is somewhat borne out by the fact that an incoming daughter-in-law was not usually aided by the wives of her husband's older brothers. Her sisters-in-law who antedated her were as likely to turn on her as to band together with her in opposition to their common mother-in-law difficulty. Thus, in an elementary form, by treating their new sister-in-law as an outsider, they focused attention on their own prior membership in the family.

During the later part of the *chung-nien* period the Chinese woman in the ordinary course of events also became a grandmother. The relation thus created was in marked contrast with her previous relation to small children. Now she was in a position to derive the maximum pleasure afforded by children with a minimum of responsibility. Responsibility for the care of the children belonged to the daughter-in-law. The grandmother was free to amuse herself with the child insofar as she chose to do so without concerning herself with the details of the child's care. This was more strictly true of gentry families than of peasant families. In peasant families if the mother were ill or busy with the other matters, the child's care devolved upon the child's grandmother.

Sometimes the mother-in-law-daughter-in-law situation backfired, as it were, and the mother-in-law was dominated rather than the reverse. Such a reversal was much less likely in the "traditional" period than in the "transitional" one. It could occur only in those situations in which the daughter-in-law could gain personal sway over her husband. In such cases the lot of the mother-in-law was a difficult one indeed. Such a reversal was also much less likely to happen in gentry families than in peasantry families. The larger number of members present in the former meant that such a wife would have to succeed in dominating more people than in the peasant family. In addition, there were more persons in the gentry family to back up the strength with which the individual member of the family would resist the attempt of a daughter-in-law to seize control. It was not easy, however, for a mother-in-law to maintain her despotism in all cases. The wife was rarely in a position to dominate her mother-in-law, but she could in many cases get her husband to ask for his share of the property and set up a new family. Such a request for division was not likely to take place while the father survived, but it was a frequent cause of family disruption after his death. Among the peasantry, after the father's death, there might well be no other adult member of the family beside the mother, her son, and her daughter-in-law; then the daughter-in-law had only to win her husband to gain control, because through him she could dominate. In the last analysis, if a daughter-in-law revolted and was not restrained by her husband or her father-in-law, she could achieve relief from her mother-in-law.

While the *chung-nien* period was one of great relief for women, there were still foci of insecurity present. The *chung-nien* woman was ordinarily a mother-in-law, and, while the position brought with it authority, it also brought its quota of worries. During the time the woman was a *chung-nien* she took over complete control of the household. She was responsible for the smoothness with which the family operated. In her relations with her daughter-in-law, for example, she had always to keep in mind the possibility that too harsh treatment of the daughter-in-law might bring about the girl's death or outside interference in her behalf. She had to be on guard lest dissension between concubines and wives threaten the stability of the family. It was she who worried over the birth of her grandsons and the perpetuation of the family line.

All of these things were, however, petty by comparison with what had beset her path in her first years of marriage. Her comparatively assured position was reflected in the suicide rate. As has been stated above, during the *chung-nien* period the unusually high relative rate for women fell off almost to zero.

The male *chung-nien* was sensible of no sharp break with his past, unless his father died during the period and he became a *chia-chang*. His succession to the position of *chia-chang* was, however, an eventuality which might well have happened previous to his becoming a *chung-nien*. In any case, if it had not happened previously, it took place now. During the *chung-nien* period of the man's life the full perquisites of power in the family were his. If his father had died when he was in an earlier age group, the man had probably been dominated to some degree by his mother. During his *chung-nien* period, however, his mother and father were both likely to be dead. Now he completed the education of his sons, and he saw them married and assuming adult status. He became a grandfather and knew the pleasures of that role. He took over the ceremonial responsibility for the performance of the ancestor worship rites in his family unit. In the marriage of his children he played an interesting role; ceremonially, he played the main role in these marriages. Actually, as has been pointed out, his wife inevitably played the major role in the choice of the wives of the sons. The man played a somewhat larger role in the marriage of his daughters, although his wife frequently played a major role there also.

The fact that a father usually played a larger role in the marriage of his daughters than of his sons had several interesting aspects. The father was definitely responsible for seeing to it that both his sons and daughters were married when a proper age was reached. In the peasant households the problem was differently posed than in gentry ones. Among the peasants, grown daughters added little to the family economy and cost much. It was to the family's advantage to marry a daughter to the highest bidder, as it were. The income from a daughter's marriage would serve to provide wives for sons and perhaps some funds over for the purchase of land or the like. Hence the price to be obtained was, from the family point of view, often more important than the soundness of the daughter's future environment. The peasant mother was, however, in close relations with her daughter, and the relationship might well have tended to delay the marriage of the daughter had the mother had the primary responsibility in these respects.[69]

A similar factor entered for the gentry, though here there was no

---

[69] The intensity of the solidarity is exemplified by the frequency with which wives stole from their husband's families to give to their mothers. This was so great a problem that it formed one of the *ch'i ch'u*, i.e., the seven bases of divorce. See Sun Pen-Wen, *op. cit.*, I, 128.

question of payment. The marriage of daughters into families more powerful than their own was a frequent method of gaining favor. Such a marriage was particularly likely if the daughter were especially attractive or talented. Families of high status could turn the process about and clinch the loyalty of another family by giving a daughter in marriage to a son of that family. The marriage of one's son focused attention on the new member to be introduced into the family. The marriage of one's daughter focused attention on obtaining the best advantage for the family from her marriage and only secondarily on obtaining the best marriage from her point of view, though consideration of her interests was by no means ignored. In a sense one might say that the son's marriage, while certainly of importance for the "foreign relations" of the family, was of primary concern as a matter affecting the "interior" of the family, whereas the reverse was the case in a daughter's marriage. Since the mother would be primarily concerned with the induction of the new member, she played the important role in the choice of a daughter-in-law. Since the father was responsible for the relations of the family with the outside world and the betterment of the family position, he generally took *de facto* as well as *de jure* control of the daughter's marriage.[70]

Although the period was not a difficult one for a man, there was, of course, the possibility of strain developing between him and his sons. Such strains were less likely to be felt while he was a *chuang-nien,* because of the extreme youth of his children during a good part of that time, although toward the end of that period his elder sons sometimes raised the problem. Such strains did not, however, sit heavily upon the father's shoulders. His position was so overwhelmingly strong relative to his son's position, both in the family and in the society at large, that there was almost no possibility of his authority being successfully challenged. In a sense a wife had a far better chance of succeeding against her mother-in-law, rare though that was, than a son had of successfully rebelling against or dominating his father. The daughter-in-law might receive the support of her own family or might be able to infatuate her husband and operate through him. There was no such possibility for the young son against his father. The relationship was a completely weighted one. Such strain as the relationship incurred fell almost entirely upon the son; the father, indeed, was often unaware that such a strain existed.

[70] There were of course many exceptions to this general pattern.

It must be noted here that the Chinese of both gentry and peasantry classes were not beset by the worry which has so dominated persons in the West since industrialization took a firm grasp of that society. The Chinese were not much concerned over their old age. The vital step in provision for one's old age was the birth and rearing of sons. The existence of one's sons guaranteed one's care in old age. It was not the responsibility of the individual Chinese to provide for his old age or for his wife's old age. It was the responsibility of his descendants. The various tales of filial piety illustrate this point, and one of them goes so far as to allude to a son who decided to sacrifice his own son that he might be able to feed his aged mother. His argument was roughly that he and his wife might have another child but could get no other mother. His extreme filial piety was rewarded by the gods, and the sacrifice of his son avoided.[71] The lesson involved was thereby driven home to the generations upon generations of Chinese who recounted these tales.

The Chinese of *chung-nien* status had to worry about his old age only if he lacked children. If he had a daughter, he could "adopt" a husband for her. If a *chung-nien* had no children at all, he adopted a son outright if possible. Usually the adopted son was a relative of his through the male line of the family, for example, a second or third son of one of his brothers. It was not easy to adopt a boy of good promise outright, and it was difficult to adopt a son-in-law who had equal status with a husband who might have been otherwise acquired for one's daughter. Men in China never liked to change their surnames or their families, or to permit their sons to do so. On the other hand, since so many sons among the peasantry were left without land, it was not too difficult for a father with land to adopt a son-in-law. Such adoption was often the only way such landless sons could establish a family for themselves on a firm basis.

Lao-nien Shih-ch'i. Whatever was in store for the *lao-nien* in the "transitional" period, in "traditional" China the eminence of their status was conceded by all. A person was regarded as a *lao-nien* roughly from the age of fifty-five on. The *lao-nien* in "traditional" China occupied the most secure status possible outside the stage of infancy. The authority borne by the *lao-nien* was great not only by virtue of the fact that they had usually graduated to positions of structural headship by the time they reached such an age, but also because of the great veneration attached to

[71] Doolittle, *op. cit.,* pp. 456–457.

old age in the society in which they lived. Oddly enough, the position they occupied came dangerously close to creating instability. The *lao-nien* had a maximum degree of authority, but in the nature of the case they could not assume a role of equivalent responsibility. They were too old. It was easily possible that they would not survive to take responsibility for their acts. It may be observed that two factors apparently kept this situation from becoming a dangerous one. In the first place, the conditions of longevity were such that there must have been relatively few aged persons. Miss Lang has pointed out that in imperial China the aged were by no means so numerous as the romantic pictures of China would have one believe.[72] In the second place, there was a distinction in treatment of the aged in gentry and in peasant families. Both accorded very great respect to the *lao-nien,* but the *lao-nien* were less likely to be heeded among the peasants.[73] *De jure* authority and responsibility lay with the male *lao-nien* and to a much more qualified degree with the female *lao-nien* as well, but respect, formal deference, and security were actually theirs rather than the exercise of authority.

It was necessarily so. No division of locus between authority and responsibility can in the long run be stable in any society or in any part of a society where the questions of authority and responsibility are of importance. It is possible for the aged to hold both *de jure* and *de facto* authority, but the same is not true of responsibility. The facts of senility and the imminence of death forbid the *de facto* bearing of responsibility by the aged, however sincere the intention of the individual to do so. True gerontocracy cannot survive in stable form beyond the scope of those individual virtuosi of longevity who are able to maintain their vigor and full power until death and who have similar virtuosi to succeed them. Since no systematic fashion of producing such virtuosi has as yet appeared, nor does one promise in the future, the true gerontocracy of long stable duration seems out of the question.

In general this view is borne out by the frequency of patterns of retirement as a concomitant of old age. Even in societies such as "traditional" China, where the reverence and authority of old age is carried to an extreme, there was such *de facto* retirement. Retirement often appears in some such form as the feeling that the aged are not to be bothered with the

[72] *Op. cit.,* p. 16 (quoted above, p. 57).
[73] See *supra,* pp. 64–65.

daily details of life. Their time is for their own pleasure and reflection. A considerable portion of authority, however, lies in the determination of the daily details of life, and everywhere in administration this fact poses a major problem centering about the delegation of power, for not only is much power inherent in control of the routine, but also such control seriously affects decision on the nonroutine matters. So it was with the *lao-nien.* The everyday routine was too trivial to be brought to their attention, and, when large issues were submitted to them for their advice and decision, the inescapable background in which the problem was posed was that of the everyday decisions that were not in fact made by the *lao-nien.*

One factor stands out above all others relative to the *lao-nien,* if the situation is viewed from the standpoint of the members of the family. All responsibility for the family was removed from their shoulders. From the point of view of the members of society outside the family unit the male *lao-nien* might bear the symbolic responsibility for the family, but even here the mantle fell in actuality on other shoulders. The *de facto* relief from responsibility meant release from virtually all the cares of ordinary Chinese life unless, of course, the whole family was on the verge of starvation. If there were any margin of subsistence at all, it was likely to go to the *lao-nien,* but they were not expected to furnish income or services to the family.

The *lao-nien* stage was often an unusual one for women. It was often a stage in which a woman was released from male domination. The ancient formula held that as a child she was subject to her father, as a woman to her husband, and as a widow to her son. It was not unknown for a wife to dominate her husband, but, when she did, her domination was not socially approved. On the other hand, it was probably more infrequent for a son to dominate his widowed mother than vice versa, despite the ancient formula. It is not difficult to see why this particular subordination was set aside or why its avoidance received more or less emphatic approval. By the time her sons were mature and she widowed, a Chinese woman was likely to be a *lao-nien.*

Three things made it unlikely that her son would attempt to subordinate his mother if an issue arose between them. In the first place, there were the ties that had bound mother and son throughout their lives together. The son had been raised in patterns of filial piety which dictated his deference to both his mother and his father. He was quite well habituated to obedience to their wishes. In addition to being used to the authority of his mother as well as of his father, the ties of affection were exceptionally strong between him and his mother. During the segment of his life when discipline fell most heavily upon him, it fell from the hands of his father rather than his mother. In fact, it was to his mother that he turned in that time for comfort and escape, and it was she who gave it to him. He had also been trained to place the family before personal considerations, and, from his point of view, the family meant the wishes of his parents, for they were in the position of defining the family interest for him. Thus, for example, he was accustomd to bending his wife to his mother's will. His wife sometimes attempted to gain freedom by having her husband snatch authority from his widowed mother, but if he were used to giving in to his mother in the past, he was hardly likely to cease to do so now when the loss of her husband made her all the more deserving of his deference. From the outsider's point of view any attempt on his part to override these factors and dominate his mother against her will would have been the fault of *pei-te*, "failure to love those to whom one is bound by natural ties." Under any but extreme provocation persons outside the family were apt to consider a son's commission of the sin of *pei-te*, a cardinal sin, indeed, far worse than a mother's desire to dominate her son contrary to Confucian canon.

The second and third factors on this score were the factors of age and generation. The son owed his mother deference not only for the reasons given above but also because of the general deference decreed by society for the younger toward the more aged. The aged commanded respect regardless of their station in life. The domination of the older by the younger was not generally approved unless some specific factor gave precedence. It may be observed that such precedence by a son over his widowed mother was specifically provided in the Confucian canon, but the generalized respect for age was undoubtedly stronger than this exception in the ordinary case. Much the same was true of the generation factor. Older generations took precedence over younger ones. Generational precedence, in fact, was one of the effective exceptions to the general age rule. In the operation of clan affairs, for example, a member of a younger generation might be older than a member of a preceding generation, but the member of the preceding generation would have precedence. The widowed *lao-nien* combined both age and generation factors relative to her son. She was older and of an earlier generation. In addition, it must be recalled that she was not only older but was "old" as well. Relative age carried its weight, but the fact of considerable age carried at least as much weight if not more. The honor due the aged was (and is) an inescapable feature of the society, and symbolism of it was deeply embedded in the language. The term *lao* or "old" figured prominently in the language as an honorific prefix to things not intrinsically aged. The prefix *lao* gave the honor of age to what followed. Thus a person referred to the father of a friend as *lao-po,* literally: "old elder brother of my father," [74] though the father in question might be a man in his thirties or forties. The factors of age and generation precedence were not of overwhelming importance to the son alone. They were equally important to the other members of his social sphere.

Under these circumstances a widowed *lao-nien* who chose to dominate her son was likely to succeed. This is not to say that all widowed *lao-nien* dominated their sons. It is undoubtedly true that the question was not even posed in many cases where it could have arisen. But undoubtedly in a majority of cases the son and his mother saw eye to eye, as it were, and hence the question of dominance did not arise. After all, the mother had also been indoctrinated with the belief that certain things were appropriate to her role and others were not. The question of relative dominance was not likely to be raised unless this line were crossed. On the other hand, one cannot ignore the fact that hers was almost the only situation in which a woman could really shake off male domination and assume domination over males without incurring definite social disapproval. Moreover, any attempt to "put her in her place," save in an extreme case, would probably have been socially disapproved. A sufficient number of widowed *lao-nien* took advantage of the situation to make the domination of sons by widowed mothers a familiar sight in China.[75] When it happened, it must have added zest to the role of *lao-nien* for in

[74] It is interesting to note *en passant* that this usage also drags in the factors of relative age and generation difference.
[75] The novel, *Dream of the Red Chamber,* is centered around the situation created by the domination of Chia Cheng by his widowed mother.

such a situation the female *lao-nien* not only realized the ordinary fruits of her age group but threw off all the frustrations of the younger woman's role in the Chinese family.

In gentry families all ease was provided for the *lao-nien*. They were pampered with all the comforts of life that were available. The best food and clothing were theirs. They had the admiring recognition of their families. Their wishes were heeded, and their words were listened to both patiently and eagerly. They had their grandchildren to amuse them. They were considered in every respect to be treasured ornaments of the family. Even though they no longer bore actual responsibility, theirs were the seats of honor on all occasions, and theirs was the constant attention of all. Beyond question the Chinese family structure was well adapted to care for the aged.

Among the peasants the lot of the *lao-nien* was not so good as among the gentry. The differences here, however, were largely due to and proportionate to the relative tightness of the peasant's economic situation. The comfort margin of the peasants was almost nil, and therefore the *lao-nien* were denied many things that their family members felt were rightly due them. But privileges were theirs wherever possible. Nevertheless, peasant *lao-nien* were at times even expected to work. At such times, they were given only the lighter tasks, and everything possible was done to ease their burdens. The most notable contrast between peasantry and gentry recognition of *lao-nien* authority has been mentioned above.[76] The economic leeway of the peasants was smaller than that of the gentry, and therefore the relative possession of *de facto* authority by the *lao-nien* was less marked among the peasants. This did not, however, seriously affect the general institutionalization of the ideal Chinese social patterns relative to age.

That it did not was probably the result of two factors. In the first place, relatively few persons lived long enough to achieve *lao-nien* status, so that the problem was not inevitably or frequently enough posed to break down the ideal pattern. It is reasonably certain that life expectancy was greater among the gentry than among the peasantry, but here again the margin of income above the bare subsistence level was much greater, so that the greater frequency of *lao-nien* among the gentry was balanced by a greater ability to lodge authority with them. The second factor was

[76] See *supra,* pp. 64–65.

that there was not necessarily a conflict situation where the locus of *de facto* authority with the *lao-nien* was a crucial issue. By this time father and son or mother and son saw eye to eye in most matters. The greater experience of the *lao-nien* was respected and esteemed by the younger family members, and relatively few decisions between them were likely to pose acutely the problem of the locus of authority. In addition, the *lao-nien* were likely to be more interested in repose and comfort than in the daily exercise of family authority. Old age was a time for reflection and tea drinking. The *lao-nien* had a right to a release from the ordinary cares and concerns of the household, and the exercise of authority was often one of the more arduous of such concerns.

In the family structure the *lao-nien* were of great importance. Whether the individual Chinese family professed Taoism, Buddhism, Confucianism, or all three to some degree, in almost every case ancestor worship was always followed. There were persons who rebelled against the patterns of ancestor worship, but they were few. Even today the position of those *ch'ing-nien* who scorn the ancestors is considered most radical. The *lao-nien* were a family's closest connection with the ancestors. The closer they came to being ancestors the more honored was their role. Presentation of a coffin to one's aged parents was considered a highly filial gift, not a brutally aggressive hint of impatience.

The presence of *lao-nien* and infants in a family was satisfactory reassurance of the stability and continuity of the family. In a land where the basic kinship structural unit bulked so large in the total social picture, the integrative aspects that *lao-nien* gave to the family patterns was no small matter. As infants symbolized and promised future continuity, security, and stability for the family and for the society, so did the *lao-nien* symbolize and evidence the same of the past. There were all sorts of ceremonial occasions for the *lao-nien*. Each year their increased venerability was the basis of congratulation for themselves and their families. Special birthdays such as the sixtieth, the seventieth, the eightieth, and the hundredth were subjects for great celebration. Neighbors, friends and relatives gathered to do honor to the *lao-nien* and to their families. To have *lao-nien* in the family was the crowning glory of the kinship structure. Anyone could have children, but only those who best observed the "Will of Heaven" could, presumably, hope to have *lao-nien* to lend dignity and glory to their families.

RELATIVE AGE CONSIDERATIONS

The distinction of age groups in "traditional" China, while marked in contrast to the West, was not the sole orientation of the kinship unit to the factor of age. One's age position relative to one's fellow family members was also important. There were three factors which were most likely to be determined on the basis of relative age. Firstly, leadership roles were oriented to such considerations. Secondly, precedence and privilege had important relative age determinants, and, thirdly, responsibility roles had relative age determinants. In addition to these three factors, the solidarity in the family also was biased by relative age considerations. A generalization may be put as follows: Among persons in the family otherwise undifferentiated as to role, the difference of relative age differentiated them in the matters of leadership, precedence, privilege, and responsibility as a minimum; and though this was the minimal differentiation so caused, it sometimes extended far beyond this point and affected relations between persons who had roles which were otherwise differentiated. For example, two brothers in the same "absolute" age group in China had differentiated roles, but the institutionalized differentiation of their roles was dependent upon the fact that one was older than the other. Two brothers of different "absolute" age groups were also differentiated as to role but in this case the differentiation sprang from two sources: (1) the difference in "absolute" age groups and (2) the difference in relative ages. Considerations of relative age were most often combined in their effects with more than one other basis of institutionalized differentiation, but in any case it alone sufficed to account for role differentiation of some sort.

One finds in China no single term for brother or sister. There are only terms for older and younger brothers or sisters. The general term for brothers is the combination of the terms for older brother and younger brother: *hsiung-ti*. Older brothers are indicated in everyday language by the term *ko-ko* which is used instead of *hsiung-hsiung* but has an identical meaning. The term *ti-ti* is used for younger brothers. The same is true for sisters. In addition one's elder brothers, if there are two or more of them, are also differentiated. The eldest is called "first elder brother"; the next in age is called "second elder brother." Again the same is true of sisters. Cousins of similar and different surnames are all so differentiated.

The process is carried on into older and younger generations. There are different terms for one's paternal uncles depending upon whether or not they are older or younger brothers of one's father. The same is true for aunts, and so it goes throughout the relational system. The importance of the kinship term differentiation emerges more clearly when one considers that the terms, rather than the names of individuals, are used in ordinary daily address of the persons concerned. The use of kinship terms was the symbolization par excellence of the lack of importance of the individual as compared with the family, and the importance of kinship obligations as compared with personal feelings. The relative age consideration was a primary basis for determining the obligations and privileges of such relationships.

It is instructive to see how the usage was carried over into the relationships between friends. So overwhelming was the importance of the family in "traditional" China, and is even today for that matter, that the relations between friends came to be phrased in kinship terms. A friend of roughly the same age was generally called "brother." A friend of considerably older age was called "uncle" or even "father." Here again the relative age question entered, and the honorific prefix *lao* (old) was used. If one were not very well acquainted with a friend, then one referred to him as *lao-hsiung*, "old older brother," because one gave one's acquaintance honor by addressing him not only as *lao* but by emphasizing that he was in the position of older brother to one and hence in the position of leadership, honor, and so on. Only among quite intimate friends would the term "younger brother" be applied, regardless of whether the friend was older or younger than one.[77]

[77] The use of terms which are proper to one domain of social relationships for relationships of a domain other than that for which they were originally intended furnishes another of those interesting and helpful spotlights for social analysis (See that mentioned in Chapter I, footnote 33). Just as the process of adoption may furnish convenient insight into the roles into which one is adopted, so can this use of terms furnish clues for students. What is it, for example, in the role of friend in China that causes the term "brother" to be applied? Consideration of such matters throws light not only on the role of "friend" but on that of "brother" as well. Such a technique must be carefully used, if one is to avoid obvious pitfalls, but when properly applied it offers a type of perspective internal to the system under consideration and furnishes an additional path for the gathering of information. It is hardly conceivable that the institutionalization of such a "displaced" use of terms could be a matter independent of any analogous content of the roles involved. In addition to the light thrown on the roles themselves, careful consideration of such clues may throw light on the basic features of the social structure as well. Thus it

This study will not attempt to delineate the various terminological differentiations made in the system of kinship terms of "traditional" China. These have been presented by Dr. H. D. Feng in an article written for the *Harvard Journal of Asiatic Studies* [78] and the full terminological elaboration of this subject may be bypassed here. The important question for the present study is the manner in which the relative age factor affected the kinship structure. Here three effects have been distinguished as primary, and a fourth mentioned as subsidiary to them. Considerations of the fourth effect will be deferred for the most part until the section devoted to solidarity.

The first three factors mentioned above fall more or less naturally together in any consideration of this matter and will be so treated. It is everywhere inevitable that these three factors be to a degree determined by order of birth, at least during childhood. This is the result of the obvious commonplace that the older child goes through the ordinary experiences of life before his younger siblings if all are normal. Thus, other things being equal, there is a tendency for an older brother to lead his younger brother. The older child knows the ropes, as it were. Situations strange to his brother are familiar to him. He knows what is expected. He can and does advise the younger brother. The younger child learns that up to a point it is easier to follow the lead of his older brother than take his own way in an unknown situation. Precedence and privilege are similar. The older child is earlier prepared for the various stages of life, and there are always some privileges which in the nature of the case cannot be safely granted until a certain age has been reached. Again much the same is true of responsibility. A certain minimum of maturity and status is required for the proper carriage of responsibility by any individual. It is therefore

---

has been noted above that friendship terminology in China tends to be taken from kinship terminology. Compare this with the United States, for example. In the United States it is not common for one to refer to one's friends as "brother" or "uncle," but particularly close relationships between father and son tend to take over the terminology of friendship and business. Such fathers and sons describe their relationships as those of "pals," "partners," and the like. Just how fruitful it would be to pursue this comparison is a question for research, perhaps, but one thing is obvious from the outset and that is that the family structures of the two societies play vastly different roles in the total social structures concerned.

[78] See H. D. Feng, "Chinese Kinship System," *Harvard Journal of Asiatic Studies*, 2, 2(July, 1937), 141–276.

possible to hold an older child responsible before it is possible to hold his younger siblings responsible. Depending on the culture concerned there is a point past which these minimal forces do not operate, but within that range these patterns are usually so well established as to persist into the later life of the persons concerned. The "traditional" Chinese family went far beyond the minimum required in these respects. This was most notable in the family's treatment of sons because the sons stayed in the family, ideally speaking, whereas the daughters married out, but the relative age factor affected daughters as well.

In order to avoid consideration of generation difference from creeping into this treatment at this point an attempt will be made to show the working of the relative age factor among siblings of a given generation. The most notable figure in this respect in the "traditional" Chinese family was the eldest son. Chinese society most emphatically did not institutionalize primogeniture so far as family property was concerned. All sons inherited equally, in theory at least, though often a somewhat larger share went to the eldest son. There was, however, a strongly institutionalized tradition of what might be called "ceremonial primogeniture." The eldest son, and he alone, took over the role of chief performer of the ancestor rites for his generation. He also became the representative of the family in its relations with the outside world after his father's death or retirement. If the brothers divided up the family at that time, he ceased to represent them in daily matters, but whenever the brothers acted as a unit, the eldest brother took the lead and represented the group in its relations with the outside world. This primogeniture in ceremonial roles generally included care of the ancestral graves. Grave care required some extra income and often resulted in the eldest brother having a somewhat larger share than his brothers. The differential treatment had a different effect on gentry families than it did on peasant families which were living at the physical margin of subsistence. When a peasant owned or had rental rights to barely enough land to support one small family, it made little sense, if he had more than one son, to divide the property among his sons. In such cases the younger sons often turned over their shares to the older brother, who in turn took over the obligation of caring for the ancestral graves and caring for his parents in their old age. As a result some peasants were constantly being forced into a landless status, and it was not insignificant that a discrimination on the basis of age entered the process of creating landless peasants. The same problem did not, of course, arise among the gentry.

Another factor of great importance similarly determined by relative age differentiation was marriage. In the Chinese family the older sons had the right to marry before the younger sons, and the same was true of the daughters. A brother could marry before his older sister, and vice versa, but this did not alter the general case. In a sense brother competed with brother for wives, and sisters were in competition with sisters for husbands. The marriage problem was generally of much greater importance among the peasants than among the gentry, since the gentry could count on marrying all their sons and daughters unless they were seriously defective physically or extreme moral outcasts.

Another precedence or privilege which fell to an individual by order of birth was headship of the family after the death of the father or upon his retirement. At that time the oldest son took his place. This was consistent with the fact that the ceremonial position of his father fell to him. This factor was more important among the gentry than among the peasantry. The pressures tending to break apart brothers after the death of the father were considerable. In the ordinary case such pressures disintegrated gentry and peasantry family units. Certainly it disintegrated peasant units, for peasant families lacked the economic base for holding together a large family unit.

The relation of brothers' wives was one factor tending to drive the family apart. The wives did not take their roles on the basis of their relative ages but rather from that of their husbands. This was consistent with the generally vaguer attention to age as a role determinant among women, and the fact that a woman's status was always dependent upon some man. The wives of all the sons were ordinarily sorely tried by their mother-in-law. In addition, the wives of the younger sons had a status inferior to that of the wives of older brothers, and they were thus doubly tried, for a genuine pecking order existed. Upon the death or retirement of the mother-in-law, a younger daughter-in-law could hardly be expected to welcome her sister-in-law as a new authority over her. When the father-in-law died and the opportunity for division arrived, the wives of younger brothers were prone to urge their husbands to demand a division of the property.

One rather interesting opportunity often fell to younger sons among the peasantry. Among peasant families with small holdings there were rarely sufficient funds to educate the first or second sons. If conditions were good, however, and if subsequent sons were growing up in the period when their older brothers did not yet have the expense of their own wives and children, there was the possibility of using whatever surplus existed for the education of a younger brother who showed aptitude. This was not a frequent occurrence, perhaps, but if there were education to be had in the ordinary peasant family, a younger son had somewhat more chance of getting it than his older brothers.

The responsibilities allocated on the basis of relative age were important. The ceremonial role of the oldest son has already been mentioned as has his headship of the family. In the former case the welfare of the ancestors and hence, in the Chinese view, of the whole family fell on his shoulders. In the latter case headship carried with it responsibility for the family in its relations with others, and often it meant the assumption of the major economically productive roles of the family, particularly if these were managerial, as in the gentry class.

During childhood and youth one of the prime responsibilities falling upon the older children was that of taking up increasingly mature roles at an early age. The effect on the termination of the *ying-erh shih-ch'i* has already been mentioned. Of equal importance, however, was the fact that the older children were pressed into service to care for their younger siblings. This was far more frequently the case in peasant than in gentry households, for the gentry had servants who could be used to care for the children. Among the peasants, however, caring for younger siblings was one of the most important contributions older children could make to the family livelihood and welfare. It was (and is) a common sight to see tiny children carried and tended by children not a great deal older than themselves and certainly too young by Western standards to take over such supervisory functions. This responsibility tended to fall more heavily upon the older girls than upon the boys. If there were no older girls, the boys were so used. The tendency to place a portion of the responsibility for the younger children upon the older was, no doubt, a factor in the leadership which generally devolved on the older children. It was also a factor in the solidarity which grew up amongst the siblings. The most intimate bonds of solidarity were likely to lead to the eldest sister, although those among brothers were, ideally speaking, expected to be greater. Even in cases where the actual nursemaid function fell to an elder sister, the elder brother was to an important degree held responsible for the conduct of his younger siblings, especially that of his brothers.

The authority of the older children over the younger ones was secondary to that of the parents, but it was nevertheless effective in operation at least as long as the family did not split up. The authority was graduated up the age scale of the siblings, but the main possessor of authority was the eldest son. It must be noted that despite relative age considerations, sisters tended to be subordinated to brothers unless placed in charge of them specifically.

In any concrete case of a Chinese family the criterion of relative age was hardly likely to be the sole determinant of role differentiation. It was sometimes, as in the example of two brothers, within the same "absolute" age groups, but in the ordinary case it was likely to be found in combination with other differentiating factors. In some cases the other factors can be clearly shown to have taken precedence over relative age, but in most of these relative age became an important reinforcing factor. Thus the distinction between father and son played a far more decisive role in their differentiation than did consideration of their relative ages, and the same was true of son and mother, but mistreatment of a father or mother by a son was not only stigmatized as unfilial (the cardinal sin of China) but also as showing a lack of respect for persons older than oneself.

ROLE DIFFERENTIATION ON A GENERATIONAL BASIS

Unlike the family structure of the United States which, perhaps, focuses the minimum possible attention on generational differences as role determinants, that of "traditional" China placed great emphasis on such factors. In the United States family structure, relative age, insofar as it figures in the family, takes precedence over generational distinctions, and certainly solidarity considerations do likewise. Thus one respects the older generation, but in citing their precedence the accent is on their relative age rather than the absolute generational difference. One obeys one's father because he is one's father and is older than one, not primarily because his generation is a different one. In "traditional" China the picture was different. Generational considerations took a definite precedence over age considerations, whether they were those of absolute age groups or those of relative age groups. Thus it was quite conceivable that *ego* have a brother younger than his own son, but his brother would take precedence over the son in all situations in which he (the brother) would have, had he (the brother) been considerably older than the son. This factor was of great importance in the distribution of family roles, but it was, perhaps, of even greater importance in the relation of the family unit with the other family units which comprised a *fang* or *tsu*. The matter of precedence in those organizations was of economic and political significance as well as of significance on the level of family ceremonials. One's generation membership was of more importance in determining one's role in the *fang* or *tsu* than was one's age. Other factors operated, but the ceremonial headship always went to the eldest male of the eldest generation of the direct line of descent in the *fang* or *tsu,* even if he were younger than some *fang* or *tsu* member of a succeeding generation.

The great emphasis placed on generational precedence by Chinese society made possible a source of strain within the family structure. Because of the inclusion of several generations in a single family unit and because of concubinage, remarriage, or long continued childbearing, the important generation criterion might contradict factors which usually reinforced it. Thus a given family could contain nephews older than their uncles, mothers younger than their step-daughters or daughter-in-law, and so on. Such a cutting across the usual structural lines was generally troublesome. Apparently these cases, while not unusual, were sufficiently rare and the general elasticity of the family system was great enough so that a general reformulation of the structural pattern was not forced. Since concubinage was a major source of such cases, the incidence of these cases was much greater among the gentry than among the peasantry.

One of the most important factors which crystallized along generational lines was the locus of political factors, that is of power and responsibility within the family group and to some extent in its relations with the outside world, particularly with outside relatives of the family. This was not a reversible relationship in "traditional" China. The possession of power and responsibility by persons not generationally defined as possessing them could never redress the relations between different generations in an institutionally approved fashion.

In discussing absolute age groups above, something of the gradual increase in the holding of power and the bearing of responsibility with the transition from one of these age groups to another and with one's development within these categories has been sketched. A glance back over that material and the brief material on relative age determinants will suffice to show that in all save two important cases (husband and wife and the relative age of siblings) the power-responsibility relationships were intergenerational rather than intragenerational, and that in both of these the relationship was most decidedly subordinated to the intergenerational ones. In general, power in the family increased with generational status, and the same was true of responsibility to outsiders for the family. This was true *de jure* all along the line and was true *de facto* until old age forced an abdication of sorts by the eldest generation. Within the family, the younger the generation the greater the responsibility of its members to family members of older generation. Responsibility of members of the older generation was never owed directly to members of the younger generation.

Tied in closely with generational division of power was generational division of economic roles. Again, much of the material has been presented in the section on age group differentiation. In general the older age groups in China had the more strategic and the more important economic roles. This bolstered the generational distribution of political roles. Two types of economic roles were especially important from the political point of view. Both had to do with the productive aspects of economic roles. One was the production of plans and management of the economic activities of the family,[79] and the other was the actual physical production of goods and services. In both, the older generations ordinarily played greater roles than did the younger, without notable exception or modification unless some injury or illness incapacitated the older generation members or until they retired with increasing age. The father ordinarily did as much work as did his sons and performed the economic aspect of the executive functions almost entirely by himself. He obviously did so prior to the physical maturity of his sons, but he also continued after that time.

With the increasing maturity of the sons the discrepancy between generations as regards physical performance diminished or even vanished, and, as the father aged, the balance turned in the other direction. The

[79] It is obvious that this aspect of the economic structure is most intimately tied to the political structure. The person or persons who performs the function of management of the economic life of the family must have power in that sphere.

change was true to a lesser degree of the executive functions, but it obtained there too. A father might still retain his full physical vigor at a time when his son attained his full physical vigor; they might perform equal physical labor. The father's executive functions, however, would continue to be greatly in excess of those of his son. It is important, however, that the executive function of the father also fell off and assumed a symbolic or honorific role rather than a primarily effective one. The process exactly paralleled the generational division of power noted above and that done on the basis of age groups as well.

As the members of the older generation went into old age, the generational precedence as regards the distribution of power and responsibility broke down, or rather changed, from a position which combined *de jure* and *de facto* political precedence to one in which the generation bearing the *de facto* power and responsibility was younger than the generation bearing it in the *de jure* sense. Just as the respect for the old *chia-chang* symbolized his *de jure* retention of political precedence which he in fact did not exercise, so in the economic sphere the old man remained symbolically the economic head of the family even when his productive role had actually become inconsequential. One of the most interesting recognitions of this was to be found in the fact that although the land and property of the family was owned by the family rather than by the *chia-chang,* and although the sons inherited equally, no matter how ineffective the old man became both politically and economically within the family, division of the land and property of the family prior to the death of one or even both parents was in general frowned upon. It did on occasion occur, but when it did, the family in which it occurred was considered unfortunate and weak. Division of the property meant economic and political dissolution of the family unit and the overt assumption of the primary political and economic roles by the dividing sons for their own family units in which they became the *chia-chang.*

The differences between peasantry and gentry patterns in these respects were notable. The peasants lived by their physical labor primarily, and the executive functions in their economic roles were comparatively less important than their actual physical contributions to the household economy. It was emphatically otherwise in the gentry family's economic structure. The basic income of the gentry family was of a sort which required administration but not physical exertion. The net effect was to make the executive function the sole important one. As a result three things could take place in gentry families which could not take place in peasant families. In the first place, a member of a younger generation could be left out of effectively productive economic roles altogether until the family reins were turned over to him by his father's death or retirement. In the second place, the members of the older generation could continue to perform the full economically productive male roles of the family until a later period in life. In the third place, the performance of economically productive roles by the sons was not vital to gentry families until a considerably later stage was reached in their development than in the case of peasant sons. The power structure paralleled this pattern and in the gentry families the generational maintenance of precedence in matters of authority and responsibility was also continued until a far greater age and with greater force than was the case with the peasants.[80]

Much of what has been said of the generational distinction of male productive roles applies generally to women, but here a difference must be kept continually in mind. The productive economic roles of the women in China, both gentry and peasantry, were predominantly concerned with household matters. This was completely true of gentry women, and among the peasantry the work done by the women in the fields did not figure so importantly as did their household work. Much the same sort of distinctions were present relative to the division of productive function into physically productive and executive functions and much the same sort of generational distinctions and qualifications obtained. There was also the same sort of distinction due to gentry and peasantry differences, that is to say a heavier emphasis on the executive functions and a longer maintenance of *de facto* economic and political functions in the former case than in the latter.

There were some generational aspects of women's roles which were not found in the roles of the men. These aspects were due to the fact that the female members of the younger generation changed families. The wife was first in charge of female members of the younger generation who were her own daughters. As time wore on, the daughters married out of

---

[80] See Fei Hsiao-T'ung, "Peasantry and Gentry: an Interpretation of Chinese Social Structure and Its Changes," *The American Journal of Sociology*, III, 1, pp. 4 and 5. The term "family" as used here by Dr. Fei is slightly at variance with the term as used in this study, but this does not affect the argument here.

the family and were replaced, depending on the number of sons in the family, by daughters-in-law who assumed similar younger generation status. As a result, women in both the economic and political aspects of their roles, experienced two personnel changes in the generations with which they were most immediately concerned. One occurred when they left their mothers and came under their mothers-in-law, a change of the older generation; the other occurred when their daughters married out and their sons brought wives into the family, a change of the younger generation. From the generational point of view the changes meant that a woman of the older generation assumed a training role twice, once relative to her daughters and once relative to her daughters-in-law, and that a woman of the younger generation assumed the role of student or subject twice, once to her mother and once again to her mother-in-law. The men did not experience any such important lack of continuous personnel in the generations under or over them.

Generational distinctions were also of importance on the consumption side of the economic picture. Here again relative to all family members, the older generation took precedence. The oldest generation took precedence even over the infants. A man and his wife might stint themselves for their small children and would certainly stint themselves for their parents, but they would also stint quite small children in order to fulfill the consumption needs of the children's grandparents. In general it is quite valid to observe of "traditional" China that the older the generation the greater the priority of its demands for consumption. The gentry were, of course, in a different position than were the peasants. In gentry families the economic situation was ordinarily such that it was not a question of stinting one generation to give to another. Therefore in the gentry families generational precedence in consumption took the form of ceremonial or symbolic representation. For example, the members of the eldest generation were offered food first; the greatest delicacies were picked out for their dishes; their desires as regards the preparation of food and the composition of menus were asked and heeded. In general, the members of younger generations were careful not to exceed in the richness of their apparel that of their parents.

While consumption of food and clothing and the like did not seriously threaten a gentry family with important intergenerational discrimination on any save an honorific basis, consumption channeled into such nonproductive uses as gambling, extrafamilial sexual indulgence, drinking, and especially, perhaps, opium smoking, was quite another matter, even in gentry families. To an extraordinary degree one of these forms of consumption was likely to involve one or more of the others, and all were extremely costly in the long run. The male members of the oldest generation could not be stopped easily by the members of their family from indulgences of this sort. The older generations could stop the younger, but not vice versa. If a member of the oldest generation was not held down to moderation, he could destroy the economic basis of his entire family, and the other family members could do little to prevent such excesses.

Among the peasants the forms of economic dissipation mentioned above were even more ruinous than among the gentry, since the economic base of the peasant family was so much more restricted. All such expenditures were ones which to a peculiar degree demanded cash in payment. Barter or payment in kind did not satisfy their demands. Since cash was the hardest thing for a peasant to accumulate, such indulgences drove him almost at once into the arms of the moneylenders whose usury was such that their victims were soon reduced to a state of tenancy or worse. The generational precedence in these respects was therefore more important to the peasants than to the gentry, but it was a difference of degree.

The peasant situation was so close to the subsistence level, moreover, that attention could not always be paid to generational precedence in consumption. In a starvation situation the old would be seen to first, perhaps, but in an ordinary situation, if the choice were between a consumption whim of the older generation and the maintenance of sufficient vigor in the working generation for the everyday needs of farm labor, the everyday needs won out.

In ceremonial matters generational distinctions meant everything both among the gentry and the peasants. Long after all other generation precedence was honored only in the breach, the precedence of the earliest generation in ceremonial roles continued to be effective. In fact, only complete senility or illness removed the eldest male from leadership in the ordinary ceremonial roles. In the face of *de facto* observations of generational precedence, especially among the peasants, the retention of prominence in ceremonial roles undoubtedly went far to stabilize the general family structure. The symbolic position of old women as "ancestors to be" and the ancestor worship roles of old men no doubt were factors in the care of the aged. Desertion of one's parents meant in effect the voluntary severance of the ancestral line. One of the latent functions at least of the ceremonial generational precedence was to make the older generation essential to the younger. This was true long after its members ceased to aid the family in any material fashion and was important as long as ancestor worship was effective.

ROLE DIFFERENTIATION ON THE BASIS OF SEX

Some minimal role differentiations oriented to the distinction between the sexes are to be found in all known societies and in all known kinship structures. The "traditional" Chinese society followed in general an extremely common pattern of sex differentiation, and it followed this pattern with vigor and consistency. The "traditional" Chinese structure was not notable for any specifically unique formulation of sex differentiation, though it might be valid to observe that few societies have been quite so consistent and careful in their observances of these matters on such a large scale.

The "traditional" Chinese family structure was beyond a shadow of a doubt patrilocal, patrilineal, and patriarchal. Whatever the merits of the long argument about some dim matriarchal and/or matrilineal and/or matrilocal period in Chinese history may be, it certainly has not been the case for more than twenty centuries or so.[81] In determination of matters relative to "traditional" Chinese society and its remnants in general, and to the Chinese family in particular, the male was (and is) the point of reference. This was clearly indicated by the phenomenon of adoption of sons by families, or even single men without children.

The fact that the residence of the mature adult was determined by the residence of the males and the fact that family continuity was in terms of males, coupled with the social facts of incest and the general surname exogamy practiced in China, meant that a major distinction in roles other than male determination of living place and family descent had to take place. It meant that the woman was cast in one role that a man did not

[81] See Marcel Granet, *La Civilisation Chinoise* (Paris, 1934), p. 405, and H. Maspero, *La Chine Antique* (Paris, 1927), p. 120.

experience, namely that of changing from the family in which she was reared, her family of orientation, to the family in whch she reared children of her own, her family of procreation. The two families were not separate for the man. He knew only one continuous family, featured, to be sure, by changing personnel (wives marrying in and sisters marrying out) but by no sharp lines of demarcation. In "traditional" Chinese society the woman ordinarily was cast in the role of having to break with one family and start as a stranger in another. Her role in her family of orientation as a person who would eventually leave it altogether and her role in her family of procreation as a stranger among the fully initiated was crucial to the entire Chinese kinship structure.

A great deal of extremely loose talk and writing about the position of Chinese women has had wide circulation in the West. One of the most erroneous ideas so promulgated has been the idea of great security inherent in the woman's position in China.[82] The Chinese family structure has provided great stability for the family as a whole and for Chinese society in general, perhaps as much stability as any such structure can provide, but this has not been achieved without the generation of stresses and insecurity. Of the two great foci of such insecurity the status of women is perhaps the greater,[83] and some of its effects will be shown in the remarks on "transitional" China.

Here it will be necessary to repeat some of what has been said in the foregoing sections. One of the most important factors to be kept in mind is that the material herein given is the general picture of the results of the institutionalized patterns which make up the social structure. There will, of course, be exceptions on the concrete level, but such exceptions will not subvert the general picture here presented. Even this, however, has been the case in one instance already mentioned above, when widowed

---

[82] See, for example, the remarks made by such people as Miss Pearl Buck. In the August, 1946 issue of *Woman's Home Companion,* p. 2, Miss Buck observes as follows: "But I found I did not really know Chinese women until I came home and began again to know American women. *This gave me perspective and made me realize how powerful the Chinese woman is. Whatever her station she is secure.* She knows just what she is supposed to be and she is just that." (The italics are by the author of this study.) Miss Buck has perhaps been so dazzled by the present restlessness of American women as to lose some of her acuity relative to China. Even on a comparative basis her statement is open to serious question.

[83] The other is the generation strain between members of the male line, especially that between fathers and sons.

mothers dominate their sons. Reasons for this domination were suggested above together with further reasons as to why it had not succeeded in subverting the wider formulations on this score. It is the only case which has been discovered in the course of this research where the ideal position on sex role differentiation has been systematically upset, but that does not outlaw the individual contraversion of the patterns arising from particular personality aggregates and particular situations.

Thus the fact that a given woman dominated her husband or failed to feel isolated or insecure when she entered her husband's family is not enough to invalidate the general argument here. On the other hand, widespread examples of such factors meeting with social approbation and encouragement would raise serious questions. One crucial point of view is that of the political variable. The line between men and women and that between boys and girls was sharply drawn in the political sphere of family structure. Much detail on this point has already been mentioned in what has gone before. In a general sense it may be underscored here. In the family patterns of "traditional" China the locus of power and responsibility was overwhelmingly in the hands of the males. The ancient formula was clear and precise. The *san-ts'ung* or "three dependencies" of women were that on her father as a child, that on her husband as a married woman, and that on her son as a widow.[84]

The male side of the family held supreme power. They also held ultimate responsibility for the family, but the men monopolized power and responsibility only from the most generalized point of view. Women held power roles in actuality by delegation. The household was the woman's sphere, and power in it was turned over to her. Also power over the women of the family institutionally resided in one woman, the wife or mother of the *chia-chang*. Interestingly enough, after the *ying-erh shih-ch'i* the males of the family were under male domination rather than female domination, and it is further interesting to note that, ideal formulations to the contrary notwithstanding, the effective differentiation on the basis of sex did not begin until after that period of life. Within the feminine sphere of the household the power and responsibility of one woman and only one was significant in the institutionally approved case. This woman also bore the responsibility for the feminine sphere. The females under the woman in power had only such power as she saw fit

[84] Mai Hui-T'ing, *op. cit.*, pp. 332–333.

to delegate to them, and ordinarily she delegated just enough so that they might fulfill the duties she required of them. The emphasis in the case of all women was overwhelmingly on responsibility. This was equally true of the one important feminine focus of power, the mother-in-law. Her power was most definitely delegated by her husband, and, while she was responsible to him in the household sphere, he was held responsible in all matters relative to the family by all persons outside the family unit including relatives and nonrelatives alike.

The truth of this sort of observation, despite the work of people who, like Lin Yutang,[85] write so charmingly of the wife-dominated Chinese husband, is hardly open to question. Miss Ida Pruitt in her book, *A Daughter of Han,* gives overwhelming detail in the case she describes of the lengths to which a husband can go in such matters, and the woman described by Miss Pruitt is unusually strong-willed and capable.[86] Furthermore, there are endless books which describe the lot of families in which the males have fallen into the ways of vice. When the *chia-chang* was a wastrel, he could and did reduce his family to ruin and destroy utterly all feminine control of the household and children. He could even sell his wife, and cases of this were by no means unknown. His wife alone could not effectively restrain him in any of these extremes if he chose to ignore her. This is not to say that any such excesses on the part of a Chinese *chia-chang* were institutionally approved. Most emphatically they were not, and such a man fell under community censure. Often such a man would be restrained by his *tsu* organization by threat of removal from the *tsu* rolls or by actual use of force. Such extremes marked only a small number of cases statistically, though there were a sufficient number to receive remark not only by foreigners,[87] who might be expected to note such excesses, but by the Chinese themselves. The importance of such cases for the purpose in hand is that they clearly demonstrated that the "socially berserk" Chinese man did not lack the power to overrule the women of his family even in their special sphere. One has only to contrast this with the situation in the United States where, despite the greater power and responsibility of the males, the distribution of the two factors is nothing like so one-sided. The community through its courts

[85] *My Country and My People,* pp. 137–171.
[86] *Op. cit.,* esp. pp. 55–86.
[87] See Smith, *op. cit.,* p. 307.

will not permit of such capricious exercise of power as was permitted in "traditional" China.

Thus in the matter of role differentiation on the basis of sex the picture in the political sphere was asymmetrical. In all the periods of life in which differentiation was carefully drawn, the males either held supreme power in the family or were subordinated to males. Women on the other hand held considerable power only as mothers-in-law (or widowed mothers) and were subject to a dual subordination. They were always subordinate to males in the family hierarchy [88] (save in the interstitial widowed-mother status), but at the same time they were subordinated to other women in the hierarchy until they reached the status of mother-in-law and wife of the *chia-chang*.

The differentiation of economic roles on the basis of sex distinctions was also an important feature of the Chinese family structure.[89] From the point of view of sex differentiation four major factors emerge from consideration of "traditional" Chinese families: (1) the productive roles of women were overwhelmingly confined to the household, (2) the men took precedence in the roles of consumption, (3) all executive roles were in the hands of the men save that of running the household, which was delegated by the *chia-chang* to his wife and was subject to his supervision and control, and (4) women were often placed in the position of being economic liabilities to their families of orientation.

Finally, one may observe that the "traditional" Chinese family drew a vital sex distinction in the sphere of ceremonial roles. In the first place, the women had a position of primacy in no single crucial ceremonial role in Chinese society. All the important ceremonial roles could be fulfilled only by men. Although ceremony was of the utmost importance in the Chinese family, a Chinese woman in a real sense never played a central role in such ceremonials until she died, and even then not unless she died as a mother of sons. Thus, ceremonially speaking, relative to her family the Chinese woman as girl, wife, and mother was always during life peripherally cast.

In the matter of sex differentiation of ceremonial roles, the differences

[88] Mothers-in-law frequently had their sons discipline their wives. This sacrificed husband and wife solidarity to the solidarity between son and mother. See I. Pruitt *A Daughter of Han*, p. 31.

[89] This matter is taken up more thoroughly in the sections devoted to economic role differentiation and that on the economic substructure of the family.

between gentry and peasantry have not been too noteworthy. The main distinctions between the two have risen rather from the degree to which ceremony was observed in the two classes. The degree, of course, differed, as has been brought out above from time to time. Insofar as the peasants observed ceremonies, however, the same attitude relative to sex differentiation of roles was observed.

In ceremonials of the type conveyed by the term "etiquette" the striking feature of sex differentiation of roles was not that women played peripheral roles but that they played subordinate ones. It was the etiquette aspect of ceremonials that Westerners in China never failed to comment upon. Obviously women could not have been left out of these prescriptions. The etiquette of women was no less important in the Chinese family than that of men, but it was subordinate to that of men. Other factors of status being equal, the sex difference was strategic in determining whose etiquette was that of an inferior and vice versa. In these respects also there were few differences between gentry and peasantry. The differences which did arise arose from the lesser observance of the *li* by the peasants. The *Li Chi* observed that "the *li*" does not "go down to the common people," [90] but in so saying it absolved all the common people from responsibility for the full observance of the *li*, women no more or less than men. Insofar as they did observe it, the same relative sex subservience appeared among the peasantry as among the gentry. The lesser concern for etiquette among the peasants tended to obscure this factor, however, and sometimes gave a superficial impression that much greater equality in such matters existed among the peasants than among the gentry.

ROLE DIFFERENTIATION ON AN ECONOMIC BASIS

In what has gone before something has been said of the manner in which factors such as age, sex, and generation affected the economic roles of the Chinese "traditional" family. Now the question must be put in another way. How did the facts of the economic structure determine role differentiation? In discussing this aspect of family structure, two distinctions must be kept in mind: (1) the distinction between the activities of production and consumption, and (2) the distinctions among different

[90] Quoted above. See p. 100.

types or degrees of production and consumption. The term production as used here will be taken to mean any activity which affords as its result a direct income of goods and services or an indirect income of command over the goods and services of others. The term consumption as used here will be taken to mean the dissipation of goods and services.[91]

In "traditional" China the distinction between production and consumption was sharply drawn. The persons who produced for the family did not consume in any direct proportion to their production either as to amount or kind. All the income produced by the various family members was pooled, and disbursements were made therefrom by the *chia-chang*. Within the sphere of production the most important distinction was that drawn on the basis of sex differentiation. It was the distinction between household work and nonhousehold work. Ideally, women did the one and abstained from the other. Actually, this was the case insofar as the gentry were concerned, but peasant women, as we have remarked, often labored outside the household at peak periods of labor demand. Such labor was never carried far, however, and work outside the household never became the principal productive work of Chinese women, save in the case of servants whose household was really part of that in which they worked. The effect of the feminine confinement to household labor is clearly seen in the description of the life of a Chinese working woman by Miss Pruitt.[92] The woman concerned was forced to work outside her own household by the fact that her husband was a wastrel and a scoundrel. She had either to support herself and her children or starve. She usually worked as a servant, but sometimes she even begged or sold things on the street. The feeling of indignation which she displays over having had to do this and the reactions others had to her clearly indicate the fact that the role in which she was cast was not an institutionalized one for a "traditional" Chinese woman.

The importance of the household work as a productive line of endeavor must not, however, be overlooked. In the gentry families it re-

[91] These definitions, while suited to the purpose in hand, are not necessarily well adapted to other uses to which the words are often put. For the present purposes the important questions are how income of goods and services comes into the family and how goods and services are used by the family. Larger questions such as exploitation of labor, socially approved goods and services, and so on, are not germane to this issue, though they are to other issues of equal importance.

[92] *Op. cit.*

solved itself into little more than the executive role of management because of the availability of servants, and this factor has biased Western appreciation of the role. Among the peasants, however, the importance of household work was great indeed. A wife was much less expensive than a servant for the peasants. Without some mature woman in the family the vital household segment of the family economy could not be realized. This was one of the reasons why the death of one's wife while still young was a tragedy in the life of a peasant. The bulk of the production relative to the procurement of the needs of life was carried on by the men of the family. The bulk of its preparation for family use and the rearing of new family members fell to the feminine side of the family. Such a division was a matter that was vital to the stability of the "traditional" structure. All the materials with which the women worked in their productive roles were procured for them by the men in their productive roles. As a result, the men had an extremely strong economic basis for power, for a woman ordinarily could neither consume nor produce without male help. The production roles open to women in the "traditional" Chinese family were to an extraordinary degree controlled by the men of their own family.

At peak agricultural seasons women assisted in both planting and harvest, but in their assistance the distinctions between the sexes were maintained, and certain jobs were done solely by women and small children. These nonhousehold jobs were not a threat to the family structure because they were neither of sufficient duration nor quantity to provide the women with a possible basis of economic support alternative to that afforded by the men in her family.

On the other hand, another type of nonhousehold work did offer something of a threat. This was domestic industry. Domestic industry was highly deceptive, for in its initial stages it was hardly distinguishable from household work. The peasant women from time immemorial wove the cloth for their families' clothes and made their clothes as a part of their household life. If they made more clothes than they needed, they sold the surplus. In "traditional" China domestic industry among the peasantry probably did not go much further than that save in the production of silk. In domestic industry women, however, were still largely dependent upon the men in the family for their productive roles. On the other hand, the true domestic industry system brought in raw materials furnished by otherwise unrelated entrepreneurs for fabrication into products of no necessary relation to the household economy. As a result, the women who participated in such work were not solely dependent upon male family members for productive jobs. It by no means cut them free, however, to the degree that factory jobs did later. The domestic jobs were performed in the household, and the men were in a position to participate in the process and to control it. It was a simple matter to prevent the income of such labor being used to establish a basis for independence. At the same time, domestic industry did give women more of an economic value than they otherwise had.

The economic role differentiation from the generational point of view has already been discussed above.[93] Suffice it to say here that just as men dominated women economically, so the older generations dominated the younger ones. By control of the economic roles in the family, the older generations could severely inhibit revolt. One hears of harsh treatment of sons who deeply resented it and feared it, but they did not leave home and strike out for themselves. To Americans, this connotes lack of character, but these sons were by no means always lacking in strength. They simply had no place to go and no alternative means of employment.

One distinction between men and women in these respects should be noted here. Men always were able to look forward to the time when they would succeed to the position of holding the economic reins of the family. Women could only look forward to reaching the position of mother-in-law or a dominant widowed mother. The latter position gave them some freedom perhaps, but relatively few achieved it, and, when they did, the pressure was long since gone. Thus in a real sense the women could never legitimately look forward to a time when economic role differentiation would cease to involve for them a subordinate, dependent family status.

The executive functions performed relative to the family economy were definitely productive roles in the sense used here, and this fact must not be obscured by their close connection with political roles. The economic executive role was an important differentiation among family members. Political, generational, and sex differentiations cut along precisely the same lines. In the gentry families the executive roles were much more significant as economic roles than in peasant families, since

___
[93] *Supra*, pp. 142–146.

the executive aspect of economic roles was merely one aspect of the peasant family economy. Among the gentry, who lived on income from the ownership of property or the holding of office and whose servants performed the basic household tasks, the executive roles became on the productive side of the economy virtually the whole of the productive function. Thus the amount of power and responsibility, especially the former, which fell to the main holders of such roles was greatly accentuated. In peasant families, while women contributed less, productively speaking, than man, their contribution was essential.

Dr. Mai Hui-T"ing, in speaking of the "large family living together" (*ta chia t'ing t'ung chu*), names five evils. One is that the structure is a source of danger to the family economy. Of this danger he says: "Since the large majority of the members of the large family rely on the productive efforts of one person, the *chia-chang,* there are many who eat but few who earn." [94] Dr. Mai introduces the point in order to castigate the lack of self-reliance it indicates and to point up the potential economic danger to the family of having one income earner and several parasites. The obverse side of this, however, is the matter as stated here. When the sole or main important productive economic role falls to a single person and authority over it resides in the same person, the position of that person in the family must be quite strong. When, in addition, there is no alternative way of making a living for the other members of the family, a structural unit results which will resist and contain severe internal stresses and strains. This was the case in "traditional" China, especially in the gentry families, and, as has been noted above, the gentry families carried the concentration of productive economic roles and of power roles further and maintained them longer into old age than did the peasant families.

Another distinction appeared, in part corollary to the one just treated, between gentry and peasantry families. It had to do with the role differentiation of the children from the economic point of view. In gentry families neither the boys nor the girls played any essential productive role in the family economy, unless the gentry family existed on the bare economic margin of gentryhood. The gentry boys were sent to school, and the gentry girls were trained to become gentry wives. Peasantry children on the other hand, were early pressed into economically productive roles, though, as has been noted above,[95] the roles of the girls especially were not suffi-

[94] *Op. cit.,* p. 58.   [95] *Supra,* p. 78.

cient to offset their marginal status in hard times.[96] In addition, the importance of the production roles of peasant children had one major implication for social mobility. It was one factor which entered the expense of education, the major path of social ascent, for peasant sons. Before a peasant family could school a boy there had to be funds for his expenses, means to make up the loss of his labor, and means to support him if he failed and came back unfit for farm work.

On the consumption side of the Chinese family, the structure was less sharply differentiated than on the production side. As in so many predominantly agricultural peasant societies, the family income was pooled. The source of the income and its distribution among family members for the purposes of consumption were to a high degree uncorrelated. The lack of.correlation is, of course, true to some degree of all societies, but there are societies in which the degree of correlation is quite high, at least by comparison, as in the modern American family. In the family of "traditional" China the question of who earned the family's income was never institutionalized as having a significant bearing on who was to spend it or for what it was to be spent. As far as the basic necessities of food, clothing, shelter, and the like were concerned, no distinctions as to rights to consume were made. Distinctions of precedence were made, and they became more significant the greater the family margin over subsistence. Precedence in the economic roles of consumption was established in terms of age groups, relative age, generation, and sex as has been brought out above, and the various distinctions made above between gentry and peasant families held true for this sphere as well.

Within the family the *chia-chang* had complete control over consumption, but ordinarily he delegated control over a sizable and important sphere of such activities, that is, the household to his wife. This was of much more importance among the peasants than among the gentry in one sense because among the peasants the household consisted of the overwhelming majority of family expenditure on consumption. But it was of

---

[96] The economic marginality of the peasant girl was a function of three factors: (1) the most productive roles were male roles; (2) ordinarily, when she was young, there were enough vigorous adult females in the peasant household to fulfill the vital feminine roles; and (3) just as she reached maturity and the other females began to fail, she married out of the family. Peasant girls did, however, perform household functions, care for other children, and produce, sometimes, a monetary income when married.

more importance among the gentry families in another sense for it meant that a more considerable amount of spending power came into the hands of a woman. Gentry household expenditures were large. The position of the *chia-chang's* wife in a gentry family was perhaps the strongest institutionalized economic position held by a woman in "traditional" Chinese society. The cash she commanded was intended solely for household purposes, but as long as things went smoothly she might be left to her own discretion. It was only as the feminine head of a household that a woman in the "traditional" Chinese society held command over spending power, and it was only in gentry families that this meant any considerable command over cash.

The most important single thing to keep in mind relative to the economic role structure of the "traditional" Chinese family is that it was by no means the sole or even the major determinant of status in that family.[97]

[97] The economic role-structure can never be the sole determinent of status in either a family or a society, naïve misinterpretation of Karl Marx to the contrary notwithstanding. Furthermore, it is frequently not the major determinant of social status, correct interpretations of Karl Marx to the contrary notwithstanding. It is, however, always a strategic variable, for in the last analysis neither the necessities of life nor the luxuries are free goods, and a certain economic basis is required for any organization. This fact which seems to be immediately obvious to students today owes its familiarity in considerable part to the intellectual impact of Karl Marx. For this all students of the social sciences owe Marx a great debt. The immediately obvious nature of this point once it had been made has served ever after to obscure a point no less important, namely, that the economic aspects of society are much dependent upon factors noneconomic in and of themselves and that thus the whole set of variables are interdependent and relatively few of them can be shown to be in a simple relation of dependency upon one or another variable. The predominance of the economic variable in the eyes of students and laymen alike of the last century has not been a matter of chance.

The last century covered a period in which all over the globe societies of various sorts were invaded by a group of societies possessing a more or less common economic structure, and in every case that structure proved disruptive to those it encountered, and dominance and success lay with the nations who had it, not with those who lacked it. Thus for at least a century, men have seen a culture conquest picture of one sort. As more and more nations become industrialized, however, the importance of other variables is becoming more and more obvious. The fact that for the past century an historically unique structure has shown unusual potency in its ability to dominate and disrupt other culture patterns has given to the economic aspect of social life an importance and precedence rarely if ever equaled in any previous society and has tended to obscure the importance of other variables. The importance of other variables may, perhaps, be indicated by the contrast in the relative ease with which Japan, superficially at least, acquired the industrial patterns of the West and

In the "traditional" Chinese family of peasantry and gentry alike, several elements took definite precedence over the economic content of the various family roles. It was, however, true that the structure of economic roles was such as to buttress these other considerations. For a stable situation to exist in either family or society, such reinforcement must be present, for in its absence the elements subject to strain in the system are thereby given a vantage point from which to resist the system. In the absence of the strains inherent in the Chinese family structure, the changes made possible by the contacts with the modern Western culture would never have taken place on a scale so far outreaching the scale of the actual industrialization which has taken place. The "traditional" Chinese society, full of its centuries as it is, is being toppled not by a force fully met, but by one which has as yet struck it only a glancing blow.

ROLE DIFFERENTIATION ON A POLITICAL BASIS [98]

It is not intended here to do more than pull together the various remarks made in the foregoing material on political roles. In the "traditional" Chinese family of both peasantry and gentry, the basis of political role differentiation was clear and distinct. Men were the institutionally authorized source of all authority, and a man was always the person responsible for the family and the behaviour of its members to other relatives and to the outside world. Among the men precedence in authority and responsibility was determined by relative age, age group membership, and generational factors. The power roles were of an autocratic sort. As one descended the power scale, the limitations on the exercise of power became greater, but at the top of the scale the power was virtually complete. On the other hand, as power diminished, responsibility to persons outside the family also diminished radically, but responsibility to other family members increased. The *chia-chang* on the other hand was not responsible to family members for his conduct, but he was responsible to members of the society outside the family.

By all odds the two most important factors affecting the allocation of power in the "traditional" Chinese family were those of generation and

---

the great difficulty China is having with the same problem. It would be invalid to ignore this; it would, however, be equally invalid for social scientists in a wave of disillusionment to ignore the crucial structural role of the economic variable.

[98] Many of the factors touched on here are systematically treated in Chapter VI.

sex. It is not insignificant that the greatest stresses in Chinese society focused on the same factors. Women held power roles in the Chinese family by delegation. Their power always, in theory at least, depended upon that of some man. Nevertheless, the women had an important sphere of the family to manage, and in order to manage it they had to have some authority. This authority was given by the *chia-chang* to his wife. The political role which the wife of the *chia-chang* played was none the less important because of her responsibility to her husband. The most obvious difficulty involved in the structuring of her role lay not in her responsibility to her husband, but in her complete and often tyrannous command over her daughter-in-law. The responsibility of the women in general was such that one major difficulty arose. The wife of the *chia-chang* was responsible for the household, but she had no command over the men of the family who were in a position to disrupt the household. If they did, she could not do more than request the intervention of the *chia-chang*.

As regards the generational distribution of political roles among both men and women, the older generation took precedence. In the family political pyramid, responsibility was from the bottom up and power from the top down. Below the *chia-chang* and throughout the structure, responsibility tended to exceed authority, whereas from the point of view of the family group, the authority of the *chia-chang* exceeded his responsibility. Such a situation is not ordinarily a stable one. The stability of this one was ensured by three factors. In the first place, it was well-known that the *chia-chang* would support a subordinate member of the family in his performance of a given duty, even though the subordinate lacked such authority ordinarily; and, in the second place, all the institutionalized sources of legitimacy for authority as well as those of economic roles and the like which could serve to buttress the power structure were concentrated in the person of the *chia-chang*. Finally, the values accompanying the role of *chia-chang* motivated his responsibility for the use of his power in the interests of the family, even though no family member could compel it. This, coupled with other structural features of the society, gave to the political role structure an ability to withstand strain that it might otherwise have lacked.

Aside from generational and sex differences, relative age criteria were also of significance in the political role structure of the Chinese family. Relative age was of rather more importance on the male side of the family than on the female side, since relatively less power lay with the women and girls. The most important relative age relations were those between brothers. Older brothers took precedence over younger ones in both power and responsibility. Of special importance was the position of eldest brother. From the point of view of the other children, the eldest brother was the person of authority who followed their parents in the hierarchy of power. At the same time, his position carried with it responsibility to the parents for the younger children, and his inheritance of the *chia-chang* position carried with it full family responsibility.

Among the daughters-in-law a departure from the usual relative age patterns took place. The daughter-in-law position was probably the lowest position in the power hierarchy of any two generations of a given Chinese family.[99] At the same time her responsibilities were quite heavy. There can be no question that particularly in the daughter-in-law role the "traditional" Chinese family institutionalized a serious imbalance in the locus of power and responsibility.[100] Daughters-in-law took precedence or lack of it not in terms of their own respective relative ages but in terms of those of their respective husbands. The precedence as between two daughters-in-law was important. Since the eldest son ordinarily married first, his wife was the daughter-in-law longest in the family. As his wife, she took precedence over the wives of his younger brothers, but her precedence was made even more effective by her longer residence in the family.[101] Even if the wife of a younger brother was older than the wife of an older brother, the wife of the older brother took precedence. Prior to their

[99] Two generations are specified because, of course, the daughter-in-law held some power over her own children.

[100] It extended into the economic realm as well since the mother-in-law delegated much of the more productive side of her economic role to her daughter-in-law. This was true to a greater degree in peasant families than among the gentry because in the peasant families the physical labor and concrete household production of the women played a larger role in the family economy.

[101] When the wife of the eldest brother was acquired after that of a younger brother, the situation was even worse because she came into the family and took an easier path of precedence over a daughter-in-law who had already been "going through the mill" as it were. This was virtually certain to cause friction between the two daughters-in-law.

marriages, however, the wives had been accustomed to ordinary relative age precedence. The abrupt change played its part in the friction between sisters-in-law which was so frequent and prominent a factor in the strains leading to a division of property among brothers.[102]

Another noteworthy violation of relative age precedence in political roles among women was the fact that the daughter-in-law, regardless of relative age, was lower in the political hierarchy than any daughters who might still remain in the family. This situation also led to friction in the family and served to make the daughter-in-law's role more difficult. An even more disruptive, though less frequent, situation of this general type was that in which the *chia-chang* remarried after the death of his first wife and thereby introduced a mother-in-law who was younger than her daughter-in-law and newer to the family. There resulted a situation which almost certainly became a focus for all sorts of aggressions and seriously threatened family harmony in many ways. The power it gave a "stranger," and often a younger one into the bargain, over wives of the sons who were already partly established as family members was not the least of its sources of disruption. Women who had endured the trials of the daughter-in-law role could hardly fail to resent a woman in the family who was not only exempt from those trials but also in a position to mete out further ones to them.

Age group considerations seem to have been of far less importance in the determination of political role structure than the factors mentioned above. It is true that the exercise of certain powers and the carrying of certain responsibilities were more or less correlated with age groups, but even so questions of relative age, sex, and generation were far more important. The fact that relative age, generation, and sex took precedence in the definition of one's position in the political role structure of the family was an interesting structural feature of the society. All these factors varied in their assortment from family to family. Absolute age group membership was in a sense common to all members of all families. In a family structure like that of the United States, the emphasis in the political role determination of the individual depends more upon such universalistic criteria as capabilities than was the case in "traditional" China. In China

---

[102] Sister-in-law friction was more important among the gentry than among the peasantry. The gentry were much more likely to be living in families including more than one married son than were the peasants.

particularistic factors such as how many brothers one had, whether one's father was living or dead, and the like, were more important than capabilities in determining the political roles of the individual in his family, but to a high degree these particularistic factors enter such solutions in all families in all societies.

CHAPTER FOUR

THE KINSHIP SUBSTRUCTURE
OF SOLIDARITY

THE FAMILY AS A UNIT OF SOLIDARITY
IN "TRADITIONAL" CHINESE SOCIETY

THE basic unit of kinship solidarity is always the family unit in the sense in which that term is used here, but in "traditional" Chinese society it was also the basic unit of solidarity for the entire society. This is by no means true of all societies. In Tokugawa Japan, for example, several relations involving solidarity took precedence over that of the family. Of these relations the primary example was the relation between a retainer and his feudal lord.[1] In "traditional" China this was not the case, however. One of the most frequently reiterated anecdotes about Confucius is about his encounter with the ruler of one of the then extant fragmentary Chinese states. The ruler, attempting to impress Confucius with the virtue of his citizens, is reputed to have boasted that in his state a son would report his father to the authorities if his father had committed a crime. Confucius replied that the virtue of his state was greater because no son there would ever accuse his father of a crime.

The story does not imply that the concealment of crimes was a virtue. The Confucian system held that a proper family in which filial piety was well inculcated could not produce a member who would act contrary to the interests of the state in the long run. The continued currency of this tale down into modern days and the various laws punishing sons who inform on their parents furnish testimony to the fact that the Confucian view of the importance of family solidarity has remained in force through the years and centuries. The solidarity of the family unit relative to the aspects of Chinese society outside it is one of the most important factors in the

[1] See R. Benedict, *The Crysanthemum and the Sword* (Boston, 1946), pp. 136–140 and 199–205.

analysis of the social situation in "transitional" China, for since there was neither any other overriding solidarity in the society nor any equal to the solidarity of the family unit, any breakdown of that solidarity inevitably had far-reaching effects.[2]

The only conceivable break in the pattern of solidarity lay in the relations of the family with the higher organization of kinship units, such as the *fang* or *tsu*. A *chia-chang* might follow a *tsu* ruling concerning his family, but his family members would not obey a *tsu* ruling as opposed to one of the *chia-chang*. The problem was not even posed in "traditional" China. The importance of *tsu* solidarity was not the *tsu* as against one member of one of its component families, but rather the solidarity it maintained relative to the parts of the society outside its membership. Inside the *tsu*, when controversies developed between *tsu* members, they were handled in terms of family units rather than in terms of individuals.

THE SOLIDARITY RELATIONSHIPS

The great focus of solidarity in "traditional" China was the family unit, not only as regards outsiders but also as regards the internal workings of the structure. The "traditional" Chinese family vis-à-vis the outside world gave an impression of "all for one and one for all," but within the structure of the family unit itself the picture was different. The type and degree of solidarity differed enormously depending on the parties to the relationship. Since the main emphasis in this study is placed on the solidarity relationships within the family, relatively little attention will be paid to those with persons outside the unit. Obviously the number of relationships in any given family unit depended upon the number of its members. By and large, gentry families contained more than peasant ones. Since, however, both families cherished the same ideal of family size and composition in "traditional" China, it will suffice for the present to set forth the most strategic relationships for these purposes.

A given family might or might not have included all of these relations. Thus, for example, the solidarity between brothers was of the utmost importance despite the fact that many men, even in "traditional" China, must have been born and reared in families with only one son. Specific

[2] Again the contrast with Japan is instructive. Industrialization seriously affected family solidarity in Japan as it did in China, but with considerably milder effects, since it did not remove the major source of solidarity in Japan, but only one of several.

differentiations between the gentry and peasantry with respect to the actual implementation of these solidarities will be pointed out from time to time. The following relationships will be treated in this section: (1) father-son, (2) husband-wife, (3) father-daughter, (4) mother-son, (5) mother-daughter, (6) father-in-law–daughter-in-law, (7) mother-in-law–daughter-in-law, (8) brother-brother (elder brother-younger brother), (9) sister-sister (elder sister-younger sister), (10) sister-brother's wife, (11) brother-brother's wife, (12) uncle-nephew, (13) uncle-niece, (14) aunt-nephew, (15) aunt-niece, (16) brother's wife-brother's wife, (17) husband-concubine, (18) other family members-concubine, (19) grandparents-grandchildren, and (20) other relations. Of the various relationships the solidarities between father and son, husband and wife, mother-in-law and daughter-in-law, and brother and brother were, structurally speaking, the most important solidarities in "traditional" Chinese families. If any one can be singled out as the most important solidarity, it was that between father and son. Interestingly enough, this relation happened to be one of the major foci of strain in the "traditional" Chinese family structure.

Father–Son. It is to be expected that in any family structure described as patriarchal, patrilocal, and patrilineal, the relationship between father and son would necessarily be a strategic one. In any such structure one of the sons must succeed to the father's role in the course of time. There is always the possibility of rivalry between father and son in such a situation, and this possibility alone would make the solidarity of their relationship a matter of the first importance. There are other reasons too. If the father is to hold the power as he must in a patriarchal family, then at least in the matter of strength [3] the father's solidarity with the other family members must be the most important in the family structure. Like all solidarities, the father-son relationship can be viewed from the point of view of either party. In only a few cases of kinship solidarity is the relation institutionally identical from the point of view of all parties, and this was not true of any solidarity relationship in the "traditional" Chinese family system. [4]

From the father's point of view the solidarity between himself and

[3] The term strength is used here in the sense in which it has been defined above, p. 15.

[4] The relationship between two brothers of reasonably close ages in the American family is as close to an institutionally identical solidarity as family relationships come. In many societies, however, the solidarity between friends is of this sort.

his son was of the utmost importance. Through his son he continued the family, and the continuance of the family was the value to be placed above all others. The interest of the father in these respects was first of all in training his son to follow in his footsteps as head of the family. Since in China ceremonial primogeniture was the institutionalized pattern, although inheritance was equal in all other respects among sons, the existence of more than one son made some difference in the father's relations with his sons, and vice versa. The surprising thing is, however, that any primogeniture could have existed and yet differentiation among sons could have remained so slight.

The Chinese father well understood the fact that sooner or later after his death his sons would, in the overwhelming majority of cases, divide the family. Moreover, the institutionalization of equal inheritance of property by all the sons was a provision which could only be overridden in the most extreme cases, unless it was done by the mutual consent of the brothers. Structurally this made for a rather unusual pattern. It meant that the relations with one son had to be emphasized, but that it could not be emphasized too much. By virtue of the rather unusual combination of ceremonial primogeniture and equal inheritance by sons, Chinese society was able to locate definitely the responsibility for the continuance of the line of descent of the family. It was in addition able to prevent the indefinite continuance of hereditary accumulations, and able to prevent the accumulation of a class of propertyless cadets who might have formed a reservoir of discontent and thereby threatened the family structure and the general social order into the bargain. This particular institutional pattern has probably been the most important single factor in the social structure tending to prevent any large scale pattern of feudalism in China for the last two thousand years.

The pattern was not, however, without its own tensions. The institutionalization of the role of the eldest son gave him certain privileges and certain duties not shared by the other sons, and since he was to succeed his father in the role of *chia-chang,* he might legitimately have expected the solidarity between himself and his father to buttress this factor. This was not always the case. In the more formal aspects of solidarity it was so observed, but often the *chia-chang* would show marked preference for a younger son, and the intimacy between the father and that son might far exceed that between the father and his eldest son. In peasant families which were rising economically, such a situation could become quite tense. The family might have been in a position to send the youngest son to school, whereas they had not been in a position to do this for the older boys. The greater respect that the father might show toward his academic though currently nonproductive son was likely to result in manifestations of jealousy.

The content of the relation between father and son was expressed by the Chinese phrase *fu tz'u tzu hsiao* which in literal translation is "father kind, son filial," and can be more freely translated as "a kind father makes a filial son" or "a father should be kind and sons should be filial." From the point of view of both father and son the first criterion of filial piety was the obedience of the son—the unquestioning and undeviating obedience of the son to the father. The kindness of the father, whatever it might mean, was distinctly subsidiary. Almost no cruelty or breach of conduct on the father's side seemed to reduce the son's institutionalized obligation in this respect.

The son owed his father a great deal more than obedience and the respect which is such a necessary correlate of obedience in all structures not maintained by coercion. He owed his father material support in his father's old age. Throughout the life of the father, the son owed him every comfort and aid which he was capable of providing. The individual Chinese in the "traditional" period was not an individualistic person. He lived for and in terms of his family. More specifically, the son could be viewed as living for his parents, especially his father, and hence his ancestors.

The father on the other hand was by no means a completely unfettered petty tyrant. This is not to argue that such tyranny was either absent or infrequent in the "traditional" period. The "traditional" Chinese family structure, however, did not leave the father's role undefined and unlimited. Every individual in China faced in two directions—toward his ancestors and toward his posterity. It is true that the heaviest emphasis lay on the orientation of younger generations to older ones, but the balancing factor was clear, unequivocal, and inescapable. Characteristically, the neatest formulation of the balance was phrased in terms of the obligations of the younger generation toward the older ones. Mencius had put it so: "Of the three unfilial acts the greatest is to lack posterity." The obligations of the father in his relations with his son and the rest of his family were defined not by any debt to them, but by his filial obligations to his own parents and the members of preceding generations.

The subtlety of this aspect of Chinese social structure is not to be ignored, because in addition to its intrinsic interest it provides insight into general problems of social structure. In a structure oriented, as the Chinese structure was, to age precedence and generational precedence, particularly in regard to the allocation of power, this device served to prevent the callous or capricious treatment of the younger people and people of later generations without disrupting the general orientation of the whole society in the other direction. "If parents are so much more important than sons in China, how can sons be so important?" Chinese social structure posed this question and answered it by holding, "Nothing is more important to a man's parents than his children and their children and their children's children." This structural principle assured the functional prerequisites of the low status (but important) family members by tying the prerequisites to the proper honoring of the high status members. Its absence would have required a redefinition of the entire political structure of the family.

Chinese society emphasized one factor above all others in its view of the father's side of the father–son relationship. The father was institutionally expected to set the proper moral example for his son. For the purposes of the present analysis, however, the matter cannot simply be left at this point. The value of filial piety so well inculcated in youth demanded that posterity be raised to maturity and fitted for a place in the family. This motivation saddled the father with two types of obligation toward his son, material support and training both in the manner of earning a living and, more important, in the moral precepts of the society. The material support of the sons was, economically speaking, the key of the solidarity of this relationship. The father had obligations far beyond that of providing food and clothing and shelter for his son during that period of his life when the son was too young to earn his own keep. There were two obligations of primary importance: (1) the provision of a wife for his son and (2) the provision of some inheritance for his son. Both economic obligations were immediately tied up with the continuity of the family line.

The provision of wives and inheritance for his sons were not obligations which anyone forced upon the father. Some fathers failed in these obligations, though not so often in the matter of providing wives as in that of leaving an inheritance. If the failure was the result of economic pressures beyond his control, the father and his family received the pity and sympathy of his neighbors and his other kinsmen, but, if the failure were the result of any dissolute conduct on his part, the father received the contempt of all who knew him. The son, however, lacked the power to force his father to fulfill these obligations. Only social pressure and the set of values which determined the father's motivation ensured that he live up to the accepted standards.

Quite obviously, the burden of the material obligations fell differently upon gentry and peasantry fathers. The economic factors were not ordinarily a serious burden in gentry families. Nevertheless, the obligations often became a sore point in a degenerating gentry family. A gentry father who dissipated the family income and thereby endangered the economic foundations of the family was likely to strain his relations with his sons and might even push them into revolt.

The training of the son by the father was a more complex matter than his material support. Among the peasants (and among craftsmen, merchants, and so on) the father usually trained his son if the son were to follow in his father's footsteps. The gentry on the other hand were occupationally bound to learning, and therefore part of the son's training was delegated to teachers. What has been said above of the training of boys in their *yu-nien* period may be applied here. The dominance was great, and the tasks involved were difficult. The discipline of the training was not such as to improve the relations between father and son.

At least as important as the occupational training, however, was the inculcation of the moral values of the society and the preparation of the son for his future place in the family unit. This training was supposedly accomplished by example and by the son's strict obedience to and respect for his father's words. In his role as moral judge and lawgiver the Chinese father was at his most awesome. There was no appeal from his words and his formulations were handed down as dicta without explanation or justification.

Among the peasants the greater part of the training fell upon the father, but the gentry father delegated much of it. Regular teachers took over the actual occupational training as has been mentioned, and they also performed a considerable part of the moral training. The Confucian system of learning considered the formation of character an integral part of the learning process, and teachers held a position of moral authority as well as intellectual authority. One aspect of learning among the gentry was the great attention paid to the complex code of *li* and to the dignity and reserve essential to the conception of the "gentleman." The discipline involved was difficult. The peasants were not similarly involved in such discipline, for the obedience and respect of a peasant son were *li* enough for the majority of purposes, and in general the ritual intricacies were ignored. This largely spared the peasant father-son relationship the strain which the gentry family system avoided only partly by the employment of teachers.

The strength of the solidarity between father and son was remarkable in its degree and in its arrangement. From the son's point of view, it was not only his strongest family solidarity, but it was the strongest solidarity he knew in the society and took precedence over all others. The contrast between China and Japan in these respects is particularly marked. The strength of the father-son solidarity was great in Japan both in the Tokugawa Period and in the subsequent period prior to the recent war, but it was by no means the strongest solidarity of any given individual. This basic structural difference between China and Japan went to the core of both societies and along with a few other factors served, despite a myriad of superficial similarities, to make the societies of China and Japan radically unlike one another. The differences which resulted in the striking contrast in the Chinese and Japanese rates of industrialization stem in part from this factor.

Although the strength of the father-son relationship was predominant from the son's point of view, it was not from the father's point of view. The father had a much stronger relation to his father. Interestingly enough, as observed above, the strength of the father-son relationship from the father's point of view was derived institutionally not from the relationship itself, but from the father's relation to his father and the ancestors of the family. It is not intended to argue that the father knew no personal affection for his son. He often did, but the strength of the relationship, institutionally speaking, was not dependent upon such affection. Next to and because of the ancestors it was the current and future family which held the allegiance of the father. It was one of the intriguing structural balances of the "traditional" Chinese family that to an extraordinary degree the father's obligations focused his allegiance on his son as the individual who was to inherit the *chia-chang's* position as core of the family. The interesting part of the picture from the structural point of view lay in the fact that although the allegiance of the father was focused on the son to a sufficient degree to balance his power with responsibility, it left the father free, through the indirect method of the focus, to correct the son should the son's conduct threaten the future of the family.

There were other relations which at times superseded in strength from the father's point of view his relations with his son. There was, for example, his relation with his wife. There were many cases in which the strength of the father's relation to his wife was not so great as that to his son, but in the case of the wife considered as a parent, the father would support her side. Thus, it was demanded of the son that he respect his mother. This too was noticeably at variance with the Japanese pattern where male disregard and dominance of females extended to mothers as well as to other women, although Japanese mothers, particularly if widowed, were sometimes able to dominate their sons in a manner not unlike that sometimes seen in China.

Closely related to the strength of the relationship was the question of its intensity. After the *ying-erh shih-ch'i* the relationship was clearly one of avoidance. The degree of avoidance tended to be somewhat relieved as the son became a mature individual, but intimacy of contact, physical or mental, and any overt display of affection were studiously avoided by both parties to the relationship. The solidarity of father and son was not characterized by the term "love" as that term has generally been applied in family relations by the West. Respect, awe, and fear are terms more validly descriptive of the relationship as seen from the son's point of view. It was not required that a son "love" his father in the Western sense. If he did, so much the better, but what was expected was respect for the father and obedience to him. Even if "love" was a feature of the relationship, any overt expression, such as features the Western patterns, was absent from the Chinese pattern. Chinese father and son rarely touched one another after the early part of childhood and generally expressed themselves on such matters in more or less formal terms, if at all. The degree of respect which characterized the son's institutionally expected attitude toward his father was high. The fact that his father said or did a thing was the basis of its validity from the son's

point of view. Contradiction and doubt were no less unfilial than dis-
obedience.

From the father's point of view the relationship was also one of
avoidance rather than one of intimacy after the early childhood of the
son. The father's affect toward the son can hardly be described as respect
or awe and certainly not as fear. The father tended not to think of his
son as an individual so much as he thought of his son as playing certain
important family roles. He did not respect his son as an individual, but
he was much concerned for his son's future family roles. Nevertheless it is
highly likely that a considerable amount of affection in the Western sense
characterized the attitude of the father toward his son, though any overt
expression of it was strongly suppressed. The father certainly displayed
such affection overtly during the early childhood of his son. As he took
over the direct supervision of his son's life, affection was replaced by at
least the appearance of dignified reserve and separateness. It is highly unlikely that the emotional basis of the display of affection lavished by the
father on his son during his son's early years should have disappeared in
so short a space of time. The pattern in these respects had a learned
rigidity about it.

The solidarity between father and son in the Chinese kinship structure
had to be quite strong and intense because it was the basic relationship
for the maintenance of family continuity. It had to be especially great in
the Chinese case because the family structure of China was to such an
overwhelming degree the most important single structural category of the
society. At the same time father-son solidarity had to be such that its
extreme strength and intensity could combine with a structure which
placed the emphasis not on the interests of any one individual in the
family but upon the family group as a whole. Respect is the affect best
suited to such purposes. It permits a high intensity in the relationship and
forges a strong positive bond between the individuals concerned, but it
does not commit them to any primacy of concern for any individual's personal interests, as would be the case with a bond based on "love." Respect
in the nature of the case is more easily preserved and fostered by avoidance
than by intimacy. It is perhaps too much to agree with the cynical view
that familiarity breeds contempt, but, if the basis for contempt or for
challenging respect is present, intimacy is more likely to make it obvious
and inescapable than is avoidance. It is by no means intended to maintain

that "love" in the Western sense was never found between father and son but merely that it was not required. No doubt it often existed, and as pointed out above, the level of intimacy between peasant fathers and sons greatly exceeded that among the gentry.

This general argument must not be taken to imply a causal priority to one of the elements involved in the argument as opposed to another. It would be teleological to assume that a structure arose needing only a solidarity pattern to complete it, and that the pattern was subsequently supplied in accordance with the needs of the structure. The solidarity structure is a necessary and inevitable part of the social structure and of the kinship structure in any empirically conceivable case. The determination of the circumstances which produced in China a particular form of kinship structure with its particular patterns of solidarity is an important matter about which little is known, but it is not the question at stake here. This study is concerned rather with what were the component parts of that structure and how those parts were interrelated. What has been stated above is that a given pattern of affect was present and that it was more stable in the structure in which it was found than any of the usually suggested or immediately possible alternatives would have been.

The type of solidarity which existed between father and son in "traditional" China may have been the best solution possible, given the general structure of the society, but certainly notable strains between father and son were created as well. There is every reason to believe that these strains were maximized among the gentry, though they certainly existed among the peasants, particularly when the son was in his *yu-nien* period. From the point of view of the son the source of his frustration was the father, for it was the father who made demands upon him, refused his desires, punished him, and reviewed his daily conduct with a critical eye. The reserve and dignity maintained by the father also prevented the father from becoming a source of reward in any intimate sense. Any overtly affectionate response and recognition received by the son at this time of his life came from his mother or his sisters or from his paternal grandparents. From his father a son was usually satisfied to receive reserved acceptance of his conduct and to avoid any show of displeasure by his father.

In addition to the fact that the father was a source of frustration and punishment from the son's point of view, the father himself occupied a position which, from the son's point of view, was free of all frustrations. The fact that the son could count on some day holding such a position may have lowered father-son rivalry in certain respects, but it did not alter the fact that when life was hardest for the son, it seemed relatively unencumbered for the father. The importance of the strains between father and sons is borne out by what has happened in the "transitional" period. The two most radical types of proposals in the "transitional" period have been those for the emancipation of women and those for the freedom of sons from parental domination. Revolt has been unusually widespread among gentry sons, partly no doubt, due to their greater education and more frequent contact with new ideas, but it is at least an interesting coincidence that the strains in the father-son relationship were greater and longer prolonged among the gentry than among the peasants.

Husband–Wife. Odd though it may appear from the Western point of view, the relation between husband and wife was neither the strongest nor the most intense relationship in the family. In fact from both points of view the relationship was weak until it was of quite a few years' duration or until the husband became a *chia-chang* and the wife's mother-in-law died. The primary orientation of the married couple was toward the production of children. The husband did not choose his wife nor she him. Whether or not mutual desire featured their sexual relations was quite immaterial to the formation of the bond. In addition, the wife was expected to care for her husband's household and raise his children. This was done under her mother-in-law's direction so long as the mother-in-law lived and did not retire, but the wife was expected to take over both the functions and their direction in the future. In the third place, the wife was in the family to serve her husband's parents. In the fourth place, she owed her husband complete obedience though she was expected to give priority to his parents' commands. Also, she was expected to promote the welfare of the family in any way required of her. Only as a remote and subsidiary consideration was she cast in the role of a companion to her husband, and any overt show of affection on his part for her was viewed as a definite breach of good taste. All these factors were nevertheless part of her solidarity with her husband, for they derived from her relationship with him.

The strength of the relationship between husband and wife from the point of view of both parties was peculiar. From the wife's point of view the relationship was of greater strength than from the husband's point of view. Like her son, she was completely subject to her husband's commands. It is true that in actuality the strength of her relationship with her mother-in-law was greater than that she had with her husband. At the same time, in any case in which the matter became relevant, no open dispute between the authority over the wife of her husband versus her mother-in-law was likely to arise. The mother-in-law used the son to enforce her authority. In the tale of Chiao Chung-Ch'ing, a translation of which appears in a book by Florence Ayscough,[5] the wife displeases the mother-in-law who orders her son to send the wife away. The son does not wish to do so but is ordered to do so by his mother who says:

> Is miserable son without veneration?
> How dare he utter aid-wife words
> Already, toward me, you fail in gratitude, rule of right conduct.
> You will not follow me! . . . indeed? [6]

The son is wilted by this argument and does as he is told, the whole tale ending in the tragic suicide of the son and his wife. While the sympathy of the poem is with the young couple, there is nothing in the poem to suggest that a revolt against filial piety would have been a more acceptable solution. The poem merely implies that parents should be less harsh with their sons and mothers-in-law less arbitrary and inconsiderate of their daughters-in-law. The continued popularity of the poem, which is supposedly of later Han Dynasty authorship, is an indication that the situation of which it speaks so eloquently is still one which deeply moves its audience and that its audience finds in it an extreme case, perhaps, but a recognizable one of a rather familiar problem.

The strength of the relationship from the husband's point of view was very different. So long as his parents lived, his relationship with his wife was weak relative to his relations with his parents. It was, however, the strongest relationship, institutionally speaking, that he had with any woman other than his own mother. Relative to the younger generation the husband-wife relationship was quite strong. A husband was expected to support his wife in such matters unless her position threatened the family interests. At the same time, the husband was in no way bound by his

[5] *Op. cit.,* pp. 250–262.
[6] *Ibid.,* p. 252.

wife's wishes. There were seven grounds on which he could divorce her and only three grounds on which she could prevent this, but in actuality he could rid himself of her at any time.

The intensity of the relationship between husband and wife was also a complex matter. Obviously no relationship involving a continued and repeated performance of sexual intercourse could have its basis in a pattern of avoidance, but every care was taken to confine the intimacy of the relationship to a specific sphere. Romantic love was no part of what husband and wife expected in marriage. The degree of reserve maintained between husband and wife was remarkable. Respect was a more frequently encountered affect, particularly as regards the wife's emotional orientation to her husband. Of course, among the peasantry, where there was less privacy, intimacy between husband and wife was greater. The sharp division of spheres of action between men and women was an important factor toward the maintenance of such reserve. In gentry households the husband and wives frequently had separate apartments. Under such conditions the husband's contact with his wife could be limited to visits to her apartments for sexual purposes and for conferences about household and family affairs.

The degree of emotional intensity in the relationship was rather low, particularly during the early years of married life, so far as the institutional patterns were concerned. It is perhaps true that husbands were often romantically in love with their wives in the Western sense and that their love was often reciprocated. If so, it increased the strength of their solidarity and its intensity. Structurally speaking, however, this intensity was quite frequently a source of trouble, because a growth in the strength of their solidarity permitted it to challenge other solidarities in the family. From the structural point of view it was necessary therefore that the solidarity of the husband and wife be strongly deëmphasized, at least until the husband's parents died. The relationship of husband and wife was particularly prone to become quite intense and have in its emotional intensity a basis for great strength (or weakness, if hate rather than love was the emotion generated), involving as it did sexual intimacy as one of its most highly emphasized components. In the West, romantic love as a component of marital solidarity has been accompanied by a kinship structure which has made husband-wife solidarity the most important solidarity in the family. It is perhaps not going too far to suggest as a general theoretical conclusion that wherever romantic love is so emphasized the kinship structure of the society will be found to institutionalize husband-wife solidarity as the strategic solidarity of the family.

There was one striking factor about husband-wife solidarity. Its strength gave a strong impression of increase with age. From the Western point of view, with its emphasis on the romantic sexual attachment of husband and wife, this may seem odd at first, since the romantic sexual element of the relationship certainly tended to decline with age and familiarity. Furthermore, the strength of the solidarity in the Chinese case seemed to continue to grow even if the husband took a concubine in the ordinary case. This impression was by no means an illusion, and it was certainly independent of any romantic sexual content. The matter was relatively simple. As the couple grew older, two forces operated simultaneously on the relationship. First, the members of the older generation to whom the husband owed an allegiance superior to that he owed his wife began to die so that the number of such persons diminished and eventually disappeared. A *chia-chang* with no living parents or brothers in the family unit had no stronger relationship with anyone in the family than with his wife. It remained weak in terms of the wife's power relative to his, but, since relative to other family members her acts were in his name, and since they were expected to act as a unit, the strength rather than the weakness of the relationship came to be emphasized. Second, she held a parent's position towards the younger generation, and in this relation her husband would support her where he might have ignored her as a wife. Filial piety was of such importance that one was not only expected to observe it oneself, but also was expected to inculcate it in the generations under one's supervision. The inculcation of filial piety served to increase husband-wife solidarity further, at least towards the younger generation.

The gentry family situation was somewhat different, at least in degree, from that of the peasantry. Since the gentry actually lived in large families of several generations and observed the *li* with some rigor, husband-wife solidarity during the early part of marriage tended to be weaker than among the peasants. There were more older generation and fraternal solidarities to take precedence over their solidarity, and the indignity of any overt expression of affection in the presence of others was more highly stressed. Furthermore, peasant husbands were in the direct company of their wives a great deal more than was customary for gentry husbands.

When the marriage had progressed in years, however, something of the reverse was the case. The gentry placed greater emphasis on the rigid observance of the canons of filial piety than did the peasants, thereby strengthening the wife's position as parent. In addition, to have command over a gentry household was to have a far more powerful position than the corresponding position among the peasants, since among the gentry such a position might carry with it considerable economic administration and power. In both cases, however, the solidarity increased in the latter part of the marriage relation.

Father–Daughter. The solidarity between father and daughter was of slight institutional importance in the family structure. On the daughter's part it involved complete obedience to her father, and on the father's part it involved the provision for the girl's support until her marriage and the arrangement of a marriage for her. It must be remembered, however, that a daughter was only a temporary member of her family of orientation. A daughter owed her father obedience only until her marriage, at which time authority over her passed to her husband's family through her husband. During her childhood in her family of orientation her father's obligations toward her could be and often were transgressed by her sale or the lack of proper concern for her future after marriage.

The strength of the relation was from the point of view of the daughter institutionalized as the strongest relation she had prior to marriage. On the other hand, her father's obligations to her were of a much slighter nature to begin with and were far more casually enforced. The strength of the solidarity, even from the daughter's point of view, was often obscured by the fact that she frequently had little or no contact with her father.

The intensity of the father-daughter relationship was also slight in degree, institutionally speaking, for both followed a pattern of avoidance. A great deal of respect and awe was expected, and no doubt given by her, but it was institutionally less significant than might have been expected because of the relatively slight contact between father and daughter. Again, this was truer of the gentry than of the peasantry. Peasant fathers saw much more of their daughters than did gentry fathers, but it is doubtful that they paid a great deal more attention to them.

The noninstitutionalized aspects of father-daughter relations are, perhaps, of more interest than the institutionalized ones. In gentry families, the informal relationship between father and daughter often became both strong and intense. Intimacy in such cases replaced avoidance, and love and affection replaced respect and awe. This was a case of great romantic appeal to the Chinese. When an intelligent daughter caught her father's eye in a gentry family, education was an almost inevitable part of the relationship. Her materials of study were those of her brothers, but her discipline was far less severe, since her education was not pointed toward the government examinations, and she more nearly received a "liberal education" than did her brothers.

An intimate relationship between father and daughter might become structurally subversive. It might have resulted in a daughter being improperly trained for her role as a woman and in interference with relationships the solidarity of which was of much greater importance to the family. Two things prevented this. In the first place, her mother remained the person to give her training in feminine roles, and since the mother was outside this relationship, the necessary discipline could be maintained. In the second place, long range disruption of more important solidarities by the relationship was prevented by the marriage of the daughter and the removal thereby of the possibility of a disruption of institutionally prescribed patterns. While the possibility of such a relationship seriously affecting the daughter's family of orientation in the long run was thus minimized, the effect on the daughter was apt to be more prolonged, since it made adjustment to daughter-in-law status more difficult to bear.

Such a relationship was rather infrequent among the peasants. One of the reasons for this was almost certainly the fact that the peasant father, unlike the gentry father, lacked the leisure time necessary for the cultivation of such a relationship. Lack of time was probably not the whole story, however, since even peasants often had idle periods. It is interesting to speculate on the origin and basis of the type of informal bond which sometimes grew up between father and daughter in gentry families. The *chia-chang*, institutionally speaking, held a position demanding uncommon emotional reserve. But there can be little doubt that the position of the *chia-chang* was far less reserved in the peasant family and that the father entered an informal intimate emotional exchange with family members to a far greater degree than was normal among gentry families. Aside from those few human beings who are virtuosi of dignity and reserve, the maintenance of such a position is either impossible or at the very least a great strain. It is, perhaps, legitimate to suggest that, in the informal intimacy which frequently characterized the relation between father and daughter in gentry families, the gentry father found a certain release from his rigorously maintained role. Since, structurally speaking, his daughter was the least strategic family member so far as the continued existence of the family was concerned, and since any disruption that such intimacy might cause could not be too prolonged because of the daughter's early marriage, it was possible for the father to find such release with his daughter with the minimum possibility of family disruption. The very strong societal injunction dictating the marriage of daughters upon the attainment of physiological maturity, or very shortly thereafter, minimized the danger of incestuous relations developing from such a relation. The differential incidence of this phenomenon among peasant families, accompanied as it was by somewhat lesser strains in the respects mentioned, lends at least a tentative substantiation to this hypothesis.

Mother–Son. The mother-son relationship was likely to have its most significant aspects on the informal uninstitutionalized level. Institutionally, the relationship required obedience and respect of the son and kindness and care of the mother. In strength the relationship was notably inferior to that borne by each to the husband and father respectively and to other relations as well. A rather high degree of intensity was expected from both sides of the relation, and its accepted emotional character was affection and respect.

In actuality the situation was not nearly so formal as it has been pictured, and affection tended to predominate. Whatever the usual reasons for attachment of mothers to their children in general and their sons in particular, the Chinese mother had special reasons for attachment to her son. More than any other single factor, he bettered her status in her husband's family. Now it must be remembered that in infancy all Chinese children, whenever circumstances permitted, were foci of affection and attention of the warmest sort. Since at the end of his first period of life the boy in the Chinese family passed on to the supervision of his father, he was likely to have his view of his mother as a source of warmth, comfort, and affection emphasized by the beginning of this paternal discipline. His mother was not charged with the essentials of his discipline and hence was in a position throughout his life to furnish him gratification with a minimum of frustration. Only at his marriage was she in a position to frustrate his wishes, but even should she have done so, the ultimate authority for her action came from the boy's father, and this fact was not likely to escape the boy's attention: The close attachment of mother and son, despite the general Chinese feeling for reserve in all family relations, was frequently featured by much the same sort of "love" found in the relationship in the West, though in the West this is formally institutionalized as correct. Chinese mothers came to figure prominently as intermediaries between fathers and sons. Miss Lang quotes the *Li Chi* to indicate the difference between the relation of father and son and that of mother and son:

Here now is the affection of a father for his sons;—he loves the worthy among them, and places on a lower level those who do not show ability; but that of a mother for them is such, that while she loves the worthy, she pities those who do not show ability:—the mother deals with them on the ground of affection and not of showing them honor, the father, on the ground of showing them honor and not of affection.[7]

This solidarity between mother and son would hardly have been possible within the Chinese kinship structure had the mother been charged with responsibility for the son's discipline. The effects of the relation were far-reaching. It seems to have served from the mother's point of view at least something of the same function performed by the informal intimacy between gentry fathers and daughters. The mother was a relatively isolated member of the family who was dominated by people who treated her rather coldly. In her relations with her son she found some release from this isolation. While sexual relations were never permitted to result from this relationship, the extreme treatment of daughters-in-law by their mothers-in-law was no doubt compounded of a jealousy which smacked of an incestuous attachment, psychologically at least. In a society which minimized intimate emotional response in human relations as did China, those displays which are countenanced are likely to be relied upon heavily.

The question of the position of the widowed mother has already been discussed at some length above, and little elaboration of that discussion is here required. The warm emotional relation between mother and son played its role in that situation, however, just as it did in the ability of the mother to exceed any wifely influence.

[7] *Op. cit.*, p. 29.

So intimate and overtly affectionate a relationship as that between mother and son might have been expected to create strains in the family as well as provide a certain emotional release for the parties concerned, but such was not actually the case. The mother might become a buffer between her husband and her son, but she was not likely to back her son in defiance of her husband or to incite him to such defiance. The father on his side was not likely to be jealous of his son's relations with his wife because the father's relations with her were not dependent primarily on any feeling of affection or sentiment.

Mother–Daughter. The mother-daughter relationship has tended to be obscured or ignored because it was of so much slighter significance in the Chinese family than such relationships as that of father and son, husband and wife, mother and son, and mother-in-law and daughter-in-law. Nevertheless, it is worth a great deal more attention than it has generally received because it formed a good part of the background against which the crucial mother-in-law–daughter-in-law relationship took place. Technically speaking, the complete obedience of the daughter was owed by her to her father, but as a member of the feminine part of the household, it was to her mother that the obedience and respect were more actively called for. The mother on her side was expected to rear and care for her daughter and train her for her future role.

Institutionally, the strength of this relationship was not great on either side. The daughter owed prior allegiance to her father as a girl, and her mother was expected to pay prior attention not only to her parents-in-law and her husband, but to her sons as well. After the daughter's marriage even this strength was negated on both sides to an extraordinary degree because a daughter's ties with her family of orientation were viewed as almost completely severed by her marriage. At any rate, they were not institutionally expected to be a major factor in determining the conduct of either mother or daughter after the marriage. The intensity of the relationship was institutionally correspondingly light. It was not, however, an avoidance relation, for there was, in addition to respect, both love and affection.

In actuality the relationship was both stronger and more intense than might have been expected. While a mother may have loved her sons more than her daughters, she had much more intimate and frequent contact with her daughters than with her sons. Daughters provided their mothers with an outlet for and source of emotional warmth. The relationship was not always severed by marriage as might have been expected. As noted above, particularly among the gentry, some contact between mother and daughter was continued after marriage. Proof of the continued non-institutional strength of the relationship is to be found in the fact that one of the seven grounds for divorce was stealing from her husband's family by the wife.[8] The fruits of such theft were frequently turned over to her mother by the daughter.

Since the mother was responsible for her daughter's training and discipline, the question of why the same sort of objectivity required of the father in his supervision of the son was not necessary in the relation of mother and daughter might well be raised. The structural strain that would have been placed upon a daughter's family of orientation by short-comings in her training and discipline were negligible and of short duration by comparison with those that would have resulted from a similar deficiency in her brother's case. For the sake of the face of her parent's family she needed to know certain techniques and patterns of behavior, but these could be taught her without the objectivity required by her brothers' more rigorous discipline and more important future in the family.

Father-in-law–Daughter-in-law. The factors involved in this relationship tended to be obscured by the mother-in-law–daughter-in-law relationship. Ideally, the daughter-in-law bore her primary burden of responsibility to her father-in-law. As a member of the feminine side of her husband's household, however, her main relations were with her mother-in-law rather than her father-in-law. Institutionally she owed him complete obedience, subservience, and consideration for his every wish. His comfort was expected to be one of her prime preoccupations. He, on his side, owed her virtually nothing save respect for her sexual inviolability as his son's wife. Her comfort and treatment was no concern of his save insofar as he, in his position of *chia-chang,* was responsible in a general way for the health and well-being of all family members.

The strength of their relation from the point of view of her obligations to him was supreme, surpassing that of her obligations to her own father, her mother-in-law, and her husband. It was not often that he and his wife would disagree about what was expected of her, but if they did,

[8] See Sun Pen-Wen, *op. cit.,* I, 128.

his word was law. From his point of view the strength of the relation was weak. Any family member merited his consideration before she did. Unless she could influence him in a noninstitutional fashion through pressure from her own father and brothers, she had no hope of changing any course of action on which he might decide.

The relationship was one of avoidance. The son's father ordinarily left the feminine side of the family alone most of the time, and his daughter-in-law was one of the last persons with whom he was likely to come in contact in the family. There was, of course, some difference between peasantry and gentry families in these respects because of the difference in privacy, but in either case the father's contact with his daughter-in-law was not emphasized. Like her husband, she felt respect, awe, and fear for her father-in-law rather than love and affection. The degree of intensity of these emotions was high in her, but the relationship was of low intensity from the father's point of view. Fortunately, perhaps, the father's relative separation from the feminine side of the household tended to prevent any more intimate relationship. Any such intimacy would have been a serious threat to the stability of the family structure because it would have struck directly at the key relations of that structure. It would have raised the problem of sexual rivalry between father and son and between mother-in-law and daughter-in-law. It would have threatened the accepted political solutions of the kinship structure and the entire position of the mother-in-law on which the household organization depended. Few attachments could have proved more disturbing. Father–daughter-in-law incest was apparently one of the few cases in which defiance of one's father was justified.[9] The mother-in-law's position served the function of giving her full power in a sphere in which she would have to bear full responsibility, but it also served to reduce to a minimum rivalries which could have been intense and would certainly have been disruptive.

Mother-in-law–Daughter-in-law. So much has been said already of this relationship that it is, perhaps, overly cautious to pick it up again at this point. Nevertheless, certain facets of this relationship should be stressed from the point of view of solidarity. The content of the relationship requires little elaboration at this point. The daughter-in-law owed complete obedience and respect to her mother-in-law. Her mother-in-law

[9] See F. L. K. Hsu, "The Problem of Incest Tabu in a North China Village," *American Anthropologist*, 42, 1, 122–135.

owed her nothing in return, merely bearing the responsibility of seeing to it that the daughter-in-law was kept in a good enough state to permit her to bear healthy children. She could even ignore this with little possibility of interference.

The strength of the relationship was great from the daughter-in-law's point of view and slight from the mother-in-law's. The mother-in-law was always in a position to have the daughter-in-law sent away, and the three factors ordinarily protecting the wife against divorce were no genuine barrier to such treatment. The power thus given over to the mother-in-law, removed as it was in actuality from any effective responsibility, was one of the major sources of difficulty in these relationships.

The matter of intensity of the mother-in-law–daughter-in-law solidarity was rather complex. Respect of the daughter-in-law for her mother-in-law was expected, and the mother-in-law on her part was supposedly kind. The relationship was not one of avoidance, but reserve was expected insofar as possible. Intimate contact was unavoidable, particularly in peasant families. The relationship was much like that of a master and a body slave. Avoidance was not practiced, but intimacy was not mutual. In actuality the emotional content on both sides of the relationship was likely to be high. Frequently the emotions were not those of respect and kindness but of fear and hatred on the one hand and contempt on the other. This, of course, was the picture at its darkest. Actually, a far more amicable working arrangement than this must have been the rule, for there was a limit to the length that even so stable a system as that of the Chinese family could go in its imposition of strain. Nevertheless, difficulty in the relationship was extremely common.

In earlier discussions some of the forces which tended to cause strains in the mother-in-law–daughter-in-law relationship have been mentioned. It is also worth noting that when such strains became unbearable in a given case, the results could not be so disruptive of the family as the breakdown between other members could have been. In an extreme case a daughter-in-law had two possible ways out of the situation. One was suicide with its negative but absolute solution. The other was to run away. This latter was far less effective because there were very few places she could go, and from most of those she could be returned upon discovery. Assuming she were successful in such a revolt, however, the situation was not as serious as a revolt of a son against his father would have been. In the latter case family disruption was the direct result, and if the son were an only son, his loss might prove irreplaceable. The loss of a daughter-in-law was serious enough, especially in a peasant family where the economic burden of the loss was so much greater, but a daughter-in-law could always be replaced if funds were available. Had the daughter-in-law held a less peripheral role in the family, it is doubtful whether the family system could have withstood the strains developed within it by this relationship. There is little reason to doubt that even at the height of the "traditional" period daughters-in-law would have preferred to live apart from their mothers-in-law.

Brother–Brother. The relationship of brothers was, next to that of father and son, one of the most crucial relations in the preservation of the ideal type of gentry family in "traditional" China. The ideal was to keep as many generations as possible living together, and, since the family was patrilineal and patrilocal all the male interrelationships were of necessity accented. If the family prospered and multiplied, it was, of course, impossible to continue it indefinitely because such a family after a few generations reached a size for which the kinship structural organization was simply inadequate. The Chinese recognized this, and ample provision was made for the division of property by brothers at such times. At the same time, the maintenance of even two or three generations living together required a strong fraternal bond.

The position of an elder brother relative to a younger brother has been discussed above and the peculiarities of the position of the eldest brother have been mentioned.[10] The relationship was a highly coöperative one in theory at least. There is reason to believe that the obedience of younger to elder brothers was of considerably less importance than the united front that brothers were expected to present to all other persons save their parents. Only the interests of parents or other older generation members in the direct line justified a breach in the mutual support of brothers.

Inside the family unit, therefore, the strength of the relationship was less than it was relative to outsiders. Relative age made some difference as to the strength of the relationship between one brother as opposed to another, but the emphasis was probably less upon this than upon the mutual obligations to one another. A Chinese expression puts the matter in the following form: "Older brothers are friends; younger brothers are

[10] See pp. 137–140.

respectful" (*hsiung yu ti kung*). In practice the lack of emphasis on obedience of the younger was certainly borne out, particularly in the periods of life after the *yu-nien* period. A younger brother could request a division of property of his father, but his father could refuse it, whereas an elder brother could not refuse it unless he drew on some noninstitutionalized basis of strength. Even if the brothers separated, however, they retained an obligation to demonstrate their solidarity relative to any outsider.

The effective content of the relationship was what has been loosely called "fraternal love" in the West, together with respect, especially towards the eldest brother. The relation was one of considerable intimacy. Brothers expected to be able to consult and confide anything and everything to one another. Companionship between brothers was a prominent feature of their relationship. The relationship was much like that of close friends in the West, except that in that case one chooses the membership of the group for oneself, whereas in this case the membership was set by forces beyond the control of any member of the group. The degree of intensity of the relationship was expected to be high though often in actuality it was not.

The relationship between brothers was a source of both stability and instability in the family. The coöperative spirit of mutual help and guidance which it fostered was a prerequisite of maintaining any large-scale family unit at all. This feeling, along with the presence of the father, greatly increased family strength. The positive solidarity among brothers made it easier for a father to hold together a family containing several married sons and their children. When the father died and the responsibility for the maintenance of the family fell upon the eldest brother, the situation was much changed. The authority of the eldest brother was not sufficient to overcome conflict, should any one of the brothers care to carry the matter to an extreme. The fact that brothers could carry off a family split whereas sons ordinarily could not probably lay in two factors which were closely interrelated. The institutionalized strength of the relation was considerably less than that of the father-son relation, and the brothers had an institutionally approved right to demand an economic basis for themselves independent of the authority of the eldest brother. This right lay in the right to demand a division of property. Thus in a fraternal quarrel economic pressure could not be used effectively to settle the issue in the manner in which it could be used in the father-son case if necessary.

There was another factor at work here. The precedence of an elder brother and the precedence of the *chia-chang* differed. The authority and prestige of the father was such that it could easily support the position of the *chia-chang*. Furthermore, the father was ordinarily in the position of *chia-chang* at some time during the son's fairly early development. The relation between brothers was different, however. In the first place, the position of *chia-chang* carried with it a power and a prestige far in excess of that inherent in the position of elder or eldest brother. The eldest brother took over the *chia-chang* position upon the death of the father, but this cast him in a radically different role than any he had played before.[11] As *chia-chang* he could not preserve the intimacy of his fraternal relationships. Furthermore, the past intimacy of those relationships made his position more difficult. He was suddenly elevated to a position of great authority, but his brothers were not accustomed to him in anything like so powerful a position. At the same time all the brothers had been to some extent frustrated by their previous relationship with their father. Since their father combined in one individual the roles of father and *chia-chang,* there was likely to be considerable amount of suppressed aggression focused on the *chia-chang's* position. The *chia-chang's* position in any case involved its holder in being the source of such frustration. The display of aggression toward the father was well inhibited, but it was not nearly so strongly inhibited relative to an elder brother. The strength of solidarity between elder and younger brothers was simply not great enough to survive the strains involved in the eldest brother's being cast in the father's role.

The frustration and austerity involved in the *chia-chang* role were by no means the only strains that had to be borne by the fraternal relation after the death of the father. The strains created among brothers' wives, for example, were almost certain to result in feminine pressure for division. In the absence of the father-in-law and mother-in-law it had a good chance of being effective.

The necessity in "traditional" Chinese family structure of having the eldest brother's position subject to great change must not be regarded as

---

[11] If the father became *chia-chang* upon the death of the grandfather, the father's relation to his son was not changed in anything like so radical a fashion because of the far greater emphasis on authority, avoidance, reserve, and the like.

entirely a source of weakness. Clearly the accretion of family members had of necessity to reach some limits. The institutionalized right of brothers to demand a division of the property together with the right of equal inheritance provided a means whereby reformulation could take place by peaceable institutionalized means. Had revolt and force been the only means of making such an adjustment, the solidarity of *tsu* units would have been needlessly sacrificed. The pattern provided a peaceful method for an inevitable adjustment, and as much interfamilial solidarity as possible was thereby salvaged for the larger patrilineal kinship organizations.

Sister–Sister. The relationship between sisters was not one of long duration. In the ordinary case it was terminated at marriage. After marriage the sisters might meet on visits home, but such visits were relatively rare and by no means certain. Precedence was granted on a basis of relative age, just as among brothers, but the relationship was not nearly so well defined as that between brothers, nor was it so vital to the family. Like the relation between brothers, that between sisters was coöperative and intimate, a sort of institutionally rather than individually selected friendship.

The sororal relationship was usually quite affectionate and intimate, and although the strength of the relationship was relatively slight, its intensity, so long as the sisters lived together, was generally great. The relationship was so completely severed at marriage, however, and the separation of women from independent control of the economic bases for power was so complete that the intensity of the relationship had no chance to be reflected in strength. At every turn the society gave priority to other relationships.

Within the confines of the "traditional" Chinese family the warmth of the sororal relationship created certain difficulties of adjustment for the women. In the first place, there were the strains involved in the breaking of the relationship at the time of marriage. In the second place, the warmth of her past environment made the girl's position in her husband's family all the more difficult to bear by contrast.

Sister–Brother's Wife. Relatively little has been said of this relationship in the literature on China, and not much seems to be known of it. The relationship was not of great structural importance in the family. In the ordinary case the relationship was likely to be of short duration, particularly in peasant families. Girls were married at the age of fifteen or sixteen or even earlier. Boys were married somewhat later than that, and peasant boys often had their marriages delayed for several years beyond that for economic reasons. Therefore, unless a father had a concubine or a second wife, his daughters were about to marry out of the family at the time or soon after the time that his sons married. But concubines and second wives were luxuries largely denied to the peasants, and this situation was less likely to arise among them than among the gentry.

Since both daughter and daughter-in-law held very low status roles in the family, the precedence of one over the other was not very meaningful. If the brother's wife were acting in some role in which she acted for her husband, she would take precedence over her husband's sister, perhaps, but actually the sister's place in the family was, at least during the daughter-in-law's early years, the more firmly established of the two, and she was usually the person with precedence. No more seems to have been demanded of their institutional relationship than that they not be a source of friction. The strength of the relationship, institutionally speaking, was negligible. The effective content was also left relatively undefined. As regards outsiders they were expected to maintain a common front, as were all family members.

In actuality the relationship was often a cool one or one of lukewarm friendship. Sometimes the extremes of love and hate characterized the relationship, and in such cases the intensity could be great indeed. If there was hatred between the two, the net effect could be disruptive since the sister was in a position to make the wife's burdens greater. All in all, however, the relationship does not seem to have been such as to give rise to any marked problems or features of the "traditional" period. It was inevitably a transitory relationship and usually one of short duration. All the persons concerned with it were, of course, well aware of this fact, and the knowledge was undoubtedly a factor which prevented the relationship in the ordinary case from taking on too serious a nature from the point of view of either participant.

Brother–Brother's Wife. This relationship was one of considerably more importance in the "traditional" Chinese family than that between sister and sisters-in-law. In the first place, when the brothers lived together in one family, the relationship was likely to be of long duration and cover the major part of the adult lives of both participants. As a result, the relationship was of greater importance among the gentry than among the peasants. Among the latter the relationship was often nonexistent because the two brothers concerned lived in different families. In the second place, the relationship bore directly on that of brother to brother, and the importance of the fraternal solidarity has already been reviewed.

A brother's wife owed her brother-in-law respect and consideration and, in general, service when such service did not conflict with her obligations to her husband or her parents-in-law. If the brother-in-law were her husband's elder or eldest brother, she owed him greater deference than would have been the case otherwise. The brother-in-law on his side owed his fraternal sister-in-law a certain amount of respect, especially if she were the wife of an elder brother. If in addition she were the wife of the *chia-chang,* the respect due her was increased.. This may be put generally by the statement that insofar as the sister-in-law acted as her husband's representative (for example, in the management of the *hu*), she merited the respect due her husband from his brothers. Actually, however, she was expected to act in such a way that no overt issue over authority could arise between her and her brothers-in-law. Another type of respect was due her regardless of the relative age status of her husband, namely, physical respect of her person and general respect of her sensibilities, above all the former. The solidarity between wife and brother-in-law was not in general strong save as it reflected fraternal solidarity, but its negative strength was great. Any sort of physical relations between brothers and the wives of brothers came under a general taboo, and sexual contacts were strongly subject to the incest taboo. The function of this taboo in minimizing rivalry between brothers is obvious enough. Actually, however, a large Chinese family with several brothers and their wives presented grave problems in these respects, and cases of incest of this sort were by no means unheard of.

Difficulties between the two were to some extent minimized by the institutionalization of avoidance. This avoidance was not buttressed by awe and fear as was father–son avoidance. It depended in large part upon the availability of privacy for the female members of the household as a group relative to men and the tendency of the women ordinarily to be accompanied by other women of the household. The contacts which existed of mature persons of mixed sexes, save in the case of husband and wife, and mother and son, and the like, were never supposed to be of two persons alone. They no doubt took place, but they were frowned upon.

When married brothers in peasant families did live together, the lack of privacy in such a household undoubtedly promoted a far more intimate relationship between brother-in-law and sister-in-law than characterized gentry families. At the same time, the incest taboos were strong among peasants too, and it may be argued on the other side of the question that the greater privacy of gentry households made clandestine implementation of such intimacy more feasible than it was among the peasants.

The importance of the relationship between a brother and his brother's wife was not primarily concerned with the two persons themselves. Its overwhelming importance lay in the manner in which this relationship affected the solidarity of the brothers. The household duties of the sister-in-law did not ordinarily affect her brother-in-law in a direct personal fashion. The great emphasis in their direct relationship was a negative one, the avoidance of trouble. Trouble arose generally in one of two forms. The first of these, sexual rivalry between brothers, has already been discussed. The second of these was a sharp dislike of brother for brother's wife or vice versa. When this occurred, it was sometimes an outgrowth of the frustration of sexual desires. This was not its only source by any manner of means, however, unless the monistic interpretation that all heterosexual rivalries and jealousies are sexual in origin be maintained. Wives were sometimes quite jealous of the advantages which, real or fancied, they felt went to their brothers-in-law at their husband's expense and consequently at their own. Although these frictions were frequently economic in origin, they were not inevitably so. In some cases frictions grew out of the relations between the wives of brothers and was, therefore, primarily a friction indirectly generated, though none the less disruptive for all that.

Uncle–Nephew.[12] This relationship was of greater importance in gentry families than in peasantry families. Again this was not merely because of the greater attention to etiquette in the gentry families but was also a function of the fact that in many peasant families uncles and nephews were not members of the same family units. Hence the solidarity became an interfamily rather than an intrafamily matter. The solidarity of

---

[12] Within the Chinese family unit as defined here, only the relationship between paternal uncles and nephews arises. Relations with maternal uncles in China were by no means unimportant, but they will not be discussed here.

paternal uncle and nephew was marked by considerations of both the generation and relative age of the uncles. As regards the first, the uncle received from his nephew much the same respect and obedience due a father by virtue of the fact that the uncle was a male family member sharing generation status with the father. Whether or not the uncle were an older or younger brother of the father also made a difference, and the Chinese employed different terms in order to distinguish between paternal uncles on this basis.[13]

Ostensibly the relationship of a paternal uncle and his nephew was simply a somewhat less intense version of the father-son relationship. Respect and awe were institutionally decreed to a high degree, and avoidance rather than intimacy was considered correct. In actuality the relationships between paternal uncles and nephews within a family unit were often more intimate than those of father and son. The responsibility of an uncle for his nephew was so much less than that of a father for his son that such intimacy did not seriously threaten to disrupt the family structure, and insofar as it existed, it probably served as a release for the nephews if not the uncles. There were two possible sources of disruption in this sort of relationship, however. It could under certain circumstances increase rivalry between brothers and between cousins. In either case the stability and integration of the family was affected accordingly.

The relationship between paternal uncles and nephews was likely to be of greater importance if the father and grandfather of the nephews were dead. Then the eldest uncle took over the headship of the family and assumed as far as the nonadult nephew was concerned much the same position as his father had held. The case of the adult nephew was somewhat different. If his grandfather and father were dead, the adult nephew could demand of his uncle his father's share of the family property. Thus, although the strength of the solidarity between uncle and nephew was somewhat stronger than that between brothers because it was bolstered by the all-important generational criterion, the uncle's position as *chia-chang* was subject to the same inherent weakness of that of a brother who became *chia-chang*. Even if division took place, however, the relationship remained important. When the uncles and nephews lived in separate family units, the nephews still recognized the precedence of their

[13] The term *pe-pe* was commonly used for a father's elder brother and *shu-shu* for a father's younger brother.

uncles in matters where large aggregations of family units were concerned. The most important cases of this recognition probably arose in *tsu* affairs. In the preservation of its importance in the interfamily sphere the uncle-nephew tie was not unlike that between brothers. Both ties were extremely prominent ones in the nepotism of China which has so caught the eye of Western investigators.

Uncle–Niece.[14] This relationship seems to have been of relatively slight importance in the structure of the Chinese family. For much the same reasons given in the section on uncles and nephews this relationship was not as likely to arise in peasant families as in those of the gentry. In gentry families, however, the relative segregation of the women and the outside interests of the men meant that a niece was not likely to have any significant relations with her uncles. Like her brother she owed him, in a modified form, the same sort of obedience and respect she owed her father. Again, as in the case of her brothers, the death of her father greatly increased her uncle's importance in her life, particularly the uncle who was *chia-chang,* for he was in a position to determine her marriage in large part. In such situations her uncle often took up her father's role completely, and the type of affectionate intimacy which sometimes characterized the relations of father and daughter was known to arise between uncle and niece.

Ordinarily, however, the emotional content of the relationship was respect and general avoidance. The relative lack of contact meant that the intensity of the solidarity was not likely to be great though on the formal level the niece was expected to pay her uncle a great deal of respect. A further factor weakening their relationship was the marriage of the niece into a different family. If her father were living, her uncle might play no part in either her betrothal or her marriage. After her marriage her contact with her paternal uncle was virtually obliterated, unless her father were dead and her uncle stood *in loco parentis.* This factor was in marked contrast with the relationship between uncle and nephew which was not similarly disrupted.

On the other hand, just as in the cases of nephews and uncles, when the relationships between uncle and niece varied from patterns of avoidance, the uncle, lacking paternal responsibilities, was often in a better position to spoil or indulge his nieces. There is some reason to believe that in

[14] Again paternal uncles are those under consideration.

"traditional" China, as in the West, the uncle, especially young uncles, were likely to become foci for romanticism. In "transitional" China in the case of an uncle with a modern Western education and a niece beginning or looking forward to such an education, the relationship became even more of a focus for the romanticism of adolescence.

Aunt–Nephew. Again this relationship was one more likely to assume prominence in gentry families than in peasant ones since peasant families were less likely to have all the necessary individuals in one group. Here two types of aunts may be distinguished—father's sisters and father's brother's wives. The first of these will be called paternal aunts in this study, and the second will be called avuncular aunts. In the former case the relationship within the family unit was necessarily transitory since the aunt married out of the group. When the relationship existed, the nephew owed his aunt obedience and respect if no person of greater precedence gave conflicting commands. At the same time, the relationship, confined as it was likely to be to relatively early childhood, was really not much concerned with either respect or obedience. It was usually characterized by warmth, intimacy, affection, and indulgence. The relationship was likely to be warmly remembered by the nephew in later life, and if circumstances permitted, he might visit his aunt. At any rate, the type of avoidance and respect which characterized the uncle-nephew relationship and the type of segregation which often separated uncles and nieces did not operate between aunts and nephews. Not only were these aunts not separated from their nephews, but in the early years of the nephews at least, the aunts frequently participated in their care and rearing. As a result, although the institutionalized strength of the relation was slight, the intensity of the solidarity was likely to be great and important for both parties to it.

The discrepancy between the strength and intensity of the relation created a situation which must often have been frustrating from the point of view of both the women and the men involved, and is but one other example of a type of frustration widely distributed throughout the Chinese family structure. The boys, especially, and the men in general in Chinese families, were accustomed to find emotional warmth and affectionate response of a high degree of intensity in precisely those relationships of weakest strength in the kinship structure. Something of the same thing was true of the girls and the women in general. As a result, whenever a conflict arose between one's relations with a highly loved person with whom one's solidarity was relatively weak and one's relations with a person with whom one's solidarity was strong but the emotional intensity involved was either slight or, more likely, of a more negative sort, such conflict was, institutionally speaking, inevitably resolved by taking the side of the stronger but less intense or more negative emotional relationship. A fairly frequent feeling of "betrayal" on the part of loved ones was unavoidable in such a situation. At the same time it was a "betrayal" which both parties to the relationship clearly understood to be inevitable and apparently accepted as right. The novel and legendary literature is full of such frustrations, and almost inevitably the solution is found either in the acceptance of the frustration or in the suicide of the persons concerned, usually after compliance with the demands of the stronger solidarity.

The case of avuncular aunts was somewhat different. The avuncular aunts, although they came into the family as strangers, were likely to have longer relationships with their nephews than did the paternal aunts. Coming into the family in the low status of daughter-in-law as these aunts did, the strength of their solidarities with their nephews was likely to be even weaker than that of nephews with their paternal aunts. They came into the family as the lowest of the low whereas their nephews were the pride and joy and hope of the family. When, however, the avuncular aunts operated as representatives of their husbands relative to their nephews, they carried the authority of the uncle and the strength inherent in that solidarity. In addition to the factor of the longer duration of this relationship another factor must be mentioned. The paternal aunt's relations with her nephews might well be prolonged after her marriage, but the important ones preceded that and hence were usually confined to the early childhood of the nephew. This was not the case with the avuncular aunt. If the family held together, she saw her nephew raised to maturity. Moreover, if she were a second wife of her nephew's uncle or the first wife of an uncle nearly the same age as her nephew, quite another order of problems was raised. The possibility of a sexual attraction between the two was interjected. Such a relationship came under the incest taboo. While the disruption which could be caused was less serious than that caused by such a relation between a son and a concubine or second wife of his father, it was nevertheless quite serious. If nephews and their avuncular aunts were at all close in age, segregation of them was given greater emphasis than otherwise.

Another problem was raised by the relation between avuncular aunts and nephews. An avuncular aunt was sometimes jealous of the position of her nephews relative to her own sons. This was particularly likely if the nephews were sons of an older brother of her husband. The nephew who was a son of the eldest brother or of the *chia-chang* was the best focus of such feelings because such a nephew, despite the equal inheritance of property by sons, definitely held a favored position. Just how important the matter was would be extremely hard to say. It would be a mistake to overemphasize any of these strains, but the frequency with which the student meets references to the conflict between members of different conjugal units leads one to believe that to some degree all the factors mentioned here have some bearing on the matter.

Aunt–Niece. The structural relations between aunts and nieces were of less importance than those of aunts and nephews. It made less difference whether the aunt were a paternal or an avuncular one. The primary reason for this was the fact that the relation was a temporary one in any case. Paternal aunts married out of the family and so broke the relation. The nieces of avuncular aunts married out of the family, and thus this set of relations was broken, though on the whole it was likely to be of longer duration than those of paternal aunts and nieces. In either case a certain degree of respect and obedience was due the aunt, though the strength of the solidarity was small save where the aunt acted in her husband's name.

The relation between paternal aunts and their nieces was largely confined to the early childhood of the nieces, and therefore they were a part of the warmth and attention with which the young child was surrounded in China. In the ordinary case, however, the aunt left the family before her niece entered the *yu-nien* period or during its early stages. The relations involving avuncular aunts continued from the entrance of the aunt and niece into the family by marriage and birth respectively until the marriage of the latter. Both aunt and niece were part of the feminine household and so were thrown together a great deal. Just as in the case of nephews, some jealousy clouded the relationship if the aunt felt her niece was receiving better treatment than her own daughter or son, but the issue was less likely to arise than in the case of nephews since girls, because of their essentially transitory family relationship, were far less likely to become a focus of such competition. In general, the relationship shared in the intimacy and warmth that characterized the relations in the feminine side of the household. The feminine side of the household could and often did become a scene of intense rivalry and jealousy for reasons which have been mentioned from time to time above, but save for the relation between mother-in-law and daughter-in-law, intimacy rather than avoidance was institutionally expected despite the fact that its realization was extremely precarious.

Brother's Wife–Brother's Wife. This relationship was peculiarly likely to be a source of unrest in the family in which married brothers lived together. Ideally speaking, these sisters-in-law were expected to have a relationship based on mutual respect, coöperation, and affection. The continued unity of the family, particularly after the death of the brother's father, depended to a considerable degree on their ability to live in harmony. When relations between sisters-in-law went well, the picture was simple enough. The solidarity involved had little strength because it could be overridden not only by various male members of the family but also by the mother-in-law; but when harmony was achieved, there was a high degree of affection and a quite intimate relationship.

On the surface one might have expected a strong motivation for close and intimate bonds between these women. They shared whatever misery and frustration was involved in the position of daughter-in-law, and that common lot might well have served to unite them by a strong bond of mutual sympathy and given them a forum for at least verbal release from this important source of frustration and aggression. Actually the reverse was probably more often the case. The sources of conflict between sisters-in-law would seem to have been considerably more potent than the forces calling for unity. Although other factors were involved, the crux of the situation was the personality of the mother-in-law. If the mother-in-law were exacting and harsh, the chances of sister-in-law conflict were greater. There was a real motivation for one daughter-in-law to reinforce the mother-in-law's treatment of another daughter-in-law. The first daughter-in-law had, other things being equal, an advantage over subsequent daughters-in-law in that by the time of their arrival she was already somewhat acclimated to the family. The sister-in-law of longest residence in the family could to some degree minimize her own status as a stranger by emphasizing that of her sister-in-law.[15] Such action could not have failed to make relations between the two more difficult.

Another aspect of this difficulty lay in the fact that there was always a possibility in the case of a harsh mother-in-law of sisters-in-law taking an opportunistic point of view and competing for favor by playing sister-in-law against sister-in-law and sister-in-law against mother-in-law. The possibility of so shifting burdens to another and avoiding unfavorable attention always existed. At this point it must be noted that the institutional structure of the family biased the sisters-in-law in favor of the opportunistic course of action rather than the course of unity. Such was the power of the mother-in-law that, were she a harsh and unjust person, her daughters-in-law could rarely hope to alleviate their situation either singly or as a group, and, therefore, the path of unity was restricted to a more or less negative, albeit important, method of release of emotions. The opportunistic course, however, offered greater possibility of relief. If a daughter-in-law could shift the burden of her own duties or failure to a sister-in-law or become a favorite of her mother-in-law at a sister-in-law's expense,[16] positive release was possible for her. Furthermore, the ideal was that she please her mother-in-law, and little attention was paid to her methods of achieving it. Such considerations were certainly a factor in making the large households so notorious for the intrigues and conflicts which featured the relations between family members.

There was another source of conflict between sisters-in-law based on the fear or jealousy of preference shown to the husbands or children of one another. Such conflict was unavoidable, perhaps, and only strong and tactful measures could prevent it from disrupting the family. It was complicated after the death of the parents-in-law by the fact that the wife of the eldest brother then assumed the mother-in-law's headship of the *hu*. While her control was never as great as that of the mother-in-law, her sisters-in-law were definitely her subordinates, and after the experience of mother-in-law domination they were not likely to care for domination by

[15] See above p. 123 for discussion of this factor in relation to the mother-in-law's treatment of the daughter-in-law.

[16] It was unlikely that she could shift her responsibilities or blame for her failures to persons in the family other than a sister-in-law. The higher family status of other members gave them an advantage over her. Their word was more likely to be accepted than hers. In fact, one of the hard aspects of the daughter-in-law's lot was the tendency of the other members to shift their responsibilities and blame to her.

one of their own number. The way out, of course, was to persuade one's husband to split up the family and set up his own unit in which his wife could take over the headship of the *hu*.

For these reasons at least, and possibly for others as well, the relationship between sisters-in-law was by no means always a coöperative, warm relationship. Even when the situation was ideal, the balance maintaining harmony was precarious, and this helped make the unbroken continuation of a family for four full generations unusual even among wealthy gentry families.

Husband–Concubine. The taking of a concubine was often a most casual affair in a Chinese family which could afford such a luxury, and the concubine's status was by no means that of a wife. The concubine owed her husband great respect and complete obedience. Much more than a wife she was something of a body slave for her husband. He on his side was expected to treat her kindly. Her children had equal legitimacy with those of his wife and assumed regular places in the relative age precedence picture with their half brothers and sisters. Sometimes the children of the wife were shown preference, and the concubine's children were teased about their mother's inferior status, but such treatment was considered unjust and improper. In addition the concubine could, if her husband chose, become his full wife upon the death of his previous wife. If she did, her position was greatly improved, but it was probably also disruptive of family unity, though perhaps no more so than the introduction of a totally new wife would have been.

The strength of the relationship was great in terms of the husband's domination of the concubine, but the husband's obligations to his concubine were even weaker than those to his wife. Their relations, while physically intimate, were not necessarily characterized by intimacy apart from their physical relations. Any real companionship between the two was frowned upon, but it sometimes existed. Institutionally speaking, their solidarity was expected to be both weaker and less intense than the relation between husband and wife. Often the concubine saw little or nothing of her husband save for their periods of physical contact. Although the strength of their solidarity was expected to be less than that existing between husband and wife and the emotional intensity milder, it was not always so in reality. A man often chose his own concubine. Therefore there was more opportunity for the relationship to be based on patterns of romantic love than in the case of a wife chosen by someone else, and the emotional intensity of the husband-concubine relationship might not only be positive and great, but might far exceed that of husband and wife. Although a man was not supposed to neglect his wife in favor of his concubine,[17] nothing was said if he had a warmer emotional relation with her. On the other hand, if he permitted the strength of his relationship with his concubine to exceed that of his relationship with his wife, his action was certainly frowned upon.

Other Family Members–Concubine. The concubine's position in the family was a precarious one. She could easily become a focus for aggression, and she had little defense against it. Her status was inferior to that of a wife, and she was supposed to be subordinate to her husband's wife. Relative to her husband's wife she was in a position which combined aspects of a servant role along with family membership, but at death she was entered on the ancestral tablets. If she were chosen by the wife or taken at the wife's behest, the chances of smooth relations between them were greatly improved. Since she was subject to the wife's authority much as a daughter-in-law was to her mother-in-law, a jealous wife could make a concubine's life miserable in the extreme. In the *Dream of the Red Chamber,*[18] a wife named Phoenix does just this to a concubine her husband has taken without her consent.

In general a concubine was likely to be a source of disruption in the family. Her relations with her husband's wife and other concubines were subject not only to sexual rivalries but also to jealousy over the position of their respective children. It made some difference whether or not the concubine was of nearly the same age as the wife or much younger. If she were nearly the same age sexual rivalry might be sharpened, and if she were much younger she might pose the problem of sexual rivalry between father and son. In general, her relations with the other males of the household were expected to be of the avoidance type. If they were not, all sorts of rivalries could be started. Of these the most seriously disruptive type of rivalry was that between father and son, but sometimes brothers came into conflict with brothers, uncles with nephews and cousins with

[17] In the novel *Chin P'ing Mei,* there is a famous scene in which the first wife rebukes her husband for not spreading his attentions more equally among all his concubines and herself instead of giving all his attention to his favorite, Golden Lotus. See II, 579.

[18] *Op. cit.,* pp. 273–296.

cousins over concubines. Since such relations violated the incest taboo, any such incident which came into the open was quite serious.

A concubine could become a source of family strain in ways other than by coming into conflict with the wife or by being consciously or unconsciously a source of sexual rivalry among the males in the family. She might upset the ordinary structure of relative age and generational roles. If a concubine were introduced by the *chia-chang* after his sons were married, she might be younger than their wives, but as their father's concubine she would have a certain precedence in some matters over the daughters-in-law. Upon the death of the *chia-chang's* wife she might even become their mother-in-law. If she did, no matter how kindly she was toward them, she was sure to be a target for their envy and resentment. Her children were a threat to their children since her children had a status of brothers and sisters of the daughters-in-law's husbands. Since there was equal division among male heirs, her sons cut down the inheritance of their sons in a proportionate degree.

Concubines of family members other than the *chia-chang* also posed the problems of rivalry and jealousy, though perhaps not so acutely. The various possible permutations and combinations in these respects were numerous and complex, varying widely with family size. The conflicts, of course, centered on the relations of the concubine with the mature members of the family. With the children her relations were different. She was frequently given the somewhat more tedious aspects of the care of the small children of the family. If she vented her own pent-up feelings on the children, she could upset them considerably, but this does not seem to have been often the case. On the contrary, the concubines of the family often figured as a source of affection and indulgence for the smaller children, but here again the situation was complex and the scattered hints which are available are unintegrated and inconclusive.

Grandparents–Grandchildren. The solidarity of this relationship seems to have had great strength. Since the grandparents took precedence over the parents from the parents' point of view, they were always in a position to enforce their will. At the same time the situation was different from the relationship of the child with his parents. This was particularly true of the grandfather's role.[19] The child, of course, owed his grand-

[19] Only the paternal grandparents enter consideration since the maternal grandparents lived in another family.

parents obedience and great respect. Relations between grandparents and grandchildren, however, were frequently based on intimacy rather than avoidance. Sometimes the grandfather, like the father, maintained his reserve and his grandchildren respected him and kept out of his way as much as possible, but often the case was otherwise. A grandfather had one great advantage over a father. Although he had great privilege as to his use of his grandson, he did not have to take direct and immediate responsibility for the boy's training and care. Therefore a warmth and intimacy frequently absent between father and son was possible between grandfather and grandson. There is little reason to doubt that these relationships were frequently both warm and intimate and were characterized by great positive emotional intensity. When such was the case, it furnished the outstanding and almost unique example in the family of the positive correlation of great strength of solidarity and great positive emotional intensity.

This relative advantage of grandparents over parents raised an interesting possibility for opportunism. The relations between father and son were subject to great strain as suggested above, and the only possible release from such strain lay in abandonment of the family, which was generally unthinkable and impractical, or in appeal to some higher authority. The only higher authority that could really operate effectively in such a situation was that of the grandparents. A son was particularly likely to seek in this relationship an easement of his situation with his father. Pao-Yü, the hero of the *Dream of the Red Chamber,* typifies the consciousness of the possibilities of exploiting this situation. Pao-Yü feared his father and wherever possible used his grandmother, whose spoiled favorite he was, as a screen to protect him from his father's wrath. His father was also aware of the elements of the situation, and on one occasion he beat Pao-Yü quite severely, but he first ordered his servants to stand guard and see that no word of it reached his mother.[20]

The possibility of manipulation of the family situation no doubt played its role in the family intrigues of China. Such manipulation was likely to be futile in the long run since one's parents generally survived one's grandparents and could regain command. The frustration parents had previously suffered in these respects was not calculated to make them more lenient with the manipulators. Furthermore, such manipulation put

[20] *Op. cit.,* pp. 173–181.

strains on the relations between the parents and the grandparents. Since the strains existing between the father and his father and the mother and her mother-in-law were often considerable, such intrigue augmented important strains already existent. Miss Yao Tz'u-Ai in her discussion of mother-in-law–daughter-in-law conflicts cites interference with the discipline of the grandchildren as a major source of difficulty in these respects.[21]

The integrative aspect of these relationships must not be overlooked, however. The warmth and affectionate response afforded grandchildren by their grandparents was important in and of itself, but it was especially important because it afforded a source of such gratification and because the persons forming this source held high status. It has been mentioned above that the sources of such warmth and response were usually vulnerable to other solidarities, but here was a source which was not similarly vulnerable. The only factor which could effectively cut off this source of affectionate response was the death of the grandparents. This was a significant factor in the integration of family structure. To some extent the strain between father and son was offset by the fact that the son had an ally in his grandfather. There was an obverse side to this, as mentioned above, but it must nevertheless have made considerable difference that a man came into his own when his father died, but when his grandfather died he often lost a source of affectionate and intimate support.

Unlike a great deal of the material above on uncles, aunts, and concubines which applied less generally to the peasant families than to those of the gentry because of the smaller size and economic situation of the former, the grandparent-grandchild relationship was prominent in peasant families. Disruption of child discipline by the grandparents was probably much less prominent, however, in peasant than in gentry families. This may be explained by the earlier curbing of the power of the aged in peasant families. Thus the strength of this solidarity must have suffered a *de facto* reduction. At the same time it was offset by the greater intimacy of peasant fathers and sons.

Other Relationships. An attempt has been made to treat the basic types of kinship solidarities encountered in the smallest membership unit of the kinship structure. In actuality these units were capable of wide variation in the number and kinds of members they contained. Any attempt

[21] *Op. cit.,* pp. 268–270.

to enumerate all possible variations would be unnecessarily lengthy and specific. The above relationships may be taken as the basic generalized ones and the remaining variants may be derived from them. One of the most prominent of these variants may be taken as an example. The gentry family included oftentimes a large number of cousins of the same surname and occasionally cousins of different surnames.[22] Institutionally speaking, the solidarities between these cousins were simply modified versions of the various sibling relationships (brother-brother, brother-sister, sister-sister) described above. Some additional allowance was made for whether or not the father of one cousin was an older or younger brother of the father of the other and for the relative ages of the two cousins.

As the variants receded farther and farther from a given individual's (ego's) direct line of descent, these relationships were modified (usually weaker and less intense) versions of the relationship of corresponding age, sex, and (perhaps, especially) generation in the direct line of descent. In the case of cousins this has already been illustrated. What in the West would be called paternal grand-uncles would in China have had solidarities with ego much after the fashion of his solidarity with his grandfather, but with some modifications in strength and intensity depending primarily on who held the *chia-chang* position and hence which member of the grandfather's generation was the oldest. Similarly the relation between ego and a male cousin's wife was a modified version of ego's relation to the wife of one of his brothers.

On the other hand, as the variants went higher or lower in the direct line of descent, the modifications were of a different order. Usually such modifications were stronger as the relation went higher in the generational scale. Thus if ego's great grandfather still lived in the family, he owed him even greater respect and obedience than he owed his grandfather. In the direct line of descent the variants were naturally confined to earlier or later generations of grandparent or grandchild, in a stronger or weaker direction depending on which generation the person taken as ego belonged to.

The variants which have been discussed are based upon greater or lesser proliferation of the lines of descent and the number of family members, but another type of variant was also possible. It was quite

[22] A cousin of a different surname was likely to be a girl brought in, often with the intention of future marriage to one of the family sons of her own generation.

within the realm of possibility that the institutionally acceptable relative arrangement and distribution of solidarities might be controverted. Particularly with regard to the factor of intensity, variation was likely to take place, if indeed it was not inevitable. The larger the number and variety of family members, the greater was the possibility and probability of such variations. It is possible for institutional structures to decree and enforce that relationship A take precedence over relationship B, but it cannot be effectively decreed in any specific case that individual X love, hate, or respect individual Y more than individual Z. The institutional structure may be such as to expect X to act in this fashion and motivate him in this direction, but, if for one of a number of possible reasons, X does not conform in either his emotions or their intensity, the institutional structure cannot enforce the requirement. On the other hand if the various aspects of the social structure involved are not such as to motivate conformity in these respects on the part of a large percentage of the persons coming within its purview, the institution will in the long run have to change.

In view of the inability of any institutional structure to enforce a given degree of emotional intensity in a specific concrete solidarity, the marked distinction drawn by the institutional structure of the "traditional" Chinese family between the strength of a solidarity and its positive or negative emotional intensity is a striking feature. At the risk of certain difficulties mentioned above, the institutional pattern sacrificed personal feelings to the preservation of the family unit. The ideal sought was a large and stable family unit, one which could divide along definite lines and could avoid disintegration based solely on the personal whims of its members. Had the structure focused on the emotional intensity of solidarity, it would have inevitably biased the family structure in the direction of a sort of individualism based on family preferences. In a large family of many members certain emotional intensities not in conformity with the ideal patterns or arising from situations not covered by those patterns were inevitable, and such factors were in the long run disruptive of family unity if unchecked. By the institutionalization of respect and even avoidance, but above all by the institutionalization of an overriding precedence for those solidarities on which the continued stable existence of the family structure depended, the institutional patterns of "traditional" China ensured the existence of the structure until its stability was threatened from quite a different quarter than the emotional preferences of its members.

CHAPTER FIVE

THE KINSHIP SUBSTRUCTURE OF ECONOMIC ALLOCATION

IN a foregoing chapter on role differentiation, quite a number of things have been said about the economic aspects of Chinese family life; the economic variable as a defining factor in role differentiation has been discussed with some elaboration. It is now necessary to take up much of the same material, but from a different point of view, the structural components of the process of economic allocation which featured the family structure of "traditional" China. To a greater extent than has formerly been the case this section requires the introduction of factors outside the family units proper. The necessity is not so great in the "traditional" period as it is in the "transitional" period, but it is significant nevertheless. It has its origin in two factors discussed in that part of Chapter I devoted to the general aspects of the substructure of economic allocation. Dividing this substructure into the structure of production and that of consumption, one finds that the structure of production brought the Chinese family into contact with the general structure of occupational roles and the structure of production of the whole society; the structure of consumption brought the Chinese family into contact with the general structure of trade and exchange of the whole society.

Actually in "traditional" China the degree to which the outside contact went in any family was rather limited by modern Western standards and was much more limited in the case of the peasantry than in the case of the gentry. If one is to understand the "traditional" period in any degree, it is essential to understand and appreciate the relative degree and structural significance of the self-sufficiency of the family. The Chinese family was an extremely tightly knit group, and it placed overwhelming structural emphasis on the loyalty of group members to one another. Therefore the degree to which its members could rely on their own efforts to secure their economic requirements without involving themselves with outsiders was of great importance to the family structure.

Since there were sharp differences between the peasants and gentry in these respects the case of the peasants will be outlined first and the gentry variations then discussed. This is something of a reversal of general procedure in this study, but whereas in the general matter of institutional patterns the gentry set the ideals from which variation took place, the peasants were the major determinants of the economic structure of the society. It may be shown within the next few years that both Western and Oriental scholars have characteristically underestimated the role played by merchants and traders in China, but even if the balance is considerably redressed, as seems necessary, the picture of Chinese economic structure as overwhelmingly based on peasant agriculture is hardly likely to be disturbed.

To a large degree the peasant family of "traditional" China was economically self-sufficient in both production and consumption. In the field of agricultural production the relationship of peasant family members to persons outside the family was virtually obviated save for neighborhood coöperation unless the family members had been reduced to the status of hired agricultural laborers. If the family entered any form of nonagricultural production as it commonly did, that too was ordinarily done on a family basis and if not, was likely to be done on a neighborhood basis. Although at peak seasons neighbors sometimes gathered together to help one another out, and although local "public works" projects were carried out by either voluntary or drafted labor of the local residents, the vast majority of production in "traditional" China was carried out by the coöperative efforts of a single family group. The family work group was maintained to a surprising degree even in merchant and handicraft activities, especially the latter. Handicraft work was generally carried out on a small scale by workers who, if not actually members of the same family, lived together in great or lesser imitation of a family. All members of a *hu* were not necessarily relatives, but they tended to be treated on a paternalistic basis. The hierarchy of servants in gentry families, for example, seems to have varied directly with the hierarchy of the people they served, and an apprentice to a craftsman tended to be treated as a sort of inferior son of the master.

The structural significance of such a work group lay in the fact that it minimized contact with outsiders for the purposes of production, and required that, so far as occupational roles were concerned, the average peasant had to be something of a jack of all trades. It is not insignificant that the production side of the Chinese economy has always been so predominantly agricultural in nature. Any other situation would have placed great strain on the Chinese family structure, since it would have required a far larger number of economic interdependencies with non-family members even if the production of family members could have been kept on a family basis. Production of a commercial, handicraft, or industrial sort not only absorbs too much time of the productive family members to allow a family to be self-sufficient as regards food, but commonly such enterprises have tended to locate in centralized urban areas. The premium thereby placed on the immediately accessible land for home and work sites has made it virtually impossible for the average worker to live conveniently near to the best or better locations for his primary nonagricultural occupational roles and to a site suitable to allow his family to be self-sufficient in agricultural products. Modern industry and trade make the problem more acute, but the basic problem is equally inherent in any society whose economic structure is not overwhelmingly agricultural.

The relevance of economic self-sufficiency to the long stability of the Chinese family structure or to the stability of any such family structure cannot be overemphasized. Such a family structure required the inclusion of as many aspects of life as possible within the family structure of administration and control. The degree of economic self-sufficiency was crucial because a relatively slight decrease in the degree of such self-sufficiency was likely to mean a disproportionately great increase in the number of contacts with outsiders both as regards production and consumption. Increased contacts were in turn not only likely to focus a greater amount of attention away from the family, but were also likely to afford possibilities for greater independence of the family members, should internal pressures make such independence desirable.

The average Chinese peasant family did not confine its operations to agriculture. The agricultural seasons and methods were such that there were considerable periods of freedom from agricultural chores. The fact that the average Chinese family raised little if any livestock beyond a few chickens and perhaps a pig (and in relatively prosperous families a donkey or water buffalo) meant that this source of year-round occupation was lacking. In their "spare" time the male workers, whose job it was to care for the fields, occupied themselves with the production of the nonagricultural requirements of the family. They repaired the house, built furniture, made baskets, containers, and various tools, and took care of a thousand such matters. Despite the fact that this involved the farmers in many aspects of handicraft work, the work lacked at least three aspects of what is customarily considered the true handicraft role: (1) it was unspecialized, (2) the level of skill was frequently much lower than that of ordinary handicraft work, and (3) such production was not intended primarily for sale but for home consumption and was considered a subsidiary occupation to farming.

The structure of production also involved the household roles of production such as management, cooking, sewing, care of children, and the like. As has been brought out above in the chapter on role differentiation, these tasks fell to the women of the family. The important consideration was that all these roles of production were filled by family members rather than by outsiders, thereby maintaining the self-sufficiency of the family.

On the consumption side of the picture the Chinese family also operated as a self-sufficient unit insofar as possible. Here, however, certain limitations were severely set. Three of these were intimately connected with production. The first of these was payment for rent. A considerable number of Chinese peasant families farmed either partially or wholly as tenants. A sizable percentage of the yearly income, usually payable in rice or cash, was required to pay rent which placed a severe drain on the family. The second of these was the yearly tax payment. Taxes were not only heavy but were also capricious. Unfortunately, from the point of view of the peasants, they were capricious in the wrong direction. Often taxes were collected more than once in a year. The peasants had little or no positive control over the levy of these taxes which represented a net loss to the family and the community each year. Taxes were payable in cash or in rice, and at times the tax burden reduced many families to tenancy or worse. The third of these limitations on self-sufficiency with respect to consumption consisted of the few items which the average peasant household had to have but could not produce. They included iron for tools (and often the shaping of the tools), ceremonial objects such as paper money for sacrifices, and a few food items of which the most important was salt. These were sometimes paid for in kind, but often had to be paid for in cash.

The requirement of cash was important because cash was a commodity which could be produced only through intermediaries, and often it was required at a time when conversion was either impossible or unprofitable (for example, just before a harvest or during a season of glut). If cash were required and was not available through exchange, the peasant was usually forced to resort to a money lender. The interest rates were usurious to a degree sometimes exceeding one hundred per cent interest per year. In fact so usurious were interest rates that a peasant who once got into debt rarely got out through agricultural efforts alone. The only security for such a loan was usually the peasant's land, and thus his land gradually passed to the money lender, and the peasant gradually became a tenant. The payment of interest was not unlike payment of rent, and as a result peasants often did not know whether their status was that of debtor or tenant.[1]

Since the acquisition of cash required exchange, it increased the number of relations between the family and outsiders. Often the number of relations were increased several times by the need for conversion of goods to cash. Usually these relations were kept to a minimum. The average peasant in China rarely went further away from home than the local market. These markets were of several types, and one or another of them was always to be found within a few *li* of any village on one or more days each month.[2] Most of the local markets had a fairly stable membership, and in his dealings with them a peasant in many cases saw only familiar faces. If the peasant went farther afield than the local markets, he found himself in an alien world and one into which, without some entree through a friend or relative, he stood little chance of entering successfully.

These three requirements which brought the family members into contact with outsiders in the matter of their expenditures were kept to a minimum, and in addition such contacts were generally made by one

---

[1] Chen Han-Seng, *Landlord and Peasant in China* (New York, 1936), pp. 60–95.

[2] Mr. Yang Ching-Kun in his paper entitled *A North China Local Market Economy* (Institute of Pacific Relations, New York, 1944) has afforded Western students some excellent if brief material on local markets in China.

person, the *chia-chang*. Women were kept out of such contacts as far as possible, and, although peasant women had more such contact directly than gentry women, they were far more restricted than men.

The gentry presented a different picture in "traditional" China. Compared to the degree of self-sufficiency of the peasant families, that of the gentry families was quite limited. As noted above, in the production of income the gentry did not contribute directly by their own efforts in any household labor or otherwise, although they did perform managerial tasks. These tasks involved the members of such families in much broader contacts outside the family than did the production side of the peasant family economy. To some degree the contacts were minimized by the virtual exclusion of women from such spheres. More important, however, was the fact that all the major aspects of such contacts were usually concentrated in the hands of a single individual, the *chia-chang*. We have already pointed out some of the implications of this concentration of income-deriving roles in gentry families and the contrast of this situation with that of peasant families in which all the males shared the burdens of production. Now it must be added that, in a somewhat artificial manner, it gave the gentry family something of a semblance of the same self-sufficiency that existed in fact in the peasant family, because it limited outside contacts to the family member least likely to disrupt the family by his use of them.

Another group of factors aided in insulating the gentry from a lack of self-sufficiency in production. The outside contacts in which the gentry were involved by virtue of their sources of income were not likely to furnish any appeal or opportunity as an alternative way of life. No gentry member was likely to seek escape from a gentry family by taking up a tenant's status, for example. Merchants as a class had extremely low prestige, and gentry dealings with them were likely to involve one's official position and/or influential connections rather than an actual investment in the enterprise.[3]

The income from the use of political position, the prestige of intellectualism, and influential connections for private aggrandizement has

[3] Commerce in China required a sort of "protection" not at all unlike that afforded prostitution, gambling, and other of the less savory aspects of city life in the United States before and since the turn of the last century. In China, as in the United States, the income possibilities of such political "protection" were enormous, and many bona fide gentry were silent partners of this order in commercial ventures.

been commented on at great length by many scholars, Western and Eastern, present and past. Such income sources have no doubt not been carefully enough analyzed, but the fact of their existence is certainly unquestionable. In a sense this source of income offered the real possibility of alternative support to gentry members who wished to free themselves of their subordination to the family. Although graft and corruption often came to override and dominate the examination system which, ideally speaking, was the correct road to political power and prestige, this path was one of the main paths of social mobility and the sole one with criteria which were in theory at least universally determined and objectively judged.

Since all good gentry fathers urged their sons to study for the examinations, and since inevitably a certain number of them passed, why did not sons irked by the restraints of the family seize upon this opportunity to free themselves of it? No doubt some did, but it still did not afford a real threat to the family structure. The major factor which prevented this path to political power and prestige from disrupting the family structure lay largely in the fact that the intellectual and disciplinary background of the bureaucracy was overwhelmingly oriented to and in support of that family structure which it might otherwise have subverted indirectly. The civil service had as its model a family. The emperor was in the position of *chia-chang,* and the various scholars were as his sons, grandsons, and so on, depending on their place in the hierarchy. Disloyalty in such a hierarchy was analogous to unfilial conduct. The bulk of the intellectual training for the hierarchy lay in the Chinese Classics, and these works were taught for their value in teaching right conduct and not for their value in stimulating independence of thought. Thus the persons most likely to succeed initially were not the best potential rebels, and once they were established in the hierarchy, the more independent spirits were less likely to rise. In addition, unfilial conduct toward his family could result in the dismissal of an official. One may say that this represented an indirect intrusion of particularistic factors in the bureaucracy, and so it did. The fact remains that the one set of occupational roles most likely to appeal to members of the gentry and offer them a basis for economic independence of the family was insulated against its use for such purposes.

There remains the possibility of the use of the prestige and connections of the educated man apart from his actually holding office. This did afford a source of income which to a degree was independent of the family. The exclusive resort to such a source of income did not have high prestige. Gentry on the down grade frequently made use of their learning to mulct the peasants. Such men were called *lieh-shen,* a term of great opprobrium in China. Schoolteaching, of course, was another alternative. None of these were really threatening to the stability of the gentry family, however, because they too were progressively less available to the unfilial son. Influence, connections, and teaching jobs, while not out of the question for the rebel son, were less likely to accrue to him. The people who counted in such matters were almost sure to frown on just such conduct as his.

On the consumption side the gentry family was far more vulnerable than on the production side, especially by contrast with the peasants. Again steps were taken to minimize the outside contacts of the women, but this was not achieved entirely, the less so when the family dwelt in a large city. With the male side of the family, controlling such outside contacts was not even attempted. The gentry had far vaster resources to devote to consumption than the peasants, and that alone radically changed the situation as regards self-sufficiency. For example, the household tasks which were performed by family members in peasant families were performed by servants in the gentry families. This meant that the group performing these tasks was not the group enjoying their fruits. This in turn meant the introduction into the family of a whole distinct group of people apart from family members. Actually these servants were as completely integrated into the family as possible. Maids sometimes became concubines, and young servants were even adopted into the family on account of exceptional talent or merit.[4] This integration of the servants into the family life has contributed to the statistical problem of distinguishing household and family, a distinction discussed above; but it also returned to the gentry family a semblance of the self-sufficiency which

---

[4] In the *Dream of the Red Chamber,* when the maid, Loyal Goose, of the Matriarch commits suicide upon the death of the Matriarch she is ordered buried as the Matriarch's granddaughter, and Pao-Yü is ordered by his father to honor the maid as his elder sister. The fact that the maid was dead did not make her incorporation into the family either less real or less effective. She became thereby one of the ancestors, an unimportant one perhaps, but important as an ancestor nonetheless, and no longer a servant. See pp. 356–360.

featured the peasant families. Any actual tasks performed by gentry women in the household, such as the making of shoes, working for the mother-in-law, and the like were, as observed before, more important for their symbolization of status than for their economic significance.

All the goods consumed by the gentry had to be brought in from outside. As a result, the family required contacts with various local petty tradesmen. Many of the purchases were delegated to the servants. This kept the contact of the women with outsiders to a minimum. On the other hand, there were other expenditures either unknown or strictly limited in peasant families. Although the indulgence in the pleasures of wine, women, and gambling were by no means unknown to the peasant man, he was very much limited in these respects. The purchase of costly clothes, jewels, art objects, and the like were completely out of the reach of peasants.

Despite the fact that the relative lack of self-sufficiency of the gentry family both in production and consumption was not of a sort necessarily disruptive of family stability, there can be little doubt that the perspective of the members was broadened by these contacts and that a basis for comparison was afforded them which was lacking to the peasants. Especially were those gentry living in large cities subject to distractions of various sorts which might tend to draw the interests of the individual away from his family. In China, too, the complaint was heard that in the large cities families degenerated, that the sons were more filial and the wives less provocative in the more rural settings. Since the gentry were exposed to such disintegrative forces rather than the peasantry who rarely neared the urban centers, it was perhaps significant that the gentry families maintained the *li* with so much more discipline. The rigid discipline of the *li* certainly created strains, but just as certainly it held the family together. Without this discipline city gentry families might have disintegrated far faster than they did.

The actual structure of production and consumption in the "traditional" Chinese family merits closer inspection. Certain of the aspects of self-sufficiency are so crucial for the understanding of what is taking place in "transitional" China, that more must be said of it. In a sense production of income has been more strategic for the purposes concerned than consumption. There is probably some reason to maintain that in general the structure of production has a somewhat greater effect upon the total social structure than does the structure of consumption. Obviously this point must be used warily, for the two aspects of economic life are most intimately connected and exert a mutual influence of great importance on one another. A major factor in this matter is the general necessity of spending more time engaged in the one aspect of life than the other. That a greater amount of time and effort has been required for production than that devoted to consumption has been an inescapable feature of the lives of the vast majority of individuals in virtually all known societies.[5] This was certainly the case in China. With the exception of the gentry who had the economic basis for avoidance of the problem, all others in the society spent on production a large multiple of the time and effort spent in consumption. The working hours of the peasants and the craftsmen were long and hard, and days of respite were few. It is true that peasants had periods of enforced "idleness," but to a considerable degree they were taken up by hard work on tools, housing, or the like. To be idle in China, unless one was relatively well off, was a tragedy. It may be readily granted that the average peasant spent his hours away from the fields in very inefficient forms of production, but he probably spent a large proportion of them in toil. Tea drinking was for the wealthy and the aged, including in the former category the marginal gentry whose economic foundations were fast disintegrating.

Not only did the peasant devote much time per year to production, but a great many years of his life, as well. Child labor existed throughout China among the poor with very rare exceptions, and the labor period of life extended until physical disability made further work impossible. One has only to consider the proportions of a peasant's income taken by taxes and rent to see how strictly the personal consumption of these people was limited. Rents probably averaged forty per cent or more of production on rented land, and taxes were what the traffic could bear. Peasants owning their own land usually paid such high taxes that there was little

[5] It is not insignificant that the Western Bible with its own approach to the problem of evil as well as other problems begins with a justification of the fact that man is unable to spend all or a vast majority of his time in the delights of consumption. From the point of view of economics, Eden afforded a setting for life which made possible a maximum of consumption for a minimum of effort. Mankind was perplexed by the problems posed by the lack of free goods in nature long before the day of the classical economists of Western Europe. In almost all ethical and religious systematizations such considerations have played a vital role.

to choose economically between their status and that of tenants. The government was supported in large part from the land tax, and the gentry were supported almost entirely by rents and by the graft that could be squeezed out of the land tax. The merchants and artisans found their domestic customers almost entirely among the gentry, so that indirectly their income came from the same sources as that of the gentry. While the peasants probably constituted over eighty per cent of the members of the society, the amount taken out of their personal consumption by this structure was still considerable.

To the degree that production occupies more time and has greater effect on the social structure than does consumption, the interrelation of the two may bring about startling effects. A relatively small change in consumption may bring about considerable changes in production. At the same time, changes in consumption may be brought about by slight changes in production. This factor is mentioned here merely for the aid it may afford in understanding the rather far-reaching effects which sometimes result from rather small changes in economic structure.

The gentry picture has been briefly sketched above, and it has been shown that while the contacts were more varied and the outsiders contacted more numerous, the impact of the contacts on the family was minimized. The gentry, however, came into contact with one type of occupational role for which no counterpart existed in the rest of Chinese society. The gentry through their education came into contact with the examination system and the bureaucracy of the government. There has been no attempt to set up any taxonomy of occupational roles, but something of the discipline and sphere of the peasant occupational role has been discussed and those of craftsmen and merchants mentioned. In all these the choice of personnel was conducted on a particularistic basis, and the possibility of alternative employment on universalistic grounds was minimal. The essential criterion for employment was a person's identity. What he could do was secondary. Ability was not left out of the question entirely, especially in craftsmanship, but even here, when one apprentice proved inept, another was chosen on the basis of particularistic criteria. In farming, ability or apitude entered to an even lesser degree. The techniques involved required patience rather than skill, and hard labor above all else. Anyone with a reasonably sturdy frame could learn the necessary manipulations, if his training and inurement to hard labor began early enough.

The one factor making for universalism on the local rural scene was not the institutionalization of universalistic criteria, but a balance of forces between family and neighborhood considerations. An individual's primary obligations were always to his own family, but in village life many families had to live in close contact with one another. In this contact there were always functions to be performed which required community participation. In many parts of China the care and maintenance of the irrigation system was an outstanding feature of these community concerns, but local law and order and similar considerations were also of importance. Ruthless pursuit of individual family gains would have inevitably resulted in local conflicts. In villages composed entirely of families belonging to a single *tsu*, the *tsu* organization prevented such conflicts or settled them when they arose, and in villages of families not related by a single *tsu* organization, a council of elders performed a similar function. The balance of family interests so achieved introduced an element of universalism in the performance of community tasks and the maintenance of community standards.

The government examinations and the bureaucracy were quite another matter. In theory at least these were avowedly and self-consciously universalistic. In the first place, anyone was eligible to compete. In the second place, success in the examinations was dependent solely on ability within the field of the examinations. Finally, choice for government position was based solely upon the results of the examinations, and subsequent advance was dependent solely upon the adequacy of one's performance within his previous positions. Actually the system was far from realization of these ideals. Entry to the examinations was by no means unrestricted.[6] Certain

[6] Although scattered remarks on these various limitations of the universalism of the examination system appear in various works by Western students, the most careful documentary study of these factors is to be found in the extensive work by Professor K. A. Wittfogel and his Chinese History Project. Unfortunately, this work has not yet been published. A considerable portion of it is at present in process of publication, and a great deal more awaits future publication. Professor Wittfogel has kindly permitted me to see a large amount of this material, and while he and his coworkers can in no sense be held responsible for the views suggested here, it was this work which confirmed the scattered references found on the subject and added greatly to whatever insight into this structure I had gained. The work of Professor Wittfogel and his colleagues is far more detailed than any material here, and not only has the virtue of making available a vast amount of documentary material heretofore unavailable to Western students, but also has submitted much of this material to statistical techniques and other forms of analysis as well.

types of persons and their descendants were excluded. Criminals and their sons, for example, were always ruled out. The groups excluded from competition varied not only from dynasty to dynasty but also within a particular dynasty. Theatrical persons and their sons were often on the list of ineligibles. Most important from the point of view of the structure of the society was the fact that merchants and their sons were often excluded, but the sons of peasants seem never to have been excluded. The significance of the former lies in two facts at least. It was symbolic of the rather low status of the merchants in Chinese society. It also connoted the fear of the gentry that eligibility for the examinations might be an avenue for the entrance of members of the merchant group into the real seat of power in Chinese society. There is reason to believe that the occupational role of merchants afforded the maximum opportunity in "traditional" China for contact with and susceptibility to patterns that were at variance with the patterns held right and good by the gentry, and that the gentry were aware of the fact.

Of at least equal importance with the status implication involved in the exclusion were the consequences of this closure of the examination system to the merchants. Since the one general structure of power in the society which extended beyond the neighborhood sphere was that of the imperial bureaucracy, and since the membership of the bureaucracy was in large part drawn from the successful examination candidates, the merchants were, therefore, often excluded from institutionalized participation in the political life of the society as a whole. At the same time the bureaucracy, holding as it did absolute power in the name of the emperor, was not only charged with the regulation of commercial affairs necessary to the running of the government, but its members were also in a position within broad limits to use it for their own ends. This, of course, forced the "protection" type of alliance between merchants on the one hand and the gentry in general, and the bureaucracy officials in particular, on the other.

Another consequence of the closure was that it motivated the retirement of successful merchants, and the assumption by them of landholding status. When accompanied by a certain amount of bribery, landholding status could gain the entrance of their sons to the examination system in spite of the exclusion laws. Thus the insecurity of other forms of investment was by no means the only factor involved in the investments in land by the merchants. To the degree that the landholding activities were emphasized and the merchant functions played down or not participated in openly and directly, the eligibility of these men and their sons for gentry membership was greatly enhanced. Another immediate implication was the bias of wealthy merchants against training their sons to take over their functions in commerce. The road to approved power and prestige lay through the examination system. The training required for it was likely to vitiate one's usefulness as a merchant, but any merchant who could gain such entrance for his son would, if his son were successful, have bettered the position of his son and his family, have honored his ancestors, and have achieved as much as was deemed possible for a man living as he did.

The fact that the sons of peasants seem never to have been excluded was equally significant for the society as a whole. It meant that theoretically at least the way of ascent was open to the peasants. Actually, it was by no means so open. Education was expensive, and as noted above, there was the additional cost involved in the loss of the student's labor. There remained the further hazard that if a man failed in this field, it was probably too late at the time of his failure to train him to fit into the peasant role. As a result of the various limitations on eligibility, both formal and informal, actual candidates were overwhelmingly culled from gentry families. The popularity of the tale of the poor peasant's son who succeeded and rose to the top of the ladder had in China something of the same element of truth but more importantly the same element of romanticism as the tale of the self-made man in the United States.[7] Of course to the degree that bribery and corruption entered the system, the gentry were still further likely to monopolize the eligibility for the examinations, for theirs were the wealth and connections necessary to get their own candidates accepted or others refused.

[7] Professor Talcott Parsons has suggested an interesting analogy in these respects between the United States and China. In China, the gentry ways of life remained the ideal way of life, despite the fact that few peasants could realistically expect to attain this ideal. In the United States, the way of life of the relatively prosperous middle-class group has remained the ideal way of life for all the members of the low income groups, despite the fact that, statistically speaking, the expectations for attaining the ideal are small. The opportunities in the case of the United States are still greater than in the Chinese case, perhaps, but the difference is in many respects a matter of degree.

There were formidable safeguards against particularistic factors entering the grading of the examinations when the system worked best.[8] When corruption was widespread, however, there were many ways of tampering with the examinations. Insofar as the objective universalistic machinery could be tampered with, the gentry were in a better position to do so either in their own favor or in the favor of protégés than was any other group in the society.

The third aspect of the bureaucracy, the choice of men for positions on the basis of examination standing and the promotion of men on the basis of past performance, was also ideally framed in such a way as to minimize particularistic considerations. Here again, however, the structure was susceptible to corruption, and again the gentry were in a better position to manipulate it than was any other group. Other factors entered here, however. Quite apart from overt bribery, which was reckoned no less a sin by the Chinese than similar corruption of the civil service in the United States, particularistic factors could enter in the choice of new men and in the choice of men for promotion. There were always more successful examination candidates than there were government positions, and many of these had similar rating. The choice of a candidate related to the examiner directly or to a friend was, therefore, not difficult to justify on objective grounds. Similar factors entered the judgment of past performances and the promotion of the various officials. Furthermore, there was some overt official circumvention of universalistic criteria. At various times in history a certain number of positions were set aside to be filled by *yin* appointments, literally, "shade" appointments. A certain number of positions could be filled by the sons or other close relatives or even unrelated protégés of especially meritorious (in effect, successful) officials. As the corruption increased, the ratio of *yin* appointments to bona fide successful examinations candidates seems to have risen.

It is not puzzling that the examinations and the bureaucracy failed to maintain universalistic standards and became highly particularistic. The miracle is that, in a society overwhelmingly particularistic as Chinese society was, it could have functioned at all.[9] The keystone of Chinese social

[8] See S. W. Williams, *The Middle Kingdom* (New York, 1899), pp. 543–572. Dr. Williams's book is a mine of information on the civil service examinations, the bureaucracy, and many other aspects of China.

[9] There is some reason to believe that highly universalistic structures inherently tend to degenerate in the direction of particularism. Modern Western industrial

structure was the family, and it was a highly particularistic structure. In the long run the extremes to which the bureaucracy went to secure objectivity were not sufficient to maintain universalistic standards. When the standards broke down, they broke down along precisely the same lines that particularism was institutionalized. Graft and corruption in the structure took two major forms: (1) nepotism, and (2) seeking primarily to advance the interests (especially wealth) of one's own family rather than to perform the job in hand to the best interests of the imperial government.

In connection with the source of economic production, we must consider attachment to the land. There were many reasons for the attachment in "traditional" China, and the high value placed on land ownership tied into the social structure in many ways, several of which have already been mentioned. Only through the ownership of land could a peasant assure himself that he and his family could operate as a unit. Tenancy was only a second best because eviction was always a possibility. Actual circumstances altered the situation somewhat because any large-scale attempt by a landlord to evict tenants or to demand an unusually high amount of rent from them would be met by neighborhood resistance. The inferiority of tenancy may have been one reason why peasants accepted ruinous mortgages rather than outright sale of their land and immediate tenancy. To be forced out of tenancy was to be forced into the

---

society has carried the institutionalization of universalism further than any other known society, but the level has been extremely difficult to maintain. Of course, it cannot be maintained indefinitely in a society in which nepotism is a virtue, unless nepotism ceases to be a virtue in certain fields of action. Modern Western society, however, has found that tendencies toward particularism crop up again and again in far more subtle forms than nepotism. Recent works on labor management relations, for example, have gone into the importance of clique structures, always highly particularistic, for industrial organization. Industrial organization is by and large a stronghold of universalistic standards, so much so that attention to the significance of clique structure was probably long diverted by just this factor. The professions, the government services, industry, business, and the educational structure, to mention only a few aspects of Western life in which a major degree of universalism is institutionalized, all have elaborate social structures insulating them from the intrusion of particularistic factors. Since it is apparently so difficult to maintain such standards in a society which institutionalizes them over so broad a part of its activities, it may be presumed that it was much more difficult to maintain universalistic standards in only one sphere of action in the Chinese case.

status of a laborer. This precluded the maintenance of the family unit of production with any certainty and so precluded normal family life as well.

The division of labor in production was another important aspect of the kinship structural unit. The tendency of production in the society as a whole to divide along more or less self-sufficient family lines has been mentioned above, but the division of labor within such units was also significant. Most of the relevant material here has already been discussed in previous sections of this study, particularly in the analysis of role differentiation. Only a few of the factors will be reiterated. From the point of view of the economic substructure the most important facts about the division of labor in family production was that it was largely determined by particularistic criteria. A few examples will suffice to illustrate the point. In the first place, household work was woman's work, as was the care and rearing of infants. The training of the older children was differentiated according to sex. Boys were trained by men and girls by women. In the second place, the oldest male of the oldest generation took over the family management as a whole, and his wife or mother managed the household, regardless of ability. In the third place, the economic relations between the family and outsiders were largely conducted by the *chia-chang* or by family members to whom he had delegated such functions. The list might be lengthened indefinitely. Even as regards tasks involving physical skills, the allocation of roles was not on a universalistic basis but was on the basis of particularistic status. Thus son and father alike plowed, and the fact that one was more skilled than the other did not ordinarily result in specialization on that basis.

The division of labor roles on a particularistic basis was not confined to the family substructure of economic production. It was generally true throughout the society. The one major exception, ideally speaking, was the bureaucracy, but even the bureaucracy tended to break down to a serious degree. The fact that production roles, that is, employment, were distributed largely on the basis of particularistic criteria strongly bolstered family stability. This was true of employment inside and outside the family. Inside the family the *chia-chang* was in a position to dominate such distribution and hence avert deviation to a large degree. In outside employment the bolstering effect hung on the fact that the main basis of the particularistic criteria was the particular status of an individual's family. Therefore the resort to outside employment as a means of winning independence of the family was curtailed.

Consumption within the family was equally well integrated with the rest of the structure. It has been shown that family production was by no means a matter of "from each according to his ability" and that family consumption was by no means a matter of "to each according to his needs" unless the terms "ability" and "needs" are so defined as to make the contrary impossible. There was, nevertheless, institutionalization of the "common fund." That is to say the income of the individual family members was pooled. For the most part the degree of self-sufficiency in production of the vast majority of families, when coupled with the way in which production roles were distributed, meant that it was generally impossible to differentiate the income of the family on the basis of individuals. It was perhaps possible to make observations such as: "The men contributed the food and the women the cooking of it." It was impossible in most cases, however, to say that a given individual contributed a given number of bushels of rice. It was not even possible with complete accuracy to say that the women did not participate in the production of the food, for at some seasons they did help. Thus to a considerable degree the income of a family unit came already pooled [10] into the family. There were some few sources of income in specific peasant families of which this was not true. A given member might work part time as a servant for another family or as an agricultural helper and be paid wages, or a given family member might hold a small amount of cash out of the family funds and lend it out at interest and so receive an income. Such income was not always put into the common family funds, but it usually was, and institutionally speaking, the *chia-chang* could require that it be.

The family income was distributed from the common fund. In the case of the peasants, rent and/or taxes took a large proportion of the income. What was left went largely to the minimum physical requisites of life: food, clothing, and shelter. Any margin over and above them usually went for ceremonial expenditures, interest on loans, if any, procurement of a wife for a son, medicine, and the like. Often ceremonial expenditures were made even at the expense of expenditures on food, clothing, and shelter. Most of the consumption of the basic prerequisites for life was direct consumption of articles produced by the family members, as has been pointed

[10] This obviously applies more accurately to the peasants than to the gentry.

out in the preceding section on self-sufficiency. Some of them required cash, and it was obtained by the sale of products produced by the family. The common fund was often administered by the wife or mother of the *chia-chang*. It was not controlled by her, however. Institutionally speaking, it was controlled by the *chia-chang* and administered by the wife or mother at his direction. Since so large a portion of consumption of the low income groups went for food, clothing, and shelter and since these, especially the first two, were usually prepared and cared for by the feminine side of the household, it is not difficult to see why administration of the common fund should have drifted into the hands of the feminine head of the household. When a larger portion of the income tended to be cash, the power of the feminine household head was increased, though she could be stopped if the *chia-chang* acted quickly and firmly enough.

In the average peasant family the amount of income over and above the margin of subsistence was so slight as to create little or no problem as to its distribution. Particularistic criteria operated in the determination of consumption right up to and below the margin of subsistence. The presence of infanticide is a case in point. It is significant that female infanticide and not male infanticide was a prominent feature of hard times in China. Male infanticide may have occurred, but it was by no means so prevalent as female infanticide. Furthermore, geronticide, matricide, and patricide were not only rarer than infanticide but were also regarded as horrendous crimes, and any idea of meeting the subsistence problem in such a way would have been considered scandalously perverted and criminal.

Not all the peasants lived exactly at the physical margin of subsistence, although enough lived sufficiently close to it to make relatively slight crop failures result in numerous famine deaths.[11] In the distribution of any

[11] It has been a notorious feature of famines in the Orient in general and China in particular that the wealthy do not perish in them. Very often famines result from the fact that grain has been hoarded by speculators and landlords or removed from an area for taxes. Such famines are usually precipitated by a crop failure, but this need not be the case if the landlords or tax gatherers have not taken an unusually large toll of the agricultural production of an area. Such shortages are inevitably complicated by lack of transport facilities to haul grain from one section to another. Of course, many famines have resulted from unusually serious and widespread crop failures. Nevertheless, the consistency with which the wealthy survive these disasters argues effectively that the system of distribution is seriously at fault. In a

excess over the physical margin something of a problem arose, to be settled by the *chia-chang*. Institutionally speaking, he was the final arbiter in these respects, and there was no appeal from his decision. Even the expenditures above such a margin were usually made in accordance with old and familiar custom and along the lines of particularistic differentiation.

The limited funds available for consumption lessened the problem in an obvious way, but the limited number of types and amounts of commodities available within any given price range also restricted the problem. A modern industrialized economy increases the number and variety of alternative objects for consumption beyond all the bounds of other methods of production and has increased the problems of allocation of consumption no less than those of production.[12] The fact that "traditional" China was not industrialized lessened the problem, perhaps, but the level of production of the society was sufficient and varied enough to pose some problems. The greatest danger to the stability of the family involved in consumption was not that one member would be slighted, but rather that such surplus as existed might be turned to uses harmful to the family in the long run. The *chia-chang* was in a position to stop others, but he could not be stopped by anyone else in the family.

Gentry consumption patterns were different from those of the peasants. In the first place, the situation differed in the matter of pooling the family income. The income of a gentry family did not come into the family with its source undifferentiated, nor was it directly consumed with little intermediation of exchange. Income from offices held by individual family members could be attributed directly to an individual. Income from lands and investments came into the *chia-chang* or his representative. Some homeogeneity was achieved by virtue of the fact that income from land and other investments was viewed as family income

---

recent Chinese famine it was by no means uncommon to see persons quietly starving to death in front of shops filled with grain. In the recent book of T. H. White and A. Jacoby, *Thunder Out of China* (New York, 1946), the Honan famine of 1943 is described in some detail (see pp. 166–178). There is no denying the crop failure which increased the devastation of this famine, but it is equally obvious that there can be no full understanding of this tragedy solely in terms of that crop failure.

[12] In fact, a considerable school of modern economics seem to hold that modern Western society has handled the problem of production far more easily and with far greater skill than it has handled the problem of consumption.

rather than as belonging to any specific individual. The *chia-chang* was in complete control of it, however, and could use it as he saw fit. Technically he did not regard it as "his" income, perhaps, but neither could any other family member.

One of the most obvious forms of consumption by the gentry families which was not duplicated by the peasants was the consumption of the services of others for household production—the use of servants. The use of servants introduced a new element of consumption, and simultaneously changed the whole picture of household production. It brought a whole group of nonfamily persons into close daily contact with the family members. As noted above, the effects of this were minimized to some degree by the accordance to these servants of a sort of "second-class" family membership which resulted in highly paternalistic relations between family members and servants, and the inclusion of all in the *hu*.[13]

In addition to the presence of servants, gentry households were noticeably different from peasant households in the matter of housing. Usually sufficient funds were available to permit a much higher degree of privacy. Gentry houses were really compounds and often consisted of many buildings connected by passages or paths, all of which were enclosed by an outside wall usually formed largely by walls of the various buildings within. The greater privacy permitted far more segregation of women and men, and afforded greater opportunity for many activities which were facilitated by the possibility of privacy.

The surplus over and above the large household expenditures in a gentry family was under the direct control of the *chia-chang,* or of a person to whom he delegated the control. The surplus was sometimes reinvested, but much of it was often spent on other forms of consumption. Schooling for sons was a frequent item of expenditure, and in general

[13] The "second class" family membership of servants is frequently found in groups characterized by wealth, many household servants, and family units of continuous stable existence extending over many generations (in theory at least). The phenomenon is especially marked when the servants live on the premises. The household servants of the British aristocracy and the ante-bellum South in the United States are cases in point, though any number of others could be found. It might be suggested that the functional basis of this phenomenon is to be found in the fact that any persons in such close daily contact with the family life of members of such a family must be integrated with those members in terms of the categories of the family structure. At the same time, full induction into the family structure would interfere with their functions as servants.

large expenditures for recreation and ceremonial purposes were prominent items. More important, however, was the fact that considerable sums were often doled out for personal expenditures, usually to the males of the family. This had two somewhat conflicting aspects. On the one hand it emphasized the dependence of the recipients on the *chia-chang* and on the family, and on the other hand it permitted the recipients to engage in activities independent of the family to a degree not found among the peasants. The former, to a certain degree, may well have served as a formidable deterrent to initiative among male gentry dependents.[14] The latter certainly opened a path for the influence of these dependents by outsiders.

Another important aspect of this surplus was that it provided the means for improvement of the status of the family. The availability of funds for education was an obvious example of this, but not the only one. The lot of the average peasant was such that no matter how diligent he and his sons might be, if more than one son per generation survived to maturity, the property inheritance patterns would inevitably result in the property disenfranchisement of sons of the male descendants or the reduction of all to a tenant or agricultural laborer status, barring some source of income outside the peasant's own land. Gentry families were subject to economic pressure too, but their surplus income, if great enough and if wisely enough handled, offered the possibility of increasing the property as fast or faster than male descendants increased. Actually this was achieved in relatively few cases for more than a small number of generations. Chinese society offered mobility downward as well as upward, and the mobility down was easier and probably more frequent, except in periods of unusual prosperity. At any rate the downward tendency was sufficiently marked to require considerable diligence in the management of family funds to offset it. If the process of reinvestment of income was not kept up, the ordinary rates of reproduction would overtake the family fortune.

Actually, however, despite the danger involved for the family's future, the *chia-chang* frequently failed to invest enough of the surplus to assure the maintenance of the family fortune in his time. The surplus was often consumed in ways unproductive of income, and family capital was often invaded for such purposes. Virtually all handicraft work and international

[14] *Supra*, p. 156.

trade during the "traditional" period was consumed by the gentry, either for household or other uses, and a tremendous amount of expenditure went into gambling, pleasure seeking of various sorts, ceremonial expenditures on a competitively lavish scale, and conspicuous consumption in all its permutations and combinations. Many of these forms of indulgence were of a type subversive of family stability. The percentage of gentry families which were tumbled from high places by gambling, opium smoking, drinking, and extramarital sexual relations was probably much greater than the percentage of peasant families reduced to economic ruin from similar causes. This, insofar as it was true, was probably not due to any stronger moral fiber on the part of the peasants, but rather to their lack of the economic means to get started in such forms of indulgence.

It is perhaps justifiable to reiterate certain points in summation. In the first place, to a large degree the structure of economic production of "traditional" Chinese society was in terms of family units. The peasantry, forming more than eighty per cent of the population, were divided into family units that carried self-sufficiency in both production and consumption to great lengths. The gentry nowhere equalled the record of the peasants, but their departures from it were hedged by patterns which preserved the appearance and effect of economic self-sufficiency as far as possible. Something of the same thing was true of handicraftsmen, merchants, and the like. In the second place, the division of roles in both production and consumption throughout peasantry, gentry, and other groups was almost entirely based upon particularistic criteria. In the third place, the possibility of any sort of employment outside the family was relatively slight, and the possibility of employment outside the family on a universalistic basis was to all practical purposes nonexistent. In the fourth place, the only specifically and strongly institutionalized exception to the particularistic family basis of employment in "traditional" Chinese society was the government bureaucracy and its civil service recruiting system. At the same time, the tendency of the bureaucratic structure to break down into particularism, both as regards recruitment and advancement, was radical and marked. In the fifth place, institutionally speaking, family income was pooled under the control of the *chia-chang,* but the differences in source and composition of the income made considerable difference between gentry and peasantry. In the sixth place, virtually all peasant income after deduction for rent and/or taxes was spent on consumption of food, clothing, and shelter. These matters were usually administered by the feminine head of the household. In the seventh place, the difference in surplus of income over household expenditures between gentry and peasantry affected not only consumption but also production, and had far-reaching implications for family stability. In the eighth place, in gentry families there was inevitably greater opportunity for individual retention of income from the family fund and greater delegation of expenditure to family members other than the *chia-chang* and the feminine head of the household. And finally, although the economic control of the *chia-chang* was a powerful means of containing strains within the family unit, to the degree that it was used it increased the possibility of disruption by any factor providing the possibility of an alternative source of income on universalistic grounds.

CHAPTER SIX

THE KINSHIP SUBSTRUCTURE OF POLITICAL ALLOCATION[1]

THE allocation of power and responsibility in the "traditional" Chinese family was clearly and explicitly institutionalized both among the gentry and among the peasantry. Had the case been otherwise, the structure could not have existed stably for a period of some two thousand years. This stable system focused on three of the possible criteria of political allocation, namely, sex, generation, and relative age. Of the three, the last was of rather less importance than the other two. It is important to note that economic position, either as regards production or consumption, was not, institutionally speaking, a determining criteria.

We will discuss the political structure of the "traditional" Chinese family in terms of the three questions defined in the first chapter of this study, namely the questions of locus, definition, and procedure,[2] and within these categories elaborate the criteria of sex, generation, and relative age.

THE LOCUS OF POWER AND RESPONSIBILITY

Both gentry and peasantry families were male-dominated institutional units in which the pinnacle of authority was occupied by one person who, ideally speaking, was always a man. In actuality, as shown above, this was sometimes negated by a widowed mother, but, nevertheless, the general institutional pattern was clear enough. Moreover, the inheritance of power was through the male line, and the power positions of feminine

[1] The concepts used in this section are those defined in the initial chapter of this study (pp. 28–31). The data relevant to this section has for the most part already appeared in various sections of what has gone before. In particular, reference should be made to the section devoted to role differentiation (especially the segments of that devoted to role differentiation on the basis of age, generation, sex, and political criteria).

[2] *Supra,* Chapter I, pp. 30–31.

members of the family were allocated to them in large part as a result of their relations with the various masculine members of the family. It is not difficult to understand why women's positions were dependent upon the men to whom they were attached. In the vast majority of Chinese families, whether peasant or gentry, the women fell into two categories: (1) those who were destined to leave the family and (2) those who were brought into the family to stay until the end of their lives. The political status of the former was relatively low because, in addition to the fact that their age, sex, and generation were all of a sort that granted low status, their transitory position meant that great authority or responsibility could not long be theirs. Their status in the family, like that of all children, was primarily a function of their father's status aside from these other factors.

The political status of the second group of women was even more obviously dependent upon men, being determined by the husband's position in the family. This statement may seem to conflict with the general remarks made heretofore about the relations between mother-in-law and daughter-in-law, but closer examination will show that there is no contradiction. The daughter-in-law came under the control of the mother-in-law because of her relation to her husband, and in extreme cases the will of the mother-in-law was enforced through the son.

The pinnacle of power had to be transferred from man to man, and, since it was impossible to predict which male members would survive to inherit power, any dominance of any of them by a woman would have meant the possibility of a woman in effect succeeding to power if it came that man's turn. Thus while a son's father lived he was definitely subordinate to his mother as well as his father. After the father's death the mother was theoretically subordinate to her son, but actually the situation often continued as before, the son being subordinate to his mother.[3]

Male dominance in the matter of power was paralleled by the struc-

[3] *Supra,* pp. 129–132. Dominance by an elder sister could not have this effect. During the early childhood of a man he might be placed under the supervision and control of an older sister, in which case, within certain limits, she certainly dominated him. This situation was not, however, threatening to the stability of the general pattern for two reasons. In the first place, such dominance ended long before the male was eligible to hold the pinnacle of power, and in the second place, his sister inevitably married out of the family, and hence the possibility of her continued dominance was removed.

ture of responsibility from one point of view, while from another it was the exact reverse. Responsibility for the family and the actions of its members was owed to relatives and other persons or groups outside the family on the one hand, and to the ancestors on the other. Here the burden of greatest responsibility fell upon the person of greatest power, the *chia-chang*. Thus the major locus of power and the major locus of responsibility were focused upon the same individual, and a variance in their loci was avoided, down through the hierarchy of the structure. In this way the male side of the family always bore greater responsibility than the female side.

The second point of view, that of the family members within the family sphere, is the view of the obverse side of the power structure within the family, and from this point of view responsibility varied inversely as power. Thus wives were responsible to husbands, but the reverse was not the case. In the Chinese family the coördination of the loci of power and responsibility was not achieved by simple reciprocity between the parties to a given relation. The responsibility within the structure was never owed directly to the person over whom power was held. The way in which a father's responsibilities to his ancestors included responsibility for the proper treatment of his son has already been discussed,[4] and, in general, responsibility to the ancestors was comprised of elements of just this sort.

The second major criterion for the allocation of power and responsibility within the family was that of generation. The most important general remark to be made here is, of course, the fact that, other things being equal, the oldest generation took precedence in these matters over the younger ones. This applied throughout the structure. If the position of *chia-chang* be used again as the primary example, it may be observed that that position was held by the oldest male member of the oldest generation in the family. The emphasis on generation was of special importance in gentry families which were likely to include several male members per generation, and several generations. In such a situation, the criterion of male dominance was not sufficient to determine the succession. In peasant families the problem was less difficult. Even so, the unequivocal dominance of the younger generation by the older throughout life was of great importance, and the stability of the total structure was closely tied up with it.

[4] See pp. 168–172.

In a family in the United States compared to the "traditional" Chinese family, the dominance of the older generation holds for the early life of the individual, but it does not hold for the later life of the individual. When an individual reaches adulthood, if he is self-supporting, and it is institutionally assumed that he will be, and especially if he is married into the bargain, he is no longer required or expected to be under the dominance of his parents, nor are they expected to continue to attempt to dominate him. Respect, love, and attention for the older generation is continued, perhaps, but nothing more. There is strong reason to believe that this pattern is closely tied to the general patterns of an industrialized society. As will be shown below, something of this sort has begun to seep into China during the "transitional" period, and its incompatibility with the "traditional" Chinese pattern is all too obvious. The functional incompatibility of these two patterns is one factor seriously limiting the "compromise family system" (*che chung ti chia t'ing chih tu*) which has filled so much of the rather romantic writing of Chinese social scientists about reform of the Chinese family.[5]

In general, the balance of power and responsibility from the generational point of view was maintained in precisely the same manner as in the case of male dominance. That is to say, internally the responsibility was owed by the younger to the older generation, and power was distributed in the reverse of this. Externally, the responsibility was borne by the older generation. The orientation which kept the capricious use of power to a minimum was not toward the government or one's neighbors, or even one's *tsu* organization, but it was that toward one's ancestors. It not only kept male dominance responsible but also kept generational dominance and relative age dominance responsible. The ancestors, be it noted, were not sharply differentiated as to sex, relative age, or even generation. There was such differentiation, of course, but whether or not one was or was not an ancestor was infinitely more important than such distinctions within the category. Furthermore, orientation of responsibility to the ancestors was not differentiated on the basis of these three factors. A man did not, for example, seek the welfare of his descendants in order to honor his male as opposed to his female ancestors or even to honor the one

[5] E.g., Mai Hui-Ting, *op. cit.*, pp. 77–82; Sun Pen-Wen, *op. cit.*, pp. 110–192; P'an Kuang-Tan, *Chinese Family Problems* (*Chung Kuo Chih Chia T'ing Wen T'i*), (Shanghai, 1929), pp. 115–123.

more than the other. Such action was due the ancestors as a group. It therefore seems reasonably safe to say that if one criteria stood out above all others in its relevance to the political substructure of the Chinese family, it was that of generational precedence. The precedence of the older generation was at least as important as that of male precedence in the determination of the allocation of power within the family, and in some respects was more important, but in the allocation of responsibility, especially in the maintenance of a coördination of the loci of power and responsibility, the generation criterion was of much greater importance, since it defined ancestor status in large part.

The manner in which the coördination seems to have been obtained suggests some general formulations on this score of interest beyond the sphere of the Chinese case itself. If the proposition be accepted that a considerable discrepancy between the loci of authority and responsibility renders any structure in which it is found unstable, either in the direction of a breakdown of authority on the one hand through inability to enforce its ruling, or through the capricious use of authority resultant from lack of an effective restraining responsibility on the other hand, then it may be further observed that in any political structure in which authority is distributed from the top down and responsibility from the bottom up, as opposed to a structure in which the distribution of power and responsibility are reciprocal and equal, there must be on the part of the power holders at the top of the structure a strongly institutionalized responsibility which is owed to a person or persons (or to a group or groups) who is empirically existent or whose existence is posited by faith. The responsibility must be capable of preventing the capricious use of power by the power holders at the top of the structure. Whether prevention means resort to physical force in the last analysis or motivating the power holders in directions other than capricious use of their power may make considerable difference for the structure, but one or the other is a prerequisite, if the structure is to be stable. One implication of this for general social science investigation is the fact that no stable political structure of this type can be well understood without examining that portion of the pattern of responsibility which lies outside the structure concerned.[6]

[6] This consideration has been neglected in most treatments of the family and certainly has not been well developed in the treatment of concrete national political

It is interesting to speculate in this connection what the situation might have been in the event that Western missionaries had succeeded, as some tried, in doing away with ancestor worship in China. At the very least it may be said that a radical reformulation of the political substructure of the Chinese family would have been necessary, and, while a new stable pattern might have evolved, it could only have done so after a fairly far-reaching social revolution, either peaceable or bloody, had taken place.

The third major criterion of the locus of power and responsibility in the "traditional" Chinese family was that of relative age. By and large in the family it operated within the limits laid down by the criterion of sex and generation and reinforced them. Thus uncles were in fact usually older than nephews, and, while one could not predict that brothers would be older than sisters, husbands were usually older than wives (and consequently fathers than mothers, uncles than aunts, and so on),[7] and mothers-in-law were usually older than their daughters-in-law. Had the relative age factor not been in the position of reinforcing rather than opposing the other two criteria in the vast majority of cases, it is hardly likely that it would have been able to continue in effect,[8] for its frequent negation by one or the other two would have weakened it greatly, and in the long run, perhaps, eliminated it altogether.

In general, the three criteria—sex, generation, and age—established the locus of power and responsibility in the Chinese family, whether gentry or peasantry, with relatively slight differences, save for the difference in the *de facto* power of aged parents, which has been discussed above.[9] Before leaving the subject, however, a word or two must be said about the political substructure of the family as viewed from the outside, but not from the point of view of the *tsu* and ancestors (in both of which cases the generation factor clarifies the situation). Two structures were of

structures. Considerations of this order lie at the heart of many current practical problems such as the relation of a military force based on compulsory service to the citizens of a republic, the relation of individual member states to an international government, and a host of other problems of greater or lesser importance.

[7] Despite the fact that peasants seem often to have married women older than themselves, it is generally agreed that the marriage age of women was younger than that of men.

[8] The difficulties sometimes caused in these respects by the acquisition by the *chia-chang* of a very young second wife and other relative age disequilibria have been mentioned above, e.g., pp. 141.

[9] See pp. 132–133.

special importance: the imperial government, and the immediate neighbor-hood of the family. Individual contact with these two structures was mostly in terms of the state with a given family or of the neighborhood with a given family. Individuals were considered largely in their capac-ity as representatives of the family.

It is not proposed to go deeply into the relations of the Chinese family and the imperial government. In general, the government was an interest-ing combination of centralization and decentralization. The hierarchy was centralized, but the relation between the people and the government was decentralized. Government officials had considerable local autonomy. The government representatives did not go down to the villages, however, but rather to the chief town of the county (*hsien*) only, and the vast majority of the people lived in villages away from the county seat. By and large, the major concerns of the *hsien* magistrate were the collection of taxes and the maintenance of order. All district magistrates attended to these two functions, but the manner in which they were carried out and whether or not the district magistrates did anything beyond these two functions were largely dependent upon the personality of the individual magistrate. In general, government dealings with the people were in terms of some organization such as the *pao chia* organization, that is to say a structure made up of a hierarchy of councils, the first level being a council of heads of families, the second a council of representatives of the first councils, and so on. The councils were made responsible for the various things the government desired within the areas they occupied, and through them responsibility devolved upon individual families.

Relatively few things were decided solely on the basis of individuals. Debts were family responsibilities. A father could be held liable for his son's debts and vice versa. Even crimes were not always tried on an individual basis. At various times in Chinese history it has been common practice to hold a whole family guilty for the misdeeds of a single member, and there have been attempts to eradicate an entire *tsu* on such grounds.[10] Taxes were also levied against families rather than individuals, largely because ownership was a family rather than an individual matter. The government held the family head responsible for his unit in many things and theoretically could have held him accountable for anything. In actuality, if he paid taxes and kept the peace, his contacts with the govern-

[10] Hu Hsin-Chin, *op. cit.,* p. 149.

ment were likely to be few, and even if he did not keep the peace, he was as likely to be disciplined by members of his *tsu* or his village as by the representatives of the imperial government.

The influence of the neighborhood was, perhaps, more important for the average individual and for the average family than was the imperial government. The operation of the Chinese neighborhood has been little studied and is little known or understood. Mr. Shih Kuo-Heng in his unpublished work has laid emphasis on the neighborhood. Sometimes the neighborhood consisted of members of only one *tsu,* in which case the neighborhood and the *tsu* organizations were usually conterminous. When such was not the case, the neighborhood usually had a council of elders selected by common consent of the group. The elders were almost inevitably *chia-chang* though not all *chia-chang* in the neighborhood were members of the council. The council handled local matters and local disputes. It tended to offset the self-interest of the members of any one family and bring about something more of a group point of view.[11] The particularism of the neighborhood thus neutralized to some extent the particularism of the family. In political matters as well as in others the neighborhood also dealt with families rather than individuals, and when a group decision had to be enforced, it was, wherever possible, enforced through a *chia-chang* rather than directly.

THE DEFINITION OF POWER AND RESPONSIBILITY

From the general point of view of this chapter the definition of the factors of power and responsibility, that is, the range of action covered by power and responsibility, need not be discussed in detail, for that detail has appeared above in various guises. On the general level under consideration perhaps the most important thing to note is the fact that both power and responsibility relations in the "traditional" Chinese family were functionally diffuse rather than functionally specific.[12] This is of special im-

[11] The village councils were frequently dominated by the wealthier peasants and by the gentry or by gentry representatives. The councils were not infrequently subverted to the ends of the more powerful and wealthy villagers. By and large, however, they did to some extent mediate the particularism of the village families.

[12] The terms "functionally diffuse" and "functionally specific" as well as the terms "universalistic" and "particularistic" are used throughout this study in the manner defined by Professor Talcott Parsons in his article, "The Professions and Social Structure," *Social Forces*, XVII, 4, 457–467.

portance when related to the fact that in essence the structure of power and responsibility in the "traditional" Chinese family was rigidly authoritarian and autocratic.

Institutionally speaking there was no question about the preëminence of the *chia-chang* in the family, both as the primary holder of power and the primary bearer of responsibility. At the same time the sphere of his power was in essence unlimited. The *chia-chang* was not limited to any specific ends which justified his power over family members, nor was he similarly limited in his responsibility for them. Furthermore, the burden of justification for such diffuse power did not lie with him in his relations with those over whom he wielded power.

To a certain degree, the functional diffuseness of the political structure is a universal trait of kinship structure. The pattern arises from the fact that the actual permutations and combinations of action by family members within the family sphere cannot be minutely enough predicted to cover all acts crucial to the structure itself, and, even if they could, minute and detailed enough institutionalization to make political action functionally specific would require a code of such complexity that the ordinary human being could never become intimately familiar with it. In situations of this sort, where the values sought are vague and their empirical referents are by no means completely defined, any attempt at the institutionalization of a functionally specific structure of political allocation would of necessity end in hopeless confusion.

There is nothing whatever unique about the functional diffuseness of the Chinese family structure, but there is a contrast between "traditional" China and the modern West in the amount of the total action of the society which is carried out in family terms. Thus, no matter how diffuse the power structure of the family in the United States, it covers only a small part of the life of an individual in that community. Economic and religious action, for example, lie outside it almost entirely. The average Chinese, on the other hand, was involved in relatively few contacts with nonfamily members, but, more important, almost none of the contacts which did take place with nonfamily members were in nonfamily terms. Therefore the functional diffuseness of the political structure of the Chinese family meant that the average Chinese was used to such a situation and expected it in the overwhelming majority of all his actions.

The power holders and responsibility bearers in the structure were not universalistically defined. The position was not open to any person who could comply with given qualifications which in themselves did not inherently limit the choice to a single individual or group of individuals. On the contrary, the positions of *chia-chang* and feminine household head were limited to one particular individual each, the oldest male member of the oldest generation on the one hand, and the wife or the mother of that person on the other. In general, each particular position was open to one and only one individual. In the ordinary course of events each male in the family sooner or later rose to the position of *chia-chang* and each female to the position of feminine head of the household.[13] Thus while any given individual was accustomed at some time of his life to be completely subject to others, in particular to one other, he was not accustomed to general submission. He also expected to be in the power position himself at some time in his life. Since his submission was so exclusively tied up with the family, it was not a simple matter to continue it in the absence of the family structure or the absence of the higher power holders in the family, and it was not a simple matter to replace it.

Contrary to what might be expected, the range of the peasantry patterns in the political aspect of family life was if anything more inclusive than those of the gentry. This was true in spite of the more careful observance of the *li* by the gentry. The difference was intimately connected to the differences in self-sufficiency between the two groups. Theoretically the range of action covered was the same, but actually the individual male member of the gentry came into far more contact with outsiders than did the average peasant. Furthermore, he was far more likely to come in contact with outsiders at times and in places where he could not be directly subject to the family structure. He was more often far from home and relatively out of communication with his family. In addition, a member of the gentry was more likely to be in one sphere, the bureaucracy, in which other responsibilities had to be given something of a priority. In order to achieve freedom from family biases or control in the bureaucracy, the government specifically outlawed the appointment of an official to serve in an area in which his family made its residence. Had the official served in his family locality, the difficulty of insulation against a family manipulation of officials would have been greatly increased.

[13] This point must be qualified in the case of those gentry families which did not divide among brothers upon the death of the last male of a previous generation.

PROCEDURE RELATIVE TO POWER AND RESPONSIBILITY

The methods of exercising power and bearing responsibility must always be specifically institutionalized in any stable structure. If such institutionalization is absent, the structure is always vulnerable to change via a usurpation of power. At the same time, it is prone to disintegrate because the implementation of power and responsibility will be haphazard and capricious rather than systematic and predictable. In the matter of political procedure, the institutionally approved use of force is always a question of paramount interest.[14]

The "traditional" Chinese family structure was quite unambiguous about the use of force. The *chia-chang* held the power of life and death over family members and was institutionally justified in using force to implement his orders. If he killed a family member, he could technically be called to account by the district magistrate, but in reality such action was infrequent. Beating was an accepted method of discipline, and it was often carried to great extremes. Sons, especially, were frequently beaten, and sometimes were even beaten to death, though such a murder was hardly likely to be premeditated. Wives caught in adultery could be killed by their outraged spouses, and daughters accused of fornication could be so severely punished that their death would result, or could even be killed outright. Persons below the level of the *chia-chang* in the political hierarchy had much less right to use force, and such use of it as they made was subject to the review of the *chia-chang*.

The use of force by persons against their superiors in the family hierarchy was a most serious crime which could be punished by the district magistrate. Patricide was, perhaps, the worst possible crime in the society and was punishable by death or torture or both. Apparently no use of force by a superior justified retaliation in kind by the victim of such force. Most of the force used in a Chinese family was monopolized at the very top of the hierarchy, and therefore the amount of force actually used was generally a function of the personality of the *chia-chang*. A kindly *chia-chang* was not likely to permit his sons to treat his grandsons more harshly than he had treated his sons. In fact, the converse was often true, since the grandsons were often favorites of their grandfather. In any case, the *chia-chang* could set the tone for the family in these respects, and

[14] See Chapter I, pp. 28–31.

other family members were no more likely to challenge his authority or ignore his example in these respects than in any other.

Although force could be used with little or no supervision from outside the family, it was by no means the most usual or the most prominent method of obtaining compliance with the demands of those in authority. Most of the demands were undoubtedly fulfilled without any resort to force or any overt threat of it. In fact, there seems to have been little use of overt threat in any case. Commands were seldom put in a form which promised retribution in advance if they were unfulfilled. There can be no doubt that fear of those in authority was a powerful factor in securing compliance with their demands, but it is questionable whether it was primarily fear of physical coercion, although in some cases such a fear was real. Probably in the majority of cases the fear of incurring the displeasure of the person in authority was more effective. His displeasure was hardly less difficult to bear when it was displayed in nonviolent forms. It often resulted in ridicule of its victim, the moral indignation of others, and a serious curtailment of the amount of recognition and response given its victim by other family members.

Fear, no more than force, is a sufficient explanation of the fact that ordinarily the exercise of institutionalized authority and the compliance with institutionalized responsibility encountered few obstacles in the family. Fear, like force, did not characterize the interrelations of all persons between whom there were obligations of obedience. A man was not ordinarily afraid of his elder brother, unless, perhaps, that elder brother was also the *chia-chang,* and even then the man was not likely to fear him as a father would be feared. Furthermore, it may be observed in general that fear cannot be exclusively relied upon to buttress a stable structure any more than force can, since both inherently breed forces subversive of the structure in which they are so used.

A great part of the compliance observable in a Chinese family was quite voluntary. The inculcation of the value of filial piety no doubt laid the basis for fear, but it also laid a more positive basis of compliance on the part of family members. Just as the unfilial were stigmatized, the filial were objects of praise. An individual could gain recognition and response by filial conduct as surely as he could lose it by the reverse. In fact, there was no higher praise than that implied in the word "filial." Filial piety was in a sense the key to the whole structure of authority in the family. While the obligations of a younger brother to an older one were not directly a matter of filial piety, they were indirectly, for failure to observe them would disrupt family harmony, and that would have been most unfilial. By such reasoning any act which violated the institutional patterns could be construed as unfilial.

There was another factor at work beside the positive motivation of individuals. The family situation was extraordinarily well defined. The basic patterns of the family were so well established, and had been established for so long, that by the Ch'ing period at least all adults were well aware of the various demands of the structure. In fact, such knowledge was usually gained long before adulthood. Moreover, the precedence of the family was so universally recognized and the sphere of action encompassed by the family was so large a portion of the average person's total life experience that the possibility of a conflict of institutionally approved loyalties was probably reduced to as low a point as in any known society. Thus the persons lower down in the hierarchy were able to anticipate a great deal of what might otherwise have required specific commands. In any stable organization such anticipation is both possible and necessary. The Chinese family merely carried it somewhat further over a longer period of time than most organizations of its sort. Orders, when given, were not necessarily given in a peremptory tone. Often commands were most indirect. The *chia-chang* knew his words were carefully analyzed, and commands, praise, and adverse criticism were often left implicit in mild impersonal observations. The exercise of authority by use of vague indirect language or other forms of expression was of necessity more prevalent among the gentry than among the peasants who lacked the leisure necessary to cultivate such sensitivity to nuances. Even so the discipline of all "well run" families was such that no order required great emphasis. Such a structure was calculated to put a minimum of strain on the persons exercising power.

The strains of the family structure were, nevertheless, considerable. But they were eased by the strength of the indoctrination of the family members in the sacredness of filial piety, and force was usually available to make up for any gap in this indoctrination. There was, however, another factor which helped to enforce the general structure of authority and responsibility. The factor was in a sense not inherent in any particular concrete element of family structure, but arose from the general integration of family structure with the total structure of the society. This factor has been mentioned before.[15] The potential rebel had no place to go outside the family. Any act which cut off an individual from his family at the same time cut him off in large part from any possibility of the establishment of new relations. Even if a person left with the blessings of his family members, the farther he went, the less likely he was to be able to reëstablish himself, because the average family was confined in its particularistic relations to a relatively small geographic sphere.

In summation, a few general remarks may be made of the general relevance of the various aspects of the political substructure for the strikingly prolonged stability of the Chinese family. The whole structure of authority and responsibility was well-integrated with the other aspects of family structure and with the general structure of the whole society. The locus of power and responsibility was institutionalized with great clarity, and thereby any possibility of confusion over the distribution of power and responsibility among given family members was minimized. Succession to position of authority and responsibility was also clearly institutionalized, and thereby the disruption of the structure by the death of old members or the introduction of new ones was virtually eliminated. The political substructure had the advantage of being closely and accurately integrated with the general structure of prestige and precedence of the family, the only conceivable major institutional conflict being that between a widowed mother and her son for domination of the family. Even in this case, the patterns were such as to make any real conflict highly unlikely.

The distribution of power and responsibility within the family proper varied inversely, but balance was restored to the structure by virtue of the fact that the power at the top owed responsibility to significant structures outside the family. The government was one of these, but the *tsu* organization and especially the concept of allegiance and responsibility to the ancestors were of vastly greater importance. The balance was therefore obtained largely in terms of filial piety which in turn was crucial for the whole structure of power and authority within the family as well as for other aspects of family life. Finally, the matter of locus was settled in a fashion which was well integrated with the general structure of the society. Thus the institutionalization of the locus of power and authority

[15] See p. 218.

was such as to reduce to a minimum sources of instability within the family itself and sources of instability inherent in the integration of the family structure with that of the general society.

The range of action and the procedures of the political sphere were equally well defined and well integrated with the general social structure. The wide range of action covered by the family pattern and its precedence over other patterns reduced the possibility of conflicts of loyalty, and the clear institutionalization of locus obviated such conflicts within the family. The wide range covered also minimized the enforcement problem by virtually eliminating the possibility of flight as a solution to strains. The use of force was approved with little or no restriction on the amount to be used but with clear understanding of who was to use it. Fear was also a means of enforcement, but neither fear nor the use of force accounted for the major level of compliance. Among the strong sources of positive institutionalized motivation, the value of filial piety was the key to the positive motivation. All in all, there was in "traditional" China little or no reason to expect change from sources inherent in the family structure unless they were preceded or accompanied by changes in the general structure into which the family was integrated.

CHAPTER SEVEN

THE KINSHIP SUBSTRUCTURE OF INTEGRATION AND EXPRESSION

IN the rather arbitrary distinction which we have drawn between the factors of integration and expression for the purposes of this study, the former has been primarily oriented to "the methods and techniques of the socialization of children and of the acclimation of persons taken into the kinship units by marriage, adoption, etc., and the general inculcation and maintenance in the members of the units of the values, attitudes and procedures, of the kinship structure." [1] The latter has been primarily oriented to the "type and limits of reaction, symbolic or otherwise on the part of the individual and/or the group in terms of the kinship structure, of the various aspects of the concrete kinship structure with which he comes in contact, or with other aspects of experience." The close interrelationship of the two factors must be kept in mind lest the integrative aspects of expression or the expressive aspects of integration be ignored.

INTEGRATION

Two main patterns may be distinguished in the structure of integration in the "traditional" Chinese family: education and religion. The interrelation of these two was necessarily close since a considerable part of the content of the educational pattern was the inculcation of the religious pattern. For the purposes in hand the individuals in any given family may be divided into two groups—those introduced to the family by birth and those introduced to it from other families by marriage or by adoption after or at the point of maturity. [2] The basis of the distinction was im-

[1] See above, Chapter I, p. 33.
[2] The adoption of a young child is a possible exception to these two categories. The younger such a child is, the more nearly he or she must be treated as any other

portant for the Chinese family. In the Chinese family, as in the family structure of most societies, a child was taught the basic patterns of the family and of the society in his family of orientation. The women, however, married out of the family of orientation into new families. Thus every woman had ordinarily to undergo not only the educational process of her family of orientation but also one in her family of procreation. In the family of procreation the emphasis was not on her general education, which was supposedly provided by her family of orientation, but upon her integration into a new family.

The content of family education consisted of inculcation of knowledge of the values, habits, and techniques of the family and of the society, and motivation to conformity with the institutionalized family patterns. The keystone of the structure was the inculcation of filial piety. From the earliest ages, all children were taught to revere and obey their parents. Stories were told them as soon as they could understand, and the stories usually illustrated the meaning of filial piety in all its varied ramifications, from physical self-sacrifice to awe and humility. Closely connected to the factor of filial piety was that of family orientation. The individual early learned to put his family first, regardless of the situation. The individual learned that in a sense any procedure was fair game if it did not involve harm to the family or some family member or other relative.

The methods of education in the Chinese family are by no means well understood. Such material as is available has already been given above.[3] Its most notable aspects were six in number. First, there was the mildness of discipline during the *ying-erh-shih-ch'i*. Second, there was the supervision of men by men and women by women, subsequent to infancy. Third, there was the harshness of the supervision of sons by fathers and of wives by mothers-in-law. Fourth, there was the extreme use of teaching by example rather than by use of generalized principles. Fifth, in gentry families an important part of the education of sons was given over to an outsider, although this was not the case in peasant families. And finally, throughout the educational process, the emphasis lay on the interests

---

child in the family of roughly comparable status in other respects. The older such a child is, the more nearly he or she must be treated like the introduction of any mature outsider.

[3] See especially pp. 66–93.

of the family as a continuing structure rather than upon the interests of any individual.

Very closely coördinated with the educational patterns touched on so briefly above and throughout this study were the religious patterns [4] of the family. It is not inevitable that the religious structure of a society be oriented to the kinship structure of the society, but it was the case in one major sector of religious activity in China. The sector concerned was, of course, ancestor worship. It is not necessary to become involved in the question of the relative predominance of Buddhism, Taoism, or Confucianism. In a sense this controversy has been created by the Western habits of thinking in terms of religious exclusiveness. Another equally fruitless controversy from the present point of view is whether or not Confucianism—the term generally applied to ancestor worship—is in actuality a religion. In the sense of religion used here,[5] it is. There is reason to believe that ancestor worship antedated Confucius, who declared himself no innovator but rather a recorder and a reviver. There is also reason to believe that almost the entire membership of "traditional" Chinese society gave lip service, at least, to ancestor worship. This included peasants as well as gentry. It is doubtful that the average peasant consciously thought of himself as a Confucian as the average gentry member tended to do, but the keeping of ancestral graves, shrines, tablets, and like paraphernalia was well nigh universal. There is no acceptable statistical evidence to be presented on this score, but as yet no one has presented any appreciable evidence to the contrary, and laymen and scholars without end have commented on the phenomenon.

The practice of ancestor worship was simple in its essentials. Complex rituals had grown up about it in some quarters, especially among the gentry, but in essence it was singularly uncomplicated. It minimized speculation on any future life though it contained definite concepts of an after existence. Confucius himself was widely renowned for having declared a lack of interest in that aspect of ancestor worship. The religion consisted of worship and other action oriented to the deceased members of previous generations of the family, but the worship was conceived as

[4] Religion is here considered only insofar as relevant to considerations of family structure.

[5] I.e., action directly oriented to nonempirical ultimate ends.

throwing emphasis not on the future life, but on the present one. The primary concern of the ancestors was for the family. One's primary duty was to honor the ancestors. One honored the ancestors by improving the condition of the family and by maintaining its patterns and its unity. It is interesting to note that a tremendous amount of the actual action of ancestor worship was in the form of reports to the ancestors about the past conduct of family members and the general state of the family. The ancestors were not on the whole conceived of as punishing evil or rewarding good, but the frequent reports made to the ancestors undoubtedly served to force the individual to reëxamine his conduct in view of the ultimate values he held. It enforced, in a manner of speaking, a self-critical examination of conduct. The orientation to the ancestors and the values they represented was strong, and, insofar as it was strong, critical self-examination was likely to be quite effective in maintaining and reinforcing conformity with the general values concerned.

In many different and small ways ancestor worship focused attention on the family. For example, it made the family status of the living a matter of great concern. The older family members were viewed as on the threshold of ancestor status, and this made it extremely important to know just how these persons were related to one, and accentuated the honors due the aged and the members of older generations. Since it was important to know who one's ancestors were, families had to keep genealogies, and that activity in turn reinforced family interest. The manner in which the institutionalization of ancestor worship restored balance to the political structure of the family has been discussed at some length above. Ancestor worship was in effect the canonization of the value of filial piety. While ancestor worship focused attention on the living in an important sense, it did so in terms of the institutional standards and patterns of the dead. Furthermore, such definition was sufficiently well identified with concrete empirical procedures so that little room was left for the exercise of discretion. This meant that the introduction of the new was inhibited to an important degree. It is not proposed to argue the merits and demerits of this aspect of the religion, but simply to observe that it was a strong positive stimulus to the maintenance of the *status quo ante,* and, insofar as the *status quo ante* was stable, it aided the perpetuation of that stability. It is interesting to contrast this feature of Chinese society with the industrialized West. In the West the emphasis is also placed on the living, but the standards involved are to a much higher degree oriented to the future rather than to the past.

Ancestor worship was by no means the sole form of worship encountered in the Chinese family, although it was the sole one completely oriented to the family and in terms of it. Three others need to be mentioned because of their effect on family integration. These are the worship of household and field gods, Buddhism, and Taoism. Ancestor worship on the whole deëmphasized the aspects of religion which integrate individuals to uncertain and uncontrollable situations and to the problem of evil.[6] The orthodox Confucian position of the Ch'ing period outlawed such considerations to a radical degree, and, while elements of the considerations undoubtedly crept into ancestor worship to some degree, satisfactory solutions to the problems were not to be found there. The orthodox Confucian scholar theoretically eschewed speculation and appeals to nonempirical forces beyond the bare minimum involved in ancestor worship, but even the most rigorous scholars rarely stuck to the letter of this law. They built their houses on the basis of the *feng-shui,* the nonempirical aspects of the forces of wind and water, and indulged in many other similar concessions. Some of the more rigorous scholars no doubt indulged in such practices merely to preserve the calm of other family members, friends, and servants, but they used them all the same. Furthermore, they did not seriously attempt to curb such practices by others, and while they themselves often refused to participate consciously in Buddhist or Taoist worship, they did not inhibit other family members or household servants from doing so if they chose.

The household and field gods were of a familiar pattern. They were conceived as safeguarding the household and crops from harm and misfortune, if they were carefully propitiated. A good part of such practices was carried out by women, and the household gods in the form of little images were usually kept on a shelf in the kitchen part of the house. The male side of the household had its counterpart of such objects of worship in the various gods of the fields and the patron gods of the various arts and crafts. These gods varied widely over China, both in names and attributes, but in some form or other they were more or less universal.

[6] The attention here given these three as religious structures must of necessity be most cursory. It is hoped that some of the difficulties of oversimplification can be avoided, but in so abbreviated a treatment some error is unavoidable.

Even in gentry households their worship was carried out, but in such households the worship was more likely to be carried out by servants than by family members. From the point of view of this study, the main function of such worship was primarily that of integration to the uncertainties of everyday life and most especially those involving natural phenomena. It is interesting that such forms of worship were less practiced by gentry family members than by others, and it may be suggested that the explanation lies partly in the fact that the degree of uncertainty of the gentry in these matters was, if not lower, certainly less pressing than for the peasants and craftsmen.

The worship of the household and field gods warrants careful and detailed study, since a consideration of their attributes would throw light on the problems and uncertainties that were of greatest concern to the Chinese in varying circumstances in varying parts of the country. It is not possible here to go further into that aspect of the matter. From the present structural point of view one important observation about this sort of worship must be made. It was not characterized by any self-consciously developed theology, and there was little or no organization uniting in terms of these beliefs those who shared them. The lack of organization was important because it meant that participation in such worship did not involve the individual practitioner in any significant relations outside the family membership.[7] The worship of these gods was able therefore to ease anxieties and prevent the accumulation of aggression to some degree without interfering in any way with the basic structural features of the family. In thus adding to the integration of the family members it made a positive contribution to family stability.

Buddhism was quite a different matter. Whatever the varying content of Buddhistic theology, and it varied widely, it always contained a certain element not contained by either of the two forms of religion mentioned above. In the first place, it contained an answer to the problem of evil in the world. In the second place, it contained an explicit ontology. In the third place, it contained a cosmology, and in the fourth place, it contained a path of salvation. Of these the first and fourth were by far the most important from the point of view of this study. The problem of evil in

[7] Both Taoism and Buddhism did involve such relations to some degree, and herein may have lain the source of some of the orthodox Confucian opposition to these forms of worship.

the world has been a matter of concern to mankind in all societies in some form or other. From a functional point of view it may be suggested that an answer to the problem of evil serves to maintain the validity of the basic institutional patterns of society by integrating the members of society to the fact that, no matter how carefully the institutional patterns are observed, there will be deviation from them, that the institutional patterns of reward and punishment are often contraverted by forces beyond an individual's knowledge or control, and that the forces of nature other than man also visit catastrophe upon man. The patterns of ancestor worship reinforced the values of Chinese society, but it did not explain how the wicked could prosper. Moreover, it failed to afford emotional consolation at the bereavement occasioned by death. Ancestor worship certainly recognized death and instituted mourning, but ancestor worship merely stated the formal ritual requisites of mourning and did little or nothing to fill the emotional gap left in the lives of family members by the departure of the deceased. Buddhism did. Buddhism was to a considerable degree oriented to the treatment of death. Where ancestor worship concentrated on the veneration due the deceased in his new status as ancestor, Buddhism concentrated its attention on the loss felt by the bereaved and the effect that the expression of this loss could have on the future life of the deceased.

It is interesting to observe that except in periods of unusual religious fervor, Buddhism seems to have shown its major appeal for the lay populace in its appeal to women. This was in keeping with the fact that the family structure of China posed the problems of bereavement more acutely for women than for men. A man's status was largely dependent on factors inherent in his own particular relation to his other family members. The woman's status was largely dependent on the particular relations of the man to whom she was attached. Furthermore, the emotional development of women was much less inhibited by reserve than was the case with men. Lastly, in the general subordination of women and their great emotional dependence on their children, the problem of evil and the sense of loss at death was greatly increased. The point need not be dwelt upon, however, because men as well as women, even if to a lesser degree, indulged in Buddhist practices on a large scale.

Intellectually Buddhism also had an appeal of its own because of the tendency of orthodox Confucianism to throw out the problems of ontology and cosmology and satisfy itself with a practical interest in things as they existed. Buddhism shared this appeal to some extent with Taoism. Real involvement on this level of Buddhism usually led into asceticism, however, and the general appeal was somewhat limited. Both Buddhism and Taoism did, however, serve as refuges for those who looked beyond the "traditional" values of the family structure and sought their meaning.

In the matter of salvation Buddhism had a dramatic appeal to the Chinese people, an appeal which was closely connected to the Buddhist answer to the problems of evil. The popular forms of Buddhism strayed from the strict ascetic Buddhist formulations and placed a far greater emphasis on salvation by appeal to the various supernatural entities in the Buddhistic hierarchy. The average Chinese peasant had little chance of improving his material lot in life, but Buddhism did offer him a method of assuring for himself a golden lotus seat in paradise in the life to come. In a society in which social mobility was in theory always open but in fact always more or less blocked, such doctrines had great appeal, the more so when the accepted avenues of social ascent became clogged.

Buddhism in China came to have virtually limitless variations, and a great part of the ascetic character which clothed the origins of the religion was sloughed off. Charms of all sorts were obtainable at the temples, and the ministrations of the Buddhist clergy could be bent to virtually any situation. There was great appeal in this, and that appeal was heightened by the fact that Buddhism provided a whole body of professionals to carry out these activities in an elaborate and dramatic fashion.

Unlike ancestor worship and worship of the household gods, Buddhism involved family members in a set of relations with outsiders and with outside organizations. Furthermore, not all its ideas were compatible with the basic values of the family structure. The ascetic aspects of Buddhism were especially subversive of the family. Intellectually, of course, Buddhism was in considerable conflict with orthodox Confucianism, and the intellectual conflict was intimately bound up with the conflicts between the two on moral grounds. These factors account for part of the opposition to Buddhism on the part of the Confucian specialists. The stability of the family system was no doubt a factor in curbing the influence of Buddhism among the people. Buddhism, when practiced, was almost never practiced to the exclusion of other religions. Such practice would have been incompatible with the accepted Chinese family patterns. On the whole, however, Buddhism probably enhanced the stability of the Chinese family because, when indulged in piecemeal, as it were, it afforded integrative measures otherwise lacking in the structure.

Taoism, like Buddhism, offered answers to the problem of evil and the like, but it could not be a thoroughgoing answer for the average Chinese, because its answer lay in repudiation of the world of ordinary affairs and a turn to otherworldly asceticism. Taoism unlike Buddhism never worked out an acceptable compromise in this respect. The ascetic aspect of Taoism did attract certain individuals who decided to flee all worldly entanglement, but in its answer to the problem of evil Taoism depended pretty much on complete renunciation.

There was another aspect of Taoism which had great popular appeal. It was something like the worship of the household gods in that it provided integration to problems of uncertainty. A great part of Taoism was simple thaumaturgy, that is, the employment of nonempirical means for the attainment of empirical ends. In addition to a pantheon of saints, Taoism came to be intimately involved in astrology, medicine, fortune-telling, and all such activities. Wandering Taoist practitioners filled the land, and Taoist doctrines infiltrated the dogmas of other religions. Taoist experts were called in frequently to apply their techniques in emergency situations of all sorts.

Like Buddhism, Taoism involved the individual in relations with persons outside the family circle and in relations with an organization outside the family as well. The Taoist organization, however, was an even looser organization than the Buddhist one. On the whole, Taoism also probably added to the family stability in its net effect when it was indulged in only partially. It was further like Buddhism in that its priesthood and collateral personnel could absorb the most determined rebels against the family structure and so insulate the society against them. At the same time, the way of life so afforded was not sufficiently attractive to the average Chinese to result in a continuous and threatening drain of people out of the family and into the religious hierarchy.

To the orthodox Confucians, Taoism was anathema, of course. The source of this opposition has long been overlaid wtih the obscuring factors of age and mysticism, not to mention such factors as jealousy. Without going into the controversy, it can be observed that a considerable amount of such opposition was inherent in the doctrinal composition of the two.

Confucianism with its emphasis on orderly conduct in the empirical world and the responsibilities of the individual to his family and to his society, was radically incompatible with the inherent anarchy of Taoism. Much has been made of the Confucian condemnation of Taoist "superstitions," but Confucianism was by no means devoid of such elements itself. By and large, sophisticated Confucians were not too much impressed by such factors, but, even when they believed them nonsense, they often followed the practices rather than upset others. The Confucian opposition to Taoism was by no means always of a physically repressive character, but the intellectual opposition was considerable, and avowedly Taoist doctrines were as far as possible kept out of the schools. Ordinarily the Confucians did not really try hard to eliminate Taoist practices by the people as a whole. The attitude was partially one of intellectual snobbery. Such superstitions were deemed more or less appropriate to the vulgar and uneducated, but it is not altogether impossible that many sophisticated scholars recognized the integrative aspects of Taoist practices.

Apart from the patterns of educational and religious activities, another major source of integration was involved in the kinship structure of China. It lay in the interrelations of the various elements of that structure with one another and with the other structural elements of the society as a whole. In a sense, educational and religious action may be thought of as conditioning an individual to participate in the other structures and helping to maintain his acclimatization to them and, of course, to the educational and religious structures as well. This can, however, never be the whole of the matter in any society. Regardless of how effectively the two structures may perform their functions, if the other aspects of the kinship structure are radically incompatible with one another, or if the kinship structure is radically incompatible with other aspects of the social structure, the stable existence of the structure is out of the question. In what has gone before there has been a continuous attempt to point out from time to time certain aspects of the mutual integration of the various facets of the structure which have been singled out analytically. If the findings of this study are valid, it may be concluded that the kinship structure of "traditional" China, when viewed as a whole, was well integrated internally and well integrated with other aspects of the society as well, despite its generation of considerable strains. By and large, the various aspects of the structure seem to have been combined so as to afford a maximum amount of support and reinforcement of those portions of it most highly esteemed.

EXPRESSION

The empirical facts about the expressionistic aspect of Chinese life are incompletely known, and it is therefore not intended to deal with them here in more than a tentative and suggestive fashion. Structurally speaking, one of the most important aspects of the phenomenon of expression in any society is the emotional reaction of the members of the society to the various phenomena with which they come in contact. In "traditional" Chinese society one fact is relatively clear. The display of emotional reaction was strongly inhibited. The Chinese placed high value on composure, poise, and self-control. Between the gentry and the peasantry there was considerable difference in the degree of observance of these standards, but the standards themselves were relatively uniform. The open display of anger frequently seen among the peasants was an accepted badge of their inferiority, and they themselves held it in low esteem.

The inhibition of such emotional display was accompanied by a highly conventionalized standard for the display of emotion, though this was by no means complete. The most notable example of formalization was, perhaps, the expression of grief. At the death of a family member, a given type of weeping was called for, but its expression was limited in both time and place. Outside the designated times and places a person's grief was expressed not by any overt emotional display but by such symbols as his clothes. The integrative aspects of this expression were obvious enough. The expressions of grief did not vary according to one's personal feelings in the matter. The persons of highest status in the family structure merited the greatest displays of grief and the most lavish funerals, thereby calling attention to the importance of the status features of the family.

Inhibition of such overt emotional expression as romantic love and anger by no means eliminated emotion. Emotions connected with positive and negative attachments among the gentry were expressed in an extremely subtle pattern of innuendo. Among the peasants this was less well developed, but a richly profane vocabulary testifies to the indulgence of emotional release.[8] Physical displays, especially of violence, were extraordinarily well inhibited, and when they did occur, were likely to be either straight criminal acts or family affairs. No physical violence between two individuals could ordinarily escape the involvement of all the family members of both and many other relatives as well.

In the noninstitutionalized expression of emotion one finds some extremely interesting aspects of the structure. The mother-in-law–daughter-in-law relationship may be taken as an example of this. The control of the daughter-in-law by her mother-in-law was institutionalized by the society, but her harsh treatment was not, nor were the aggressive displays of so many mothers-in-law considered correct. It has been suggested in what has gone before that two elements in such displays were: (1) the mother-in-law's jealousy of her daughter-in-law's relations with her son, and (2) an emphasis of the fact that the mother-in-law was no longer a stranger in the family. The partial relief afforded the daughter-in-law by the birth of her son undoubtedly increased her institutionally acceptable emotional attachment for him, and her increased emotional attachment for him was in all probability a factor in her jealousy of her own daughter-in-law.

The reciprocal attachment of the son for his mother, strengthened as it was by the strain of his relationship with his father, made his reinforcement of his mother as against his wife all the stronger. This in turn emphasized his wife's position as a stranger in the family and increased her motivation to minimize her stranger status in any fashion possible. Since the only other family members to whom she could demonstrate a superiority in these respects were her subsequent sisters-in-law, her daughters-in-law, and her husband's concubines, the probability of expression of aggression in their direction was increased. It is a mistake, perhaps, to overemphasize such matters, and one may feel this interpretation reads too much into the mother-in-law–daughter-in-law relation, but the effect of the relation undoubtedly reached well beyond the principal persons involved, and the treatment involved was of so consistent a pattern that it seems to imply some consistent pattern of expression.

About certain other modes of expression in the Chinese family a great

[8] The novel literature of China is strewn with highly imaginative and elaborate cursing, and today as in the past, oaths and imprecations are often an important component of the medley of street sounds in China.

deal more is known, though much of what is known remains incompletely analyzed. The full elaboration of the *li* consists of formalized expression without end. Clothes, gestures, actions, and the like are minutely ordered over a wide sphere of action. The *li* were incompletely observed save among the gentry, although the peasantry observed them insofar as possible. The effect of such observance was closely bound to family stability. In the first place, it reduced to a minimum unpredictable modes of expression or the free display of emotion and thereby tended to eliminate the disruptive effects of such displays. In the second place, it directed as much expression as possible along lines calculated to reinforce the institutionally accepted patterns. Finally, the fact that the gentry did carry out the injunctions of the *li* with exceptional rigor was significant in the matter of stability, because it meant that the group in China which was most strategic from the point of view of embodying ideal patterns was precisely the group which in matters of expression carried out patterns which best bolstered the stability of the structure.

Religious and educational action cannot be overlooked as types of expression. Ancestor worship was a systematic expression of the basic family values, and the other religious action patterns which were followed expressed the uncertainties and problems raised by life in the society. The general tendency of these forms of action to bolster family stability or to take forms which could not threaten more than a small percentage of families at any one time has already been discussed. The expressive side of education is too obvious to require much elaboration. There is one point that may be elucidated, however. Much of education is a consciously calculated process of indoctrination carried out with more or less full knowledge of the implications of the process. The expression involved is the self-conscious attempt to inculcate certain patterns deemed desirable. The indoctrination of the Chinese child in patterns of filial piety was an example of this type of education.

There is, however, another aspect of education in which the process of indoctrination is not consciously calculated and the implications of which are hardly understood at all. This type of education is no less important than the other, and its implications as a structured form of expression are not negligible. The institutionalization of a particular system of toilet training and the education of boys by women in an otherwise male dominated society are examples which come easily to mind. An example of this in China was the mother-in-law–daughter-in-law relationship pattern. More education was involved in this relationship than the manifest function of getting the newcomer habituated to her new family. The daughter-in-law learned how to protect herself in such a situation and to what sources she could turn for response. It undoubtedly "taught" mothers an increased love of their children, especially the boys, and had many implications for expression along that line. Similarly the relationship was an expression of the mother-in-law's now great security and at the same time a reflection of her past insecurity. Examples of this sort and their implications could be elaborated in considerable degree and would repay detailed study. These examples of expression which arise implicitly from the juxtaposition of more conscious elements of the structure are difficult to analyze because the individuals who exemplify them usually do not understand them and are often unaware of their existence. Structurally speaking, such elements are often decisive.

The patterns of amusement and artistic enjoyment are ordinarily rich sources for the study of expression. In "traditional" China these patterns of action were quite consistent with the other elements of the society. So far as amusement was concerned its most striking feature lay in the separation of the sexes. Small children played together, but ordinarily the children were separated while quite young. This separation was carefully maintained throughout the rest of life. Such relaxation as was afforded in the society was rarely carried out in mixed company. In adulthood the men sought relaxation together and usually went outside the household to such places as teahouses, where they mingled with other men. Entertainment of male friends was rarely carried on at home, and, if it were, the women of the household were little in evidence. The women, on the other hand, conducted their amusements largely in the family residence and in the company of the other feminine members of the household rather than outsiders. Sometimes women from other households were present, but the sort of free exchange of visits among women friends so prominent in the West was unknown.

There were vast differences between the gentry and the peasantry in these respects. The level of formality maintained by the gentry was higher, and their economic base permitted them a far greater indulgence in amusement. Nevertheless, much the same type of expression was to be found. The radical separation of the sexes in the sphere of amusement was an expression of the general emphasis on sex role differentiation. The fact that men went outside the household for their relaxation not only expressed their greater freedom in general, but also took them away from family observance of their more unguarded moments.

As forms of amusement men indulged in gambling, drinking, opium smoking, and extramarital sexual practices. The first three were also practiced by women who were especially fond of gambling. The popularity of these forms of amusement is interesting because they are forms of amusement particularly well adapted to an escape from ordinary daily life. In a sense, this is true to some degree of all amusement, but the difference of degree is significant. The self-restraint required by Chinese family life was not achieved without some cost, and all these forms of amusement emphasized release from such self-restraint.

Among the men, at least, amusement furnished a release from the family atmosphere. Opium smoking took its devotees completely out of the pragmatic world of everyday life, family or otherwise. Getting away from the family was also well expressed in sexual amusement. The sexual relations between man and wife were not primarily oriented to amusement, but rather to the production of posterity. This was less true of concubines, perhaps, but in general it applied. This is not to say that men found no amusement in their relations with their wives, but merely that it was not essential, nor was any overt emphasis on this permissible within the family. For sex as an overt amusement a man went outside the family where the element of feminine companionship denied to men in the family could be conducted. This was reflected in the employment of women for other forms of entertainment than sexual intercourse. The female entertainer was a widespread phenomenon, and while many or even most of these women undoubtedly engaged in prostitution to a greater or lesser degree, their other functions, such as singing and dancing, were highly esteemed.

Gambling was extremely popular in China, and the significance of it may easily be misread. Gambling, like drinking and some of the other forms of amusement, are widespread escapist amusements. China was not unique either in its degree or types of gambling. It may be suggested, however, that the popularity of it lay in its release from the certainty of daily life. The need of an individual for some form of integration to uncertainty has been much discussed by social scientists, but the need for some form of adjustment to certainty has been rather neglected. Chinese life was predictable to an unusual degree, as has been shown above. The desire for new experience of which Thomas and Znaniecki [9] speak is in some form or other frequently if not inevitably found in mankind and such a desire had exceptionally little scope or opportunity for gratification in Chinese society. This was hardly the sole explanation of gambling as a phenomenon in China, but it almost certainly played a large role in that phenomenon.

Under the term artistic, one may gather a whole group of patterns which in one sense are merely subsidiary forms of amusement, and they will be considered only in that aspect here. Some differentiation is made necessary by the fact that for general purposes amusement activities have been thought of as those pointing overwhelmingly to the production of pleasure and relaxation. Artistic activities do the same, but they also place great emphasis on the skill of execution within the medium and the ability of the finished product to stimulate the observer emotionally through his reception of the results of the process, rather than his participation in it. Here again the case in China is incompletely understood and little studied. Chinese art and literature have received some attention in the West, but very little, considering the magnitude of the field, and Chinese music has hardly been studied at all.

In focusing attention on artistic activities this study will confine its attention to relatively few aspects of the field, and the treatment of those will of necessity be sparing. In this field one must return at the outset to the gentry-peasantry distinction. Here the distinction was more than one of means and formality, though both of these were important. Literacy entered the picture, for the art of China was to an extraordinary degree tied to literacy.

In the analysis of Chinese literature one must draw a distinction between the formal or classical literary productions and the informal or popular ones. The former portions of literature were the exclusive monopoly of the educated gentry. The illiterate were cut off from the art

[9] W. I. Thomas and F. Znaniecki in *The Polish Peasant in Europe and America* (Boston, 1918), I, 73, have given attention to the upsetting aspects of certainty, but even they have not carried the matter far. The social implications of fright and anxiety are dramatic, but a study of boredom would be no less illuminating. Heretofore, the implications of boredom have been expressed not by social scientists but by a relatively small number of sophisticated literary men.

in a twofold fashion. Simple literacy was not adequate to the enjoyment of it, but rather was specialist training a prerequisite. It is not necessary to elaborate here the distinction between literary and vernacular Chinese; suffice it to say that the distinction is no less than that between modern Italian and classical Latin and in many respects greater. The classical Chinese works were highly formalized. Such was the level of specialization required for their appreciation that the persons who could truly enjoy them were confined to a minority of the educated. The most interesting implication of this lay in the fact that these persons were the persons most likely to be completely imbued with the general classical tradition and its exemplification of the family tradition. Therefore, the family elements in this form of expression are not hard to find.

The vernacular tradition was another matter. It has come to be highly esteemed in the West today, so much so that each person interested in it seems to have identified his own Oriental Proust. The vernacular tradition was closely connected with the story-telling tradition of China, and so low was its prestige among the educated who outlawed its works that it is now a problem to ascertain the authorship of many of the works. The Chinese novels are, of course, the most widely known representatives of this tradition. The important thing about the vernacular works was the avidity with which they were read. These novels to an interesting degree concerned themselves with family problems and often, as in the case of *Dream of the Red Chamber*,[10] offered romantic pictures of that life, and thereby furnished an avenue of escape for their audience. Their romantic appeal is not surprising because romanticism was almost completely eliminated from the ordinary Chinese family, which as a rule was both practical and unsentimental.

The novels were not entirely lost to the peasants because of their illiteracy. The stories contained in them were sometimes read aloud to family or village members by some literate person within their midst, or recounted by one of the myriad of professional storytellers who swarmed the countryside. The stories usually exalted the virtues of the Chinese family, but their appeal hardly lay in their didacticism. Hearing the stories, a Chinese could lose himself for a time in surroundings of great luxury and honor and in vicarious participation in great events. By and

[10] *Op. cit.*, throughout the volume, especially such passages as pp. 129–136, 92–101, 167–172, and 273–284.

large, like gambling, the popularity of this tradition seems to have centered at least in part in a retreat from certainty and the humdrum facts of everyday life. The classical literature afforded integration by its positive content and the training it involved. The vernacular literature afforded integration by furnishing an outlet for emotion and imagination which could not be expressed otherwise in the family.

Closely connected in popular appeal to the vernacular literature were the Chinese operas and other dramatic performances. These performances were more available to city dwellers than to others, but companies of performers traveled all over China and brought this form of entertainment to the villages as well as the towns and cities. The operas were tremendously popular. They combined romantic tales and gorgeous costumes with a type of musical entertainment which apparently had great appeal in and of itself. The subject matter of the operas gives some insight into their romantic appeal. Plots were frequently concerned with dramatic historical events, the rise of a brilliant young scholar from a peasant home to the top of the bureaucracy, and so forth. The vicarious satisfaction offered by the plot was increased by the gorgeous spectacle afforded by the performances at their best.

The wealthy were able to indulge their desires for such entertainment within the confines of the family. It was not unusual for an opera company to be hired to give private performances for a gentry family or for the entertainment of a few friends. For the majority of persons, however, the performances meant contacts outside the family. In the cities and towns it took one into the crowded bustling theatres filled by vendors of various sorts as well as by the audience. As an avenue of outside influence in the town and city areas, the theatre played a role in China not dissimilar to its role in Western society. Theatrical people of China were "Bohemians" in the eyes of Chinese society, just as they have been in the West. In the villages, however, the effect of such performances must have been greatly different. Village performances were occasions for neighborhood gatherings. The performances involved the individual with persons outside his family, but they did not involve him in a totally alien atmosphere. All around him were the members of his neighborhood well known to him from birth. In a sense these occasions served to cement the solidarity of the neighborhood. It was of great importance from the point of view of the family that the companies were transient features of the local scene. The fact that such companies never stayed for any length of time in any village severely limited the effect of personal contact between the players and the audience, and also reduced the possibility of influence of the theatre setting on the way of life of these people. A stage-struck city dweller could find ways to keep up his contact with the theatrical world. This path was not open to the peasant unless he completely broke with his past way of life and left home.

The itinerant storytellers mentioned above gave a similar release to the peasants and furnished similar occasions for local gatherings. The professional storyteller was not the only source of such tales, however. The art of narration was highly regarded in China as one would expect of any society in which the literacy rate was very low. Almost every Chinese family had its storyteller. Grandparents, especially grandmothers, seem frequently to have fulfilled this function for Chinese children. The status of these tales as a form of expression is obvious enough, but they went far beyond simple amusement. Many of those tales were straight bits of education as well as entertainment. The tales also gave the average Chinese a sense of the general cultural patterns of China, past and present, which was quite surprising under the circumstances. When one stops to consider the self-sufficiency of the average peasant family, the relative geographic confinement of its members, the limitation of communication facilities, and the illiteracy of its members, it is surprising that the average peasant know anything of China beyond the range of his own eyesight. He did, though, and while the structure for various reasons did not raise in the average peasant's mind any grave concern over political unity, he was relatively well aware of the culture which he represented. The tradition of narration, aided and abetted by operas and other dramatic performances helped the average peasant to know something of the history of China and something of its intellectual traditions. His information may have been highly colored and inaccurate, but it gave the patterns of everyday life a continuity beyond the local scene in both time and space.

Fine arts and music played lesser roles than storytelling. Both fields were in part tied to the religious patterns of the land. In general these sources of artistic enjoyment were less available to the peasant than to the gentry. This was especially true of painting and calligraphy, which were so intimately bound up with the intellectual traditions of China.

Interestingly enough, the very basis of its unavailability to the average peasant conditioned him to a superficial reverence or appreciation of these forms of art when he came in contact with them. So overwhelmingly prestigious were the intellectual pursuits, among the illiterate as well as the literate, that the written word itself became well-nigh sacred. Thus the tradition of beauty in writing was not so difficult even for the illiterate to comprehend as might have been supposed. The traditions of calligraphy and painting were closely related, as one would imagine in a society in which the same instruments were habitually used for both. Even so, the average peasant must have known relatively little of either painting or calligraphy, and it is doubtful that either had much relevance for family life. Calligraphy, however, certainly was relevant in gentry families. All gentry sons were supposed to learn to read and write, and an acceptable calligraphy was not only an ideal but also the object of rigorous training. Some of the more arduous aspects of the academic training of Chinese were the result of this reverence of the artistic use of the brush and ink.

Like the dramatic arts, the fine arts did bring the gentry into contact with a group of artists, and the painters and sculptors were often unconventional in their behavior. It is questionable, however, whether or not this form of outside contact played any serious general role in family stability. Even in urban centers the painters were far less numerous than the actors and singers. Furthermore, established centers for focusing the social influence of these artists were not present as they were in the theatrical world. The fine arts had no counterpart of theatres as public places of availability, and they had no systematic organization to make continued existence a certainty. There were painting schools to be sure, but even so these schools were hardly comparable to theatrical troupes. The peasants obviously had even less systematic contact with such artists than did the gentry. An occasional painter might wander into a Chinese village, but any regularity comparable to the periodic visits of storytellers or opera troupes was out of the question. Many peasants lived and died without the sight of a painter and perhaps without the sight of a finished painting.

Music was more widespread than painting. The Chinese operas have already been discussed, but there were other troupes of musicians who wandered about the land. A great deal of music was connected with Buddhist ceremonials, particularly with the rites for the dead. Music, like storytelling, entered the lives of the average person, and many Chinese played simple flute-like instruments or sang for personal amusement.

One of the more interesting aspects of singing was its use in work. In the carrying of heavy loads where a large number of men coöperated in a single operation they sang various chants together. Whatever other function these chants may have performed, they helped to coördinate the timing of the workers through a clear and simple rhythm.

Folksongs were also a widespread form of personal enjoyment, and were frequently connected to storytelling activities. Excerpts of operas were also sung in this fashion. This was a source of pleasure which was economical and which involved no great contact with outsiders. Very little seems to be known in the West of Chinese folk music, and there is reason to believe that much of it is being lost today. Even so the number of persons who found pleasure and relaxation in this form of activity must have been considerable. How folk music was integrated into family life would be difficult to say under the present circumstances. The content of the songs in all probability expressed in one form or another not only the values of the structure but also vicarious escapes from it.

Music among the gentry was in general more sophisticated. Instrumental music and dancing were developed as audience entertainments rather than participation entertainment, such as folk singing. Some gentry families were wealthy enough to maintain their own musicians who thereby swelled the numbers of the household and complicated that organization. On the whole, it was perhaps more common to hire musicians and dancers who were readily available in the town and city environments. The towns and cities also afforded establishments devoted to music, maintained on a more or less permanent basis. The opera houses were not the only establishments of this sort. The establishments other than the opera houses catered to a male clientele and frequently combined musical and feminine entertainment.

Finally, in the general category of amusement it is necessary to consider games and sport. In these forms of expression two things were obvious and noteworthy. One was the separation of the sexes, and the other was the fact that insofar as possible these activities were carried out by groups of family members. In the peasant villages the latter tended to break down to a larger degree than the former, though both were more rigidly maintained by the gentry than by the peasants. The implications of these two facts in light of what has gone before requires no further elaboration. The content of these forms of expression is another matter, however. Sports, especially in the sense of games placing emphasis on physical prowess, were of minor interest to the Chinese. The culture hero of China was sometimes a strong man physically, but ordinarily he was primarily a wise and clever man.[11] No doubt this was in part due to the Confucian formula that one's body belonged to one's parents and ancestors and therefore one should not take unnecessary risks with it, but this is not a completely satisfying explanation. A further reason may have rested in the discouragement of overt competition in most spheres of action. Children were encouraged to exemplify the *li* better than other children, but in general competition was frowned upon. Within the family, encouragement of competition might have disrupted the intricate balance of precedence, and in interfamily relationships, competition might have resulted in needless embarrassment of one group by another. Sports imply such competition to a high degree, if they do not actually require it. Performance in games need not be universalistic in nature because highly particularistic games can be devised, but particularistic competitive sports are a contradiction in terms. The physical and competitive sports which were practised, such as fencing, were relatively confined in their appeal and unusually formalized in their performance.

In general, the substructure of integration and expression implemented the various other substructures and held them together. The patterns of integration inducted new members into the family by teaching them the techniques and values appropriate to the structure and by affording in general a sense of justification of the structure and of daily experience. The patterns of expression provided for the accepted display of attitudes in the course of everyday life as well as in extreme situations. In these respects it must be remembered that expression took two important forms. First, there was the expression of the institutionally approved attitudes in the implementation of the various aspects of everyday life. In China, this was exemplified by the more or less faithful adherence to the *li,* with all its forms of expression of filial piety, respect, obedience, and the like.

[11] Even in the famous novel *All Men Are Brothers* (*Shui Hu Chuan*), the chief hero among the physically great is distinguished by his wisdom and character rather than his physical prowess.

Second, there was the expression which provided emotional release and relaxation. In the latter form of expression, the problem of the effect of such release and relaxation on the general structure was raised. Such expression can quite easily take forms subversive of the structure of which it is a part. In general, it may be said that such was not the case in "traditional" China. In "traditional" China this aspect of expression was to a high degree compatible with the general structure, and where the compatibility was not great, disintegration tended to be in terms of individuals and individual families rather than in terms of the structure as a whole.

PART THREE

THE KINSHIP STRUCTURE OF "TRANSITIONAL" CHINA AND THE PROBLEM OF MODERNIZATION

CHAPTER EIGHT

THE SITUATION AND THE NEW FORCES

IN Part II of this study an attempt has been made to sketch out in some detail the major structural components of the fundamental membership units based on kinship in "traditional" Chinese society, and to show as far as possible some of the most important interrelations and interdependencies of the structural components as they operated in the course of everyday life. The present part attempts to use the base presented above and, in conjunction with a brief description of the foreign influences at work, indicate the major directions of change of the structure and some of the major problems involved. The state of knowledge about contemporary Chinese society and the society itself are in such a state of flux that it is not possible to do a great deal more than present hypotheses about what is taking place. Statistical studies in China have heretofore been limited to extremely small samples, of which the general statistical relevance is extremely questionable. This is not intended to cast reflection upon the research which has employed them. Quite the contrary, all praise is due such workers as Professor J. Buck and Miss Lang[1] for the careful use they have made of such material and the insight gained thereby. It is merely intended to forewarn students in the field that the few statistics available offer no more than hypotheses and certainly no definitive conclusions. Unfortunately, on most of the points of major concern here, nothing of a statistical nature exists at all.

Because of this situation the method followed here has placed major reliance for its hypotheses about "transitional" China on the base from which the changes started and the new forces introduced into the society. The former has been developed above, and the latter will be developed in this chapter. As regards these latter only the most general aspects of the new forces which have made themselves felt in China over the last hun-

[1] *Op. cit.*

[273]

dred years will be considered, for to carry consideration to much lower levels of generalization would require a precision of data both as regards the current situation and the past which simply is not available today.

"Transitional" China presents an extremely interesting problem. It is not difficult to obtain general agreement that far-reaching changes are afoot in China today, and it is relatively easy to show that the current situation is unstable and necessarily of a transitory nature. But why, after so many centuries of stability, should the change have come largely within the last hundred years, and more especially within the last fifty years? China has on more than one occasion been completely conquered by foreigners with societies radically different from her own, and has been ruled by such people for several centuries at a time. The effect of such domination on the basic patterns analyzed above has apparently been slight. In fact, these patterns have heretofore so dominated the conquerors as virtually to obliterate the patterns of the foreign rulers. Now it is often suggested that it has been the invasion of Western customs which has upset Chinese society and is producing dramatic changes. The suggestion is in part undeniable, but it is by no means a sufficient answer. There is every reason to believe that not just any Western pattern could have brought about such changes. It is interesting that the patterns of modern industrialized society are no less unique in Western history than in Oriental history, despite the fact that they appeared earlier in the West. Neither East nor West has ever seen any society like it before.

However slight or great the contact between East and West may have been in ancient times, it has long been known that since the time of Marco Polo many representatives of the West have gone to China. Of the representatives, those of the Catholic Church in particular carried the intellectual traditions of the Europe of their day, including its scientific knowledge. Beyond the casting of cannon, the revision of the calendar, certain revisions in astronomical practices, and the like, these representatives made no considerable inroad whatever on Chinese life. Certainly prior to the nineteenth century the features of Chinese life discussed above had not been touched by either the general influence of these Westerners or by their science and technology. Marco Polo was insistent on the fact that in his day the West had little if anything to offer China on a technological basis, but that China had much to offer the West. There is no ground for attributing these views to that romantic traveler's love of the exotic. China's technological superiority to the West at that period would hardly be seriously contested. China maintained technological equality or superiority until the technological forces of the industrial revolution in Europe began to move forward in the eighteenth century, and it was not until the nineteenth century that the West was able to demonstrate any decisive superiority over China.

This phase of history is symbolized by a rather notable pair of diplomatic documents. The documents were handed to Earl Macartney, who in 1793 went to China as an emissary from the British Empire to seek better trade relations between that empire and China. Earl Macartney refused to perform the usual obeisances and was permitted by Emperor Ch'ien Lung to refrain from them. Here concession ended. The British emissary was treated as any other tribute bearer, and his requests for greater trade relations and an exchange of national representatives was refused in two mandates addressed to King George III. The mandates, while couched in terms which must have been a harder blow to British pride in some respects than the successful American revolution, were cogently reasoned. Ch'ien Lung wrote in part as follows:

Yesterday your Ambassador petitioned my ministers to memorialize me regarding your trade with China, but his proposal is not consistent with our dynastic usage and cannot be entertained. Hitherto, all European nations, including your country's barbarian merchants, have carried on their trade with Our Celestial Empire at Canton. Such has been the procedure for many years, although Our Celestial Empire possesses all things in prolific abundance and lacks no product within its own borders. There was therefore no reason to import the manufactures of outside barbarians in exchange for our own produce. But as tea, silk, and porcelain which the Celestial Empire produces are absolute necessities to European nations and to yourselves, we have permitted as a signal mark of favor that foreign *hongs* should be established at Canton, so that your wants might be supplied and your country thus participate in our beneficence.

After taking up the requests in detail and refusing them, Ch'ien Lung added:

It may be, O King, that the above proposals have been wantonly made by your Ambassador on his own responsibility, or peradventure, you, yourself, are ignorant of our dynastic regulations and had no intention of transgressing them when you expressed these wild ideas and hopes. I have ever shown the greatest condescension to the tribute missions of all States which sincerely yearn after the blessings of civilization, so as to manifest my kindly indulgence. I have even gone out of my way to grant any requests which were in any way consistent with Chinese usage. Above all, upon you, who live in a remote and inaccessible region, far across the spaces of ocean, but who have shown your submissive loyalty by sending this tribute mission, I have heaped benefits far in excess of those accorded to other nations. But the demands presented by your Embassy are not only a contravention of dynastic tradition but would be utterly unproductive of good result to yourself, besides being quite impracticable. I have accordingly stated the facts to you in detail, and it is your bounden duty reverently to appreciate my feelings and to obey these instructions henceforward for all time, so that you may enjoy the blessings of perpetual peace. If, after the receipt of this explicit decree, you lightly give ear to the representations of your subordinates and allow your barbarian merchants to proceed to Chekiang and Tientsin, with the object of landing and trading there, the ordinances of my Celestial Empire are strict in the extreme, and the local officials, both civil and military are bound reverently to obey the law of the land. Should your vessels touch the shore, your merchants will assuredly never be permitted to land or to reside there, but will be subject to immediate expulsion. In that event your barbarian merchants will have had a long journey for nothing. Do not say that you were not warned in due time! Tremblingly obey and show no negligence! A special mandate! [2]

The condescension of the mandates is obvious enough from what has here been quoted, and the fact that at that time Great Britain did nothing about the matter is significant in and of itself. What is more important from the present point of view is Ch'ien Lung's remark anent China's lack of dependence on this trade. Even at the beginning of the nineteenth century Europe had little in the way of exports that could appeal to the traders of China. The industrial revolution was underway, but many of its major inventions had only just been made or were still in the future, and the great applications of mass production lay far in the future. Like the West of that time China had iron tools and probably had had them for at least as long a period of time. It was, after all, not until 1797 that Charles Newbold in the West received a patent for the iron plow. The steam engine did not make its appearance until the last part of the eighteenth century, and its application to industry had not gone far before

[2] This and the foregoing quotation are taken from pages 4–5 and 8–9 respectively of H. F. McNair's *Modern Chinese History Selected Readings* (Shanghai, 1927).

the nineteenth century. As late as 1830, France had only six hundred steam engines, and in 1847 had only 4853 of them. The steamboat appeared only in the first quarter of the nineteenth century along with the steam locomotive. Electricity was primarily the subject of an intellectual pastime until the appearance of the electric motor and generator in the second quarter of the nineteenth century. The sewing machine, which more than any one single invention directly and immediately affected the lives of clothesmakers (usually women) all over the world by affording the means whereby clothes could be manufactured more cheaply than made at home by hand, was not even available in a crude form until the middle of the nineteenth century. A glance over the chronology of Western invention will serve to remind one that almost all twentieth century technology is a product of the last one hundred and fifty years, especially of the last half of that period. The roots, of course, go far back of that and the process has a rapidly cumulative rate of acceleration. Within the scope of the nineteenth century alone the technology of man and his physical equipment underwent more changes than in all the known years of his previous existence, and the twentieth century has already repeated the process at least once.

When Ch'ien Lung told the British ambassador that China had nothing to ask of Britain and nothing to learn of her, he was in part incorrect because Britain had then the germination of the power and the technology which was to surpass China's hopelessly within the nineteenth century. Ch'ien Lung can hardly be taken to task for not seeing this, however, for no one in the West seems to have seen it either, and he was after all acting in the pragmatic Chinese tradition. Had the British had to demonstrate their superiority in 1793 it is hard to see how they could possibly have done so. At this time even British textiles (the spinning jenny dated back only to 1767), which were later to become so great a factor in the Far Eastern market, had little appeal for the Chinese, and only in opium and bullion could Great Britain finance her trade with China. The mechanism of industry in the West had not yet reached the point which would permit it by greater efficiency to overcome the cost of transportation and sell better goods more cheaply than handicraft or jack-of-all-trade peasant labor could produce them.

By the end of the third decade of the nineteenth century the earliest stages of industrial society had already reached a point which gave Great

Britain technological superiority over the Chinese in the use of force, and the British lost no time demonstrating this superiority. Perhaps it is questionable whether or not the British would have been so successful had the society they opposed been less ridden by graft and more characterized by talent in its leaders. Ch'ien Lung's rule might have made some difference. Tao Kuang was not a ruler of great capacity. This question is rather beside the point, however, for even the best of Chinese rulers and even the most powerful day of Chinese society could not have prevented British soldiers, armed by the infant Western technology, from seizing and maintaining local superiority at any point they chose.[3] Western arms were ahead of peaceful manufacture for export, perhaps, but not far ahead. And after the third decade of the nineteenth century manufactured goods began to flow into China in increasing amounts and increasing varieties.

The influx of new and cheap commodities had three closely connected effects insofar as it touched the life of the peasants. In the first place, it changed to some degree the habits of consumption of the people by giving them new types of consumption. Textile products were perhaps the best example of this. Cloth had always been used by the Chinese, but formerly it was largely made at home by family members at times when farming required little attention. The introduction of machine-made cloth made cloth available in certain areas at prices cheaper than home labor could produce it. In the second place, the production picture of the family was changed to the extent that new goods replaced the old ones previously made at home, for certain spare-time occupations were taken away. In the third place, the peasants were involved in new economic transactions outside the family sphere. These new transactions involved a new source of outflow of family goods and services, either in the form of barter or cash. To an increasing degree this came to result in further need for cash on the part of peasant families.[4]

The extent of the three effects need not be overemphasized. There are no reliable figures for peasant production of this sort, and the extent of the invasion by Western goods relative to the old types is not known even today. Certainly in the nineteenth century a tremendous number of

[3] The Japanese, of course, were able to do just this for almost the entire duration of their 1937–1945 war with China.

[4] Some of the implications of the need for cash have been discussed above. See pp. 211–212.

peasant families were not directly touched, and even today there are areas of China in which the consumption and production habits of the peasants have been little changed by the importation of goods manufactured by modern technical methods. The influence was first felt in the areas adjacent to the large seaports of the China coast and in the areas adjacent to the large navigable rivers reaching back into the Chinese hinterland. The effects of the influx of manufactured goods were considerable wherever they made their way, but in the long run it is doubtful whether such an influx could have done more than drain Chinese resources out of the land and disrupt the peasant economy by reducing the value of peasant labor even further. This would have brought more families to economic ruin faster, and might so have precipitated revolt and unrest. But like all past revolts based on such factors, it is not likely that the rebels would have struck out along new social lines. As of old, only renovation of the previous patterns would have resulted, for no alternative would have been offered.

After the first part of the nineteenth century the contact with the West was not limited to the exchange of commodities as previous contact had been. One obvious factor about Chinese society impressed all Westerners. Human life and hence labor were incredibly cheap. Although the standard of living of the West at this time was cheap, that of China was far cheaper. Furthermore, the standard of living in the West was rising faster and faster as the nineteenth century wore on, while that in China rose slowly, if at all. By the third decade of the twentieth century, the gap was almost beyond belief, and the average Chinese lived on a material basis which the average American or Englishman believed incapable of supporting life. The Western industrialized societies quickly forgot that a scant hundred years or so before their people had by and large lived close to the physical margin of subsistence too. The cheapness of human labor in China meant nothing so long as labor in the West was equally cheap, and even later it would have meant little had not low labor cost in combination with the superior efficiency of the new machine over the old craft methods been more than enough to cover the transport costs of goods and machines. As things were, there was incentive to carry on industry as well as trade in China. This, together with the influx of new commodities, afforded a real basis for change.

Originally production of manufactured items for export was handled by domestic industry and by the crude beginnings of factory production as it had been in Europe. As time went on, the domestic industry continued rather as it had from time immemorial, but factory production changed as machinery changed and focused its output on the home market. Along with this development of manufacture went development of communications and public utilities. China came to know the steamship and the railroad, the telephone and the telegraph, the radio, the electric light, and even the automobile and the airplane. These products and elements of modern industry did not extend far into China by comparison with the way in which they permeated life in the industrialized sections of the West and even in Japan. The fact that all China in 1936 had only about eleven thousand kilometers of railroad conveys only a part of the story,[5] for such railroads as existed were less efficient in every way than railroads in the West. A thousand kilometers of railroad in China was not at all comparable to a thousand kilometers in the United States. Nevertheless, to an increasing degree, the people in China came in contact with the machines of the West and the ideas and habits that accompanied those machines. As the technology of Europe and the United States outgrew industrial infancy and turned to modern mass production, this too was reflected in China. At the same time domestic industry was virtually obliterated in the West by these developments. In China the cheapness of labor and the restricted spread of modern industrial technology left a sphere for this type of production which flourished along with the other.

The new developments were more or less added to "traditional" Chinese society. Many things went with these contacts with the West, but this study will restrict itself to a few of the most significant elements. For present purposes these elements may be divided into three sorts: those introduced largely because they were implicit in Western trade and industry; those introduced as explicit Western ideals by school education and the like; and those brought in by direct observation of the daily lives of the foreigners who came to live in China. Of those three the last two exerted their primary influence on the well-to-do members of Chinese society, the old gentry, and the larger commercial families. The first affected everyone who came in direct contact with them and an even greater number who had such contact only indirectly.

[5] See *The Orient Yearbook* (Tokyo, 1942), p. 764.

Western trade and industry are dominated to a remarkable degree by the machine technology which underlies them both. One of the prerequisites of the technology is the enforcement of universalistic criteria over a good part of the lives of the people in any society employing this technology. Another prerequisite is that functional specificity be introduced on a large scale in such a society. To some degree both of these elements exist in all societies, but no known society has given them so large a role as has modern industrialized society. "Traditional" China was highly particularistic, and its major social relations were functionally diffuse.

Modern industry is not concerned with who a person is. Modern industry is concerned merely with whether or not he can perform certain specific technical functions with a particular level of skill. The use of machinery brings this about, for it makes no difference to either a truck or a drill press whether its operator is a sinner or saint, prince or pauper. Whoever he may be, if he pulls the correct levers, pushes the right buttons, lifts the right material at the right time, the machine will do its job. If he does not, the machine is nothing more than so many pounds of metal or concrete or wood. Unlike handicraft society in which a new worker is likely to have to live intimately with the family of the master, the machine process makes no such demands. A machine worker need have no contact with fellow workers outside his working hours, and he might be doing very different things than the persons working with him. It is not inconceivable that handicraft work be carried out on as universalistic a basis as modern industry, though it is not likely, but it is inconceivable that modern industry be carried out on a large scale on any but universalistic grounds. The prevailing particularism of China was at one and the same time a major barrier to the spread of modern industry and a major cause of the disruptive effect of modern industry on Chinese society in general and the Chinese family in particular. Insofar as particularism in certain spheres held fast, the universalism necessary for effective industrialization was impeded, and insofar as industrialization was successful, particularism in certain spheres was broken down.

Much the same sort of situation holds with regard to functional specificity. Machine technology requires its institutionalization for several reasons. In the first place, machine industry cannot place primary emphasis on the relation between persons. It emphasizes the relations between men and machines. Relations between persons, except insofar as they implement that between men and machines, are at best extraneous to the process and at worst interfere with it. In the second place, machines are characterized by the fact that, however ingenious and complex they may be, their functions are both limited and predictable, and therefore relations beyond those necessary to perform the limited predictable functions are again at best extraneous and at worst an interference. In the third place, the recruitment of machine workers has to be carried out on a universalistic basis rather than on a particularistic one if operation of the process is to be efficient. Therefore the possibility of combining workers and employers, or workers and workers, with diffuse relationships outside their occupational roles is limited, and as a consequence the necessity of a functionally diffuse relation in the occupational capacity is minimized.

There is some distinction between the commercial and technological aspects of a modern industrial economy in the matter of the level of universalism and functional specificity required. The business aspects of the economy permit a greater degree of particularism and functional diffuseness than do the actual industrial processes. The difference, while noteworthy, should not be overemphasized, because the close relation between business and industry requires that both assume much the same patterns in these respects. Business when carried out in conjunction with handicraft or nonmechanical agricultural economies can be and has been highly particularistic and highly diffuse in function, but the possibility is strongly inhibited by the transfer to a modern technological base. One of the basic reasons for the inhibition is the question of control. In Western society modern industry developed under the control of businessmen who, with certain exceptions, were not technologically competent in the mechanical processes which formed the basis of their business operations. The control which businessmen exercised over the technological processes, however, required that within broad limits the selection of business as well as industrial personnel be on a universalistic and functionally specific basis. Administration of industry by persons chosen on grounds other than administrative ability would have meant the disruption of the technological processes themselves.

Another reason for the presence of universalistic criteria and functional specificity in modern business lies in the degree and kind of productivity of modern industry. The mechanical ingenuity of the last one hundred years produced commodities in amounts and of a complexity hitherto undreamed of in the history of mankind. The net result was to force the average business into an involved system of accounting and a widespread net of contacts such as had featured only the largest commercial enterprises in the Western world before this time. It is not by accident that modern accounting practice traces its origin, not to the small shops and traders of Europe, but to the Fuggers and the Hanseatic League. The new level of complexity required the recruitment of a large body of business personnel solely on the basis of ability to keep track of the myriad of commitments involved in everyday business life. In addition the advances in technology invaded actual business practice and surrounded businessmen with mechanical paraphernalia more ingenious and baffling than any involved in the physical processes of production before the industrial revolution. The competitive basis of a good part of modern business has been a further factor in enforcing recruitment for efficiency. Although the competition has also resulted in attempts to prosper by manipulation of particularistic factors, nepotism and other lapses into particularism could not be carried too far save in rather small business concerns. A certain number of relatives and friends could be tucked away in corporate sinecures, but the strategic positions for the functioning of the enterprise had to fall to men of ability, or the enterprise was likely to suffer, and that quickly too, unless protected by some special monopoly condition. In business generally particularism in recruitment of personnel came to be limited to advancing some persons of ability more quickly than might otherwise have been the case, or to the provision of sinecures insulated from the enterprises.

Aside from the universalism and functional specificity implicit in Western business and industry, let alone the Western scientific professions, many material factors were directly changed by the introduction of these new forms of economic organization. In the following material these factors will be taken up only insofar as some fairly defensible hypotheses about their effects on kinship structure and vice versa can be made. Some of the more obvious changes may be mentioned. Communications is an important example. Although the network of modern communications devices in China is crude by modern industrial standards, it is infinitely superior to anything that existed in China prior to this time. Heretofore some spectacular courier services were usually confined to rather limited governmental purposes. Some merchants had their own devices to speed communication, but neither goods nor messages in quantities considered routine today could be transported by any save the old slow methods of preindustrial Europe. The Chinese certainly have in the past done exceptionally well with what they had at hand. The Chinese canal system is an engineering feat for which Europe had no real equal until modern times, but even so the old forms could not compete with the new.

The production of light consumers' goods was also changed by the new techniques. Textiles and tools could be produced by the new machines in factories at prices with which neither spare time home nor handicraft labor could compete. In the cities where industries were established, new forms of production of light commodities were introduced, and in cities and rural areas the old forms began to dwindle. Heavy industry also came in and gave the Chinese something totally new. Heretofore large-scale projects in China had been raised to large scale simply by the multiplication of human labor. By the old methods the digging of the Grand Canal and the digging of a rice paddy irrigation ditch were differences of degree. The introduction of the steam shovel made them differences of kind. The steel industry was introduced, and mining was carried out to a degree and by techniques never before seen in China. All these signs of the new industry were confined to relatively restricted areas, usually along the coast and bordering the large rivers. By the standards of a highly industrialized nation there was little industry at best, but even so small an absolute amount was an explosive when mixed into "traditional" Chinese society.

Western ideals as well as Western technology were brought into contact with those of the Chinese society during the "traditional" period. The ideals of universalism and functional specificity have already been mentioned as implicit in industrial technology. Many of the ideals of the West were introduced directly through the educational institutions established by Westerners and Chinese alike. Books and periodicals carried Western ideas through the land. Those who could read informed those who could not. The ideas underlying modern science came in. Even the most reactionary Chinese could see sooner or later the material advantage afforded by modern technology and its basis in modern science, so that Chinese as well as foreigners came to support the introduction of such technical education. Education could not be brought in alone. It required definite habits of thought. One of the most striking of these was the critical approach, which once inculcated was not easily confined to a particular area. Western ideas of political freedom, of individualism, of self-reliance, and the like, filtered into the Chinese scene with all the imprecision with which they were found in the West, but were sufficiently well-defined so that their contrast with Chinese ideals could not be overlooked. The Western treatment of women was another concept which was in sharp contrast with prevailing Chinese ideas. The Western woman certainly does not have political or economic status equal to that of a man, but she approaches it in a way that is revolutionary from the "traditional" Chinese point of view. Individualism, the idea that the individual rather than the family should be the primary focus and basis of decision, was equally revolutionary from the point of view of the "traditional" Chinese society.

Universal education as a desirable social end was also novel in China and threatened to wipe out a major basis of social distinction in the land. This idea had a peculiar subversive quality, because the devotion to learning that characterized the society as a whole was such that no member of the society could well afford to oppose such a move too vociferously. The kind of education proposed was another matter. Universal literacy was an aim, but this was not to be a literacy based on the old classical curriculum. The advocates of new education looked toward education for use in a modern world in which the classic curriculum of China would be doomed to become a field for particular scholars only, and would no longer be part of the equipment of every educated man. Such a movement threatened not only to sweep away a special advantage confined to a few but also threatened to change the whole content of education, and reduce all the prevailing experts to obsolescence. Education of the old Chinese style was so complex and so removed in certain of its aspects from everyday life that its inculcation could not be made available to all. Furthermore, the old ways of production and distribution did not permit the average peasant a standard of living which could support education for all children. The greater productivity of modern industry gives promise of such a standard of living, but it has not yet been realized. Education in China is far from universal even today, but more people are learning to read and write than ever before in Chinese history.

Western religions were also introduced in China. This has not been a recent matter altogether. There has been some missionary activity in one form or another in China for centuries, and it far antedates the introduction of industrial technology. Neither Christianity in its various forms nor Judaism seems to have had any appreciable appeal for the Chinese. The Jews who settled there centuries ago were absorbed into the society and few traces of them have persisted. Certainly they caused no changes in general Chinese institutions.[6] The Christian sects of various denominations have made a deeper impression. They have built churches, schools, hospitals, and orphanages. They have done the people all kinds of social services, often at the cost of much abnegation on the part of the devoted persons involved. They have made converts, but again one can point to no basic change in Chinese institutions which stems from the specific religious character of this·influence. The schools they set up have had an influence of other sorts, but their religious influence seems to be slight. It is hard even to know how to reckon the number of converts because Christianity is an exclusive religion. Participation in it excludes participation in other religions, theoretically at least. It is difficult to estimate the number of announced Christians in China who have given up all other forms of religious action.

When the religious element is taken in conjunction with the general set of ideals introduced from the West, the picture is somewhat different. The Western view of the inherent dignity and sacredness of the individual is not distinct from the Christian tradition. Equally important is the close connection of the Christian religion with a universalistic ethic. There was little opportunity for the ideals to have an appeal for the Chinese people, however, unless accompanied by other aspects which permitted of a way of life alternative to the "traditional" Chinese way. Prior to the industrial revolution, the West had not produced any alternative way of life which could compete in these respects. Furthermore, so far as the ideals are concerned, they cannot be viewed as complete innovations. China has had a long tradition of ethical and religious leaders, and these various ideals have cropped up before in Chinese history. They did not win out then, and they showed no signs whatever of making any headway when introduced from the West until the West provided a radical alternative in social organization as well.

Another source of introduction of the social patterns of the modern industrialized societies was the observation by the Chinese of the daily

[6] See S. M. Perlmann, *The History of the Jews in China* (London, 1913).

habits of Westerners who came to live in China or to travel there. The effect of such observation is difficult to judge in any case, and particularly so in the case of China, where reliable information is so limited. A great many foreigners settled in China for extended periods of time. The majority of them settled in the large coastal cities where the principles of extraterritoriality with its freedom from subjection to Chinese law aided them in the preservation of their own customs. Except for the exotic trimmings of the sights seen in the streets and the "picturesque native" servants, the lives of these people were as much as possible like the lives they would have lived at home. The favorable rates of exchange and the standards of living of the Chinese made it possible for them to live on a scale far above that which they would have been able to support at home, but this in turn merely increased their ability to import their own "native" ways of life. Some of these representatives of a foreign culture lived in remoter sections of China or traveled into such areas. Of these many were missionaries who were specifically concerned with educating the Chinese in terms of the ways held right and good in the West. Ordinarily even they maintained their own ways as far as they could, and the foreigner who "went Chinese" was a relatively rare phenomenon.

The foreigners gave the Chinese in the large cities a prolonged first hand contact with Western customs, and even many Chinese in more isolated areas saw such people. Familiarity with Western customs of everyday dress, routine public relations between the sexes, the care of children, forms of recreation, types of housing, and the like, became a part of the lives of many Chinese. The concentration of both foreigners and industry in the larger cities meant that the very Chinese who were most subject to the other influences from the West had the best first hand view of Western life. As China became more and more interested in the foreign ways, many of the customs were taken over. Western clothes for men became familiar even in some rural areas where such clothes were not often worn by the local inhabitants, but the people saw them worn. Of course, there were, and are, areas which have been so completely isolated that the residents have not had such an experience, but these areas are becoming increasingly rare.

Some foreign habits were bound to be considered more striking than others by the Chinese. The Western attitudes toward women were of this sort. It was one thing for a "traditional" Chinese to hear of the treatment of women as companions, but it was quite another to come in contact with an actual case of this. When Westerners entertained Chinese, the wives of the foreigners participated. Chinese learned that social invitations to a foreigner were likely to be interpreted as including his wife, unless otherwise specified.

The motivation for change in China lay primarily in the stresses and strains created by, but contained within, the "traditional" structure. The contact with the industrialized West increased those stresses and strains by economic and military pressure. The new Western industry and trade afforded direct material ends. At the same time, the social organization and institutional patterns afforded in part at least the possibility of a way of life alternative to the "traditional" Chinese way, and to a certain extent imposed the new way on the people in direct contact with them. Finally, the physical presence of large numbers of the representatives of these new ways gave the Chinese examples of the associated patterns in all their minutiae.

CHAPTER NINE

"TRANSITIONAL" KINSHIP STRUCTURE

"TRANSITIONAL" kinship structure cannot be considered a stable integrated whole in the sense that the "traditional" structure can. The striking fact about the "transitional" picture is that it is not well-defined and is to a degree uninstitutionalized. The old patterns are giving way, but the new ones are not firmly established. A great part of the old continues to persist, and there are far more people who continue to observe the old with little or no change than there are people who have almost completely taken over the ways of the West. The vast majority of those who have been affected combine the old and the new, and all degrees of such combination are present. For reasons which will emerge from the material to follow the general finding of this study is that this combination cannot be more than a transitory stage because the points at which the two ways of life are incompatible are crucial to the stability of either.

The factors discussed here will therefore be only a selection of some of the more important types of variation taking place. Not all types will be discussed, nor all the degrees of variation. In general the outline followed in the section on "traditional" China will be followed here, but treatment will be far less detailed since those elements which have not changed markedly or are less strategic for these purposes will be left out.

ROLE DIFFERENTIATION

ABSOLUTE AGE GROUPS

Even in those families most affected by the new ways of life the structure of absolute age groups has not been completely upset, though certain notable modifications are taking place. In the *ying-erh-shih-ch'i* modern health precautions are being introduced by the more educated people, but little or no change in the picture of affection or discipline seems to have taken place. The desire for children has not been so quick to pass away as has the submission to parental control. It is, of course, not uncommon to find persons in China today who have taken radical positions in their youth but have become more conservative in later years. Rebellious sons are often demanding fathers, an inconsistency with which the West is familiar enough. No marked change has taken place in this age group. The medical changes have not spread far from the big cities, and even within the big cities only the better educated parents have made changes in these respects. Miss Lang expresses a belief that the increase of marital unions based on romantic love has tended to increase the rivalry between father and son,[1] but there exists as yet no evidence to indicate that this has resulted in any widespread change in the attitude of the father toward his children. The discrimination which formerly operated in hard times against infant girls is changing to some degree. The increased value of women as income earners in factory employment is leading to a somewhat higher evaluation on female life. Officially the government has also given more attention to female infanticide and the sale of girls, but in hard times these factors still come into play in many areas.

The *yu-nien* stage has seen greater changes than the preceding one. In the more Westernized circles the discipline of the *yu-nien* has changed considerably. The separation of the sexes is not carried out so far as formerly, and children are frequently sent to coëducational schools, where the education itself is also changing. Many *yu-nien* are now learning a different curriculum, by different teaching methods. Literacy is taught without the classics, and learning is not simple training in uncritical memory work. Arithmetic, modern history, and science have been introduced to the roster of subjects taught. The government is attempting to make such education universal, but so far little real headway has been made save in the most advanced areas.

A marked change in family life of the male *yu-nien* is appearing in China today. According to the "traditional" patterns, the boy at this stage of life came under the direct discipline of the father with the various results outlined above. As Western patterns are taken up, this diminishes because a father employed in a Western style business or industry cannot be with his son as much of the time as was the case under the old pattern. Greater responsibility for the rearing of children of both sexes is thereby placed upon the mother much as in the West. The change has certainly

[1] *Op. cit.,* pp. 248–249.

not reached any large proportions as yet, but it cannot be ignored as a trend. Furthermore, the elementary schools of China are to a noticeable, and probably to an increasing degree being staffed by women. The implication of the change in direct domination of the male *yu-nien* from male to female domination may be far-reaching. The trend is well exemplified in the United States and some of the other industrialized societies today. In China it represents a radical departure.

The female *yu-nien* is also experiencing change. Wherever public education is offered or where the girl's parents can afford to educate her, girls as well as boys are receiving the new education. In gentry families in the past only a few girls received education, but education for gentry girls is becoming the rule, for illiteracy for women as well as for men is becoming increasingly disgraceful. The spread of literacy among girls adds immensely to the prestige of girls in a society which prizes learning. More important, perhaps, is the fact that the girls touched by education are brought into contact with a whole new sphere of life formerly closed to them. Not only are the girl's contacts with nonfamily members vastly increased, but she is given a perspective on her family which was formerly lacking. In "traditional" China a girl had little or no alternative to the accepted way of life, and such was her seclusion and confinement in the family that she had little possibility of discovering any alternative, should one exist.

In addition, the female *yu-nien* is acquiring new occupational roles which greatly change her position in the family. As a *yu-nien* she is employable in the new factories, for child labor is a prominent feature of modern China, despite any laws pretending to regulate it.[2] Furthermore, the services of many more girls are now used in domestic industry. A great deal of domestic industry has been and is being encouraged for export to the West, and it is one of the major forms of exploitation of cheap Chinese labor. Hair nets, matches, toys, artificial flowers, and endless other goods are produced under this system. Whatever the merits or demerits of the system, overnight it helped make the female *yu-nien* an economic asset, for now household work and agricultural work at peak seasons are not her only uses. Between the factory and domestic industry the female *yu-nien* is now in many instances able to earn her keep.

[2] See D. J. Orchard, "Manpower in China," I and II, *Political Science Quarterly,* L, 4 (December, 1935), 561–583, and LI, 1 (March, 1936), 1–35.

The new position as an economic asset does not affect all female *yu-nien*. Factory work is highly concentrated in urban areas, and domestic industry is likely to be confined to an area easily visited by the entrepreneur who provides the raw material and sells the product. Nevertheless, the factory industry may well be having an influence in excess of the domestic industry in these respects. The factories recruit labor from a wide area and periodically send out representatives to comb the countryside for new workers. Usually some arrangement is made whereby, initially at least, the major portion of her wages is sent to her family or an initial cash sum is given. This method of recruiting workers has the result of affecting the lives of people at a distance where they would otherwise have been insulated rather well from the direct or indirect effects of the factory centers. This is one of many ways in which the new forces are affecting China far beyond the extent that their absolute amounts would seem to warrant. Although women comprise a sizable portion of the industrial labor force of China,[3] only a small portion of the total female population can be directly involved. The enhanced position of women as an economic asset, however, is affecting the treatment of many more women than are actually involved as industrial workers at any given time.

The higher evaluation placed on girls for economic reasons by the peasants is matched in the economically superior social groups. Among the wealthier people higher evaluation is based on new ideas about the intrinsic worth of individuals. The Chinese government has announced quite unequivocal laws on this subject and points with pride to its rather advanced legislation. In actuality little or no attempt is made to enforce the statutes, and they are largely ignored. For all its ineffectuality, however, the mere fact that such legislation is on the statute books indicates that a sufficient number of powerful persons have been sensitive enough to foreign views to place them there. The higher evaluation placed on girls is increasing the security of the female *yu-nien* in her family of orientation. She is less and less an essentially superfluous person, and the transitory aspect of her life in her family of orientation is less emphasized. Among all economic groups the age of marriage appears to be increasing. The poorer families are less anxious to get rid of a member who has become an economic asset, and the wealthier families are becom-

[3] See Orchard, *op. cit.*, p. 574.

ing more anxious to have their daughters profit by education before marriage. During the *yu-nien* period this results in a weakening of one of the main elements of differentiation between boys and girls of this age group, the attitude that the girls are merely temporary family members whereas the boys are not.

In the most thoroughly Westernized families the whole problem is largely dissolved. In simple conjugal family units consisting of husband and wife and nonadult children, both boys and girls are treated as equal family members, and the parents anticipate eventual departure of both from their family of orientation. The latter is extreme because even the most advanced Chinese do not easily give up the ideas of the duties owed parents by children. This type of change is reflected not only in the change in the lives of the *yu-nien* but also in the creation of an "old age" problem which is causing so much concern in China today. The growing security afforded the female *yu-nien* probably accounts for the extreme activity of the older girls in political movements in China today. The old insecurity of Chinese women is an important factor in motivating the demands for reforms, but without some change in or prospect of security independent of the old ways, it is doubtful that Chinese women could have ventured out of their past role of submission.

The changes in the lot of both male and female *yu-nien* are becoming more and more dramatic. The *yu-nien* period was formerly the most severe faced by the Chinese male, but to the extent that the family is changing toward the Western model, the strain between father and son at this time is being eased, though undoubtedly at the cost of the stability of the old style family. The growing sexual rivalry between father and son mentioned by Miss Lang probably will not equal the old strain because less attempt is made to keep father and son indefinitely contained within one family unit.

In all this one sees a spectacle quite familiar to the observer of the West. The new ways in China maximize the security of the family members at the preadult stage. China is moving toward a "youth" culture. After two thousand years of a culture definitely oriented to old age, this change must of necessity be both dramatic and far-reaching. The widespread organization of youths on a nonfamily basis and their vociferous participation in political activity is something quite new and revolutionary in China. Part of the basis for it lies in the new treatment of the *yu-nien.* Parents to a degree never before true in China are coming to live for their children as individuals rather than having children who will live for the family. These orientations are consciously held by only a small fragment of Chinese society today, but they are being taken up unconsciously by others, and they are spreading.

These considerations merge directly with the consideration of the *ch'ing-nien.* From a group of little or no importance in the past this group has suddenly become one of the most important in all Chinese society. The most notable change in the *ch'ing-nien* age group is that it now has application for peasants and gentry alike and that it has taken on a general political as well as a family role. The *ch'ing-nien* group no longer consists almost entirely of males. In modern China the young women are an important component of it. Furthermore, the *ch'ing-nien* period is not so restricted as formerly. It is no longer a period interstitial to childhood and marriage. The *ch'ing-nien* classification now extends even into the fourth decade of life. *Ch'ing-nien* has come to be something rather different from a family absolute age group. There is a definite relationship between a *ch'ing-nien* and other family members, but the term has come to have its primary significance in its implications for the society as a whole rather than for the development of the individual family member. The term is now applied to persons, male or female, roughly from the age of sixteen to some point in the thirties. Not many persons of thirty or more continue to be considered *ch'ing-nien,* but some do, particularly if they pursue active academic or political roles.

The *ch'ing-nien* are definitely tied today to modern educational and political activities. The village sons who follow the old patterns of life are no more called *ch'ing-nien* than they were formerly. The youth who study under the new education and set out to secure reforms are the *ch'ing-nien* proper of today. The frivolous aura of the old *ch'ing-nien* is by no means gone. The frivolity of a wealthy man's son in a new university is a mark of *ch'ing-nien* status still, but by and large the *ch'ing-nien* take themselves seriously, indeed, and work hard at their roles. The lack of perspective they sometimes exhibit relative to their own roles is one of their distinguishing characteristics. The demand of the *ch'ing-nien* for recognition as serious mature members of society is so insistent and earnest that it is often met with amusement by more mature members of the society. Their amusement in its turn only accentuates the action which causes it. This is a phenomenon well known in the West. The American college student has long been a familiar figure in these respects, though he has shown rather more concern for privilege and less for responsibility than have his Chinese counterparts.

In the Chinese family the new *ch'ing-nien* create a new situation. In the "traditional" Chinese family the individual *ch'ing-nien* or *yu-nien* did not dare to demand to be taken seriously or think in terms of it. He thought in terms of doing what was required and, aside from that, of leaving as much of the burden as possible to one side. Even more disruptive, from the family point of view, than the demand for recognition and respect is the insistence of the new *ch'ing-nien* on allegiance to, and concern for, matters outside the family. The concern for problems which take priority over the family unit means, of course, the end of the old family pattern. The acquisition of such concerns alone would serve to differentiate the new from the old *ch'ing-nien*. The new *ch'ing-nien* have now been a feature of Chinese society long enough for some of them to have reared families of their own. The radicalism of the early members of this group has not kept many of them from returning to conservative ideas with their own children. But the break once made is difficult to retrace, and a complete return to the old ways is probably rare.

From the point of view of the stability of the "traditional" family unit his turning to outside interests is the new *ch'ing-nien's* most subversive aspect, but there are others as well. The new education which the *ch'ing-nien* receives is often coëducation. The *ch'ing-nien* males and females have contacts with nonfamily members of the opposite sex. This is a change even for the males. The "traditional" *ch'ing-nien* had contact with women to some degree, but the contact was specifically for sexual purposes and was not with women of his own status in society. The new *ch'ing-nien* has feminine companionship of girls of his own social standing. The problem of romantic love was raised on a large scale as soon as these new youths appeared in China. The *ch'ing-nien* early demanded a voice in the choice of their wives and husbands. Today the Chinese scene contains every variation from the completely arranged marriage of "traditional" China in which neither party to the marriage sees the other until the ceremony is performed, to the marriages so common in the United States in which a young couple meet by chance and marry without the consent of their respective families or even without consulting them.[4] The arranged marriage was an important part of the "traditional" structure, and any departure from it challenged the structure, if for no other reason than the fact that it challenged the old distribution of power and the stable relationships of the family with the local community.

The *ch'ing-nien* who associated with academic and political activity also associated with the new industry. In centers like Shanghai and Canton the young workers who are active in workers' movements of various sorts are also *ch'ing-nien*. Long before the outbreak of the war with Japan in 1937, they had already become a strategic group in all the major industrial centers. New technological skills make them an important group, and the urban influences under which they live maximize the disintegrative effects of the new ways relative to the old.

From the point of view of the old style families from which most of the *ch'ing-nien* come, the new youths present an insoluble problem. The advantages given them so that they can benefit the family break down their concern for the family, and breed in them defiance of the family's "old fashioned" ways. At the same time, the advantages, especially the new education, give these youths a basis for making a living apart from the family. Interestingly enough, the *ch'ing-nien* have sprung out of major sources of strain in the old family. The male *yu-nien* was under great pressure, and the female *yu-nien* faced expulsion into a strange environment in which, as a young wife, she could expect a difficult time. It is not by chance that these *ch'ing-nien* raised the cry for living by themselves. This is closely connected with the demand for freedom in marriage as well as with the desire to get away from the old restrictions in other respects. One has only to look at the works of various Chinese sociologists to see how crucial this problem has become. Mai Hui-T'ing, for example, is vitally concerned with finding a means to cut the young people loose and still give them responsibility for their parents.[5] The experience of the West in the same respect makes the prospects for such a balance on a family basis gloomy.

In a sense the appearance of a new member of the *ch'ing-nien* marks the end of an old style family, or at least it militates against the establishment of new families on the old basis. The critical point of view acquired by the *ch'ing-nien* and the demand for independence associated

[4] See P'an Kuang-Tan, *op. cit.*, pp. 55–88.
[5] *Op. cit.*, pp. 74, 79, 82, and 322–330.

with it does not permit the continued stability of the old style family either of the gentry or the peasantry type. The *ch'ing-nien* have by no means taken over Chinese society, nor are they likely to do so within the next few years, but their numbers and effectiveness are growing. One of the most striking things about the Communist Party in China is that it has conducted a major movement based almost entirely upon *ch'ing-nien*. The Communist Party has been and remains a youth organization in China. Most of its members over forty years of age grew to maturity in the party after starting out as very young men and women. The Kuomintang was in its inception in large part a youth organization too, but the youths have gradually been purged from positions of power in the party. The character of the Communist Party is of peculiar significance in these respects because it is the first major job of administration and social organization undertaken and carried out by the *ch'ing-nien* in which the *ch'ing-nien* continue to exercise genuine institutionalized influence.

From the point of view of the modernization of China no single group is of more importance than the *ch'ing-nien*. From this group industry will have to draw the greater part of its skilled labor, and the considerable group of men and women trained in the professional roles necessary to keep industry functioning. The unskilled labor taken in by the new industry will be fashioned into *ch'ing-nien* by their new experience. The further industrialization is carried, the greater will be its effect because the proportion of unskilled labor will be reduced. Modern industrial organization will impose its universalistic and functionally specific aspects on all those who work in it and a great many others beside. It will also require a minimum of literacy from all save the most unskilled workers and in time even from those. The experience of the West with the spread of literacy is still sufficiently fresh to serve as a forewarning of what accompanies it. The spread of literacy greatly increases the difficulty of controlling the attitudes of the population at large and of obtaining conformity in their action. All the radically authoritarian movements of the last one hundred years have had to devote an ever increasing amount of time and energy to the censorship and control of the sources of information.

The *ch'ing-nien* are the members of Chinese society today best fitted to carry out the patterns of industry. They, and the persons who have passed through this stage without reverting to the old patterns, absorb in their education the attitudes persons must have to operate a modern industry. They require specific training on the job, but to a large extent they can come to the job disabused of those aspects of the "traditional" way of life inimical to modern technology. This is a matter of degree, of course, and among the *ch'ing-nien* there are all shades of variation from the old patterns. The problem of recruiting labor on a universalistic basis in China is by Western standards a terrible one, even today, but the situation is changing, and the word of this type of employment is spreading.

The *ch'ing-nien* leave home today in unprecedented numbers. Peasant youths first go to the small local towns and from there to the larger industrial centers. Many go directly, of course, but those who do not have a firmer basis for adapting themselves to the new society. In any case, they are removed from direct parental control, and in many cases the difficulties of communication are such that contact with one's family is lost for long periods of time if not completely. In this fashion young people with no rebellious inclinations whatever are forced into self-reliance. Moreover, at the same time they are forced into the making of decisions that would formerly have been made for them by others, and they are forced to discover new bases for decisions as well. The result is a radical "individualism by default." The possibility of making decisions in terms of the family or by consulting family members is removed and self-determination forced upon the individual. In China, unlike Japan, where such individualism was hedged in at every conceivable point in the social structure, only the family, and to a lesser extent, the closely associated neighborhood, served as an effective brake on the individual. When the Chinese individual was out of range of family or neighborhood, he was cut loose in a radical sense. "Individualism by default" came to characterize all sorts of age groups during the chaotic conditions of the war period of 1937 to the present, but before and during this period these factors affected the *ch'ing-nien* with particular force because they, more than other age groups, moved about the land and got out of contact with their families. To a certain extent the *ch'ing-nien* absorbed a certain amount of individualism by contact with positive Western ideals, but from the point of view of the social structure as a whole "individualism by default" would certainly seem to have been a more effective and widespread solvent of the old than "individualism by ideal."

The female *ch'ing-nien* is an altogether new phenomenon in China and an even more subversive one, in a sense, than the male *ch'ing-nien*. The girls of this group change their relation to the other age groups in the family and more or less break with the family just as do the boys. In their case, however, a radical subversion of the accepted sex roles is involved as well. This gives rise to endless problems in present day China. Since the society is neither all old nor all new, individuals in various stages of development are thrown into contact with one another. For the young men and women marriage poses peculiar problems, but the women feel the weight of such problems more than the men. The modern young man married to the "traditional" style wife and vice versa are both prominent themes of the social problem literature which characterizes China today. Its basis in fact is all too obvious for any observer to ignore it. The case of the modern girl married into a more or less "traditional" family is the greater problem for several reasons. In the first place, the girl cannot leave such a family as easily as can the young man. He can at least stay away from his wife if he chooses. In the second place, she cannot stay away from the other members of the family, most especially from her mother-in-law. Miss Yao T'su-Ai cites modern daughters and "traditional" type mothers-in-law as a combination at the base of much mother-in-law–daughter-in-law conflict today.[6] Other Chinese social scientists agree with her. In the third place, a modern young woman would probably only have concluded such a marriage against her will, and in the fourth place, a modern young man can take his "traditional" wife out of the family and convert her to the new ways, whereas the likelihood of the young woman's being able to do this with her husband is considerably less.

The female *ch'ing-nien* is also becoming more important for the training of the young. As these young women become mothers and as more and more of the child training of both boys and girls falls on the mother rather than the father, the radical social views which mark the *ch'ing-nien* are perpetuated in their children. The same sort of thing is implicit in the spread of public education and the use of women teachers in the schools. The teachers have to be drawn from past or present *ch'ing-nien* because the "traditional" women would, of course, not consider such a job.

[6] *Op. cit.,* pp. 266-267.

It is a mistake to overestimate the extent of the phenomenon of the new *ch'ing-nien,* but it is, nevertheless, a dramatic change in Chinese society. The youth movement of China cannot be ignored in any investigation of modern Chinese social structure or of modern Chinese history. Dr. T. C. Wang has written a brief monograph on the youth movement [7] in which the role of the movement in modern political events is discussed. The Chinese youth movement has been a major factor in the marshaling of public opinion since at least 1919, and its activities relative to the Treaty of Versailles and the recent war with Japan seriously conditioned government policy. Because of the fact that the *ch'ing-nien* constitute one of the most articulate groups in China, and because they are vociferous in their demand for change, they assume an importance in the total social structure far beyond that which might appear to be warranted by any reckoning of their actual numbers relative to the total population.

The changes in the *chuang-nien* and *chung-nien* groups have not been so marked as have the changes in the *yu-nien* and *ch'ing-nien* groups. The reason is simple enough. These two groups comprise the most mature and active members of any society. The responsibilities of adult behavior, and the care and training of the young continue to fall on these groups, as do general positions of authority in the society. There are two main general types of difference which affect these two groups. Both are in a sense extensions from the *ch'ing-nien* period, which today often continues past marriage and hence into what was formerly *chuang-nien* status. The first is the new type of family unit. The second is the position of the women. The new family unit is the simple conjugal family consisting of husband, wife, and nonadult children. The father heads this unit, having greater power and responsibility than the mother. The important difference is that the roles of father and *chia-chang* are always combined, and no older people exert pressure on the married couple. Furthermore, the children, both male and female, marry out of the family. The number of such families seems to be increasing rapidly in China, though there is not satisfactory statistical evidence to prove this point. Modern industrialized cities are to a notable degree functionally incompatible with either *famille souche* or patriarchal families, and in the cities of China, the simple conjugal units are becoming more and more common. To the extent that this spreads to more and more of China, the marriage cere-

[7] The Youth Movement in China (New York, 1927).

mony rather than the death of one's father is increasingly the date at which one assumes full family power and responsibility.

Closely connected with the new type of family is the freedom of the wife from domination by her mother-in-law. The security of the younger women is increased in this respect, and many of their family strains are removed. The relation of the woman to her husband is also different in families affected by modern trends. The relationship is likely to be based upon mutual desire, if not outright romantic love, and the element of companionship is more heavily emphasized. The wife becomes more than the particular feminine family member with whom the husband has sexual relations. She becomes the primary source to which her husband can turn for feminine recognition and response because his mother has been removed from the situation. On the other hand, he is less inhibited in any overt show of attention for his wife. The attention of both parties to the marriage is more directly focused on each other.

One interesting new phenomenon that arises in these two age groups is the appearance in China of the bachelor and the spinster. Save for religious virtuosi, the "traditional" Chinese society was almost completely devoid of unmarried adults, either male or female, save in those extreme economic straits when a man could not secure a wife. Neither bachelor nor "old maid" had any place in the society. The new ways changed this. Careers other than marriage were now open to women, and some women chose to follow them rather than to marry. Unmarried women in professional or worker roles are an increasingly common sight in China, and the marriage age of many other women is being postponed until much later in life than would have been possible in "traditional" China. Some women remain unmarried because they will not accept a marriage arranged by their parents and cannot arrange a suitable one themselves. In the cities the problem of finding husbands for women who will not accept arranged marriages is beginning to give some hint of the similar problem in the West.

The unmarried adults who are appearing with greater and greater frequency in China today constitute an obvious break with the old family traditions. From the point of view of the "traditional" structure it is significant that these individuals seem to be most heavily concentrated among the new intellectual groups. The great prestige of the intellectual in China makes any patterns assumed by the intellectuals of wide influence. The spread of their ideas and the independence of old family traditions implicit in the example set by these people are not lost on the rest of China. The adult who remains unmarried by preference is an extreme form of a much more widespread trend in China today. Although no satisfactory statistics are available, there is unanimous agreement by informants that the age at which both males and females marry in China is increasing. It is not uncommon in China today to find groups of students averaging over twenty-two years in age, none or few of whom are married. Granting that students form a special group and generally tend to marry later, informants agree that even as recently as thirty years ago a far larger percentage of these students would have been married long before reaching such an age. One of the obvious implications of this later marriage date is that it leaves the individual free of many of the "traditional" family obligations and responsibilities at just the time that the individual is most likely to be caught up in interests outside the family. "Traditional" families have not been unaware of this factor, and many have been the cases in which an attempt has been made to stabilize the son or daughter concerned by arranging a marriage and forcing its acceptance. This is a more or less self-conscious attempt to force the person concerned out of *ch'ing-nien* status into that of *chuang-nien*. The marriage can often be forced through, but it is extremely difficult to make the arrangement work Inevitably in such matters the tendency of parents is to choose a partner who is as "traditional" as possible. There frequently results the unhappy situation which has become a leitmotiv of the conflict between old and new in China, the marriage of a modern youth with a "traditional" one. It is hard for the observer to decide whether the lot of the "traditional" partner or the "modern" partner is the more tragic. The former cannot understand why the latter cannot adjust to the situation, and the latter usually cannot see why the former clings to the marriage. Some of these marriages have the effect desired of them, but a striking number only accentuate opposition to the old ways of life.

Another situation facing *chuang-nien* and more especially *chung-nien* individuals in the "traditional" period is the defiance of their children. There are now some modern parents who make no serious effort to impose the "traditional" patterns on their adult children but rather cut them loose from the family after the Western fashion. Such parents are a small minority, however, even in the urban centers. One of the most disturbing clashes between the old and the new is that "traditional" parents try to maintain their dominance over their children but are ever less able to do so. Their own upbringing has led them to expect of their children the type of submission they gave their own parents, but it is no longer forthcoming.

The old forces which gave the parents disciplinary weapons are less effective today. The possibility of a son's running away and being able to support himself has greatly diminished the amount of domination he will bear, and the same is true of daughters, daughters-in-law, and wives.[8] This is no doubt proving to be a serious source of frustration for "traditional" parents. It introduces a whole set of new requirements in their lives. Now they must act carefully to secure the allegiance and devotion of their children. Miss Lang has stated this well while pointing out at the same time that such revolts are by no means universal:

The possibility that they might run away has strengthened the position of the youths who have stayed at home and has given them courage to defend their rights against their parents.

"Don't be so cruel to us, father," two ricksha coolies in Tientsin used to say to their father who wanted to beat them when he suspected that they had not given him all their earnings. "What would you and mother do if we ran away?" This threat made the father, a shoemaker who told us the story, uneasy, and he began to think that his wife was right when she implored him to treat the boys better. "Times are changing," he said.

But on the whole the young peasants and coolies who have stayed at home (especially the peasants) still submit to their parents' authority.[9]

The problem of parental control merges directly with considerations of the changes taking place in the position of the *lao-nien*. The changes faced by this group are so far-reaching as to form one of the major social problems of modern China. This is an interesting sign of the extent to which the slight absolute amount of Westernization has spread its influence in the land. The aged constitute an increasing problem in every modern industrial society, and growing concern over the care of the aged is a portent in China. In such modern industrial countries as the United States one factor in this problem is the statistically established

[8] The possibility of alternative employment on relatively universalistic grounds makes this difference. This matter is treated further below, e.g., pp. 329 ff.

[9] *Op. cit.*, p. 261.

trend toward an older population resultant from an increased life expectancy on the one hand and a lowered birth rate on the other. Aside from war time exceptions, the life expectancy in China may already be increasing, but the birth rate does not seem to have fallen off as yet. Actually no one knows just what China's position in these respects is. Even in relatively peaceful periods before 1937 Chinese statistics have been a nightmare to workers in the field of demography, and one of the most recent works on Chinese population leaves the reader still uncertain as to Chinese population by as much as fifty millions to one side or the other of four hundred millions.[10] The most careful estimates hover around the figure of four hundred millions, but no one really knows. Furthermore, no one knows, or even seems to have any reliable estimates of how many persons have died from war, famine, endemic disease, "old age," and so on, in the last ten years.

It is not necessary in China that the average age of the population increase in order for the old age problems to be posed. The break up of the "traditional" family is quite sufficient. In the "traditional" family the care and support of the aged were guaranteed by the continued presence of one or more sons in the family unit, and by the fact that *de jure* the authority over the economic assets of the family and over the children themselves lay with the father. The mother, while technically subject to her son if widowed, was actually in a similar position. In the "transitional" period the large number of young people who leave home deprives many of the aged of support in their declining years. Even if they own their own land, they cannot work it, and it is usually insufficient to permit them to live on rent from the land. The aged in the cities and towns are in an even worse predicament if deserted by their children, for they ordinarily have no appreciable savings and have no land or tenant rights either.

If the defiance of parents by children is a source of frustration, the desertion of aged parents is even more upsetting. It certainly outrages the "traditional" set of values. The Chinese consider the disregard of the aged which they see in the West callous and inhuman, and when it crops up at home, it is even more shocking to them. The desertion of parents by those absorbed into industry is in a sense inevitable. The mobility required of industrial labor emphasizes the necessity for a small compact

[10] See Chen Ta, *op. cit.*

family easily uprooted and transferred. Furthermore, in order to take industrial jobs many workers are forced to leave their family homes. Their parents are often self-supporting when the children leave, and when old age incapacitates the parents, the children are lost in the cities. If the children are not lost, they are often unable to support their parents in the cities or to learn farm work.

Living with one's parents is made more difficult by involvement in modern industry as a result of the role of decision forced on the worker. The "traditional" structure required submission of decisions to the aged, but the factory cares not for the opinion or the will of the aged, and demands quick decisions of the individual. The clashes of the old and the new motivate a separation of the new family from the old. Once separated and divorced from family lands, the feeling of responsibility for the aged is not reinforced by daily contact. Furthermore, in the cities one may not know one's neighbors at all, and therefore community pressure cannot force one's support of one's parents so easily as in the rural setting.

Whatever the source of the problem, China is now faced with a major problem of providing for the aged. The "traditional" family institutional pattern was so well adjusted to the care of the aged that the question of alternative techniques for their care rarely arose. Now the question is a bitter one. The number needing aid is increasing, but sympathy for the aged is not increasing. As China modernizes, the prestige of youth is increasing and that of age is declining. Furthermore, the old family structure leaves a vacuum in these respects. While the "traditional" family values required that one would support one's own aged parents, it said nothing of one's obligations to support aged persons unrelated to one by kinship. Therefore, if an old man's sons do not provide for him, no one else in the society feels responsible for him. Now the cases are becoming more and more common. Local charity cannot handle the burden, and the general members of the community feel no responsibility for an old person unless bound to him by personal ties. No adequate government provision is being made for the old at present, although the problem is fast exceeding the ability of private charity to meet it.

Psychologically speaking, the effect is disruptive. The present aged of China are almost entirely people who have clung to the "traditional" ways. They have now reached that stage of life at which, in terms of their own institutional patterns, they have every right to expect a maximum amount of honor, consideration, and ease. The aged were used to poverty because so many families lived so close to the margin of subsistence, but it was a poverty shared by the family, and the aged had first call on whatever material goods there were. Now more and more live into old age only to find abandonment and poverty in isolation. The old-age insurance of the "traditional" family is being wiped out without being replaced. This occurs at a time when, if one judges by the experience of other countries in the process of industrialization, there is every reason to expect that the proportion of aged in the population is increasing.

The matter of suicide is an indication of the growth of the problem. Actually no one has reliable suicide rates for any significant samples of the Chinese population. Estimates of informants on suicide rates vary widely, but all agree on certain factors, and that agreement is bolstered by internal structural evidence. One of these factors is that in the "traditional" society, suicide of an aged person was virtually unheard of, and that suicides after the age of about thirty-five were rare. This certainly fits well with the picture of the maxim security and well-being afforded the aged by the "traditional" kinship structure. The available opinions point, however, to an increasing suicide rate in general, and especially to an increasing number of suicides of persons over thirty-five and well into the advanced age groups. The increased suicide of the middle-aged is most prominent in the cities. This is consistent with the fact that the more modern aspects of urban life place an emphasis on the individual responsibility of the middle-aged adult which was not previously borne alone by him. The increased suicide of the aged is also greater in urban centers than in rural ones, and this coincides with the generally lower rural suicide rates and the greater retention of "traditional" institutions in the rural areas. The rise of the suicide rate of the aged is felt by some to be greater among the men than among the women, which would certainly be in keeping with the fact that there is a warmer emotional bond between sons and mothers than between sons and fathers. Although it would be a mistake to pursue such tenuous indications too far, any rise in the suicide rate of the aged fits the picture of the greater uncertainty and insecurity of their position.

The abandonment of the aged has its effects upon the other members of the family as well as upon the *lao-nien*. The presence of the grandparents in the families in which they lived did much to perpetuate the values of the "traditional" family, for their presence provided the younger generations with a living exemplification of the values concerned. Furthermore, the affection given grandchildren by their grandparents did much to ease the rather stern relations the children sometimes had with their parents. This was particularly true of boys on whom the greatest pressure was placed during the *yu-nien* period. When modern couples break away from the old people, their children lack these forces tending to bolster the "traditional" patterns and at the same time lose certain sources of recognition and response in the family.

RELATIVE AGE DIFFERENTIATION

Relative age distinctions are losing their old strength rapidly among those to whom the new influences are spreading. This is not difficult to understand, for it has been shown above that the relative age criteria in role differentiation were of rather less significance than other criteria. Chinese who break from the "traditional" patterns are not likely to retain the recognition of the precedence of family members on the basis of relative age. The relation between brothers was the most important illustration of relative age relation in the "traditional" family, and even there the relationship could in effect be severed by the division of the family after the death of the father. Today this relationship is shattered even before the death of the father if one of the younger generation breaks away from the family. In the rearing of children the emphasis on relative age is diminishing in the more Westernized families. These "modern" couples distinguish among their children on the basis of relative age, but in so doing the tendency is to justify the distinction by reference to some universalistic factor, whereas in the "traditional" families even today the particularistic statement of relative age is justification enough.[11]

[11] This is an interesting change in view of the probable functional origin of relative age precedence. To a certain degree, particularly during early childhood, the objective difference in the ability of children to perform certain functions and shift for themselves undoubtedly varies with age. Thus, for a time at least, there is on the average a high correlation between the particularistic factor of greater age and the universalistic one of greater ability. Modern industrial society, with its great emphasis on universalism, forces a reformulation even in this sphere where the positive correlation of particularistic and universalistic criteria is high. In doing so it devalues the particularistic criteria and so lessens the force of the particularistic criteria when a period is reached in which the positive correlation of particularistic and universalistic criteria is by no means so great or so certain.

The changes with regard to generation differentiation are so intimately connected with the changes in the political and economic structure of the family that it is best to postpone consideration of them as well as of differentiation on the basis of economic and political factors to the later sections taking up those structural aspects specifically. From the generational point of view itself only one or two remarks need be made. The most important observation is obviously that the "traditional" precedence of the older generation is breaking down in modern China. To an increasing degree the injunctions of the older generation are ignored, and the margin of tolerance of their domination is diminishing. Respect for the older generation is also diminishing, and even where respect has not diminished greatly, it has to some degree been offset by a growing confidence of youth in individual judgment.

Industrialization in China as elsewhere places an obvious premium on youth, and hence the younger generation, for the recruitment of both workers and executives. The members of the older generations are, by and large, still trained in the "traditional" ways and have followed such ways too long to change readily. Many of the younger generation are being trained in the new ways, and those who are not already so trained can be trained without too great difficulty, if they are taken in hand early enough. Furthermore, the physical qualities of speed, coördination, eyesight, and the like, which modern industry needs, are to be found at their best in the young. In the worker both training and physical fitness are important. In the executive the new training is the important factor, but a premium is still placed thereby on the younger generation.

The emphasis placed on the new generation by the technological demands of modern business and industry have removed from the older generation an ancient heritage. The older generation no longer knows more of economic production than does the younger in the new fields. The young in the industrial field must be trained by the young, and the process is such that the relatively young are likely to remain the best teachers. Insofar as the new ways spread, the older generation is losing its function of inducting the younger generation into its occupational roles.

As China eventually acquires a fund of specialists trained in the new ways, the members of the younger generation will come once again to be trained by the older generation rather than by members of their own group. There will be two great differences from the old patterns when this takes place. First, the members of the older generation who will come to train the young will themselves be men and women who are trained in the new ways and whose views are consequently iconoclastic concerning the "traditional" ways. In their training and in the training they give to others, the matter of generational difference will of necessity become a matter of minor importance by comparison with the material to be taught and skill in the techniques to be learned. Second, the persons doing the training, whether members of the older or younger generation, will not in the ordinary case be family members. The attention focused on the older generation in "traditional" China by the fact that one's training came largely from the members of the older generation with whom one lived cannot be overestimated. The new training will never be able to buttress the position of the older generation *in the family* in the same way. The complexity of the industrial society is such that, in the training associated with its technological aspects, the training of the younger generation by family members of the older generation cannot be guaranteed, and in fact can occur only by coincidence if the structure is to operate smoothly.

SEX DIFFERENTIATION

In "transitional" China the changes in role differentiation on the basis of sex are revolutionary, although in actuality these changes, like all the others, have not gone far in any absolute sense. Nevertheless, the extent to which they have gone, and the apparent inevitability with which they are spreading further are dramatic enough. Legally today in China the status of women is equivalent in privilege and responsibility with that of men. Daughters even have the right to inherit equally with sons.[12] These laws have not been enforced, but the extreme position they represent serves to reinforce and reflect the considerable changes which exist in fact.

For the purposes of the present discussion the "transitional" women of China may be divided into three groups: (1) those with modern education and professional roles, (2) those employed in modern industry itself,

[12] See the *Civil Code of the Republic of China* (Shanghai, 1931), Article 1138.

(3) those affected by the domestic industry or indirectly by modern industry itself. The women in the first category are absorbing the ideas of the West about feminine equality in a direct form at the same time that they absorb the other Western ideas which are subversive of the "traditional" Chinese way of life. Many of these women do not follow out these new ways after marriage but lapse into the familiar wifely roles. The extent to which they return to "traditional" patterns depends in part upon the degree of emancipation of their husbands. These women are concentrated in cities and towns and in the wealthier groups. Though many of them submit to the domination of their husbands, the pattern is more like that of the American housewife than the "traditional" Chinese wife. Many if not most of them assert some rights in the choice of their husbands, and unions based on romantic love are frequent among them.[13] Once married they are not likely to submit to the seclusion which was formerly the lot of most proper Chinese wives. They are likely to insist on greater contact with feminine friends outside the family and on greater companionship with their husbands. If these women live with their mothers-in-law, they are not likely to submit calmly to the type of treatment formerly accepted.

The women with modern professional careers are even more radical than those who merely have a Western education. The very idea of their following a career is radical enough. These women not only demand and get the consideration and companionship of their husbands, but have in addition a standing of their own outside the family. Need for the professionally trained in China is so great that the prejudice against women in "men's roles" has not been able to keep professional women out of positions. The professional training involves the Western intellectual tradition in its aspects most subversive of the "traditional" Chinese values. Therefore the professionally-trained Chinese woman is subjected to influences which break down the authority of the old institutional patterns, and at the same time the end result of her training is to endow her with a competence which permits her to defy any attempt to force the old ways upon her.

The women employed in modern industry are also emancipated

[13] Chao Bu Wei's book, *Autobiography of a Chinese Woman* (New York, 1947), gives an interesting example. (See especially pp. 113–114). This book gives an interesting picture of a rather unusual professional woman in China.

from the "traditional" patterns. The process here does not necessarily involve any direct intellectual appeal to the individual. In her work with machines, however, the woman learns to think in empirical terms and to think critically about empirical phenomena. Her learning cannot be completely confined to a given area of life without highly organized and efficient social planning which China lacks. As a result the "matter-of-fact" point of view instilled by the daily work is carried over to other aspects of life. Furthermore, the source of income is relatively independent of family control, and a woman worker quickly learns the power such a source of income carries with it.[14] She demands and gets a freedom in her personal conduct unheard of by "traditional" girls.

Within the family the economic position of such a woman is changed. The primary contribution of the female factory worker is not what she contributes in cooking, sewing, care of the children, and the like. These things persist in importance, but now her wages are also important. She, like her husband or father or brother, makes a contribution to nonhousehold production. Furthermore, she is employed outside the family. Her economic role gives her a basis from which to resist exceptionally burdensome domination, so that her position in the power hierarchy is substantially changed. Within limits she is dominated by her husband and perhaps even by his parents, if they are present, but these limits are much narrower. In the old days her only possibilities were to submit, return to her parents, or to commit suicide. Now she has another. She can desert the family and live by herself. If she has children, she is more tied down, but the fact that she once stood on her own feet economically or the fact that she continues to do so as a part or full-time worker even after motherhood is likely to reduce substantially the amount of subordination she will submit to.

The women who work in the domestic industries or who have been indirectly affected by the machine industry are also numerous. Miss Lang observes with some correctness that "the young daughter in a Chinese peasant or coolie house looks and acts very much like the girl in olden times; the new trends usually enter her life only when she becomes a factory worker."[15] The changes, however, have not entirely passed by the nonfactory workers. Domestic industry has in many spheres been hurt by

[14] See Olga Lang, *op. cit.*, pp. 262–269.
[15] *Op. cit.*, p. 262.

the introduction of machines, but modern entrepreneurs, both foreign and domestic, have also seen in domestic industry the maximum possibility of utilizing cheap labor with a minimum of capital to produce articles for both foreign and domestic consumption. For this reason the modern period in China has seen a growth of domestic industry, although it does not exert so subversive an influence on its workers as modern mechanized industry. The fact that the work can be confined to the home tends to maintain the old family self-sufficiency in a way not equaled by the factory. There are other "advantages" as well, but from the point of view of sex differentiation, the spread of domestic industry has also given women a function in economic production other than the old household roles. Although the work is carried on in a family setting, the enhanced position of the women as an economic asset is not entirely lost to the women themselves.

In an indirect manner the enhanced value of the women as an economic asset is having a general effect beyond the families of factory and domestic industry workers. Chinese parents are coming to understand that daughters as well as sons may become economic assets. Furthermore, as communication facilities improve, women outside of urban centers learn more and more of the new ways being followed by their more modern counterparts. The stress and uncertainty of the female role in China is a matter of long standing. There is no reason to believe that Chinese women are socially or biologically an aggregation of innate masochists who enjoy the uncertainty and actual physical abuse which they are so often compelled to bear. The strains involved in the "traditional" role of women in the Chinese family provides motivation enough for trying alternative ways whenever the opportunity offers. As time goes on the actual opportunity is increasing, but word of the increasing opportunity outruns the fact. Westerners are amazed by the facility with which news spreads in the Orient with relatively little aid from modern communication devices. Much distorted gossip and rumor accompanies the core of fact, but nevertheless the word spreads. The news that women in the cities can earn an income over and above the cost of their keep has spread far and wide through the land. It is still difficult even for men to travel to the industrial centers, and women have not yet begun the long trek in great numbers. Most women factory workers are still drawn from the areas in immediate contact with the industrial centers. The use of contract labor and the travels of professional labor recruiters has in the past made some difference in this respect. The recent war and the contact it brought between local people and migrants from the industrial centers have also made some difference. The difference that will be made by another ten thousand miles of railroad, by a million new trucks and buses, by thousands of miles of new auto roads, and by the further development of China's waterways will be even greater. Modern China is going to be faced with the often-sung American dilemma of "How're you going to keep them down on the farm," and in China this will mean women as well as men.

SOLIDARITY

The substructure of solidarity in the Chinese family is also changing in the families which are moving away from the "traditional" patterns. In the most radical new families which have self-consciously abandoned the "traditional" patriarchal and *famille souche* patterns, the changes in the structure of solidarity have been great. Most of the changing families, however, suffer change in these respects without knowing why or how. Many such cases result from a simple difficulty in communication. This is an old difficulty in China, but it is immensely complicated now that more individuals than ever before are separated from their families. Other cases result from the fact, mentioned so often above, that now more than ever before persons suffering from the strains of the old family organization can leave the family with some hope of being able to maintain themselves.

The changes in solidarity between father and son are dramatic and crucial. This was, of course, inevitable, because that relationship was so important for the "traditional" Chinese family, and at the same time such a source of strain in it. Even in the areas remote from the urban centers a weakening of the strength of the solidarity is evident. Since the possibility of escape from an unbearable situation by flight is now greater than before, some fathers are becoming aware of the fact that they must be more lenient with their sons, and sons are beginning to realize that the possibility of flight is a social lever with which they can alleviate their burdens. In actuality the solidarity is probably more often broken by flight than by the more self-conscious method. In any case, the absolute obedience of son to father is a matter which can no longer be taken for granted in the same degree as formerly.

As one moves from the families who are maintaining the "traditional" patterns relatively intact, the changes are no longer negative in character. Changes in education are making marked differences. Sons of the gentry are more often educated in the new learning which does not reinforce the old pattern of solidarity. The sons of the poorer classes in the areas nearest to the urban centers are beginning in a small way to receive public education. This education also tends toward the new style. The education of the sons of the poor is a radical departure. It not only takes them away from paternal supervision for a certain amount of time, but it also gives them an increased prestige over their uneducated parents. The new ideas encountered as education progresses are further subversive of the old authoritarian bond.

The experience in the new schooling breaks down the bond between father and son in yet another way. In "traditional" China schooling was hardly an escape from paternal tyranny, for the tyranny of the schoolmaster was even greater than that of the father. Some of this persists in the new schooling, but it is diminishing as new teaching methods stressing student participation and initiative are introduced. The presence of women teachers is increasing. This is not only a dramatic change in educational practice, but when present, inevitably accentuates any harsh treatment by the father and increases the perspective of the sons on such treatment.

In the families in which the father himself is employed in modern industry still more extreme changes are to be found. The most notable of these is that the father's work takes him out of the family for an appreciable part of each day, and accordingly obviates his personal supervision of the son during the *yu-nien* period. The supervision falls in such cases to the mother or to older sisters, and he is dominated by women in a way not hitherto true. Such families are likely to be the simple conjugal type, and the absence of grandparents has further implications for the son's training.[16] The emphasis on the father-son tie is weakening, but it is not diminishing as fast as the actual strength of the relationship.

Among most modern young families there is some reason to believe that the son is becoming a rival of the father for the attention of the

[16] See above, pp. 306–307.

mother. This can only be the case in families emphasizing the bond of romantic love between husband and wife. It is doubtful that this trend has gone very far as yet, but as free marriages increase, this source of father–son friction well may increase.

Next to the father-son relationship, that of husband and wife is probably undergoing the greatest change. To an increasing degree youths are demanding some voice in the selection of their marital partners. P'an Kuang-Tan presents some statistical evidence to indicate that the majority of youths want some voice in their marriage but that, at the same time, the majority do not ask that marriage be cut entirely free from parental participation.[17] Miss Lang points out that in the peasant communities it is virtually impossible for children to choose their own mates without regard to parental views and that even in the cities complete disregard of parents is uncommon.[18] Various compromise arrangements appear in the cities. Parents select and children approve; children select and parents approve, and so forth. In the rural villages the old patterns persist, but, as other new patterns come to the rural areas, greater freedom in these respects usually comes too. So long as the villages remain untouched, the parents obviously cannot risk the upset of the whole pattern of family relations by a capricious marriage choice.

The new patterns change the whole relationship between husband and wife particularly among the young people with modern educations. These youths emphasize companionship between husband and wife, rather than an arrangement to provide heirs for the family. In the most radical of these modern families the primary orientation of the husband is to his wife and vice versa. The strength of their relationship is no longer negligible, but supersedes all others. Furthermore, these wives are not submissive to their husbands as of old. They demand and get a certain amount of consideration as individuals. Among the educated this sort of material relationship results in part from exposure to Western ideals. Something of the same thing is to be found among industrial workers, however, when both husband and wife are employed. In the case of the workers, the basis is more likely to be economic than intellectual. The employed wife early appreciates the power given her by her potential economic independence, and so is less likely to put up with the old type of subordination.

[17] *Op. cit.*, pp. 73–76.   [18] *Op. cit.*, pp. 122–123.

Closely connected to the changes in solidarity between husband and wife are those between daughter-in-law and mother-in-law. This was one of the most explosive relationships in "traditional" China, and in the "transitional" period its strain is resulting in a breakdown of the relationship. Again, the old patterns persist in a great majority of cases, but the new are appearing, and the old patterns have no effective way of stopping them without stopping the entire process. Young couples to an increasing degree insist upon their right to live alone, and this fact immediately smashes the strength of the old daughter-in-law–mother-in-law solidarity by removing the relationship almost entirely. The increased strength of solidarity between husband and wife further weakens that of the wife and the mother-in-law, since the son is less disposed to enforce his mother's will. A corollary of this situation is of course a decrease in the strength of solidarity of son and mother after the son reaches adulthood.

The new education which the wife sometimes has is a source of friction between the daughter-in-law and the mother-in-law. The daughter-in-law learns new theories about child care, housekeeping, personal behavior, and the like. In the past there were sufficient sources of conflict between these two, but the new ideas are opening up a whole new field of battle. As sources of conflict increase, other family members are to an increasing degree called upon to settle issues. To the degree that new issues arise, the young people are already influenced away from the "traditional" verities and hence are less likely to support the mother-in-law's claim to power. If the mother-in-law's power is backed up, the matter does not necessarily end there. Now the daughter-in-law has the possibility of leaving and making her own way.

The mother-in-law–daughter-in-law relationship in China has not ceased to be a problem. In the majority of the populace it persists. Even where its strength has been broken, it still exerts an influence. The break over the mother-in-law's power is a point at which the old and the new come into serious conflict. Once the problem is posed in a family, the young couple can either submit or revolt. If they revolt, they break the old family entirely, for its interlocking solidarities permit little compromise. If the son refuses to enforce his mother's wishes, she can ask his father to order him to do so. If the son defies his father, the old family structure is finished. Thus the break of the mother-in-law's power almost inevitably involves other crucial aspects of family structure.

Many of the other solidarities taken up in the section on the "traditional" family are being negated by the new family trends. The simple conjugal family unit eliminates all members save the husband, wife, and nonadult children. The change in family composition, therefore, increases the relegation of old family members to the category of outsiders. Among those who remain, however, other changes are to be found. The distinction between brothers and sisters is becoming less marked than formerly, particularly as regards the precedence of the boys over the girls. The precedence of the older over the younger is also less marked. To an increasing degree children are becoming a group of equals. Discrimination among them must to an increasing degree be justified on objective grounds. This trend is not marked save in the most radical new families, but it is noticeable none the less.

The general weakening of family solidarities is of great strategic interest in modern China. The family organization is in all societies an ineradicable stronghold of particularism and functional diffuseness. In "traditional" China the part of one's total social life encompassed by the family meant a corresponding institutionalization of particularism and functional diffuseness throughout the whole of one's social life. Modern industrialization requires a high degree of universalism and functional specificity over a wide sphere of action. The conjugal family, which seems to accompany modern industrialization wherever it goes, reduces the number of family members to a minimum. It also reduces the length of time during which any individual is a member of a given unit, for in the simple conjugal family structure both male and female have different families of orientation and procreation. This reduces the number of persons with whom any given person has very strong particularistic and functionally diffuse relationships. The family structure is by no means the sole source of the problem of particularism in China, but it is certainly the major one. The shift to simple conjugal family units and the consequent weakening of the "traditional" family solidarities tends somewhat to reduce the problem of particularism.

ECONOMIC SUBSTRUCTURE

At the outset of the "transitional" period the economic substructure of the Chinese family began to change. It is doubtful whether the intellectual forces so prominently at work among the students could have brought about the current changes in China. The persons converted to the new patterns by intellectual experience are vital to the changes because of the leadership they afford, but the far-reaching changes which seem to be afoot must rest on a broad popular base which the students alone cannot offer. China has seen many popular revolutions in the past, but these have inevitably aimed at renovation of the old social structure rather than its abolition and replacement. The social movements of the last hundred years have increasingly sought a new social organization rather than a renovation of the old. The change introduced in the economic substructure of the family has been a prime factor in the new revolutionary orientation.

The question of why the new industry was introduced to China is an interesting one. The desire for profit both by foreigners and by Chinese played a role in this, as did the efforts of men who felt that China must modernize its methods of production or be forever reduced to colonial status. As has been indicated above, the various stresses and strains within the family guarantee the new industrial efforts a source of labor. Other factors also help produce a labor supply. The procedure of family inheritance, and the prevailing practices in tenancy and usury are in many areas driving the peasants from the land. Professor Chen Han-Seng in a remarkable monograph discusses this problem at length. He gives examples of high interest rates in twelve villages in which the semiannual interest rates on grain loans vary from 50 per cent to 100 per cent and average 70.83 per cent.[19] He points out that:

In Kwantung one-third of the peasant families possess less than five mow (of land) each, nearly half of the peasant families are entirely landless, and more than 60% of all the land cultivated is rented from landlords.[20]

He states that at least seven or eight years of great deprivation of the family is required to save enough to buy one mow of medium grade land in Kwantung.[21] Professor Chen also points to the fact that the lot of of these peasants is so hard that the land itself is being mined. The peasants cannot afford to maintain it, let alone improve it.

. . . we now ask whether production itself is going upward or downward, whether the future for agriculture in this part of the world is growing brighter or gloomier. So far, no scientific and statistical data can be given to show the

[19] *Op. cit.,* p. 90.   [20] *Ibid.,* Preface, p. viii.   [21] *Ibid.,* p. 103.

exact degree of decline in agricultural production, because no such investigation has yet been made in Kwantung; but in the case of Kwei-kwan or large farms in the Pan-yu district, we know that the amount of unhusked rice produced per mow has been reduced from six to four piculs within the last thirty years. In the district of Kao-yao, Wung-yuen, and Mei-Hsien, the peasants in many a village told the writer that there had been a decline in production even within the past ten years . . . under these circumstances, the emigration going abroad and the rural exodus in general, the increasing prevalence of women laborers in agriculture, and especially the decrease in agricultural wages which . . . is sure proof of the lowering of the standard of living among the peasantry, all reflect the discouragement and even loss of labor power.[22]

Whatever may have been the motivation which led to the establishment of the new business and industry and the willingness of persons to work in it, the effects on the "traditional" family's economic substructure are undeniable and unavoidable. In the first place, the new business and industry draws its participants to large urban centers.[23] In so doing it separates the majority of them from their old family units. Migration to the cities is not generally a family matter. When one goes to the city, it is by no means certain that he will succeed there. Usually there are some ties with the family and the home which make life in the old environment more certain and desirable in some respects than in the new. Some land is left, perhaps; the ancestral graves must be tended, and so on. Furthermore, the motivation to leave and seek new pastures is not a matter moving an entire family at once. It is more likely to strike at one or two members than at the whole unit.

Once in the urban centers the forces which militate against rebuilding the old style families are powerful. The most important single force of this sort is the fact that the family members cannot count on continuing to work as an economic unit. The very universalism which makes the new economic organization an alternative to the old submission also prevents one from counting on the employment of all the working members

[22] *Ibid.*, pp. 97-98.

[23] The functional basis for the concentration of modern business and industry in large urban centers need not be analyzed here. The concentration has not been a matter of chance, however, and this factor should be kept in mind by the many planners who urge that China be industrialized as quickly as possible but on a basis of rural decentralization. There is good reason to believe that, while a certain amount of decentralization is compatible with industrialization, a large-scale industrial society is inherently urban.

of one's family as a unit. Only at relatively unskilled jobs can family members have any expectations of being left together as a unit. In modern industry family members cannot even count on being employed in the same organization or the same area. Therefore a sufficient number of family members to permit of the support of large family units cannot be sure of employment close enough so that living together is feasible. Even if the jobs are within the same city they may be far enough apart so that a common dwelling is inconvenient. To some extent in China the presence of domestic industry in the cities tends to offset this, for the domestic industry permits of the common local employment of family members or it may utilize those members who cannot find or take other jobs locally.

The incompatibility of large families of the patriarchal or *famille souche* types with modern industrialized cities is not confined to China. It is to be seen in the urban breakdown of the family patterns in Japan and in the West. A whole school of modern social thinkers has arisen to decry this tendency in the West, but no force has arisen which is compatible with modern technology and at the same time threatens to block the spread of the multilineal conjugal family composed of husband, wife, and nonadult children or to disrupt its institutionalization.

The cities of China are by no means highly industrialized by the standards of the United States or England, but they are becoming so to a sufficient degree to manifest the tendencies common in other societies in which industrialization is a major component. The fact that Chinese cities contain so much domestic industry, so much handicraft work, and so much unskilled labor, offsets these tendencies to some degree, but as modern industry spreads, the tendencies spread as fast or faster. From the point of view of the family, modern industry places an emphasis on individuals as sources of the family income of the nonhousehold sort. The household matters of cooking, sewing, child care, and the like can be done by feminine and nonadult family members as a group, but the acquisition of the materials and nonhousehold services for consumption cannot be carried out as a unit. The family members engaged in nonhousehold production produce an income in terms of generalized purchasing power with which the necessities of life and other goods and services as well may be purchased. When this happens, the core of the "traditional" Chinese family economic substructure is destroyed. The self-sufficiency of the family unit both as regards production and consumption is removed, and its lack cannot be offset as in the case of gentry families in the "traditional" period.[24]

Another factor which is breaking up the "traditional" pattern is the question of entry to occupation roles. In the "traditional" family most sons followed the occupations of their fathers, and virtually all women were destined for a place in the household economy. In the "transitional" family this is no longer the case. The son of a father employed in modern industry or by a modern business firm cannot count on learning an occupational role from his father. His father may be able to help him get a job, but even this cannot be counted upon. The element of stability involved in the "traditional" family by virtue of the fact that its members by and large followed the same occupational roles as their predecessors does not exist for the "transitional" family. This is of great importance, for it removes a functional basis for family continuity of more than one generation. The old economic structure of the family required and fostered such continuity. The new uncertainty neither requires nor fosters it. Furthermore, in the case of members of "traditional" families taking jobs in modern industry, there is a change to a radically different social environment, as well as a change from the old succession of occupational roles.

Another change is the difference in the place of women in the economic substructure. One of the most notable changes in the woman's role is the changed relation she bears to the male roles. Even the amount of mingling possible in the "traditional" family occupational roles is no longer possible. In "transitional" families in which the men or women are employed in modern industry the various family members cannot mingle in one another's productive realms. Sometimes in textile mills, for example, one member of a family will be hired, and other family members will appear at the job to aid him. This is not, however, a true measure of the industrial discipline but rather of the relatively primitive stage of much of the industry in China today. As Chinese industry approaches a par with industry elsewhere, such labor practices will have to be omitted.

The nature of the new production roles further separates men and women in the family. The standard of living of the Chinese worker is notoriously low, but in order to support even that meager level of income

[24] *Supra,* pp. 213 ff.

the worker is forced to work long hours. The factory worker knows no slack season during which he may work in and around the household while nature in effect carries the productive load. When a factory worker is not at work, he is without any income. Since his wages are low, he has little chance to save against such seasons. He therefore cannot take them voluntarily. As a result the contact of male and female family members and of father and children which marked the slack season household labor of the man in the peasant economy is gone. The family is thereby denied another vital aspect of association which featured the "traditional" family.

With the disappearance of time for household labor goes the increased dependence upon outsiders to supply family needs. Food obviously must be bought from outsiders, but so must many other articles which the peasants formerly fashioned for themselves. Industry spreads dependence on outsiders inevitably, not only because it makes goods more cheaply than they can be made by the old methods, but also because it forces such dependency upon its own participants. Modern industry brings with it a degree of specialization unknown in other economic structures. The degree of specialization immediately required is diffused throughout the society by the specialization it induces to supply the needs of its participants.

While the women are cut off in their occupational roles from the male members of their own families, they are not similarly cut off from other male contacts. In fact the contact with males outside the family is increased, particularly if the woman concerned is involved in a modern factory job. The women immediately involved in factory jobs meet men during their work and in their journeying to and from work, thereby increasing the possibility of extramarital contacts. Although in modern industry certain types of work become known as "women's jobs" and others as "men's jobs," the mingling of the sexes is inevitable unless one or the other is completely excluded from employment. The increased contact of persons with members of the opposite sex who are not family members runs directly counter to the "traditional" pattern of separating adults, especially women, from nonfamily members of the opposite sex.

The increased extramarital contact does not arise solely from the change in production roles. The change in the structure of consumption is also significant. Since the incomes of the new type of workers is in the form of money, their families must purchase their needs on the open market. Since the male family member or members must be occupied away from the home most of the day, the burden of such marketing is thrown on the women. In the old handicraft shops and in the domestic industries this dependency on the markets was also felt, even though to a lesser degree, but the performance or supervision of these outside contacts by the male family members was not similarly inhibited, and close supervision of the women was always a possibility.

Women are caught up in another interesting change by the new developments. In the "traditional" family economy the woman's economic contribution was so defined as to permit her to combine her work with her childbearing and her care of children. Her husband's work was such that he could supervise the boys after infancy. The new technology changes all that. The woman, if she works in modern industry, must give the care of her children to others, or let them grow up with a minimum of adult supervision and a resultant loss of training by adults and of a feeling of security and response on the part of the children. If the wife stays at home with the children, the urban location and the new commodities deprive her of many of her former functions.

The increased value of the feminine economic contributions to the family, and the wider possibility of feminine employment is, as mentioned above, easing the uncertainty felt by girls as they approach maturity, for their families are no longer so anxious to marry them off and turn them from a familiar to a strange environment. As a result, the marriage age of girls is increasing. The new education of girls is delaying the marriage of girls in families which can afford the luxury of education for daughters, but the possibility of nonhousehold employment is having the same effect among the poorer families.[25]

The delay of marriage creates all sorts of economic possibilities which did not formerly exist. Formerly the delay of marriage was costly to the girl's family. Now, if she can find work, the delay of her marriage may even provide a method of improving the family's general economic position. Not enough jobs have yet been created to raise the possibility of peasant families pulling themselves out of economic difficulties in this fashion, nor is this likely to be the case in the future, because the more plentiful such jobs become, the less likely the daughters will be to serve

[25] See Lang, op. cit., 263.

the family in this way. In the present, however, some families are being aided in this fashion.

The delay of marriage also makes it more difficult for men to find wives. This is particularly true in those rural areas from which women are being actively drained away for industrial work. The economic implications of this for the peasant family with an unmarried son are important. The cost of getting married is increased on the one hand, and the difficulty of finding a young woman to replace the aging mother in the household economic roles is increased on the other. At the same time, the delay in marriage may make the family more vulnerable to economic fluctuations of the outside world. If the female members of the family who are employed are thrown out of work, they become economic burdens once again.

This brings up the general point of the integration of the economic substructure of the family with that of the society at large, and with that of other societies. The extreme social decentralization implicit in the "traditional" society of China was reflected in the economic structure of the society. The various families were to an unusual degree independent of one another in economic respects. The irrigation system modified this independence in areas in which irrigation was required, but even so, the economic decentralization was great. The average peasant in the eighteenth century might well have been unaffected by a calamity in another *hsien*. He was certainly not likely to have his own economic position affected by what took place in the European economy.

As the self-sufficiency of the average Chinese family declines, the Chinese family is no longer so well insulated against indirect economic effects from the outside. Fluctuations in the business cycle can and do touch many of the Chinese peasants today. The self-sufficiency of the Chinese peasant family seriously circumscribed its ability to profit materially, but at the same time it afforded the family a maximum amount of security under the circumstances. In "transitional" China much of that security is being wiped out without any corresponding rise in the material standard of living. Dr. Fei Hsiao-T'ung in his *Peasant Life in China* shows what has been the effect of the world slump of the silk market on a relatively isolated village.[26] The same sort of thing is taking place with increasing effect all over China.

[26] See pp. 197–236, and 282.

The exposure of the Chinese family to the effects of economic forces far removed from its immediate locale poses difficult problems for the family members. In the "traditional" period, sources of economic distress were close at hand and relatively easy to identify. A bad crop, an oppressive tax collector, usury, drought, rapacious landlords, or idleness are all rather easily comprehended. The backwash of a world-wide depression is not so easy to explain, and the uncertainty added thereby may have a role in the apparently increasing appeal in China of radical programs for change. Once the self-sufficiency of the family unit is destroyed and family production is integrated with a national or international economy, it is difficult to reëstablish the old self-sufficiency of the family unit. The Chinese who are absorbed in the new economic ventures probably do not in fact return to the old ways in times of depression. Peasant life, either economically speaking or otherwise, is not a cloak to be put on or off. The life of the peasant requires long habituation and cannot be resumed as a stopgap.

In the "transitional" families there is a decline in the executive functions in the economic sphere of both the *chia-chang* and the feminine head of the household. The diminution of family size is one factor in this. Neither family production nor consumption involves as many persons as formerly. This is not, however, the whole or even the major part of the story. The *chia-chang* is no longer in a position to plan the major income producing activities of the family. The *chia-chang* cannot plan the actual work because he does not control it, and he cannot guarantee that a family member will be able to get and hold any particular job. Within the household the executive function is also reduced because so large a portion of the materials formerly produced there are now bought in various markets.

The loss of these executive functions has indirect effects of considerable importance. Not the least of the factors creating and maintaining respect for the *chia-chang* and the feminine head of the household in the "traditional" family was the fact that the other family members saw them carry out daily administration of the unit upon which they depended. From earliest childhood this administration was seen and taken for granted, and this habituation served to sanction the position of the administrator and to make the extension of these functions into other spheres seem natural and inevitable. In the "transitional" period the loss of these executive functions is therefore still another feature of the society which undermines the "traditional" sanctity of the *chia-chang* and the feminine head of the household.

The new trends in family structure have a set of economic implications which extend well past the economic substructure of the family itself. Decentralized though it was, Chinese society in the "traditional" period was not without its own generalized economic integration. The decentralization of the society and the high level of self-sufficiency of its family units focused attention on a geographical basis of integration, rather than on an integration by industries or by financial control. In a sense only government-operated economic efforts, such as tax collecting, the salt monopoly, and the like were directly integrated on a national scale, and even these tended toward a localized integration, as was exemplified by the relative autonomy of the local tax collector. Nevertheless, the particularism which dominated the society gave it integration. In the local sphere individuals were disciplined in family terms, and within any given neighborhood a family balance of power was maintained, either through the *tsu* organization or through a council of elders, or by some combination of the two. Even in the urban centers, integration was maintained in something of the same fashion. In the cities guild organizations, which were organized on paternalistic and particularistic grounds, were a large force in economic integration.[27] There were other organizations as well, but the guilds were more or less typical. The guilds, like the neighborhood, operated to a large extent through families. The guilds regulated entrance to an occupation, standards of performance, and also, in large degree, relations of the trade with other aspects of the economy. Even beggars and coolies were organized on a guild basis. Such integration of the economy as was maintained was therefore maintained primarily on a basis of family particularism. Aside from connections on that basis, the field of action was notoriously undefined, and a radical *caveat emptor* situation existed.

The new changes in the family are being injected into the "traditional" economic situation. A prominent feature of these changes is the breakdown of economic organization on a family basis, and the strength of family control over the individual. The breakdown is proceeding most rapidly in the urban centers, which are precisely the places in which the

[27] See, for example, J. S. Burgess, *The Guilds of Peking* (New York, 1928).

need for integrated social organization is greatest and most complex. Much of the breakdown is not self-conscious. For every person in China who deliberately abandons family domination and departs from the "traditional" family economic organization, there are several persons who have been forced into the position by geographical separation, family deaths, and economic pressures. These persons are forced to fall back on individual decisions rather than family decisions. It is the matter of "individualism by default" in another of its guises.

In a "traditional" rural setting a person cut off from his family can be reabsorbed by the surrounding neighborhood and family organizations into the old patterns, or can be forced out of the area entirely. In the cities this is not the case. The guilds are breaking down at a rapid pace.[28] They are not in a position to reabsorb persons who are unwillingly thrown out of the old family ways. In the first place, these persons lack the necessary particularistic connections for getting into the guilds. In the second place, the sanctity of the bonds which made the guilds effective is to a large degree dependent upon the old family discipline. In the third place, the field of the guilds is being destroyed at a progressive pace by the new technology, so that the guild organizations are faced with an increasing problem of finding employment for their own members without accepting new ones. In the fourth place, the guilds are faced with a new problem in their own field. The number of persons attracted to the urban centers by the new possibilities of employment and by economic pressures in the rural areas is so great that the guilds can no longer maintain effective monopolies. This is especially true in unskilled roles. Many laborers who come to the city seeking new types of employment are disappointed and become a reservoir of cheap labor for general purposes, old and new alike. And in the fifth place, many of the city workers are involved in jobs based on the new technology. For these workers and in these spheres there are no particularistic organizations to furnish general integration. Trade unions are growing, but their organization is by no means as inclusive or as effective as was that of the old guilds. As a result, there are no well defined social structures for integrating a phase of the economy which is growing in absolute size and which is of special importance for its direct and indirect effects on the old economy. The institutional patterns of the "traditional" structure are being broken down before the institutional

[28] See Burgess, *op. cit.,* p. 235.

patterns of the industrialized West can replace them. The result is a situation which often approaches *anomie* in an advanced form.[29] The breakdown of the "traditional" economic patterns is at one and the same time a prerequisite and an obstacle to the industrialization of China.

POLITICAL SUBSTRUCTURE

Many of the changes in the political substructures of the Chinese family during the "transitional" period have already been mentioned in one connection or another above, and need not be labored here. In essence the situation is one in which the bases of the old political integration are being destroyed. The introduction of the political ideas of the West is certainly an important feature of modern China, but these ideas can easily be given an unwarranted significance. The importance of student and intellectual leadership in the liberal movement of China is in part responsible for the tendency to weigh these ideas so heavily, but the roles of these persons is only to be understood in terms of other aspects of the structural picture of modern China.

Like the philosophic traditions of most societies of long history, that of China contains a wide variety of concepts other than those which have at any given time actually held sway in the society. The ideas of liberty, equality, and fraternity which are so widely associated with the rise of modern industrialism and modern democracy are not without a philosophic pedigree in China. The same is true of most of the other political concepts which characterize the industrialized societies of the present day. The failure of "traditional" Chinese society to institutionalize these concepts is argument enough to refute the attribution of causal priority to these ideas unaccompanied by other factors. If the ideas alone contain some mysterious causal efficacy, the absence of their previous institutionalization is difficult to explain.

Structurally speaking, the entire political picture of the family is changing, and with it that of the society as a whole. The introduction of

[29] Professor Shih Kuo-Heng in a manuscript which has not yet been published on tin mining in the Ko-Chiu area of Yünnan has presented a situation of this sort of *anomie*. This monograph is extremely fruitful for the insight it provides into the industrial problems of "transitional" China. An excerpt of this study has appeared as "Social Implications of Tin-Mining in Yunnan," *Pacific Affairs*, XX 1 (March, 1947), 53–61.

the new technology of the West with its accompanying discipline and set of ideas is probably proving more immediately subversive of the "traditional" political substructure of the family than of other aspects of the family. Often it is through its effect on the political substructure of the family that the process of industrialization in China outruns itself, in a manner of speaking. Villages to which neither the goods nor the discipline of the machine process have reached can be touched by its ability to undermine the autocratic position of the *chia-chang* and so undermine the entire integration of the family.

The key to the disruption of the political substructure of the Chinese family seems to lie in the possibility of acceptable alternative employment on a relatively universalistic basis. Future researches may disprove this hypothesis, but it would seem for the present to be consistent with the known aspects of the situation. It is not intended to imply here that even in modern industry or business in China particularistic elements in employment have been eliminated. This is by no means true, and the degree to which particularism continues to invade this field constitutes one of the primary obstacles to industrialization and the conduct of modern business in China today. Even in the United States, which is surely the epitome of an industrialized society, particularism has not been entirely eliminated from this sphere of action. China has no monopoly on nepotism. But in industrialized societies universalism is institutionalized, and it is in the process of being institutionalized in China insofar as the new technology of business and industry is spreading.

In the "traditional" family structure one element was crucial to the maintenance of the political substructure. It was the integration of the family with the society. The family had to have some means to contain its members, for if they could have fled an unpleasant situation, the power positions of the family would have had been severely limited. As has been suggested above, this means lay in the inability of the average individual to find an acceptable alternative method of making a living. Prior to the industrialization of the West, no large scale contact of China with other societies afforded any such possibility. It is not by chance that the ideas and patterns of the preindustrial West made little or no inroads on Chinese society. It is not by chance, either, that the Mongol and Manchu invasions and the foreign rule of China failed to change the situation basically. Both of these societies were highly organized for war and the nomadic life,[30] but all China could not be kept on a war footing, nor could it be converted to a nomadic or seminomadic way of life. Having few or no institutions of their own to cover such a situation, these societies were forced to choose between total destruction of China or major adoption and maintenance of Chinese ways. At one time in the Mongol invasion the alternative of destruction was seriously considered on just these grounds.[31] It was not until well into the nineteenth century that the society of Europe and America had any genuine alternative to offer on this score. Shortly in the wake of this, China was faced by the beginnings of the first genuinely revolutionary social movement in at least several hundred years. The movement is still in process, and its fate is far from settled. It already promises, however, to change virtually every important structural feature of Chinese society.

In "transitional" China the three major criteria of political role differentiation—age, sex, and generation—are all changing. None of them is completely gone, even in the most modern families, and they may never be, but they are all changing in their incidence. Since the trend in "transitional" China is toward a family unit consisting of husband, wife, and nonadult children, many aspects of the old political structure are out of the question. For example, the old generational continuity of the family unit is gone, and with it the need for the elaborate institutionalization of a continuing and stable inheritance of authority in the family. Every man's family of procreation becomes a new family.

The two basic generational strains in the "traditional" family, that between father and son and that between mother-in-law and daughter-in-law, are both changed by the new situation, for now both sons and daughters-in-law can leave home. In the "traditional" families generational domination remains in force, but the autonomy of the *chia-chang* and the feminine head of the household is no longer secure. In addition, the major avenue to economic and social ascent is no longer precisely that which best inculcates the "traditional" patterns, for modern education and modern business and professional roles compete formidably with the old classical education.

[30] The Manchus were, of course, already "Sinified" to some degree when they conquered China, so the contrast in their case was much less than in that of the Mongols.

[31] See Paul Ratchnevsky, *Un Code des Yüan* (Paris, 1937), pp. vii-viii.

In the "transitional" families the older generation continues to dominate the younger, but not in the same way or in the same degree. Domination is no longer a matter of the lifetime of the older generation, but is to an increasing degree only a matter of the age of maturity of the young. To an increasing degree the young demand personal autonomy upon maturity, and in some instances parents are even coming to expect it of them. Even the domination of the younger by the older generation prior to the time of maturity is becoming more limited. The new legal codes of China contain many humanitarian provisions against the sale, murder, harsh punishment, or coercion of children into marriage [32] which previously were not written into law. The fact that these laws are by and large unenforced does not obviate the significance of their presence. The more modern families are beginning to observe them voluntarily, and the appearance of the laws on the statute books indicates at least a concern not previously felt.

The growing "accent on youth" is a contributing factor to the changing political relations between the younger and the older generation. Although the change has not yet gone to any dramatic lengths even in the urban centers, there is a growing tendency of the older generation to view the younger generation as an end in itself and not primarily as a means of provision for the declining years of the older generation, or as a means for the continuation of the family in order to perpetuate the veneration of the ancestors. On the other side, the tendency is matched by a tendency of the younger generation to demand recognition as individuals rather than, or as well as, family members. In families in which these changes are taking place much of the old patterns of obedience is no longer meaningful. Obedience is coming to be primarily oriented to the preservation of the young from harm and the preparation of the young for mature roles in the society rather than to the reinforcement of the position of the older generation.

With the shift in attention to the younger generation, another element which alters the political substructure of the family appears. The family ceases to be the primary orientation of the individual. Much of the priority of the political substructure of the family is thereby lost. Among the young other responsibilities are being weighed against family responsibilities. Duty to one's country, duty to one's profession, duty to one's

[32] E.g. see *The Civil Code of the Republic of China,* Article 972.

ideals, and duty to oneself, all are now entering competition with the old family loyalties.

The appearance of the consideration of duty to oneself is radical in Chinese society, for in this one may find the beginnings of "individualism by ideal" rather than "by default." Individualism as an ideal does not characterize a large number of Chinese today. It is found largely among students and intellectuals. The individualism among others is likely to be of the default variety. The presence of the ideal among the students and intellectuals must not be too heavily discounted, despite the smallness of the numbers involved, for the group affected is an exceptionally strategic group in China. As a highly articulate group, and as a teaching and leading group, its influence may spread broadly through the society. Among the larger numbers of "individualists by default" the doctrine of individualism as an ideal may find ready reception, especially if attempts are made to curb the new freedom, or if the individuals involved become convinced of the futility of returning to the old ways.

In any case, the granting of priority to other than the "traditional" family considerations breaks the old pattern of generational dominance by removing the voluntary basis of compliance with the demands of the structure. It has been suggested above that even the powerful supporting features of the "traditional" Chinese situation could not have maintained such domination through the use of coercion without any positive source of motivation. The "transitional" situation combines a change in both factors. At the same time it provides an alternative basis of employment, which seriously limits the effectiveness of the old coercive structure, and an alternative group of values and allegiances, which seriously limits the institutionalization of generational priority.

The political priority of the male sex is also undergoing change. New laws limit the domination of men over women. Fathers may no longer sell their daughters or force them into marriages against their will. Wives technically have legal support in resistance to abuse by their husbands or mothers-in-law. The new laws declare women to be equal and complete citizens. The length the new law reaches in these respects is to be found in the provision by it for equal inheritance by daughters as well as by sons.[33] Again it must be observed that these laws are not enforced. The actual enforcement of these laws, especially the last one, would mean

[33] See *The Civil Code of the Republic of China,* Articles 1138 and 1223.

the immediate end throughout China of the "traditional" patterns because it would at one stroke radically alter the economic basis of the family. The appearance of these laws, like the other unenforced laws of modern China, is none the less of symbolic significance. The industrialized West, with certain exceptions, professes the ideal that women are the equals of men, and that the individual is sacred regardless of sex, but in actuality there is a decided difference between men and women, both with regard to privilege and responsibility. But the ideal is still important in understanding the society, and in China the incorporation of this ideal in the governmental guarantees of the society indicates a marked change in ideals, even if the level on which the change has taken place is a superficial one.

The legal basis of the position of women in respect to the allocation of power and responsibility is a great deal less important than the new economic basis. It does, however, have one interesting implication. Insofar as the constitution and legal code of the Chinese government claims priority over all other sources of authority in the society, it constitutes a government insistence on the fact that the time of priority of the family is past. The present government of China has shown itself in part, at least, anxious to maintain as much of the old social structure as possible, but this is hardly compatible with its insistence on priority over the family. The consequent decline in family priority has probably done more to weaken the "traditional" patterns of dominance than have the more positive provisions which are apparently aimed directly at the "traditional" formulations.

The new economic opportunities for women disrupt the old situation in which the political position of the women was always dependent upon some particular man. To an increasing degree, especially in the cities, and in the case of factory workers, their political status in the family is coming to depend upon the size and importance of their contribution to the family income on the one hand, and whether or not it is sufficient to support them independently of the family on the other. It is by no means as simple a proposition for a woman to leave her family and shift for herself as it is for a man, because China is still a male-dominated society, but the possibility exists now, whereas virtually none existed before. With the release in part from dependency for political position on some particular man goes a breakdown of the domination of wives by their mothers-in-law. There are other reasons for this breakdown, but this one is important because in the last analysis enforcement of the mother-in-law's dominance lay with her son.

One of the most important changes in the position of women is their new power in the matter of marriage. Some of the most modern girls make a complete break with the "traditional" patterns and choose their husbands without even consulting their parents. Most of the changes from the old, however, are in the form of a compromise. Marriages are arranged, but the girls as well as the boys are consulted, and their consent is required. The new privilege of women in this respect represents a serious limitation upon the former position of the *chia-chang,* and represents yet another intrusion of a factor which takes precedence over the family's former priority. Thus once again the change in the relation between two or more members of the family has implicit in it a change of the whole position of the family. It is in just such implicit factors that the instability of the "traditional" period lies. Chinese society cannot continue indefinitely with the present proportions of the old and the new, for the present proportions of the new involve still further disintegration of the old.

The weakening of emphasis on relative age is another aspect of the changed political substructure of the "transitional" family. The immediate effects of this precedence are being lost and so are its indirect effects, most notably that of reinforcing generational precedence. In the change the new family unit is by no means the sole factor at work, though it does cut the duration of such relations to a minimum. The discipline of the new occupational roles is also important. In handicraft work and in small-scale farming the improvement of knowledge and skill with age for a notable length of time keeps ahead of actual physical decline. A lattice-maker of fifty is probably a better craftsman than a younger man. Modern industry does not show a similar deference to age. Although the actual physical load of work may be considerably less in an automobile factory than on a Chinese farm, the demand for speed, alertness, and coördination is greater. These factors apparently deteriorate more rapidly with age than do the qualities demanded by craftsmanship and agriculture.[34]

[34] Modern American industry is a notorious consumer of youth. The older men still actively employed by modern industry tend to gravitate into the more craftsman-like aspects of the process, into the nonmechanical aspects of the work, or into

Something of the same thing may be said of the work strains created by the new jobs. In China this is further accented by the fact that it is a great deal easier to train a young man for the new type of work than to train an older one, because there is so much less "unlearning" to be done in the former case. Finally, the new industry cannot allow the particularistic factor of relative age to enter into the choice of persons for jobs in the degree to which this is possible in the old type of occupational roles. The possibility of younger persons having superior status to older ones in the new industrial and business organizations is much increased. Thus a conflict between the status determinants in the occupational role and the status determinants in the family role is set up. This factor operates with regard to generation as well as age, and in both cases tends to breach the sanctity of the "traditional" institutional standards of conduct.

In this changing situation the locus of power and responsibility is no longer so well balanced as formerly. There are two new situations which require primary consideration on this score. The first is that of the deviation of individuals in an otherwise "traditional" family. The second is that of the new solutions of locus toward which the new family seems to be moving. The first is undoubtedly the most important case numerically, since the vast majority of Chinese families today, even among urban industrial workers, are the result of rebellions from "traditional" families or contain notable "traditional" elements themselves.

The "traditional" families are faced by a difficult problem. The institutionalized locus of power and responsibility has not changed for the majority of members. At the same time a new set of forces completely beyond the control of any individual family has given potential deviants the possibility of successful defiance of the "traditional" patterns. This means, of course, that in the "traditional" settings responsibility remains after the power which was formerly commensurate with it has been destroyed. The locus of power and responsibility is no longer a balanced one, and instability results. This instability has implications beyond any individual deviant. The problem is not simply ended by a son's departure for the city. The entire family may be disrupted by the departure of a

---

sinecures. Certainly other factors than physical ones are involved, but the emphasis placed on youth by assembly line methods in particular and modern industry in general is hardly questionable.

single member, depending upon how important that member's various roles, economic and otherwise, are for the family as a whole.

Those who leave are not the only significant cases. Those who remain in a family, but who gain a modification of the structure, are no less important. It is these persons who gain greater control over their marriages, over their expenditures, and over their personal actions in general. The loci of power and responsibility may remain in balance, but they certainly change. Usually these changes are consciously or unconsciously designed to bring the factors of power and responsibility back into balance. Miss Lang points out that the new financial contributions of women to the family economy and the new education result in their acquisition of a voice in family affairs.[35] The modification of domination of fathers over sons has similar bases. In any case the strict hierarchical nature of the "traditional" political substructure is being modified. Mutual responsibilities and privileges are coming to be stressed within the family rather than a strict arrangement of authority from the top down and responsibility from the bottom up.

Often, however, the loci of power and responsibility get seriously out of balance. This is a matter of degree, but the sort of bickering which characterizes so many "transitional" families today may well derive from this source. The mother-in-law–daughter-in-law conflicts cited by Miss Yao T'su Ai [36] contain elements of this sort. The conflicts seem often to have their basis in a desire to test one's position rather than in an intrinsically significant issue. Both wife and mother-in-law jockey for the support of the male members of the family. The degree to which the institutionalized authority of the mother-in-law over her son has broken down without disappearing entirely, makes it difficult to settle the struggle for power one way or the other. This type of imbalance is capable of numerous variations and combinations, and the intricate interrelationships and interdependencies of the family structure serve to transmit any specific imbalance to other parts of the family structure.

In the families which are self-consciously abandoning the "traditional" patterns an acute problem is raised. The integrative force of ancestor worship has been noted above.[37] In responsibility to the ancestors lay the

[35] *Op. cit.,* pp. 263–264.
[36] *Op. cit.,* pp. 259–270.
[37] See pp. 168–170 and 249–250.

restoration of balance to the autocratic power of the *chia-chang*. In the new families, however, the strength of ancestor worship is not so great. The radical advocates of the new family are likely to be in revolt against the old faiths all along the line, and, even if they are not, the new type of family unit with its emphasis on generational discontinuity is hardly likely to retain a balance of responsibility in terms of generational obligations. Some of the conditions discussed by Professor H. D. Lamson in his *Social Pathology in China* [38] are no doubt due to the breakup of old patterns of authority and responsibility without adequate replacement. This has been an accompanying phenomenon of urbanization and industrialization all over the world. There is nothing unusual in the apparently increasing rates of divorce, suicide, juvenile delinquency, illegitimacy, and the like in China. It is a familiar story in the West.

The situation is being met after the Western fashion too. The tendency of the family to decrease in general social importance requires that the necessary balance for the political structure lie in part outside the family. Modern China is in part trying to replace the old types of responsibility to the ancestors by responsibility to the state. The fact that the state does not actually operate effectively in this sphere does not alter the outlines which the new society is taking. It merely helps to account for the fact that the present social situation is unstable and is deemed by many to be highly unsatisfactory. There can, however, be little doubt that the emphasis which is increasingly being placed upon public responsibility was formerly placed upon family responsibility.

The institutionalized political substructure which seems to be forming in the new type of families tends to resemble that found in such industrialized societies as the United States. A hierarchy of power and responsibility is maintained with inverse variation, but the power is much less absolute. Responsibility to the state is supposed to prevent excesses on the one hand as a limiting case; on the other hand, a voluntary responsibility, much after the character of responsibility to ancestors, is being fostered by a growing belief in the worth of the individual and a devotion to children as primarily of an intrinsic importance, independent of their role in perpetuating the family. Within the family itself the political substructure places a new emphasis upon reciprocity. At the same time the particularistic basis of allocation of power and responsibility

[38] Shanghai, 1935, see *e.g.*, Chapters V, VI, XIV, and XVIII.

is being deëmphasized to some extent. General ability as opposed to hereditary status is receiving increased prominence, and justification of specific solutions to political problems is increasingly couched in universalistic terms.

The new family type has another new aspect in the political substructure. Family continuity is not emphasized in the new structure. Men as well as women now have different families of orientation and procreation. At the same time neither enters the new family as a stranger among intimates. At the outset the new family of procreation consists solely of man and wife. This has an obvious functional implication. It reduces the problem of allocation of power and responsibility to two people in each new family. It also tends to eliminate a self-perpetuating hierarchical structure and force a reformulation with each new family. Furthermore, it requires that both members be cut loose from the old political hierarchy to which they belonged. Implicit in the new family structure is a termination of the power of any particular individual over another, and the termination is not dependent upon the death of one or the other of them. The institutionalization of this release from domination also changes the nature of the dominance while it exists and lowers the amount of autocracy which can be maintained.

Other changes are also discernible. The few families tending toward these new extremes have changed the relations between members in other ways. The emphasis on reserve, respect, and even force in the implementation of the political substructure is changing. Miss Lang points out that beating as a form of punishment is less prominent in the more modern families, particularly in those in which the parents have had education of the Western type.[39] The relationships are increasingly intimate, and companionship is emphasized. The subordinates no longer are simply commanded. Parents now furnish rationalizations for commands and phrase them in terms of the best interests of the governed rather than the governing persons. The whole orientation of the political substructure is undergoing a diametric change. Even when the old and new political substructures retain common features, they have a different basis. In the "traditional" period the orientation of the political substructure was toward the ancestors, the older generation; in the modern extremes it is toward the younger generations which will follow them.

[39] *Op. cit.,* see pp. 239–243.

The significance of these changes for modernization must not be ignored. There has already been mention above of the fact that the new trends in family structure minimize not only the amount of particularism in the family proper, but also its extension to spheres outside the family. This is closely interrelated with the broad sphere of universalism required by a modern industrialized society. The changes in the political substructure exhibit another such change. The new trends minimize a conflict in loyalties and obligation between the family and the structure of occupational roles. In the "traditional" period the same thing was achieved by incorporation of the occupational roles into the family structure to an extraordinary degree. In an industrialized society it is impossible to continue such a degree of self-sufficiency of family units. A family unit of the simple conjugal type minimizes the conflicts between family loyalties and those required by the new structure of occupational roles. It is hard to conceive of another type of family which will permit this minimization and maintain stability as well. The simple conjugal family provides for a separation of family members and the erection of new families at every point at which the strategic family members can theoretically take up occupational roles which might conflict with one another, or cause the family members themselves to conflict.

THE SUBSTRUCTURE OF INTEGRATION AND EXPRESSION

The "transitional" patterns of integration and expression are neither well understood nor are the facts readily available. It is certainly true that the "traditional" patterns are maintained with considerable vigor in many areas, and that in all areas elements of the "traditional" patterns are to be found. Only a few facts are readily available on the changes which are taking place, and the student is thrown back largely upon conjecture. The few figures available on such matters as education, for example, are by no means adequate, and in many cases give quite inconclusive results. Nevertheless, certain trends seem obvious enough for comments, and brief mention of them will be made here.

INTEGRATION

Education. There are two particularly interesting trends in the general process of education in China. The first is the change of the educational

[339]

procedures and the second the development of public and private education along new lines. The first of these is in large part a function of the new trends in the family and the influx of Western ideas, such as new ideas about child care. These ideas are widespread only among the most modern families. Students, intellectuals, professional men, modern businessmen, and the new industrialists, follow these new ideas. In early life the ideas are largely concerned with health. There is some acceleration of toilet training, but this can hardly be said to have gone far enough to have yet made any appreciable impression upon Chinese character.

Indulgence by children in physical exercise is one of the more pervasive of the Western ideas. Physical exercise of the competitive sports variety is to a large degree fostered through the new schools, but it is also being urged upon children by modern parents who have themselves indulged in it. The educational effect of the new forms of play is highly problematical. The new emphasis on rough and tumble physical sports is only in its infancy. The vast majority of Chinese families cling to the "traditional" patterns and deëmphasize any such activities. Where the new sports are found, certain implications are plain. The children are forced into open competition for one thing. More important, such play emphasizes the individual and individual ability, rather than the group and particularistic status. This is not to deny that some of the sports develop group feeling too. Team sports, such as basketball, are very popular among the Chinese who have access to them. Even in these, however, one is forced, in reckoning the possibilities of a situation, to reckon the potentialities of each individual. The emphasis on individual ability rather than on particularistic status is not a reinforcement of "traditional" patterns, and it is probable that the attitudes thus fostered carry over into other spheres as well.

The most striking of the changes in this sphere of the family has already been mentioned above. It is the shift in supervision of the young boys from men to women. The implications of this are not as yet clear in the Chinese case, but, if modern psychology and psychoanalysis have any validity, the effect should be considerable. The effect on girls is not so great in these respects, but the fact that the father is in general so much away from the family must have its effect on girls as well as boys. These general changes and others similar to them are not dependent upon any specific conscious absorption of Western ideas by the family members involved. They emerge from the structural implications of the new forces. Insofar as the new forces are in China to stay, or are going to increase in China, these trends must also continue or increase as well, quite apart from self-conscious attempts at family reform. The present study has unearthed no direct advocate of the supervision of young boys by women instead of men in the literature surveyed on Chinese family reform. Nevertheless, the trend is more prominent and more certain than many reforms which are enthusiastically urged on the people.

Whatever the effects of the new family educational procedures may be, some of those of the new educational program are hardly in doubt. The numbers involved are not impressive considering the size of China. One source states:

The total number of children attending kindergartens is 61,967, those in lower grade elementary schools and higher grade elementary schools are 7,118,-581 and 774,082 respectively. Other school pupils number 12,928. The grand total is 7,937,558. The total numbers of teachers employed in these schools are 1,580 for kindergartens, 345,314 for lower grade elementary schools, 50,144 for higher grade elementary schools, and 1,096 in other schools. Altogether there are 407,044 teachers.[40]

One has only to compare these figures with those of the United States of the same year to see how far Chinese education has yet to go. With a population between twenty-five and thirty-three and one-third per cent that of China, the number of school pupils between the ages of five to seventeen (inclusive) was 29,908,544, and of teachers was 1,037,605.[41] However inadequate the comparison may be, the figures are still revolutionary in Chinese history, and indicate a start toward universal education.

The education is on the whole of the new style and follows the new methods. Women as well as men teach, particularly in the lower grades, and stress literacy in terms of the vernacular rather than the literary language. Schools are coëducational to a large extent, and teach Western science and the humanities. The schools are inevitably subversive of the "traditional" family in endless ways. Miss Lang cites examples of attempts in the schools to reinforce the old patterns,[42] but the attempt is largely

[40] *The China Year Book* (Shanghai, 1934), p. 316. The reader will notice discrepancies in both totals given. That is the way with most statistics in this field at present.

[41] *The World Almanac* (New York, 1934), p. 530.

[42] *Op. cit.*, p. 244.

offset by the other things taught. In simply learning to read, the Chinese children are given a tremendous advantage over their elders, who are usually illiterate. The advantage is one for which their elders have respect, and it plays a role in the transfer of emphasis to youth. The new education also gives the children the intellectual equipment needed for them to escape the family, if they wish to do so.

The schools are widely used to inculcate government propaganda in the students, and this unwittingly breaks down the very family which government lessons on filial piety seek to preserve. In emphasizing nationalism the state gives itself a priority over the family, and this is an assault on the old patterns, whether it is recognized as such or not. Apart from government propaganda, however, the schools deëmphasize the family in other ways. In learning foreign as well as Chinese history, the students gain a perspective which the Chinese formerly lacked. Inevitably they learn of other ways of life and other ideals than the "traditional" ones.

The student movement is perhaps the best example of the influence of the schools against the "traditional" ways both of the family and the society in general. The student movement in China has been and is in the forefront of every radical and modern movement in modern China. The students have decried old family customs of marriage, the autocracy of the *chia-chang,* the Treaty of Versailles, nepotism and corruption in the government, and the domination of their elders. They have demanded government reform, freedom for the individual, war against Japan, equality for women, and so forth. All government efforts to control them and regiment their thinking has failed.[43] Education in China is accompanied everywhere by more or less defiance of the authority of the "traditional" ways. Not all students take up radical views. Many try to observe the old patterns as far as possible. Even among these, however, the burden of proof has come to rest on the "traditional" patterns, which are no longer taken for granted and left unquestioned.

The educational trend is a strategic factor in the "transitional" character of modern China. If China is to modernize, i.e., industrialize herself,

---

[43] A *New York Times* dispatch of February 26, 1947 (p. 2) states: "The most dangerous element in Peiping, from the Kuomintang point of view, is the University student body. Between 60 and 85 per cent of the students are believed to oppose the Kuomintang. Students have a long history of political activity." This is apparently the situation after years of planned and self-conscious effort, both propagandistic and terroristic, to direct the thinking of students along more acceptable lines.

the new education will have to increase rather than diminish. The new technology requires at least some literacy on the part of its workers. Unless this literacy can be hedged by such structures as those of Nazi Germany and post-Meiji Japan it will inevitably be subversive of the "traditional" patterns of the society, and even if it is hedged, it will, together with the industrial technology, be subversive of the "traditional" family.[44]

Religion. The trend in this respect is difficult to estimate. One thing is certainly true. The former religions, ancestor worship, household and field gods, Buddhism, and Taoism, are all losing their hold on the more modern members of the society. Their faith in these religions, if not entirely gone, is certainly becoming a matter of much less concern to them. Among the intellectuals the more obviously magical practices so prominently associated with Taoism are the first to go, but from the point of view of the family and of the social structure in general, the lessening faith in ancestor worship is of greater significance. Ancestor worship embodies the set of ultimate values which provided for the authenticity and binding force of virtually the entire social structure of "traditional" China.

The complete elimination of faith in the old religions is on the whole infrequent. Lessening faith in them is, however, apparently spreading widely. On the whole, lessening faith is not being replaced by any systematic orientation. The general tendency among intellectuals is toward agnosticism, accompanied by a self-conscious faith in familiar Western humanitarian ideals. There is some evidence that a worship of science and technology is growing up, but this is neither widespread nor well organized, though it may come to be so.

The general tendency among the people as a whole insofar as the old faiths lessen is unclear. No positive new faith seems to emerge. The breakdown of the old faith is a factor, perhaps, in the cynical realism characterizing the "individualism by default" which usually accompanies the breakdown of the old faiths. To some extent the political parties of China either consciously or unconsciously have tried to replace the old faiths with political faiths. The Kuomintang tries to inculcate a nationalistic brand of Confucianism, and so utilize the old patterns. The Communist Party, at the other extreme, has, of course, propagandized for faith in the Marxist ideology. With the population as a whole neither group seems to have had great success as yet.

[44] This was the case in Japan despite efforts to offset the trend.

The Communist Party has something of an advantage in this struggle because of the compactness of its ideology and because of the fact that it can present the ideology with or after economic reform measures which have great appeal to the broad mass of the people. At the same time it can use whatever appeal there is in the nationalistic slogans of the Kuomintang. Nationalism, whether leftist or rightist, has had a great appeal for students and intellectuals. This has no doubt been closely tied to the desire of these groups for the modernization and industrialization of China and the patent impossibility of achieving these ends in the modern world on any save a national basis. The peasants as a group have certainly not been converted to nationalism as yet. The "cultural paranoia" of nationalism is not well inculcated in the Chinese peasants. Furthermore, nationalism is notoriously associated with armies, and the "traditional" peasant attitude toward the military has never been favorable. Recent experience with various Chinese, Japanese, and American armies can hardly have raised the peasants to any great pitch of enthusiasm with regard to the virtues of troops in residence.

There is much talk of the spread of the organized Western religions in China, particularly of the various Protestant sects and the Roman Catholic form of Christianity. On the whole any major movement in this direction seems unlikely. There will no doubt be many converts, but the possibility of China's becoming a Christian nation in the Western sense is exceedingly slim. The established forms of religious faith are facing a severe test in the West today, and the forces bringing this about are apparently implicit in that same industrialized society toward which China is moving. Therefore, it may be tentatively argued that the same forces will hinder their spread in China. Insofar as these trends bog down in China, the Western faiths will have to combat the established religious forms of the society. In this process Western religion will labor under at least one severe disability in China. That disability is its exclusiveness. Religious exclusivism is quite opposite to the general Oriental view. Any major spread of Western religion in China, if made at all, will probably require major compromises on this score.

On the whole, the proselytizing activities of Westerners in the field of religion are likely to facilitate the breakdown of faith in the prevailing religions rather than to spread the Western religions in any strict form. The example set by the social services rendered by Western missionaries will be impressive, and skepticism of the old will be forwarded by the presentation of alternative ideals. Although the outlook for the acceptance of any of the Western religions in an organized and theologically exact form is not bright, the outlook for the ideals embodied in them is promising. The ideals involved, particularly such ideals as a universalistic ethic, the emphasis on individual dignity and integrity, and the like, have proven themselves to be to a high degree compatible with the modern forms of industrial society and, more important, have played a considerable role in the development of that society. In the Western religions is to be found a more or less systematic justification in faith of the various institutional bases of the modern industrial society. Western religion is, however, by no means the only possible justification in faith of the necessary factors, and the ideals involved can certainly be taken over without either the theological or ritual structure involved.

All the old forms of expression continue in a more or less modified form. New forms of expression in amusement, such as the Western motion picture, dancing, and sports, are being taken up in the urban centers and in the schools. Some Western influence is already to be seen in the arts, but as yet no settled amalgamation or definitive new style has emerged in any of these fields. The tendency in such areas as music and painting seems to be rather toward abandonment of the old without any systematic replacement of it.

One of the most interesting aspects of the new forms of amusement and recreation is the mixture of the sexes. Today in the more modern centers there is more and more companionship between boys and girls, and men and women. Not only do married couples appear in public together, but unmarried couples do also. Furthermore, group amusements on a nonfamily basis occur more frequently. In these new forms of expression the breakdown of the old isolation of the sexes and the relative seclusion of the family are clearly evidenced.

Other forms of expression are receiving attention. Observers remark upon the changes in dress of girls and boys. The change in girls is particularly noteworthy. The emphasis now placed on public display of physical attractiveness is new for the average women. This is not entirely confined to college students and the more radical youths. Factory workers to an increasing degree insist on such competition for the attention of the opposite sex. Lipstick, permanent waves, and physically revealing clothes are being enthusiastically taken up by the women of China. Carl Crow in a volume filled with sharp insights into "transitional" Chinese society attributes the change in the position of women in China to an advertising campaign for cosmetics.[45]

Mr. Crow may well be called to account for his attribution of causality and for his statement of the sequence of events, but his association of the new ways of expression and the changed position of women is beyond question. The new dress is associated with the new freedom, the new association of the sexes, the new trends in marriage, and so on. The line of causation is not simple but the association of the elements is undeniable.

Another form of expression which is of great significance for Chinese society as a whole is the public participation in popular political movements. In "traditional" China organized popular expression on political and economic problems was relatively rare. When conditions became unbearable, peasant revolts took place, and some of them were on a scale sufficient to unseat dynasties. But in the ordinary run of events the government did not consult the public, and the public was either uninterested or wary of expressing itself on general matters affecting the society as a whole. This was in part due no doubt to the strong impulse to view most matters entirely in individual family terms with a consequent difficulty of arousing public interest until all or nearly all families in a given area were vitally affected.

The situation is no longer so. On a larger and larger scale persons in China express their desires and frustrations in public political effort. Students and intellectuals in general are the most articulate performers, but they are by no means alone. Merchants and workers join them. In 1919 the public expression was so effective that the public prevented the signing of the Treaty of Versailles by the Chinese. John Dewey wrote of the event, stating of the Treaty and the student movement against it:

The entire government has been for it—the President up to ten days before the signing said that it was necessary. It was a victory for public opinion, and all set going by these little schoolboys and girls.[46]

[45] Carl Crow, *Four Hundred Million Customers* (New York, 1937), p. 37.
[46] John Dewey and others, *Letters from China and Japan* (New York, 1921), p. 226.

This was one of the first victories for a deliberately aroused public opinion in modern China. Since that time the technique has been used more and more. The government and its opponents devote more and more time to propaganda. Much of the public is as yet relatively untouched by the movement, but it is going ahead. In this form of expression there appears an idea seldom if ever before used in China on a large and more or less systematic scale. The urge to convert others to a given point of view is on the increase. It contains an implicit expression of concern with public issues and a feeling that one's interests and duties in such matters cannot be confined to a single family or a single locality.

The urge to proselytize has not been great in Chinese history, save at relatively rare intervals. There is today a sustained and growing effort in this direction. The current effort is almost half a century old now. Both the Kuomintang and the Communist Party demonstrate the urge to convert the public to their own points of view. As a result new ideas and new ways receive far greater publicity today. This is an important factor in carrying ideas of change to the people as a whole. In the old days such new ideas as were generated were left to spread more or less of their own accord through particularistic channels. Public expression is changing all that.

Within the field of public expression the widest variants are to be found. Nationalism is a growing expression of the public. Authoritarian ideologies of the left and the right claim much attention. There are proforeign and antiforeign elements in China today. Economic issues are seized upon. Strikes, riots, and other demonstrations are on the increase. In all these movements, even those specifically aimed at maintaining or returning to the old patterns, one common element emerges. All are modes of expression carried out on a markedly nonfamily basis and so imply or accelerate the changes of the old.

There are also signs of expression of the strains and frustrations of the "transitional" society. Many elements of this sort are to be found in the public expressions. Some of the expressions are directly connected to the sources of frustration and are both calculated and logical. Others are demonstrations of aggressions often expressed in scapegoat demonstrations of various sorts.

One other notable form of expression is an apparently changing suicide rate. Observers agree that suicide among both men and women is increasing. Observers agree that the urban rate is above the rural rate and is rising faster. This may perhaps be taken to suggest that some close connection between the "transitional" forces and the rates exists, because the forces are increasing and they are most effective in the cities. The suicide rate of men compared to women is rising. This is perhaps indicative of the growing burden of responsibility and cares placed on the individual male shoulders by the new trends in social structure. The rates for women may have been decreased relatively by a lessening of the mother-in-law problem, but they have been increased absolutely by the exposure of women to frustrations of the new society, and to the frustrations implicit in mixtures of the new and the old, most notably in marriages. The suicide rates of women still exceed those of men, or are just equivalent to them, according to observers. These estimates imply a situation still markedly at variance with the general Western rates, but tending in their direction. Finally, the suicide rates for older people definitely seem to be increasing. This is true for both among men and women. It is a hypothesis of this study that the rates are in fact increasing with age (and those of old men increasing faster than those of old women), and that this increase is a direct reflection of the increasing problem of economic and social security of the older people. This problem in its turn is posited as a result of the breakdown of the "traditional" family structure and the tendency toward the simple conjugal family unit.

The forms of expression which are growing up in "transitional" China are by and large a reflection of the disintegration of the old and the beginning of the new. Unlike the "traditional" family situation, that of the "transitional" period cannot be said to foster a mutual reinforcement between the substructure of integration and expression and other aspects of family structure, because only the untouched "traditional" families maintain any such mutual reinforcement. The new trends in expression and integration are subversive of the "traditional" patterns. The difficulty is not solely a matter of internal change in the family structure. It is also a matter of changing the total position of the family structure in the general structure of the society. In "traditional" China the family structure covered a far larger proportion of the total social structure than is true in a modern industrialized society. The incessant reference to nonfamilial structures in discussing the family structure of "transitional" China is but the symbol of the change. As the change itself goes forward, less and less of the society is explicable in terms of kinship structure, and more and more reference must be made to the general structure of occupational roles and the political integration of the society as a whole.

CHAPTER TEN

THE PROBLEM OF MODERNIZATION

IT is generally agreed that the future of China depends upon the degree to which a stable modern industrialized society can be achieved. Regardless of the source of motivation, all the major political parties of China today espouse industrialization as an end. The means to be used are more controversial. Some of the effects of industrialization on the kinship structure of China have been discussed above. Now the question of the effects of the kinship structure on the industrialization of China may be raised. Industrialization is not a process which can simply be taken for granted. In the history of industrialization some societies, such as the United States and Great Britain, have incorporated industrialization as it developed. Others, notably Germany and Japan, have entered the stream of development later in the process and taken over modern industry at a more advanced stage. China represents a society which has taken on only a minor degree of modern industry. The future of the process in China is by no means certain, either as to degree or rate of change. But one of the few certainties about the process in China is that it has already taken hold and that its effects have already been striking.

In discussions of this sort it is customary to contrast the rapid systematic growth of modern industry in Japan [1] with its slow haphazard spread in China. Much of the perplexity about the contrast results from a generally unexamined assumption that, when the two societies were "opened" to Western influence in the nineteenth century, they were basically quite similar. This, of course, was not the case, although superficial similarities were sufficient to account for the generally mistaken ideas on this score. The basic social structure of China was and is no more similar to that of Japan than the social structure of the Greek city state was to that

---

[1] The industrialization of Japan in certain of its structural aspects has been analyzed in unpublished notes by the author of this study. It was intended for inclusion here, but consideration of space and time prevented.

of feudalistic France. One of the many superficial resemblances between Ch'ing China and Tokugawa Japan lay in the kinship structure of the two societies. The differences were equally striking, but the one of most concern for the present study is the difference which existed between the two societies in the relative position occupied by the family in the total structure of the society.

In Japan the family certainly occupied a position of strategic importance, but it was definitely subordinated to other considerations in the society. This created in the society a possibility of overriding or manipulating various aspects of the family patterns for other purposes. In China this possibility of manipulating family patterns in terms of other aspects of the society was much more limited because the family structure of China was to a much greater degree the major focus of the society than was the case in Japan. It is not intended to imply that this was the sole basis of the different courses taken by China and Japan in the matter of modernization, but it is presented as a major basis of this difference, and the contrast is suggested for the insight it gives into the importance of the kinship structure of China in relation to the development of modern industry there.

China does not lack the material prerequisites for industry. In these respects China's position is far stronger than was that of Japan. Although China's known mineral resources are in many respects inferior to those of other nations, this inferiority may turn out in part to be merely the result of insufficient exploration. The topography offers some difficulty for transport and communications, but the physical factors of the landscape can hardly be taken seriously as an explanation of China's slowness, since modern technology has again and again demonstrated its ability to cope with such problems. Nor is lack of a labor force an obstacle, for China's population is notoriously large and is apparently easily motivated to participate in new kinds of enterprise. There is nothing inherent in the physical character of the people which makes them unfit for such work. American engineers and plant managers with experience in China agree that a properly trained Chinese worker is as adept mechanically as his American counterpart.

There is reason to believe that potentially China is capable of becoming one of the three or four most powerful and highly industrialized areas in the world, if not the foremost area. The possibility of atomic power has changed the whole outlook of the world for the future, but even without such possibilities, Chinese power prospects are probably better than those of any other nation in the world if estimated solely in terms of physical resources. A group of hydroelectric experts in a private unpublished study have arrived at an estimate that the development of sixteen power sites on the Yangtze River alone, ignoring many tributary sites of unquestionable power potentials equal to or greater than that of the Tennessee Valley Authority, would generate more than two and one-half times as much power as all the power generated today in the United States from all sources, hydroelectric and otherwise. These sites would be capable, according to these estimates, of producing power more cheaply than anywhere else in the world. This power could theoretically be co-ordinated with an efficient industrial and agricultural program.

The problem of putting China on a modern industrialized footing and the realization of such projects as the one mentioned above may seem grandiose, but China has in the past been a grandiose society. China has shown an incredible capacity for engineering feats. The irrigation system, the Grand Canal, and the Great Wall are not achievements to be taken lightly. The question is whether or not modern China can do a similar job with the tools of modern industry.

Modernization will require above all a great spread of universalism and functional specificity in the society. China's former feats of engineering also required a certain degree of these two factors, but herein lies a major difference between the past and the present. In the past the tools used in major projects were relatively simple. The genius involved in these works lay in their planning, and in the manipulation of huge masses of more or less unskilled labor. Anyone can dig a ditch if he has the level of physical fitness possessed by the average individual and if he is properly directed. Therefore universalism in the recruitment of manpower was not a problem in these past projects. Labor was obtained by mass drafts ordinarily, but these drafts did not imply a breakdown of the particularistic standards of the family, nor was the erection of these works a permanent feature of the society, although some of them took many years. Their direction and planning did require a selection of personnel on a universalistic basis. It was just in this sphere of Chinese life that the major institutionalization of universalistic criteria appeared, that is, in the bureaucracy. Some scholars such as Professor K. A. Wittfogel have definitely stated that the administrative and engineering requirements of the irrigation system of China caused the development of the bureaucracy of China and maintained it through Chinese history.[2] It is certainly undeniable that so complex and large-scale a project did imply an administrative problem of the first order, and it is also true that the stable perpetuation of such an organization required some objective technique of choosing its personnel on the basis of ability. It is also interesting to note that the fall of dynasties was usually preceded by a decline in universalism in this sphere of action and a growing breakdown of the irrigation and canal system, and that the establishment of new dynasties was usually accompanied by a restoration of universalism and a rehabilitation of the irrigation and canal system.

Modern industry has two requirements unlike those which the past major engineering and organizational feats demanded. In the first place, it requires universalistic criteria for the employment of virtually all its personnel, and not merely for executive and planning personnel. In the second place, modern industry is not a structure which once erected can be left more or less to itself for years at a time and periodically refurbished. The universalism and other factors required to erect a modern industrial plant are also required in its everyday operation and maintenance. Both of these requirements are closely related to one another. The basis for the generalized necessity for universalistic criteria of employment lies in the tools which must be used and the scale on which the job must be done. It is not true that just anyone can learn to run a steamshovel, and the difference between the ability of two steamshovel operators, because of the multiple factor involved in the machine, is considerably more important than the difference of skill between two men digging a ditch with hand shovels. As modern industry progresses, unskilled labor has a smaller and smaller role, and the tools which must be manipulated become more and more complex. This requires that more emphasis be placed on ability in recruitment of all workers, for differences in ability are more important, not only because of the level required to master the tools, but also because of the difference in effect made by the multiple factor so supplied.

It is for much the same reason that institutionalization of universalism must be maintained if industry is to operate. In the great engineering projects of China, the greatest problem was initial planning and construction.

[2] Professor Wittfogel made such statements in lectures before the China Regional Studies Group at Harvard University in the Fall Semester of 1946.

Maintenance was a much simpler problem, and the project could continue to operate for quite some time with faulty maintenance. The Great Wall is an outstanding example of this, but it was true of the irrigation and canal system too. It took some time for a gradually declining efficiency of maintenance to result in a silting of canals, breakdown of canal gates and dams, and a general serious disruption of the system. Modern industry on the other hand poses an exceptionally difficult and continuous problem of maintenance and operation, and relatively small failures can easily disrupt the entire structure at once.[3] Therefore modern industry may be said to require both a wider institutionalization of universalism and a better maintenance of it than ever before in Chinese society.

The "traditional" Chinese family was a highly particularistic structure, and it dominated all training in the society save that for the bureaucracy, the one sphere in Chinese society of institutionalized universalism. Widespread particularism as much as any other factor is a major obstacle to the spread of modern industry in China. It enormously complicates the operation of modern enterprise in China in two major ways. The first is the problem of employment, where particularism injects the element of nepotism on a large scale. The second is the problem of maintaining relations outside a given organization itself, the purchase or sale of goods, services, and so on.

As we have indicated, modern industry and the "traditional" family are mutually subversive. The introduction of modern industry is the first genuine threat to the stability of the "traditional" Chinese family, and the nepotism fostered by the "traditional" Chinese family is one of the greatest obstacles to an efficient industrial system. Mr. Crow in his book points out that an attempt by a businessman to introduce into a modern business firm a promising young worker who has no previous connections with the other workers is often a complete failure.[4] He goes on to point out that the new man need not be met by violence or any open show of hostility by the other workers. The new man simply finds himself in a position where no one helps him or coöperates with him. Misleading information is given him. If his job is to any degree coördinated with the work of the other members of the concern, and it usually is, he is simply unable to operate in such a setting. Every modern business and industrial organiza-

---

[3] This is one of the factors involved in the great power of organized labor in highly integrated modern industries.   [4] *Op. cit.,* p. 95.

tion in China must either exert special effort to prevent the growth of such particularistic cliques in the organization or else operate in terms of them. The first alternative adds to the burdens of the executive roles, and the second can interfere directly with the efficiency of the organization.

Particularism in China is not confined entirely to relatives. Friends and neighbors are included. A Chinese will first try to secure jobs for his relatives and then to secure jobs for friends and members of his native area. The fact that close friends tend to be viewed in terms of family solidarities has been mentioned above.[5] The local tie is equally strong. Even quite highly mechanized employments are predominantly held by workers from a special area. Although other factors are involved, this is partially explained by the intrusion of the particularistic ties of the "traditional" family into employment in the new occupational roles.

The pressure of particularism upon Chinese who attempt to run a modern organization is great. The friends, neighbors, and relatives of such a person soon learn how much power he has at his command. Even modern young professional people fall easy prey to such pressure. Few of the new businessmen and industrialists have so completely cut themselves off from the "traditional" ways that they are neither bound by the old patterns nor concerned with the opinions of those who are. When a man has any sort of connection outside his family, friends, or neighborhood, the burden of proof is on him if he refuses to use his position to help them. Failure to help them with jobs and other concessions is to demonstrate a lack of *jen-ch'ing*, human feelings. If he fails to help close relatives, he is even worse. He may be said to be unfilial or to demonstrate *pei-te*, that is, not loving those to whom one is bound by natural ties, both of which are extremes of inhumanity. His failure to be swayed may lead to his ostracism by friends and relatives alike. The pressure brought can be extreme, and all Chinese involved in the new industries are subject to it. The owners, engineers, executives, and foremen are all more or less vulnerable to such pressure.[6]

Foreign ownership and direction is no cure for the problem. The average foreigner in China knows so little of the language and habits of the people that he is entirely dependent for operation upon the aid

[5] See pp. 134–135.

[6] This information, confirmed by other informants, was given the author by Dr. Hu Hsin-Chin in conversations about her dissertation cited above.

and advice of Chinese. His only other alternative for a working force is to turn to other foreigners resident in China. Obviously this offers no solution to the problem of modernization as a whole. If the enterprise is conducted with the aid and advice of Chinese, the Chinese placed in positions of authority and influence will, of course, be subjected to the pressures of particularism. Actually many large foreign firms in an effort to avoid this problem and other aspects of the Chinese problem as well have deliberately recruited staffs from residents of their own countries, trained them specially for work in China, and set up rules and regulations of both a formal and an informal nature designed to insulate these staff members from the Chinese community as a whole.

It is impossible to estimate how much the difficulty of maintaining a relatively universalistic basis of employment has hindered and slowed industrialization and the spread of modern business methods in China. The probability is that the effect has been enormous. All concerns in China have been more or less plagued by the problem, and it is highly probable that, if it could be solved and a stable, well-institutionalized basis of universalism be brought about, the general level of the efficiency of most modern concerns in China would be raised. The inefficiencies which result from particularistic factors in employment have probably prevented the establishment of industries and enterprises which might otherwise have been founded, or brought about the failure of enterprises which might otherwise have been successful. The use by foreign firms of foreign staffs offsets the problem somewhat, but their lack of knowledge about the local people is, in all probability, productive of its own inefficiencies, most of which are probably never known even by the firms themselves.

Modern business and industrial firms are faced with another dilemma. Modern technology to a considerable degree finds economy in large-scale production. This means large-scale plants and administration. The current move in the West for decentralization of industry still speaks in terms of individual plant units of enormous size by Chinese standards, and even in the West the move for decentralization has not gone far. Ordinarily, the larger the unit of operation, the greater is the management problem. At the same time the inefficiencies which arise from particularism in employment are both more numerous and more disruptive. In a small concern when one establishes particularistic relations with one's employees, the resultant loyalty to the interests of the organization will be carried to lengths unheard of in the West. In the large concerns, where such ties are not present, the motivation of concern for the general interests of the organization is extremely difficult. The sort of loyalty and *esprit de corps* which is necessary for the most efficient operation can be best obtained in China only by resort to a particularism which is as crippling as the difficulty which would motivate its use. A major problem of Chinese industrial firms is to motivate such loyalty and *esprit de corps* by the inculcation of values which will not in themselves interfere with the technological processes of the concern.

Employment is not the only sphere in which the particularism bred by the "traditional" kinship structure is a hindrance to the development of modern industry in China. It is equally important in the relations of the organization with other organizations. Here a brief word needs to be said on the distinction made here between business and industry. Industry, as distinct from business, refers to the use of technological equipment in conjunction with human skills and effort to produce goods and services. Modern industry is distinguished from the industry of other periods largely by the striking difference in its technological equipment, and by the difference in organization and administration made necessary by that technological equipment.

Business may be taken to mean the management of industry oriented to the production of profit from operation of the industry. By and large, modern industry has been developed on a basis of business management and operation. This is not inevitably the case. There is no valid technological or social reason why modern industry cannot be operated on other than a business basis, and indeed even in the most thoroughly business-dominated societies some industry is conducted on a nonbusiness basis. There is no intention here to stigmatize either business or industry, but it should be pointed out that, while in general there is some positive correlation between the production of goods and services and the production of profits, the two are not always positively correlated. The larger the structure viewed from the economic point of view, the more likelihood there is that such a positive correlation will hold.[7]

[7] *E.g.*, a given business firm may be able under certain circumstances to profit by cutting down production in a given area, but business as a whole in the United States is not likely to benefit from a general fall in physical production. The reasons for this are too complex to be discussed here.

In China the development of modern business and industry have gone hand in hand, and a good part of the future development of China promises to be conducted in the same way. The conduct of industry is thus to a large degree left to individuals in China. Since only in the government service was there any considerable degree of universalism, institutionalized particularism dominated the relations of all save a few organizations run by the government, and even these became highly particularistic as the government became weak and corrupt. Since loyalties were overwhelmingly dependent upon family considerations and, by extension, upon relations of friendship, relations between strangers had somehow to be consummated through a person or persons with particularistic relations with both of the main parties in the relation. This was the function of the go-between in China, and the need for such services persists in China today. Mr. Crow states that:

A Chinese wants first, to do business with members of his own family, next, with his friends, and will not have any dealings with strangers if it is possible to avoid it. If two strangers are parties to a business deal then it is absolutely essential that there be a go-between, a mutual friend who will conduct the negotiations, compose differences of opinion and, when the deal is concluded, set as joint guarantor for both parties, making himself personally responsible that the contract will be carried out and the money will be paid.[8]

Here the considerations of particularism and functional diffuseness merge. In a sense the conduct of economic relations in the "traditional" Chinese setting requires the erection of an artificially contrived particularistic relation between the parties concerned to get any specific end accomplished. In the course of this procedure the relationship tends to become functionally diffuse, because the vast majority of "traditional" particularistic relations in China are also functionally diffuse. Therefore, to the degree that the "traditional" patterns persist, economic transactions are involved in particularism and functional diffuseness. Both of these hinder modern business and industry, which place a premium upon transactions with others on a basis of the material end sought, rather than on a basis of the personal relations of the parties to the transaction, and on a basis of completely terminating the relationship once that end is accomplished. The reasons for this difference between modern business and

[8] *Op. cit.,* p. 87.

industry and the "traditional" type of transactions in China are too complex to be taken up in detail, but the difference lies partly in the fact that the productivity of the technological equipment is so great and the complexity and number of contacts required to operate the organizations are of such a high order that the outside relations of the organization simply cannot be conducted on a basis of particularism and functional diffuseness.

Again, there is no way to judge how much these factors have impeded modernization in China, but in all probability the effect has been considerable. Emile Durkheim has pointed out how crucial the noncontractual elements in contracts are to modern society.[9] Unless the vast majority of contracts were voluntarily fulfilled without a resort to the courts to enforce them, modern Western economic organization would cease to function. In China today, insofar as "traditional" elements remain, the only way to gain this level of compliance is through the establishment of a type of relationship which is itself subversive to the requirements of modern business and industry. The problem is further complicated, and its effects are further spread by the fact that, in a setting in which some persons have the new ideals in these respects and others operate by the old, the persons operating by the new are at a disadvantage. Their standards require that they respect the rights of the others, but in the absence of some particularistic bond the others are bound by no such standards.

The factor of political security is closely connected to such factors as those mentioned above. In "traditional" China the decentralization of government left the local residents at the mercy of robbers and war lords who were willing and ready to use force, and at the mercy of corrupt officials who could use their official powers for their own ends. When dynasties were most vigorous, the imperial troops gave some protection, but in most periods protection depended upon the particularistic organizations of family and neighborhood. This vulnerability to the unauthorized uses of force placed a radical limit on investment in physical goods and plants. Land as the most difficult possession to destroy offered the maximum security as a form of investment, and part of the appeal of land as an investment inhered in this factor. The development of modern industry, if it is to be conducted on a business basis, must offer security for

[9] See *De la division du travail social* (Paris, 1893), pp. 192–195.

private investment. Insofar as such security is only to be achieved on the basis of particularistic and functionally diffuse relations, the process is further retarded. One of the reasons for the development of industrialization around the treaty ports lay in the fact that the presence of foreigners there and the patterns of extraterritoriality increased the security of investment. Western banks in the foreign settlements were relatively immune to the particularistic pressures of the Chinese structure and afforded a secure form of local investment alternative to land.

Ignorance, poverty, disease, bad communications, and lack of resources are not the basic barriers to the industrialization of China. They are serious impediments, but none of them is a problem for which the world lacks a remedy. The matériel and training technology of the modern world is sufficient to overcome all of these in a short period of time, if the technology is properly applied. The presence of political disunity, the necessity of readjusting the ownership of land, and the abolition of the "traditional" institutional patterns which hinder the modernization of China are not so easy to combat. The problem is essentially that the "traditional" social structure of China and that which must replace it if China is to be modernized are functionally incompatible at too many points to permit of an easy gradual introduction of the one while the easy gradual decay of the other takes place. Too often as things stand now the breakdown of the "traditional" patterns leaves a social vacuum and forces persons into a radical role of *sauve qui peut* which has the integrative features of neither the old nor the new.

There is no easy answer for this problem in China. Japan, unlike China, was able to cut loose from the Tokugawa patterns and take over certain of those of modern industrial society with less difficulty, largely because there were structures of control in Japanese society which were not immediately attacked by that process. In China the major source of control was the family, and the family was most immediately attacked by the process. It is questionable how long Japan could have maintained her course with or without a war, but China has not even an interstitial period like that of Japan.

Although the "traditional" patterns amply demonstrate their ability to impede the spread of the new patterns of modernization, they show no signs of being able either to stop them where they are or to eradicate them altogether. There are in general two main possibilities of development in

China. China can achieve a level of industrialization comparable with that of the highly industrialized Western nations. In order to accomplish this quickly, one of the best available techniques would be the renovation of the institutionalization of universalism in the national government, and the establishment and operation of the major heavy industrial installations by the national government. There is a long tradition of universalism in this sphere. Its change to accord with the demands of the new technology should therefore be relatively easy. At the same time, the government could attempt to broaden and maintain the areas in which the new social patterns apply. The schools plus efficient and honest courts and police can be made to serve this end, as well as relief for the inevitable cases of social hardship which would result. Relief of the aged and the technologically unemployed would be the major requirements on this score. Private industry could be encouraged and protected. The most essential feature of such a program would be the erection of a government which is as free as possible of particularistic elements. This would of course mean the abolition of the graft, corruption, and nepotism which are features of the present Chinese government. Regardless of which party or parties rule in China, these reforms will have to be made if industrialization is to go ahead with any speed at all. If China is unable to reëstablish universalism in a sphere of the society where it has long been institutionalized, even though not always maintained, it is not likely that other spheres of society will be able to achieve it.

In the long run the modernization of China is relatively certain. In the short run there is no such certainty. There is an alternative present, and there is a real possibility that that alternative may be realized and may delay the modernization of China for an indefinite length of time. The alternative is the possibility that a systematic and consistent program of industrialization will not be followed, or will receive only secondary consideration. It is the possibility that the financially powerful men of modern China will insist upon their private right to exploit all opportunities with a view to the immediate maximization of private income. Whether this is done on an independent basis or through government corruption will make significant differences from many points of view, but the retardation of a balanced industrialized economy in China will be effected in either case. The immediate possibilities for greatest profit in China lie in commercial speculations of various sorts. At present the general situation from both the political and the economic point of view makes the long-term investment of capital in industry less inviting than shorter-term investments subject to rapid liquidation. The lack of universalism in the governmental structure as well as elsewhere is an unequivocal deterrent for industry, but, while in the long run it is also a deterrent to modern commerce, in the short run it is not. It may in fact even increase the possibilities of profit through the curtailment of productive facilities and through the manipulation of the national structure for private ends. There is no question but that today in China a businessman may confidently expect to make more money with less risk by importing and selling automobiles than by erecting plants to build them. It is true that such a trader must worry about the possibility of losing his automobiles, but so would an industrialist in China today. The latter would also have the worry of losing his whole plant, let alone the problems of production. One of the dangers of this development further lies in the fact that from the point of view of such traders, a definite advantage will lie in the restriction of the development of Chinese industry, lest the eventual products seriously compete with their importations.

In the long run the commercialization line of development promises to be self-defeating, though it might easily impede industrialization for many years. The reason for this is not hard to find. Such commercialization would accentuate the dependency of China upon the output of the industry of foreign nations. Furthermore, it would inherently restrict its own markets, because it would continually drain money and goods from China to pay for such importations. This would mean a continuous decrease in purchasing power, so that the persons able to buy such importations would become fewer and fewer. It is hard to imagine that even the Chinese, a notoriously patient and hard-pressed people, would stand for a great deal more such pressure, and, if they did, many of them would be eliminated from the society by being pushed below the physical minimum necessary for subsistence. Apart from change by revolution, other elements of the situation would dictate change. As the dependency of China on foreign nations increased, their influence in Chinese affairs would increase. As this increased, the possibility of foreigners maintaining order in restricted enough areas to take advantage of the cheapness of Chinese labor for use in industrial production would also increase. The foreigners themselves would come again to the establishment of industry in China, and eventually this industry would interfere with the commercial interests. Such a line of argument need not be considered far-fetched. Previous Chinese experience with trade and industry has been quite close to this pattern.

Neither of these possibilities of development is exclusive. Industrialization of China will have to contain accompanying elements of commercial speculation. The commercialization possibility sketched above will only partially exclude industrialization, because it will depend on some level of modern industry. Development of communications, for example, will serve the ends of commercialization as well as industrialization. It is true that a tremendous amount of pure speculation can be supported by a society as large as that of China. Even if industrialization is definitely a matter of secondary consideration, however, the future development of China can in no case support any such pure level of speculation as has recently prevailed.

The danger in the current situation of China, if modernization is considered desirable, is that the comparative ease of combining the commercialization of China with the present situation and all its "traditional" remnants will gain at least a temporary triumph. Industrialization as a conscious program of top priority will not only make further inroads upon the "traditional" patterns, but will have to seek an institutionalization of the necessary patterns for an industrialized society as a whole. The "individualism by default," which has been bred in China by the partial decomposition of the "traditional" family and the lack of positive formulation of a new structure, motivates more strongly in the direction of a commercialization than in the direction of modern industry. Moreover, the most staunchly "traditional" interests in China are in the positions of greatest power in the recognized government today. Their position would be threatened by any workable plan for industrialization, and their sincere standards of right and wrong would be violated.

Nevertheless, the indications are that modernization will win out in the long run. China cannot isolate herself from the world today unless the rest of the world will isolate itself from China, and this is manifestly not going to be the case. Furthermore, unless some striking revolution takes place which wipes out the whole social basis of industry in the Western world, China cannot continue indefinitely unindustrialized in that world. If the Chinese do not industrialize themselves, others will do it for them. The current situation cannot persist indefinitely. The transition must work itself out to some stable formulation. The "traditional" social structure motivates some of its members to take up the patterns of industrial society and these patterns are in turn subversive of the "traditional" patterns. The process can be more or less facilitated or retarded, but it cannot be stopped short of the reëstablishment of a clear ascendency of the "traditional" structure.

Since the structure of industrial society cannot be eliminated without its general elimination all over the world, the eventual triumph of that pattern is the more probable eventuality. This does not mean that all traces of the "traditional" patterns will be wiped out. It is not improbable that quite recognizable "traditional" families, or even whole villages, may continue to exist indefinitely in remote areas. In rural areas in general they will persist longer and more strongly than in urban areas. What it does mean, however, is that many of the so-called "compromise" solutions are unstable and cannot persist. The "compromise" solutions inevitably involve elements of the "traditional" patterns and elements of the patterns associated with modern industrial society, but the ideals of the one structure can rarely be maintained by the motivation of the other. It is well enough to say that it would be good to have the freedom and size of the conjugal unit and the accent on youth of modern Western society combined with a responsibility to support one's aged parents, but how is it to be done? The first generation which achieves its independence may retain sufficient of its reverence for the aged, but what of their own children? In place of the rigid indoctrination in attitudes toward the aged, their indoctrination will be largely in the view of the aged as a burden upon the young.

Other patterns will be no less difficult to combine. If parents are asked for consent to marry, and have no real power to control these matters, that consent will become more and more obviously meaningless, and with it the whole system of arranged marriages. The weakening or alteration at one point of so carefully integrated a structure as the "traditional" Chinese family has so many implications for the rest of the structure that it cannot be stopped half-way through. Industrialization has already supplied enough of a moderation of the "traditional" pattern to start the change, and the change will not stop until a new stable pattern has replaced the primacy of the old, unless industrial society itself is stopped.

The odds are that this new pattern will be the simple conjugal family unit of the West rather than a patchwork of parts from the one and the other.

Whether a new stable formulation in terms of the patterns of modern Western society will be reached is not entirely certain. Modern industrial society requires a unique and apparently precarious balance of variables. The strains involved in it are certainly great, and within the last three decades the world has seen large-scale social movements which threatened the bases of that whole society. That threat is by no means eliminated, though it has been temporarily halted from one direction of change. It may well be that China will still be in a "transitional" stage when and if the industrial societies of the West are forced to seek a new formulation for themselves. In such a case one might conceivably look forward to another two thousand years of history for the "traditional" patterns in China, confident that the only structure man has yet contrived to threaten seriously their domination contained the seeds of its own destruction.

BIBLIOGRAPHY

This bibliography has two major components. The first of these consists of those works actually cited in the text. These works are all designated by asterisks. The remaining works furnished general background information, the climate of the study, as it were. These works, while not actually cited, were invaluable to the effort because of the general sense of familiarity they afforded.

Anderson, Adelaide M., *Humanity and Labor in China,* Student Christian Movement (London, 1928).

—— "The Recommendations of the Shanghai Child Labor Commission," *International Labor Review,* XI, 5 (Geneva, May, 1925), 665-681.

Arnold, Julian H., *Changes in the Economic Life of the Chinese People,* Government Printing Office (Washington, D.C., 1922).

—— *China, A Commercial and Industrial Handbook,* 2 vols., Government Printing Office (Washington, D.C., 1926).

Auber, Peter, *China, an Outline of Its Government, Laws, and Policy,* Parbury, Allen & Co. (London, 1934).

*Ayscough, Florence, *Chinese Women,* Houghton Mifflin Co. (Boston, 1937).

Baker, O. E., "Agriculture and the Future of China," *Foreign Affairs,* 6, 3 (April, 1928), 483-497.

*Ball, J. Dyer, *Things Chinese,* Charles Scribner's Sons (New York, 1906).

Bashford, J. W., *The Awakening of China,* The Board of Foreign Missions of the Methodist Episcopal Church (New York, 1907).

—— *China,* The Abingdon Press (New York, 1916).

*Benedict, Ruth, *The Crysanthemum and the Sword,* Houghton Mifflin Co. (Boston, 1946).

Bingham, W., *The Founding of the T'ang Dynasty,* Waverly Press, Inc. (Baltimore, 1941)

Blaisdell, Thomas, C., Jr., see Chu, C. C.

Blakeslee, G. H. (ed.), *Recent Developments in China,* C. E. Stechert & Co. (New York, 1913).

Brewitt-Taylor, C. H., *San Kuo, or Romance of the Three Kingdoms* (translation), 2 vols., Kelly & Walsh, Ltd. (Shanghai, 1925).

Buck, J. L., *An Agricultural Survey of Szechwan Province, China,* The Farmer's Bank of China (Chungking, 1943).

―― *Chinese Farm Economy,* University of Chicago Press (Chicago, 1930).

―― "An Economic and Social Survey of 150 Farms, Yenshan County, Chihli Province, China," *Publications of the University of Nanking College of Agriculture and Forestry,* Bulletin No. 13 (June, 1936).

―― *Farm Ownership and Tenancy in China,* Committee on Christianizing the Economic Order, National Christian Council (Shanghai, n.d.).

*―― *Land Utilization in China,* 3 vols., University of Nanking (Nanking, 1937).

Buck, Pearl, *All Men Are Brothers* (translation), 2 vols. The John Day Co. (New York, 1933).

*―― "Author's Note," *Woman's Home Companion* (August 1946), p. 2.

*Burgess, John Stewart, *The Guilds of Peking.* Columbia University Press (New York, 1928).

Chang Chih-I, see Fei Hsiao-T'ung.

Chang Chih-T'ung, *China's Only Hope,* F. H. Revell Co. (New York, 1900).

*Chao Buwei, *Autobiography of a Chinese Woman,* The John Day Co. (New York, 1947).

Chao Chi-Chen, "Being an Old Maid in China," *Asia,* 41 (September, 1941), 492–496.

Chen Han-Seng, *Industrial Capital and Chinese Peasants,* Kelly & Walsh, Ltd. (Shanghai, 1939).

*―― *Landlord and Peasant in China,* International Publishers (New York, 1936).

Chen Shao-Kwan, *The System of Taxation in China in the Tsing Dynasty, 1644–1911,* Columbia University Press (New York, 1914).

Chen Ta, *Chinese Migrations; with Special Reference to Labor Conditions,* Government Printing Office (Washington, D.C., 1923).

―― *The Labor Movement in China,* Institute of Pacific Relations (Honolulu, 1927).

—— Articles in *Monthly Labor Review of the U.S. Bureau of Labor Statistics,*

    (1) "The Labor Situation in China" (December, 1920), pp. 201–212.

    (2) "Wages and Hours in Five Chinese Cities" (August, 1921), pp. 3–15.

    (3) "Labor Unrest in China" (August, 1921), pp. 16–30.

    (4) "Working Women in China" (December 1921), pp. 142–144.

    (5) "Labor Conditions in China" (November 1924), pp. 36–49.

*—— "Population in Modern China," *The American Journal of Sociology,* LII, 1 (July, 1946), Part 2, Supplement.

Cheng Ch'eng-K'un, "Characteristic Traits of the Chinese People," *Social Forces,* 25, 2 (December, 1946), 146–155.

Chin P'ing Mei, 2 vols., G. P. Putnam's Sons (New York, 1940), preface by Arthur Waley.

China Yearbook, The, published by the North China *Daily News and Herald,* Ltd. (Shanghai, 1934).

"Chinese Business Woman, A," *The Chinese Recorder,* LXIII, 2 (February, 1932), 71–74.

Chou Ku-Ch'eng, *Chung-Kuo T'ung Shih (A Comprehensive History of China),* Kai Ming Shu Tien (Shanghai, 1939).

Chu, C. C. and Thomas C. Blaisdell, Jr., "Peking Rugs and Peking Boys," Special Supplement to *Chinese Social and Political Science Review* (Peking, April, 1924).

Civil Code of the Republic of China, The, translated by Hsia Ching-Ling, Chow, J. L. E., Chieh Liu, & Chang Yukon, Kelly & Walsh, Ltd. (Shanghai, 1931).

Creel, H. G., *The Birth of China,* Reynal & Hitchcock (New York, 1937).

—— *Sinism,* The Open Court Publishing Co. (Chicago, 1929).

—— *Studies in Early Chinese Culture,* Waverly Press, Inc. (Baltimore, 1937).

*Crow, Carl, *Four Hundred Million Customers,* Harper & Bros. (New York, 1937).

Davis, Alexandra, *Le Philosophe Meh-Ti et l'Idée de Solidarité,* Luzac et Co. (London, 1907)

*Dewey, J. & others, *Letters from China and Japan,* E. P. Dutton (New York, 1921).

Dickinson, Jean, *Observations on the Social Life of a North China Village*, Dept. of Sociology, Yenching University, Peking, Series SNO6 (October–December, 1924)

Dingle, E. J., *China's Revolution*, McBride, Nast & Co. (New York, 1912).

*Doolittle, Justus, *Social Life of the Chinese*, 2 vols., Harper & Bros. (New York, 1865).

Douglas, R. K., *Society in China*, A. D. Innes & Co. (London, 1895).

Dubs, H. H., see Pan Ku.

Dulles, Foster Rhea, *China and America*, Princeton University (Princeton, 1946).

*Durkheim, Emile, *De la Division du Travail Social*, Librairie Felix Alcan (Paris, 1893)

*—— *Les Formes Elementaires de la Vie Religieuse*, Librairie Felix Alcan (Paris, 1925).

Eldridge, F. R., *Oriental Trade Methods*, D. Appleton & Co. (New York, 1923).

Escarra, Jean, *Le Droit Chinois*, Henry Vetch (Peiping, 1936).

Favre, B., *Les Sociétés Secrètes en Chine*, C. P. Maisonneuve (Paris, 1933).

*Fei Hsiao-T'ung, *Peasant Life in China*, E. P. Dutton & Co. (New York, 1939).

*Fei Hsiao-T'ung and Chang Chih-I, *Earthbound China*, University of Chicago Press (Chicago, 1945).

*—— "Peasantry and Gentry: an Interpretation of Chinese Social Structure and its Changes," *The American Journal of Sociology*, LII, 1 (July, 1946), 1–17

*Feng, H. D., "Chinese Kinship System," *Harvard Journal of Asiatic Studies*, II, 2, 141–276.

*Fitzgerald, C. P., *China, a Short Cultural History*, D. Appleton Century Co. (New York, 1938).

Fong Hsien-Ding, "China's Industrialization, a Statistical Survey," *Conference Documents (4th Conference, vol. 2) of the Institute of Pacific Relations*.

—— "Chinese Guilds Old and New," *Chinese Student Monthly*, XIII, 6 (April, 1928), 14–19.

—— "Cotton Industry and Trade in China," *Nankai Institute of Economics Industry Series*, 2 vols., Bulletin No. 4 (1932).

—— "Growth and Decline of Rural Industrial Enterprise in North China," *Nankai Institute of Economics Industry Series,* Bulletin No. 8 (1936).

—— "Industrial Capital in China," *Nankai Institute of Economics Industry Series,* Bulletin No. 9 (1936).

—— "Industrial Organization in China," *Nankai Institute of Economics Industry Series,* Bulletin No. 10 (1937).

—— *The Post-War Industrialization of China,* National Planning Association (Washington, D.C., 1942).

—— *Toward Economic Control in China,* China Institute of Pacific Relations (Shanghai, 1936).

*Fortune, R., "Incest," *Encyclopedia of the Social Sciences,* 7, 620–622.

Foster, John, *Chinese Realities,* Edinburgh House Press (London, 1930).

Gamble, S. D. and J. S. Burgess, *Peking; A Social Survey,* George H. Donan Co. (New York, 1921).

Gannett, L. S., *Young China,* The Nation (New York, 1926).

*Goldhamer, H. and E. A. Shils, "Types of Power and Status," *American Journal of Sociology,* XLV, 2 (September, 1939), 171–183.

Goodrich, L. C., *The Literary Inquisition of Ch'ien Lung,* Waverly Press, Inc. (Baltimore, 1935).

—— *A Short History of the Chinese People,* Harper & Bros. (New York, 1943).

*Granet, Marcel, *La Civilization Chinoise,* La Renaissance du Livre (Paris, 1934).

Harvey, Edwin D., *The Mind of China,* Yale University Press (New Haven, 1933).

Henry, P., "Some Aspects of the Labor Problem in China," *International Labor Review,* XV, 1 (Geneva, January, 1927).

Hinder, E. H., "Some Facts Regarding the Chinese Labor Movement," *China Weekly Review,* XLIII, 11 (February, 1928), 261–263.

Holcombe, A. N., *The Chinese Revolution,* Harvard University Press (Cambridge, 1930).

Howell, E. B., *The Restitution of the Bride* (translation), T. Werner Laurie, Ltd. (London, 1926).

Hsu Chi-Lien, "Rural Credit in China," *Chinese Social and Political Science Review,* XII, 1, 1–15.

Hsu, F. L. K., "China's New Social Spirit," *Asia*, 42, 9 (September, 1942), 506–509.

—— "The Differential Functions of Relationship Terms," *American Anthropologist*, 44, 2 (April–June, 1942), 248–256.

—— "Guild and Kinship among the Butchers in West Town," *American Sociological Review*, X, 3 (June, 1945), 357–364.

*—— "The Myth of Chinese Family Size," *American Journal of Sociology*, XLVIII, 5 (March, 1943), 555–562.

*—— "Observations on Cross-Cousin Marriage in China," *American Anthropologist*, 47, 1 (January–March, 1945), 83–103.

*—— "The Problem of Incest Tabu in a North China Village," *American Anthropologist*, 42, 1 (January–March, 1940), 122–135.

Hsu, Leonard, *Ching Ho: A Sociological Analysis*, Yenching University (Peiping, 1930).

Hsu, M. C., *Railway Problems in China*, Columbia University Press (New York, 1915).

Hsu Meng-Hsiung, "The Free Women of Free China," *Asia*, 41, 3 (March, 1941), 123–126.

*Hu Hsien-Chin, *The Common Descent Group in China and Its Functions*, Unpublished Ph.D. dissertation, Columbia University.

—— "The Chinese Concepts of 'Face,'" *American Anthropologist*, 46, 1, Pt. 1 (January–March, 1944), 45–65.

Hu Shih, P'an Kuang-Tan: *Chung-Kuo Wen T'i* (*China's Problems*), Hsin Yueh Shu Tien (Shanghai, 1932)

*—— "The Indianization of China: a Case Study in Cultural Borrowing," *Independence, Convergence, and Borrowing*, Harvard Tercentenary Publications, Harvard University Press (Cambridge, Mass., 1937).

Huang Han Liang, *Land Tax in China*, Columbia University (New York, 1918).

*Jacoby, A., see White, T. H.

Kent, Percy H., *Railway Enterprises in China*, E. Arnold (London, 1907).

King, F. H., *Farmers of Forty Centuries*, Harcourt, Brace & Co. (New York, 1927).

Koung Shien-Ming, *Comment Remédier à la Situation Tragique des Travailleurs Chinois*, E. Desbarax (Louvain, 1927).

Krausse, Alexis, *China in Decay*, Chapman & Hall, Ltd. (London, 1900).

Kulp, Daniel Harrison, *Country Life in South China*, Columbia University (New York, 1925), vol. 1.

Kuo, P. W., "China's Revolt Against the Old Order, V.—The Cultural and Social Background," *Current History*, XXVI, 3 (June, 1927), 372-378.

Lachin, Maurice, *La Chine Capitaliste*, Gallimard (Paris, 1938).

*Lamson, Herbert Day, *Social Pathology in China*, Commercial Press, Ltd. (Shanghai, 1935).

*Lang, Olga, *Chinese Family and Society*, Yale University Press (New Haven, 1946).

Lattimore, Eleanor, *Labor Unions in the Far East*, American Council, Institute of Pacific Relations (New York, 1945).

Lattimore, Owen, *Inner Asian Frontiers of China*, Oxford University Press (New York, 1940).

Lattimore, Owen & Eleanor, *The Making of Modern China*, W. W. Norton & Co. (New York, 1944).

Latourette, K. S., *The Chinese, Their History and Culture*, The Macmillan Co. (New York, 1942).

—— *The Development of China*, Houghton Mifflin Co. (New York, 1917).

Lee Chow-Ying, *The System of Chinese Public Finance*, P. S. King and Son, Ltd. (London, 1936).

*Leeuw, Henry de, *Cities of Sin*, Modern Age Books, Inc. (New York, 1933).

Legge, James, *The Four Books* (translation), The Chinese Book Co. (Shanghai, n.d.).

*—— *The Li Ki*, Vols. 27 and 28 in *The Sacred Books of the East*, ed. by Max Muller, Clarendon Press (Oxford, 1885).

Leong, Y. K. and L. K. Tao, *Village and Town Life in China*, George Allen & Unwin, Ltd. (London, 1915).

*Le Play, F., *Les Ouvriers Européens*, 6 vols., Alfred Mame et Fils (Tours, 1879).

Lieu, D. K., *The Silk Industry of China*, Kelly & Walsh, Ltd. (Shanghai, 1940).

Lim Hy-Soon, *La Question Ouvrière en Chine*, Librairie Poncelet (Nancy, 1931).

Lin Mousheng, *Men and Ideas,* The John Day Co. (New York, 1942).

Lin Sung-Ho, *Factory Workers in Tangku,* Chao Chang Press, Ltd. (Peiping, 1928).

Lin Yueh-Hwa, *The Golden Wing,* Institute of Pacific Relations (New York, 1944).

Lin Yutang, *A History of the Press and Public Opinion in China,* University of Chicago Press (Chicago, 1936).

*—— *Moment in Peking,* John Day Co. (New York, 1939).

*—— *My Country and My People,* Halcyon House (New York, 1935).

Lo Tun-Wei, *Chung-Kuo Chih Hun-Yin Wen-T'i (Chinese Marriage Problems),* Ta Tung Shu Chu (Shanghai, 1931).

Lockwood, E. H., "Labor Unions in Canton," *Chinese Recorder* (July, 1927), 399–403.

Lowe, C. H. *Facing Labor Issue in China,* George Allen & Unwin, Ltd. (London, 1934).

*Mai Hui-T'ing, *Chung Kuo Chia T'ing Kai Tsao Wen T'i (Problems of Chinese Family Reconstruction),* Commercial Press, Ltd. (Shanghai, 1930).

Mason, Mary G., *Western Concepts of China and the Chinese,* 1840–1876, The Seeman Printery, Inc. (Durham, North Carolina, 1939).

*Maspero, Henri, *La Chine Antique,* E. de Boccard (Paris, 1927).

*Mathews, R. H., *Chinese-English Dictionary,* Harvard University Press (Cambridge, 1945).

McGovern, William M., *The Early Empires of Central Asia,* University of North Carolina Press (Chapel Hill, 1939).

*McNair, H. F., *Modern Chinese History, Selected Readings,* Commercial Press, Ltd. (Shanghai, 1927)

Meng, Paul Chih, "The Student Movement," *Current History,* XXVI, 3 (June, 1927), 410–412.

Monroe, Paul, *China, a Nation in Evolution,* Macmillan Co. (New York, 1928).

Morgan, Harry J., *Chinese Symbols and Superstitions,* P. D. & Ione Perkins (South Pasadena, California, 1942).

Morrison, Robert, *Memoir of the Principal Occurrences during an Embassy from the British Government to the Court of China in the Year 1816,* James Nichols (London, 1820).

Morse, H. B., *Guilds of China*, Longmans, Green & Co. (New York, 1909).

—— *The Trade and Administration of China*, Longmans, Green & Co. (New York, 1913).

*Nagano Akira, *Chung-Kuo She-Hui Tsu-Chih* (*Chinese Social Organization*), translated from Japanese to Chinese by Chu Chia-Ch'ing, Kuang Ming Shu Chu (Shanghai, 1932).

Nelson, J. H., *Changing Factors in the Economic Life of China*, Government Printing Office (Washington, D.C., 1925).

* *New York Times*, New York Times Co. (New York, February 2, 1947).

*Orchard, Dorothy, "Manpower in China I and II," *Political Science Quarterly*, L, 4 (December, 1935), 561–583 and LI, 1 (March, 1936), 1–35.

Orient Year Book 1942, The, The Asia Statistics Co. (Tokyo, 1942).

Pan Ku, *The History of the Former Han Dynasty*, translated by H. H. Dubs, 2 vols., Waverly Press, Inc. (Baltimore, 1938).

*P'an Kuang-Tan, *Chung-Kuo Chih Chia-T'ing Wen-T'i* (*Chinese Family Problems*), Hsin Yueh Shu Tien (Shanghai, 1929).

P'an Kuang-Tan, see also Hu Shih.

Parker, E. H., *China Past and Present*, E. P. Dutton & Co. (New York, 1903).

*Parsons, Talcott, "The Professions and Social Structure," *Social Forces*, 17, 4 (May, 1939), 457–467.

*Perlmann, S. M., *The History of the Jews in China*, R. Mazin & Co., Ltd. (London, 1913).

Pritchard, E. H. "Anglo-Chinese Relations during the Seventeenth and Eighteenth Centuries," *University of Illinois Studies in the Social Sciences*, XVII, 1–2 (March–June, 1929).

*Pruitt, Ida, *A Daughter of Han*, Yale University Press (New Haven, 1945).

*Ratchnevsky, Paul, *Un Code des Yüan*, Librairie, E. Leroux (Paris, 1937).

Rosinger, L. K., *China's Wartime Politics 1937–1944*, Institute of Pacific Relations (New York, 1944).

Ross, E. A., *The Changing Chinese*, The Century Co. (New York, 1911).

—— "Sociological Observations in Inner China," *American Sociological Society Papers,* V (December, 1910), 17–30.

Royal Institute of International Affairs, London: *China and Japan,* Oxford University Press (New York, 1938).

Russell, Bertrand A., *The Problem of China,* G. Allen & Unwin, Ltd. (London, 1922).

Salter, A., "China and the Depression," *The Economist,* Supplement (May 19, 1934).

Shih Kuo-Heng, *China Between Disorganization and Reorganization* (unpublished manuscript)

*—— *China Enters the Machine Age,* Harvard University Press (Cambridge, 1944).

*—— "Social Implications of Tin-Mining in Yunnan," *Pacific Affairs,* XX, 1 (March, 1947), 53–61

*—— "Tin-Mining in Yunnan" (unpublished manuscript).

*Shils, E. A., see Goldhamer, H.

Sie-Ying-Chou, *Le Federalisme en Chine,* Henri d'Arthez (Paris, 1924).

Sing Ging Su, *The Chinese Family System,* International Press (New York, 1922).

Smith, Arthur H., *China in Convulsion,* 2 vols., F. H. Revell Co. (New York, 1901).

—— *Chinese Characteristics,* F. H. Revell Co. (New York, 1894).

*—— *Village Life in China,* F. H. Revell Co. (New York, 1899).

Snow, Edgar, *Red Star Over China,* Random House, Inc. (New York, 1938).

Soh Chuan-Pao, *La Situation de l'Ouvrier Industriel en Chine,* Gembloux (Belgium, 1937).

Soong Ch'ing-Ling (Mme. Sun Yat-Sen) "The Chinese Woman's Fight for Freedom," *Asia,* 42 (July–August, 1942), 390–393 and 470–472.

Soothill, W. E., *The Three Religions of China,* Hodder and Stoughton (New York, 1913).

*Sorokin, P. A., *Social and Cultural Dynamics,* American Book Co. (New York, 1937).

Sun Fo, *China Looks Forward,* The John Day Co. (New York, 1944).

*Sun Pen Wen, *Hsien-Tai Chung-Kuo She Hui Wen-T'i (Social Problems of Modern China),* 3 vols., Commercial Press (Chungking, 1942).

Tamagna, F. M., *Banking and Finance in China,* Institute of Pacific Relations (New York, 1942).

T'ang Leang-Li, *China, Facts and Fancies,* China United Press (Shanghai, 1936).

—— *The New Social Order in China,* China United Press (Shanghai, 1936).

T'ao Hsi-Sheng, *Chung-Kuo She-Hui Shih (Chinese Social History),* Ch'ou Chieh Fu (Chungking, 1944).

Tawney, R. H. (ed.), *Agrarian China,* George Allen & Unwin, Ltd. (London, 1939).

*Tawney, R. H., *Land and Labor in China,* Harcourt Brace & Co. (New York, 1932).

Taylor, J. B. and W. T. Zung, "Labor and Industry in China," *International Labor Review,* VIII, 1 (July, 1923), 1–20.

*Thomas, W. I. and F. Zneniecki, *The Polish Peasant,* The Gorham Press (Boston, 1918).

Torgasheff, Boris, "Town Population in China," *China Critic,* III (Shanghai, 1930), 317–322.

*Toynbee, A. J., *A Study of History,* Oxford University Press (London, 1934).

*Tsao Hsueh-Chin, *Dream of the Red Chamber* (translated by Wang Chi-Chen), George Routledge & Sons, Ltd. (London, c. 1929).

Tse, N. Q., "China: Progenitor and Novice of Our Modern World," *Social Forces,* 25, 2 (December, 1946), 155–159.

Tso, S. K. Sheldon, *The Labor Movement in China* (Shanghai, 1928).

Tsu Yu-Yue, "The Spirit of Chinese Philanthropy," *Studies in History, Economics, and Public Law,* Columbia University, L, 1.

Tyau, M. T. Z., *China Awakened,* The Macmillan Co. (New York, 1922).

Vinacke, Harold M., *A History of the Far East in Modern Times,* F. S. Crofts & Co., Inc. (New York, 1928).

——*Problems of Industrial Progress in China,* Princeton University Press (Princeton, 1926).

Wagner, Augusta, *Labor Legislation in China,* Yenching University (Peiping, 1938).

*Waley, Arthur, see Chin P'ing Mei.

——, see Wu Ch'eng-En.

*Wang Chi-Chen, see also Tsao Hsueh-Chin.

Wang Chi-Chen, *Contemporary Chinese Stories,* Columbia University Press (New York, 1944).

*—— Traditional Chinese Tales, Columbia University Press (New York, 1944).

*Wang, T. C., *The Youth Movement in China,* New Republic Inc. (New York, 1927).

*Wang, Y. C., same as Hu Hsin-Chin.

Wei, T. F., "Chinese Wedding," *The China Journal,* XXXIV, 2 (February, 1941), 55-58.

*White, T. H. and A. Jacoby, *Thunder Out of China,* William Sloane Associates, Inc. (New York, 1946).

Wieger, L., *Moral Tenets and Customs in China,* Catholic Mission Press (Ho-Kien-Fu, 1913).

Wilcox, Walter F., "A Westerner's Effort to Estimate the Population of China and Its Increase since 1650," *Journal of American Statistical Association,* XXV, 171 (Washington, D.C., 1930), New Series, 255-268.

Wilhelm, Richard, *A Short History of Chinese Civilization,* G. G. Harrap & Co., Ltd. (London, 1929)

Wilkinson, H., *The Family in Classical China,* Kelly & Walsh, Ltd. (Shanghai, 1926).

Williams, Edward Thomas, *China Yesterday and Today,* G. G. Harrap & Co., Ltd. (New York, 1933).

*Williams, S. Wells, *The Middle Kingdom,* 2 vols. Charles Scribner's Sons (New York, 1899).

*World Almanac, The, published by the *New York World Telegram* (New York, 1934).

Wu Ch'eng-En, *Monkey* (translated by A. Waley), The John Day Co. (New York, 1943).

Wu Kuo-Cheng, *Ancient Chinese Political Theories,* The Commercial Press, Ltd., (Shanghai, 1928).

*Yang Ching-Kung, *A North China Local Market Economy,* Institute of Pacific Relations (New York, 1944).

*Yang, Martin C., *A Chinese Village,* Columbia University Press (New York, 1945).

* Yao Tz'u-Ai, *"P'o-Hsi Chung-T'u ti Chu-Yao Yuan-Yin* (The Main

Reasons for Mother-in-law Conflicts"), *She Hui Hsüeh Chieh* (*Sociological World*), VII (1933), 259ff.

Yung Wing, *My Life in China and America,* Henry Holt & Co. (New York, 1909).

Zen, Sophia H. Chen, (ed.), *Symposium on Chinese Culture,* China Institute of Pacific Relations (Shanghai, 1931).

*Znaniecki, F., see Thomas, W. I.

Zung, W. T., see Taylor, J. B.

GLOSSARY

Chinese Transliterations

che chung ti chia-t'ing chih tu 折中的家庭制度
ch'eng-jen 成人
ch'i-chu 七出
chia-chang 家長
chia-t'ing 家庭
Ch'ien Lung 乾隆
Ch'in 秦
Chin P'ing Mei 金瓶梅
ch'in-ying 親迎
Ch'ing 清
ch'ing-ch'i 請期
ch'ing-nien 青年
ch'ing nien jen 青年人
Chou 周
Ch'ou Chieh Fu 鄒傑夫
Chou Ku-Ch'eng 周谷城
Chu Chia-Ch'ing 朱家清
chuang-nien 壯年
Chung-Kuo Chia-T'ing Kai-Tsao Wen-T'i 中國家庭改造問題
Chung-Kuo Chih Chia T'ing Wen T'i 中國之家庭問題
Chung Kuo Chih Hun Yin Wen T'i 中國之婚姻問題
Chung Kuo She Hui Shih 中國社會史
Chung-Kuo She-Hui Tsu-Chih 中國社會組織
Chung Kuo T'ung Shih 中國通史
Chung Kuo Wen T'i 中國問題
chung-nien 中年
Chung ssu yen ch'ing 螽斯衍慶
fang 房
Fei Hsiao-T'ung 費孝通
feng-shui 風水
Fu mu chih ming mei cho chih yen 父母之命媒妁之言
Fu tz'u tzu hsiao 父慈子孝
Han 漢
hsiao chih chih tu 小家制度
hsiao-hsi 小媳
hsien 縣
Hsien-Tai Chung-Kuo She-Hui Wen-T'i 現代中國社會問題

Hsin Yueh Shu Tien 新月書店

hsiung-ti 兄弟

Hsiung yu ti kung 兄友弟恭

hu 戶

Hung Lou Meng 紅樓夢

jen-ch'ing 人情

jen nai 忍耐

Kai Ming Shu Tien 開明書店

ko-ko 哥哥

Kuang Ming Shu Tien 光明書店

kung ho han i lung sun chih lo 恭賀含飴弄孫之樂

lao 老

lao hsiung 老兄

lao-ju-jen 老孺人

lao-nien 老年

lao po 老伯

li 里

li 禮

Li Chi 禮記

Li pu hsia shu jen 禮不下庶人

Li Yu-I 李有義

lieh-shen 劣紳

Lo Tun-Wei 羅敦偉

Mai Hui-T'ing 麥惠庭

miao-chien 廟見

Ming 明

na-cheng 納徵

na-chi 納吉

na-ts'ai 納采

Nagano Akira 長野朗

nien yu wu chih 年幼無知

nü 女

P'an Kuang-Tan 潘光旦

pao-chia 保甲

pe-pe 伯伯

pei-te 悖德

p'iao-tu 嫖賭

[383]

P'o-Hsi Ch'ung-T'u Chu-Yao Yüan-Yin 婆媳衝突主要原因

pu ch'eng ch'ang 不成常

Pu hsiao yu san wu hou wei ta 不孝有三無後為大

san-ts'ung 三從

Shang ch'uang fu fu lo ti chün tzu 上床夫婦落地君子

She Hui Hsüeh Chieh 社會學界

Shih Kuo-Heng 史國衡

shu-shu 叔叔

Shui Hu Chuan 水滸傳

Sun Pen-Wen 孫本文

Sung 宋

ta chia chih tu 大家制度

ta chia-t'ing t'ung chü 大家庭同居

Ta Tung Shu Chu 大東書局

T'ang 唐

T'ao Hsi-Sheng 陶希聖

Tao Kuang 道光

ti-ti 弟弟

Ting Sheng-Shu 丁聲樹

tsu 族

tung yang hsi 童養媳

wen-ming 問名

Wu Wen-Tsao 吳文藻

Yao Tz'u-Ai 姚慈藹

Yen Shan 鹽山

yin 陰

ying-erh shih-ch'i 嬰兒時期

yu-nien 幼年

yu-nü 幼女

yu-t'ung 幼童

Yüan 元

INDEX

Ability, *see* Universalistic standards
Adoption, 33, 34, 91, 127, 215, 247
Age, absolute, 66–133, 141; in "transitional" China, 289–307
Age, relative, 134–140, 161, 187, 237; in "transitional" China, 307, 334
Age, role differentiation based on, 11, 12, 63–140, 330. *See also Ying-erh Shih-ch'i; Yu-nien Shih-ch'i; Ch'ing-nien Shih-ch'i; Chuang-nien Shih-ch'i; Chung-nien Shih ch'i; Lao-nien Shih-ch'i*
Agriculture, 209–212, 334
Amusement, 37, 260–269, 345
Ancestors, 78, 133, 168, 171, 234–237, 249–251, 259, 336, 337, 343. *See also* Ritual activities
Artisans, *see* Craftsmen
Artistic activities, 37, 260, 262. *See also* Expression
Avoidance, *see* Solidarity
Ayscough, Florence, 176

Birth rate, 304
British Empire, 275–278
Brothers, 134–136, 139, 140, 165, 307; wives of, 138, 190–193, 199–201; and sisters, 233, 317
Buck, J., 273
Buck, Pearl, 148n.
Buddhism, 251–255, 266, 343
Bureaucracy, 218, 219, 222, 224, 230, 352, 354. *See also* Government; Civil Service, Examination system
Business, definition, 357–359; investment, 361–363

Calligraphy, 265, 266
Cash, 212, 226, 278

Celibacy, 94, 301
Ceremonies, *see* Ritual activities
Chang Kung-I, 48n.
Chen Han-Seng, 318
Chia-chang (family head), 52, 109, 119, 143, 149–151, 157, 159, 160, 167, 172, 175, 178, 180, 184, 189, 192, 194, 195, 198, 203, 206; in "transitional" China, 300, 325, 329, 330, 334, 337, 342
Chiao Chung-Ch'ing, Tale of, 176
Chia-t'ing (family), 49–51, 55. *See also* Gentry; Peasantry
Ch'ien Lung, Emperor, 54, 275–278
Child labor, 217, 291
Childbearing, 113–116, 168, 186, 323; among gentry, 114, 115; among peasantry, 114, 116
Children, rearing of, 11, 33, 34, 66–84, 116, 224, 248; joint play of, 78, 260. *See also* Sons; Daughters
Ch'in Dynasty, 46, 55
China, Republic of, 41
China, "traditional," 32, 40–43, 63–269, 295, 296, 302, 330, 335, 348, 355, 357–360, 363, 364
China, "transitional," 41, 42, 71, 89, 175, 235, 273–365
Ch'ing Dynasty, 41, 54, 59, 92, 93, 112, 244, 251, 351
Ch'ing-nien Shih-ch'i (marriageable period), 84–93, 294–300
Chou Dynasty, 46
Christianity, 286. *See also* Missionaries
Chuang-nien Shih-ch'i (mature period), 93–105; among gentry, 98–105, 112, 114; among peasantry, 90, 95–97, 112, 114, 119; in "transitional" China, 300
Chung-nien Shih-ch'i (middle age), 105–127; in "transitional" China, 300

[385]

Civil Service, 214, 222
Coëducation, 290, 295, 341. *See also* Education; Integration
Commerce, 282. *See also* Industrialization; Business
Communications, 280, 283, 284, 313, 351, 363
Communist Party, 297, 343, 344, 347
Competition, 283
Concubinage, 97, 98, 124, 178, 191, 197, 201, 202, 215, 261
Confucianism, 16, 48, 130, 164, 249, 251, 256, 343
Consumption, 24–27, 145, 146, 157–159, 208, 210, 215, 216, 218, 225–231; in "transitional" China, 278, 279. *See also* Economic allocation
Craftsmen, 44, 45, 81, 209, 217, 218, 252, 334
Crow, Carl, 346, 354, 358

Daughters, birth of, 67, 69; training of, 71, 76, 78–80, 180, 184; marriage of, 89–93, 180; and fathers, 179–181; and mothers, 180, 183, 184; in "transitional" China, 291, 292, 303, 309, 323, 332
Dewey, John, 346
Divorce, 177, 186, 337
Domestic workers, 44, 45, 154, 155, 280, 291, 311, 312, 320
Dowries, 95–97
Dream of the Red Chamber, 65, 88, 202, 204, 215*n.*, 263
Dress, 345, 346
Durkheim, Emile, 359

Economic allocation, 13, 14, 22, 27, 28, 151–159, 208–231; in "transitional" China, 317–328. *See also* Production; Consumption
Education, 33–36, 66–84, 116, 224, 229; in "transitional" China, 284–286, 293, 314, 339–343, 361. *See also* Coëducation; Integration
Electric power, *see* Utilities
Emancipation of women, *see* Women, in "transitional" China

Emotions, 37, 38; inhibition of, 257; grief, 257; romantic love, 177, 178, 257, 290, 295, 301, 310, 315. *See also* Expression
Entertainers, 44
Examination system, 218, 219, 222. *See also* Government; Bureaucracy; Civil Service
Exports, 279
Expression, 33, 247, 257–269; in "transitional" China, 339, 345–349. *See also* Emotions; Amusement; Artistic activities

Factory workers, 44, 45, 155, 210, 280, 311, 312, 322, 334, 345
Famille souche, 55, 56, 58, 59, 108, 119, 300, 313, 320. *See also* Family
Family, 5, 48–60, 164, 165, 281; simple conjugal, 58, 293, 300, 317, 320, 339, 365; and *passim. See also* Kinship structure
Famines, 226, 227*n.*
Fang (subclan), 49, 50, 141
Farmers, 209–212, 218
Fathers, and sons, 76, 82, 83, 104, 118–120, 126, 133, 166–175, 248, 290, 293, 313, 330, 336, 340; and daughters, 76, 90, 125, 126, 179–181, 332; power of, 189
Fei Hsiao-T'ung, 324
Feng, H. D., 136
Filial piety, 74, 110, 127, 129, 164, 168, 176, 178, 243–246, 248, 250, 259, 268, 342
Fine arts, 265, 266, 345
Folksongs, 267
Force, use of, 242, 243, 246. *See also* Political allocation; Power; *Chia-chang*
Foreigners, 287, 356, 362. *See also* Missionaries
Fortune, R., 20
Fukien province, 50
Functional diffuseness, 282, 358–360
Functional specificity, 281–284, 352

Gambling, 86, 87, 146, 216, 230, 261
Games, 267, 268

Generation, role differentiation based on, 140–147, 187, 234–237; in "transitional" China, 308, 309, 330, 331

Gentry, defined, 42–49; family pattern, 49–51, 55, 59, 60, 143; age differentiation, 64, 65, 73–80, 83–93, 98–105, 112, 114, 125; and economic allocation, 155, 156, 158, 208, 212–216, 218, 220–222, 227–231; solidarity of family, 170, 179, 191, 193, 195; and political allocation, 232, 234, 241; and integration, 248, 252; and expression, 257, 260, 262, 266; in "transitional" China, 294, 314

George III, King of England, 275

Geronticide, 226

Gods, household and field, 251, 252, 343

Government, 218, 219, 230, 238, 245, 333, 342, 347, 359, 361, 362. See also Bureaucracy; Civil Service; Examination system

Graft, 214, 220, 223, 361

Grand Canal, 352–354

Great Britain, see British Empire

Great Wall, 352, 354

Grief, see Emotions

Guilds, 326, 327

Han emperors, 41, 176

Handicraft work, 209–211, 230, 281, 284

Heterosexual intercourse, 19, 20, 22, 86, 111, 112

Homosexual intercourse, 19n.

Household work, 109, 192, 200, 201, 211. See also Hu; Wives; Women

Hsiao-chia chih-tu (small family system), 49

Hsiung-hsiung (older brothers), 134

Hsiung-ti (brothers), 134

Hu (household), 109, 192, 200, 201, 228

Husbands, 104; and wives, 172, 175–179, 201, 202; and concubines, 200, 201; in "transitional" China, 301, 315, 332

Illegitimacy, 337

Imports, 278

Incest taboo, 19, 20, 21, 86, 88, 112, 192, 193, 203

Individualism, 285, 292, 296, 305, 331, 332, 345; "by default," 298, 327, 363

Industrial Revolution, 275–277, 286. See also Technology

Industrialization, 24–26, 32, 38, 159, 171, 227, 235, 279–282, 284, 286, 288, 297, 308, 309, 318, 320, 323, 328, 329, 335, 344, 350–365 passim

Infanticide, 67n., 69, 81, 98, 99, 226, 290

Integration, 33, 34, 106, 108, 247–257; in "transitional" China, 339–345. See also Marriage; Adoption; Education; Religion

Intellectuals, 318, 328, 332, 340, 346

Intimacy, see Solidarity

Irrigation system, 352–354

Japan, family solidarity in, 171, 172, 320, 351; war with, 296, 300, 342; industry in, 350

Judaism, 286

Juvenile delinquency, 337

Kinship structure, definition, 3–8; role differentiation, 8–14, 63–163, 289–313; solidarity, 8n., 13, 15–22, 164–207, 313–317; economic allocation, 22–28, 208–231, 317–328; political allocation, 28–33, 232–246, 328–339; integration and expression, 33–38, 247–269, 339–349

ko-ko (older brothers), 134

Kuomintang, 297, 343, 344, 347

Kwantung province, 50

Lamson, H. D., 337

Land ownership, 223

Lang, Olga, 51, 57, 64, 68, 69, 93, 128, 182, 273, 290, 293, 303, 311, 315, 336, 341

Lao-hsiung (old older brother), 135

Lao-nien Shih-ch'i (old age), 83, 84, 93, 121, 127–133; among gentry, 132; among peasantry, 132; in "transitional" China, 303, 306. See also Old age

Leadership roles, 134, 135

Li Chi (The Book of Rites), 99, 100, 118, 122, 171, 172, 178, 182, 216, 241, 259

Life expectancy, 304
Lin Yutang, 45*n.*, 150; *Moment in Peking*, 88
Literacy, 297, 342, 343. *See also* Education
Literature, 262–264

Macartney, Earl, 275
Mai Hui-T'ing, 94, 296
Manchu invasion, 329
Manufacturing, 278–280. *See also* Industrialization; Business
Marco Polo, 274
Markets, 212, 323
Marriage, 33, 34, 93–119, 175–179, 247; among gentry, 87–92, 98–105, 112, 125, 177, 178; among peasantry, 91, 95–97, 112, 125, 177, 178; in "transitional" China, 292, 295, 296, 299, 302, 310, 315, 323, 324, 334, 342, 348, 364
Mathews, R. H., 94
Matricide, 226
Men, domination of, 52, 109, 119, 143, 149–151, 157, 159, 160, 232, 234, 235, 332. *See also* Fathers; Husbands; Sons
Mencius, ideals of, 48, 68, 168
Merchants, 44, 45, 209, 213, 218, 220, 221, 230; in "transitional" China, 283, 346
Migration, rural, 313, 319
Ming Dynasty, 55
Missionaries, 274, 285, 286, 344
Modernization, problem of, 339, 344, 350–365. *See also* Westernization; Industrialization
Mongol invasion, 329
Mothers, and sons, 76, 95, 99, 105, 109, 129–131, 133, 181–183, 233, 258, 290, 299, 304, 314, 316, 334, 340; and daughters, 76, 183, 184
Mothers-in-law, and daughters-in-law, 105, 106, 108–116 *passim*, 122, 123, 138, 150, 151, 160, 162, 175, 176, 182, 185–187, 199, 200, 216, 248, 258, 260; in "transitional" China, 299, 301, 303, 316, 330, 334, 336, 348
Music, 265–267, 345

Nationalism, 344
Neighborhood, 238, 298. *See also Tsu; Fang*
Nepotism, 223, 283, 329, 342, 354, 361
Newbold, Charles, 276

Old age, problem, of, 293, 303–306, 348, 361, 364. *See also Lao-nien Shih-ch'i*
Operas, 264, 267. *See also* Music
Orientation, family of, 108 179, 183, 248, 338

P'an Kuang-tan, 315
Parents, role of, 12, 64, 169, 204, 235; in "transitional" China, 294, 302–304, 338. *See also* Mother; Father
Parsons, Talcott, 18*n.*, 221*n.*
Particularistic standards, 218, 219, 222–224, 230, 282, 283, 307, 317, 326, 329, 335, 337, 339, 352, 354, 356, 358–360. *See also* Universalistic standards
Patricide, 226
Peasantry, defined, 42–48; family pattern, 60, 143; age differentiation, 64, 65, 73, 74, 77–83, 90, 95–97, 112, 114, 119, 137; and economic allocation, 155, 156, 208–212, 217, 220, 221, 227, 229, 230; solidarity of family members, 170, 180, 191; and political allocation, 232, 234, 241; and integration, 252; and expression, 257, 263, 266, 267; in "transitional" China, 278, 279, 294, 298, 314, 323, 344
Political allocation, 13, 28, 151, 159–163, 232–246; in "transitional" China, 328–339. *See also* Power; Responsibility
Posterity, importance of, 168, 171. *See also* Childbearing
Power, 28–31, 141–143, 151, 159, 189; locus of, 232–239; definition of, 239–241; procedure, 242–246; in "transitional" China, 335–338. *See also* Political allocation
Precedence, based on relative age, 134, 136
Premarital intercourse, 111, 112
Priests, 44

Primogeniture, 167. *See also* Property; Ritual activities

Privilege, based on relative age, 134, 136

Procreation, family of, 248, 330

Production, 23–26, 142–145, 152–157, 208–218, 224; in "transitional" China, 278, 279, 284. *See also* Economic allocation

Property division, 137, 167, 194, 203

Prostitution, 86, 97, 98, 261

Pruitt, Ida, 150, 153

Public demonstrations, 346, 347

Religion, 36, 247, 249–256, 343–345. *See also* Integration

Rent, *see* Tenancy

Respect, 173, 179, 192, 194, 204, 235, 268, 308, 338. *See also* Solidarity; Expression

Responsibility, 28–31, 141, 143, 159; based on relative age, 134, 136, 137, 139, 140; locus of, 232–239; definition of, 239–241; procedure, 242–246; in "transitional" China, 335–338. *See also* Political allocation

Ritual activities, differentiation of roles, 11, 137, 146, 151, 167

Role differentiation, 8–14; based on age, 10, 11, 63–140, 330; based on sex, 11, 12, 67–69, 71, 147–153, 224, 232–234, 237, 261, 309–313, 330, 345; based on occupation, 11, 24; based on generation, 12, 13, 140–147, 187, 234–237, 308, 309, 330, 331; based on political allocation, 13, 28, 151, 159–163, 232–246, 328–339; based on economic allocation, 13, 14, 22, 27, 28, 151–159, 208–231, 317–328; in "transitional" China, 289–313, 317–339

Romantic love, *see* Emotions

San-ts'ung (three dependencies), 149

Servants, 44, 209, 215, 228

Sex, role differentiation based on, 11, 12, 67–69, 71, 147–153, 224, 232–234, 237, 261; in "transitional" China, 309–313, 330, 345

Shih Kuo-Heng, 239

Sisters, 190

Smith, Arthur H., 70, 117

Soldiers, 44, 49n.

Solidarity, 8n., 13, 18, 20, 134, 139, 164–207; content, 15; strength, 15, 17, 166–172, 177; intensity, 16, 172–174, 177, 181; of father and son, 15, 32, 38, 76, 82, 166–175; of mother and son, 76, 181–183; of father and daughter, 76, 90, 179–181; of mother and daughter, 76, 183, 184; of husband and wife, 175–179; of father-in-law and daughter-in-law, 184, 185; of mother-in-law and daughter-in-law, 185–187; of brothers, 165, 187–190; of sisters, 190; of sister and brother's wife, 190, 191; of brother and brother's wife, 191–193; of uncle and nephew, 193–195; of uncle and niece, 195, 196; of aunt and nephew, 196–198; of aunt and niece, 198, 199; of brothers' wives, 199–201; of husband and concubine, 201, 202; of other members and concubine, 202, 203; of grandparents and grandchildren, 203–205; in "transitional" China, 313–317. *See also individual entries*

Sons, birth of, 67, 69, 118; training of, 53, 76, 79–86, 92, 170; marriage of, 87–92, 118, 181; and fathers, 76, 82, 83, 104, 118–120, 166–175, 233, 248, 290, 293, 313, 330; and mothers, 181–183, 258, 290, 314; in "transitional" China, 303, 316

Sorokin, P., 3n.

Speculation, *see* Business investment

Sports, 267, 268, 340

Storytellers, 265

Students, 328, 332, 340, 342, 345, 346

Suicide, 117, 118, 306, 337, 347, 348

Sung China, 41, 48, 55

Ta-chia chih-tu (large family system), 49

T'ang China, 39, 41, 55, 59

Tao Kuang, 278

Taoism, 251, 254–256, 343

Taxes, 211, 217, 218, 225, 238

Teachers, role of, 77, 170, 215, 248; women, 291, 299, 314, 341

Technology, 275, 277, 278, 280–284, 296, 298, 308, 309, 322, 323, 327, 329, 343, 351, 356, 359–361. *See also* Industrialization; Modernization

Tenancy, 212, 217, 223, 225, 318

Thomas, W. I., 262

Ti-ti (younger brothers), 134

Tokugawa period, 171, 351, 360

Topography, 351

Traders, 209. *See also* Merchants

"Traditional" China, *see* China

"Transitional" China, *see* China

Transportation, 313, 351

Tsu (clan), 49, 50, 81, 141, 150, 190, 195, 219, 235, 239, 245, 326

Twenty-Four Examples of Filial Piety, 74. *See also* Filial piety

United States, family in, 16–18, 27, 31, 39, 56; role differentiation in, 63, 66, 140; old age in, 303

Universalistic standards, 218, 219, 222, 224, 281–284, 286, 298, 307, 329, 338, 339, 345, 352–354, 356, 358, 361, 362. *See also* Particularistic standards

Usury, 52, 212, 318

Utilities, public, 280, 352

Versailles, Treaty of, 300, 342, 346

Wang, T. C., 300

Westernization, 274, 279–281, 284, 288, 298, 303, 320, 328, 329, 344. *See also* Industrialization; Modernization

Widows, remarriage of, 46, 96. *See also* Mothers

Wittfogel, K. A., 352

Wives, role of, 102, 107, 121–124, 160, 234; and mothers-in-law, 105–116 *passim*, 161, 162, 185–187, 248, 258, 260; and family of orientation, 108, 179, 183, 248; and production, 153–155; and husbands, 172, 175–179, 258; and consumption, 226; and family of procreation, 248; in "transitional" China, 301, 303, 315, 332, 333

Women, role differentiation of, 7, 12, 25, 147–150; economic role of, 144, 145, 153–155, 211, 213, 215, 216, 224; in "transitional" China, 285, 287, 288, 290–294, 301, 309–313, 321–323, 332, 333, 336, 338, 345, 346. *See also* Daughters; Wives; Mothers; Mothers-in-law

Yang, Martin, 67, 70*n.*, 72

Yangtze River, 352

Yangtze Valley, 50

Yao T'su-Ai, 205, 299, 336

Ying-erh Shih-ch'i (infant period), 66–75, 83, 84, 120, 121, 139, 149, 172, 248; among gentry, 64, 65, 73–75; among peasantry, 64, 65, 73, 74; in "transitional" China, 289

Yüan Dynasty, 55

Yu-nien Shih-ch'i (immature period), 73–84, 170, 174; among gentry, 75–80, 83, 85; among peasantry, 77–83, 90; in "transitional" China, 290–296, 307, 314

Yu-T'ung (sons), 82, 83

Znaniecki, F., 262

Marion J. Levy, Jr., is Professor of Sociology and a member of the faculty of the Woodrow Wilson School of Public and International Affairs at Princeton University. He is the author of *Modernization and the Structure of Societies* and *Structure of Society*.

Atheneum Paperbacks

HISTORY—AMERICAN

2   POWER AND DIPLOMACY *by Dean Acheson*
4   THE ROAD TO PEARL HARBOR *by Herbert Feis*
6   ROGER WILLIAMS *by Perry Miller*
7   THE REPUBLICAN ROOSEVELT *by John Morton Blum*
17 MYTHS AND REALITIES *by Carl Bridenbaugh*
32 STRANGERS IN THE LAND *by John Higham*
40 THE UNITED STATES AND MEXICO *by Howard F. Cline*
43 HOLMES-LASKI LETTERS: THE CORRESPONDENCE OF JUSTICE OLIVER
A&B WENDELL HOLMES AND HAROLD J. LASKI 1916–1935 *edited by Mark
    DeWolfe Howe, abridged by Alger Hiss, 2 vols.*
49 THE CONCEPT OF JACKSONIAN DEMOCRACY *by Lee Benson*
51 TURMOIL AND TRADITION *by Elting E. Morison*
70 THE CHINA TANGLE *by Herbert Feis*
84 THE DIMENSIONS OF LIBERTY *by Oscar and Mary Handlin*
86 THE CORPORATION IN MODERN SOCIETY *edited by Edward S. Mason*
110 DRED SCOTT'S CASE *by Vincent C. Hopkins, S.J.*
111 THE DECLINE OF AMERICAN LIBERALISM *by Arthur A. Ekirch, Jr.*
113 HARVARD GUIDE TO AMERICAN HISTORY *edited by Oscar Handlin,
    Arthur Meier Schlesinger, Samuel Eliot Morison, Frederick Merk,
    Arthur Meier Schlesinger, Jr., Paul Herman Buck*
115 THE ROOTS OF AMERICAN LOYALTY *by Merle Curti*
116 THE POLITICS OF PREJUDICE *by Roger Daniels*
117 CENTURY OF STRUGGLE *by Eleanor Flexner*
118 BOSTON'S IMMIGRANTS *by Oscar Handlin*
123 THE AMERICAN APPROACH TO FOREIGN POLICY *by Dexter Perkins*
125 THE EIGHTEENTH-CENTURY COMMONWEALTHMAN *by Caroline Robbins*
126 THE AMERICAN AS REFORMER *by Arthur M. Schlesinger*
129 THE LEGEND OF HENRY FORD *by Keith Sward*
132 ASA GRAY *by A. Hunter Dupree*
134 THE COLONIAL MERCHANTS AND THE AMERICAN REVOLUTION—
    1763–1776 *by Arthur M. Schlesinger*
136 THE ROAD TO APPOMATTOX *by Bell Irvin Wiley*
TAP THE ADAMS PAPERS: DIARY AND AUTOBIOGRAPHY OF JOHN ADAMS·
1,2,3,4 *edited by L. H. Butterfield, 4 vols.*
TAP THE ADAMS PAPERS: ADAMS FAMILY CORRESPONDENCE *edited by
5,6 L. H. Butterfield, 2 vols.*
TAP THE ADAMS PAPERS: DIARY OF CHARLES FRANCIS ADAMS *edited by
7,8 L. H. Butterfield, 2 vols.*
TAP THE ADAMS PAPERS: LEGAL PAPERS OF JOHN ADAMS *edited by
9,10,11 L. H. Butterfield, 3 vols.*

Atheneum Paperbacks

HISTORY

3   SIX MEDIEVAL MEN AND WOMEN *by H. S. Bennett*
10 TRAVEL AND DISCOVERY IN THE RENAISSANCE *by Boies Penrose*
30 GHANA IN TRANSITION *by David E. Apter*
58 TROTSKY'S DIARY IN EXILE—1935 *translated by Elena Zarudnaya*
63 THE SINO-SOVIET CONFLICT 1956–1961 *by Donald S. Zagoria*
65 LORD AND PEASANT IN RUSSIA FROM THE NINTH TO THE NINETEENTH CENTURY *by Jerome Blum*
68 TWELVE WHO RULED *by Robert R. Palmer*
83 KARAMZIN'S MEMOIR ON ANCIENT AND MODERN RUSSIA *by Richard Pipes*
97 THE EIGHTEENTH CENTURY CONFRONTS THE GODS *by Frank E. Manuel*
103 JACOBEAN PAGEANT *by G. P. V. Akrigg*
104 THE MAKING OF VICTORIAN ENGLAND *by G. Kitson Clark*
107 RUSSIA LEAVES THE WAR *by George F. Kennan*
108 THE DECISION TO INTERVENE *by George F. Kennan*
121 DRIVING FORCES IN HISTORY *by Halvdan Koht*
124 THE FORMATION OF THE SOVIET UNION *by Richard Pipes*
127 THE THREE LIVES OF CHARLES DE GAULLE *by David Schoenbrun*
128 AS FRANCE GOES *by David Schoenbrun*

HISTORY—ASIA

44 CHINA'S RESPONSE TO THE WEST *by Ssu-Yü Teng and John K. Fairbank*
63 THE SINO-SOVIET CONFLICT 1956–1961 *by Donald S. Zagoria*
64 CONFUCIANISM AND CHINESE CIVILIZATION *edited by Arthur F. Wright*
70 THE CHINA TANGLE *by Herbert Feis*
77 BUDDHISM IN CHINESE HISTORY *by Arthur F. Wright*
87 A DOCUMENTARY HISTORY OF CHINESE COMMUNISM *by Conrad Brandt, Benjamin Schwartz and John K. Fairbank*
92 THE LAST STAND OF CHINESE CONSERVATISM *by Mary Clabaugh Wright*
93 THE TRAGEDY OF THE CHINESE REVOLUTION *by Harold R. Isaacs*
94 THE AGRARIAN ORIGINS OF MODERN JAPAN *by Thomas C. Smith*

THE NEW YORK TIMES BYLINE BOOKS

CHINA *by Harry Schwartz*
RUSSIA *by Harrison E. Salisbury*
THE MIDDLE EAST *by Jay Walz*
AFRICA *by Waldemar A. Nielsen*
LATIN AMERICA *by Tad Szulc*
SOUTHEAST ASIA *by Tillman Durdin*

Atheneum Paperbacks

STUDIES IN AMERICAN NEGRO LIFE

NL1 THE NEGRO IN COLONIAL NEW ENGLAND *by Lorenzo Johnston Greene*
NL2 SEPARATE AND UNEQUAL *by Louis R. Harlan*
NL3 AFTER FREEDOM *by Hortense Powdermaker*
NL4 FREDERICK DOUGLASS *by Benjamin Quarles*
NL5 PREFACE TO PEASANTRY *by Arthur F. Raper*
NL6 W.E.B. DU BOIS: PROPAGANDIST OF THE NEGRO PROTEST
       by Elliott Rudwick
NL7 THE BLACK WORKER *by Sterling D. Spero and Abram L. Harris*
NL8 THE MAKING OF BLACK AMERICA *edited*
A&B *by August Meier and Elliott Rudwick, 2 vols.*
NL9 BLACK MANHATTAN *by James Weldon Johnson*
NL10 THE NEW NEGRO *edited by Alain Locke*
NL11 THE NEGRO'S GOD AS REFLECTED IN HIS LITERATURE
       by Benjamin Mays

LAW AND GOVERNMENT

20   DOCUMENTS ON FUNDAMENTAL HUMAN RIGHTS *edited by Zechariah*
A&B *Chafee, Jr., 2 vols.*
23   THE CONSTITUTION AND WHAT IT MEANS TODAY *by Edward S. Corwin*
27   COURTS ON TRIAL *by Jerome Frank*
30   GHANA IN TRANSITION *by David E. Apter*
46   THE FUTURE OF FEDERALISM *by Nelson A. Rockefeller*
53   THE BILL OF RIGHTS *by Learned Hand*
72   MR. JUSTICE HOLMES AND THE SUPREME COURT *by Felix Frankfurter*
73   THE STRUCTURE OF FREEDOM *by Christian Bay*
84   THE DIMENSIONS OF LIBERTY *by Oscar and Mary Handlin*
89   MAKERS OF MODERN STRATEGY *edited by Edward M. Earle*
105 DILEMMAS OF URBAN AMERICA *by Robert C. Weaver*
110 DRED SCOTT'S CASE *by Vincent C. Hopkins, S.J.*
130 THE REVOLUTION OF THE SAINTS *by Michael Walzer*

PSYCHOLOGY AND SOCIOLOGY

21   BIG BUSINESS LEADERS IN AMERICA *by W. Lloyd Warner and*
       James Abegglen
67   ON KNOWING *by Jerome S. Bruner*
79   THE SOCIETY OF CAPTIVES *by Gresham M. Sykes*
109 AFRICAN HOMICIDE AND SUICIDE *edited by Paul Bohannan*
119 THE LAW OF PRIMITIVE MAN *by E. Adamson Hoebel*
120 THE SOVIET CITIZEN *by Alex Inkeles and Raymond Bauer*
133 THE FAMILY REVOLUTION IN MODERN CHINA *by Marion J. Levy, Jr.*

Atheneum Paperbacks

ECONOMICS AND BUSINESS

21 BIG BUSINESS LEADERS IN AMERICA *by W. Lloyd Warner and James Abegglen*

24 PROSPERITY AND DEPRESSION *by Gottfried Haberler*

34 THE DIPLOMACY OF ECONOMIC DEVELOPMENT *by Eugene R. Black*

47 ECONOMIC CONCENTRATION AND THE MONOPOLY PROBLEM *by Edward S. Mason*

78 THE ECONOMICS OF DEFENSE IN THE NUCLEAR AGE *by Charles J. Hitch and Roland N. McKean*

80 FOUNDATIONS OF ECONOMIC ANALYSIS *by Paul Anthony Samuelson*

86 THE CORPORATION IN MODERN SOCIETY *edited by Edward S. Mason*

DIPLOMACY AND INTERNATIONAL RELATIONS

2 POWER AND DIPLOMACY *by Dean Acheson*

4 THE ROAD TO PEARL HARBOR *by Herbert Feis*

15 CALL TO GREATNESS *by Adlai E. Stevenson*

34 THE DIPLOMACY OF ECONOMIC DEVELOPMENT *by Eugene R. Black*

40 THE UNITED STATES AND MEXICO *by Howard F. Cline*

41 THE DIPLOMATS 1919–1939 *by Gordon A. Craig and*
A&B *Felix Gilbert*

44 CHINA'S RESPONSE TO THE WEST *by Ssu-Yü Teng and John K. Fairbank*

54 STRATEGIC SURRENDER *by Paul Kecskemeti*

63 THE SINO-SOVIET CONFLICT 1956–1961 *by Donald S. Zagoria*

70 THE CHINA TANGLE *by Herbert Feis*

74 STALIN'S FOREIGN POLICY REAPPRAISED *by Marshall Shulman*

89 MAKERS OF MODERN STRATEGY *edited by Edward M. Earle*

107 RUSSIA LEAVES THE WAR *by George F. Kennan*

108 THE DECISION TO INTERVENE *by George F. Kennan*

Atheneum Paperbacks

THE WORLDS OF NATURE AND MAN
5 OF MEN AND MOUNTAINS *by William O. Douglas*
18 THE SUDDEN VIEW *by Sybille Bedford*
22 SPRING IN WASHINGTON *by Louis J. Halle*
33 LOST CITY OF THE INCAS *by Hiram Bingham*
45 THE SEA SHORE *by C. M. Yonge*
61 THE NEW YORK TIMES GUIDE TO DINING OUT IN NEW YORK *edited by Craig Claiborne*
81 THE NEW YORK TIMES GUIDE TO HOME FURNISHING *edited by Barbara Plumb and Elizabeth Sverbeyeff*
82 BIRDS AND MEN *by Robert H. Welker*
95 THE FIRMAMENT OF TIME *by Loren Eiseley*

PHYSICAL SCIENCES AND MATHEMATICS
13 THE AIM AND STRUCTURE OF PHYSICAL THEORY *by Pierre Duhem*
31 PHILOSOPHY OF MATHEMATICS AND NATURAL SCIENCE *by Hermann Weyl*
56 THE EARTH BENEATH THE SEA *by Francis P. Shepard*
57 SATELLITE OF THE SUN *by Athelstan Spilhaus*
59 PLAYING WITH INFINITY *by Rózsa Péter*
100 GALAXIES *by Harlow Shapley*

LIFE SCIENCES AND ANTHROPOLOGY
9 MATTER, MIND AND MAN *by Edmund W. Sinnott*
16 THE HORMONES IN HUMAN REPRODUCTION *by George W. Corner*
26 THE OLD STONE AGE *by Miles C. Burkitt*
28 MORPHOGENESIS *by John Tyler Bonner*
33 LOST CITY OF THE INCAS *by Hiram Bingham*
35 GENETICS, PALEONTOLOGY, AND EVOLUTION *edited by Glenn L. Jepsen, Ernst Mayr and George Gaylord Simpson*
45 THE SEA SHORE *by C. M. Yonge*
48 TRISTES TROPIQUES *by Claude Lévi-Strauss*
62 TERRITORY IN BIRD LIFE *by Eliot Howard*
71 HEREDITY AND EVOLUTION IN HUMAN POPULATIONS *by L. C. Dunn*
85 THE INTEGRITY OF THE BODY *by F. M. Burnet, F.R.S.*
88 SPEECH AND BRAIN-MECHANISMS *by Wilder Penfield and Lamar Roberts*
91 CELLS AND SOCIETIES *by John Tyler Bonner*
95 THE FIRMAMENT OF TIME *by Loren Eiseley*
98 IDEAS ON HUMAN EVOLUTION *edited by William Howells*
101 COMMUNICATION AMONG SOCIAL BEES *by Martin Lindauer*
106 ON THE ORIGIN OF SPECIES *by Charles Darwin, a Facsimile of the First Edition, edited by Ernst Mayr*
109 AFRICAN HOMICIDE AND SUICIDE *edited by Paul Bohannon*

Atheneum Paperbacks

PHILOSOPHY AND RELIGION

6 ROGER WILLIAMS *by Perry Miller*
9 MATTER, MIND AND MAN *by Edmund W. Sinnott*
19 BUDDHISM IN TRANSLATIONS *by Henry Clarke Warren*
31 PHILOSOPHY OF MATHEMATICS AND NATURAL SCIENCE
    by Hermann Weyl
38 TOWARD REUNION IN PHILOSOPHY *by Morton White*
52 RELIGION IN TWENTIETH CENTURY AMERICA *by Herbert W. Schneider*
60 HERACLITUS *by Philip Wheelwright*
64 CONFUCIANISM AND CHINESE CIVILIZATION *edited by Arthur F. Wright*
69 ON THE USE OF PHILOSOPHY *by Jacques Maritain*
75 RELIGIOUS PHILOSOPHY *by Harry Austryn Wolfson*
77 BUDDHISM IN CHINESE HISTORY *by Arthur F. Wright*
97 THE EIGHTEENTH CENTURY CONFRONTS THE GODS *by Frank E. Manuel*

LITERATURE AND THE ARTS

1 ROME AND A VILLA *by Eleanor Clark*
8 THE MUSICAL EXPERIENCE OF COMPOSER, PERFORMER, LISTENER
   by Roger Sessions
11 THE GRANDMOTHERS *by Glenway Wescott*
12 i: SIX NONLECTURES *by e. e. cummings*
14 THE PRESENCE OF GRACE *by J. F. Powers*
18 THE SUDDEN VIEW *by Sybille Bedford*
25 THE ROBBER BRIDEGROOM *by Eudora Welty*
29 CONTEXTS OF CRITICISM *by Harry Levin*
36 GEORGE BERNARD SHAW *by Hesketh Pearson*
37 THE TERRITORY AHEAD *by Wright Morris*
39 THE LETTERS OF VINCENT VAN GOGH *edited by Mark Roskill*
42 THE GREEN MARE *by Marcel Aymé*
50 AMERICAN ARCHITECTURE AND OTHER WRITINGS *by Montgomery
    Schuyler, edited by William H. Jordy and Ralph Coe; abridged
    by William H. Jordy*
55 PNIN *by Vladimir Nabokov*
66 SELECTED POEMS INCLUDING THE WOMAN AT THE WASHINGTON ZOO
    by Randall Jarrell
76 THE SINGER OF TALES *by Albert B. Lord*
90 ANATOMY OF CRITICISM *by Northrop Frye*
96 CONRAD THE NOVELIST *by Albert J. Guerard*
99 MARK TWAIN *by Henry Nash Smith*
102 EMILY DICKINSON *by Thomas H. Johnson*
112 THE LIFE OF THE DRAMA *by Eric Bentley*
114 SELECTED MARK TWAIN-HOWELLS LETTERS *edited by Frederick
    Anderson, William Gibson, and Henry Nash Smith*
122 REPORTING THE NEWS *edited by Louis M. Lyons*
131 WHAT IS THEATRE? (*incorporating* THE DRAMATIC EVENT)
    by Eric Bentley
135 THE HERO OF THE WAVERLEY NOVELS *by Alexander Welsh*